AMONG THE PEOPLE: ENCOUNTERS WITH THE POOR

Among the People:

Encounters with the Poor

Edited by

Irwin Deutscher
and
Elizabeth J. Thompson

Basic Books, Inc.,
Publishers
New York
London

To the memory of our colleague
MELVIN WEISS
who died accidentally with his friend Aaron Edelman
in November 1964,
and to the future of
Meiling, David, and Aaron

The Authors

HOWARD S. BECKER is Professor of Sociology at Northwestern University and project director of a study of the educational experiences of non-college youth. Among his publications are *Outsiders: Studies in the Sociology of Deviance* and, with Blanche Geer, Anselm L. Strauss, and Everett C. Hughes, *Boys in White: Student Culture in Medical School.*

JEROME BEKER is Senior Research Associate at the Syracuse University Youth Development Center. He was a National Institute of Mental Health Postdoctoral Research Fellow from 1960 to 1962 and served as Research Psychologist at Berkshire Farm for Boys. His professional interests are centered on social psychological research in education and the implementation and evaluation of promising educational innovations. He is a frequent contributor to the professional literature of educational research and practice.

RHONDDA K. CASSETTA is a Senior Research Scientist (Biometrics) in the Mental Health Research Unit, New York State Department of Mental Hygiene. She was formerly an Assistant in Prices and Statistics at Cornell University. Mrs. Cassetta is the co-author of several journal articles on mental health and on economics.

DAVID CUMMING is a graduate of Brandeis University and is presently a student at the University of Chicago Law School.

ELAINE CUMMING is a sociologist who lives in Albany, New York. She is the author of *Closed Ranks, Growing Old, Ego and Milieu,* and *Systems of Social Control.* She was formerly associated with the Mental Health Research Unit, New York State Department of Mental Hygiene in Syracuse.

IRWIN DEUTSCHER is Professor of Sociology at Syracuse University, the former Director of the Youth Development Center, and a past president of the Society for the Study of Social Problems. He is the author of numerous articles and monographs ranging over a wide variety of subjects.

LINTON C. FREEMAN is Professor of Sociology and Computer Science at the University of Pittsburgh. When the research reported in this volume was conducted, he was on the faculty of Syracuse University.

BLANCHE GEER is Associate Professor of Sociology and Education at Syracuse University and Senior Research Associate at the university's Youth Development Center. She is currently project director of a study of the educational experiences of non-college youth. Dr. Geer is a co-author of *Boys in White: Student Culture in Medical School.*

JOSEPH GELMAN writes from the background of his experience as a resident of one of our better-known institutions for troubled youngsters. He is now thirteen, living at home, and attending public school. After taking a competitive examination, he was admitted to a public high school for academically talented youths. This is his first publication.

JACK HAAS is Assistant Professor, Department of Sociology and Anthropology, Pennsylvania State University. He was formerly a Research Associate at the Syracuse University Youth Development Center.

WARREN C. HAGGSTROM is Associate Professor in the School of Social Welfare, U.C.L.A. He was formerly a Senior Research Associate with the Youth Development Center and was Director of Syracuse University's Community Action Training Center. He has had extensive experience in helping to organize labor, farm, civil-rights, student, political, and community organizations. His publications include "On Careful Reasoning in Ordinary Language," "The Power of the Poor," "Poverty and Adult Education," and other papers in related areas.

ROBERT H. HARDT is Acting Director, Youth Development Center, and Assistant Professor of Sociology at Syracuse University. He was research director of Syracuse Action for Youth, a community-based demonstration program sponsored by the President's Committee on Juvenile Delinquency and Youth Crime. He is currently involved in a study of the impact of the Upward Bound program on low-income youth of high school age.

A. C. HIGGINS is Assistant Professor of Sociology at Syracuse University and Assistant Professor of Administrative Medicine at the Upstate Medical Center, Syracuse, New York. From 1961 to 1964 he was Field Director of the North Carolina Survey of Handicapped Children. He is presently directing a study of industrial medicine in Syracuse.

PAUL MEADOWS is Professor and former Chairman, Department of Sociology, Syracuse University. His publications include *The Culture of Industrial Man, John Wesley Powell: Frontiersman of Science, El Proceso Social de la Revolución,* and numerous articles on subjects ranging from art to development administration.

viii

S. M. MILLER is Professor of Education and Sociology, New York University, and Program Adviser, The Ford Foundation. He was formerly in the Department of Sociology and the Youth Development Center of Syracuse University. He is the author of *Comparitive Social Mobility,* co-editor of *Applied Sociology,* and co-author of *The Dynamics of the American Economy* and *Social Class and Social Policy.*

STEPHEN J. MILLER is Associate Professor of Medical Sociology at Brandeis University and project director of a study of the educational experience of the intern. His publications include "Exchange and Negotiated Learning in Graduate Medical Education."

HOWARD J. OSOFSKY, M.D., is Assistant Professor of Obstetrics and Gynecology, State University of New York Upstate Medical Center, and Medical Director of the Young Mothers' Educational Development Program. He has published several articles on the psychological and sociological aspects of obstetrics and gynecology. At present, a book concerning the problems of the teen-age mother is in press.

ARTHUR PEARL is Professor of Education at the University of Oregon. He was formerly on the faculty of Howard University and served as Deputy Director of the New York State Division for Youth. He is co-author, with Frank Riessman, of *New Careers for the Poor* and co-editor, with Riessman and Jerome Cohen, of *Mental Health of the Poor.* In addition, he has written articles on schools, school dropouts, alcoholism, and drug addiction.

LEE RAINWATER is Professor of Sociology and Anthropology at Washington University and a Research Associate in the university's Social Science Institute. He is the author of *And the Poor Get Children* and *Family Design: Marital Sexuality, Family Size and Contraception,* and a co-author of *Workingman's Wife: Her Personality, World and Life Style.* For the past three years he has been directing a major study of a lower-class Negro community in St. Louis.

ARNOLD M. ROSE was Professor of Sociology at the University of Minnesota. At the time of his death in January, 1968, he was President-elect of the American Sociological Association and had served as President of the Society for the Study of Social Problems and of the Midwest Sociological Society. He was a member of the President's Advisory Committee on Older Americans and served as consultant to several government agencies. He was author or editor of fifteen books, the most recent being *The Political Power Structure of the United States* and *Academic Freedom on Trial.*

HELEN ICKEN SAFA is a member of the anthropology faculty at Livingston College, Rutgers, The State University (N.J.). A former Senior Research Associate at the Syracuse University Youth Development Center, she has done extensive research in the social aspects of housing and low-income families in the United States and Latin America. Her most recent study compares the problems of the urban poor in Puerto Rico and Syracuse. Her publications include "From Shanty Town to Public Housing: A Comparison of Family Structure in Two Urban Neighborhoods in Puerto Rico," "The Female-Based Household in Public Housing: A Case Study in Puerto Rico," and "The Migration and Urbanization of the American Negro."

LINDA F. SEIDEL is a School Psychologist in Elmont, New York. She received her master's degree in school psychology from Syracuse University, where she worked on the project reported in this volume as a Graduate Assistant at the Youth Development Center.

DOROTHY AND ADRIAN SINFIELD carried out the surveys reported here in North Shields for the London School of Economics and in Syracuse in cooperation with the Mental Health Research Unit of the New York State Department of Mental Hygiene. Adrian Sinfield is on the faculty of the Department of Sociology, University of Essex, England, and Consultant on Long-Term Unemployment to the Organization for Economic Cooperation and Development, Paris.

CHARLES W. SLACK is an educational consultant to industry and advertising. He holds a Ph.D. in psychology from Princeton University and was an Assistant Professor in the Department of Social Relations at Harvard University. He served as a consultant to the Youth Development Center. His most recent publication is "A Study of Young People," issued by Doyle Dane Bernbach, Inc., Advertising.

MORRIS H. SUNSHINE is Associate Professor of Sociology at Kent State University and was formerly a member of the sociology faculty at Syracuse University. His publications have treated community leadership, public education, and small-group structures.

ELIZABETH J. THOMPSON is associated with the Syracuse University Youth Development Center and the School of Journalism's Mental Health Information Program. She is completing studies for a doctorate in social science with emphasis on mass culture.

JAMES B. VICTOR is Research Associate at the Youth Development Center, Syracuse University, and a graduate student in psychology. He has worked with delinquent and disturbed youth in both clinical and educational settings.

CHARLES VI VONA is a graduate student and teaching assistant at Syracuse University. He was an assistant to Blanche Geer at the Syracuse University Youth Development Center from 1964 to 1966.

CHARLES V. WILLIE is Associate Professor and Chairman of the Department of Sociology at Syracuse University and a former Senior Research Associate at the Youth Development Center. He has served as Visiting Lecturer in Sociology, Harvard Medical School, and as Research Director of the Washington, D.C., project of the President's Committee on Juvenile Delinquency and Youth Crime. He has published extensively in the fields of juvenile delinquency, family structure, and community organization.

CLYDE WOODS is a graduate student in anthropology at Stanford University.

Preface

Most of us who contributed to this volume were at the time of its conception associated with the Syracuse University Youth Development Center, the Department of Sociology and Anthropology at Syracuse University, or the New York State Mental Health Research Unit in Syracuse. This book is our memorial to our late friend and colleague Mel Weiss, who, at various times, was a member of the staff of each of these three establishments. In large part, the book is a reflection of his influence on us. He viewed people not as objects, but as subjects; not as "data," but as human beings enmeshed in a complicated and troublesome world; not merely as phenomena to be understood, but as people deserving of sympathy and in need of help.

The contents of this book are not intended to be representative of the research conducted either at the Youth Development Center or the New York State Mental Health Research Unit. These are selected fragments, supplemented by a few pieces contributed by friends and colleagues who have in one way or another been associated with us or with the man who inspired us to put this volume together. None of the chapters has been previously published, although one is a revised and expanded version of an earlier article.

The disciplinary backgrounds of the contributors include the practicing professions of education, medicine, and social work, as well as the academic disciplines of anthropology, economics, psychology, sociology, and statistics. Although this range represents many perspectives, not always consistent with one another, most of the authors share in common a view of the poor as seen from among the people. They also shared in common an unhesitating willingness to make a contribution to this memorial volume.

We wish to express our thanks to our associates at the Youth Development Center, who patiently lived with this book during its formative time, and particularly to Susan Drucker for her assistance in the preparation of the manuscript.

IRWIN DEUTSCHER
ELIZABETH J. THOMPSON

Syracuse, N.Y.
April 1968

Contents

PART IV: POOR BUT HEALTHY?

PART V: IT'S THE SAME EVERYWHERE

Contents

Part I: Prologue

Editors' Introduction   There was a brief interlude in American social science during the transition from liberal reform polemics to tautological exercises in trivia, when anthropologists, psychologists, and sociologists began to discover America's underbelly. The rich documentation of *The Gold Coast and the Slum, The Ghetto, The Taxi Dance Hall, The Gang,* and other monographs of the so-called Chicago Golden Age, as well as the pioneering conceptual development of *The Polish Peasant in Europe and America* and, later, *French Canada in Transition, Black Metropolis, Deep South, Who Shall Be Educated? Race Riot*—all of these sounded the alarm. They should have alerted a nation on the way to mass prosperity that poverty and inequality were among us and could not be swept under the rug. But they did not.

These cogent messages, tolling throughout the 1930's and 1940's, were lost in the din of louder and more appealing noises. We complacently read of our affluent society and shrugged off what we preferred to think of as transient and dissipating pockets of poverty. In retrospect, this body of literature ought to be viewed not with nostalgia but with frustration and regret: frustration because of our inability to read its message and regret because we have had to rediscover all that was learned not so very long ago.

After a hundred years, inequities in human rights have caught up with us. In desperation, we are trying with new governmental and private programs to rewrite a history that is swamped in the morass of a culture that has grown around these very inequities. After untold thousands of years, we have become self-conscious about poverty in the

1

midst of plenty. But social science today, with a few rare exceptions, has lost touch with humanity. It is childish to cry and unscientific to feel, and who among us scholars would damn himself to the role of an unscientific child? Some mavericks perhaps, like the bitterly satirical psychologist who furnishes this volume with its opening chapter, or the angry educator who gives us a chapter on what schools do to kids, or the sensitive social worker who sees the world through the eyes of the poor—or like the dead anthropologist whose memory and humanity this book is intended to keep alive. But, by and large, the great contributions to understanding the American poor of the 1960's have come not from the research of social science but from the perceptions of journalists and the analyses of activists. For some of us who have contributed to it, this volume is a modest offering in the way of partial redemption.

This book is mostly about poor people and the kinds of encounters they have with the rest of us and we with them. Most of the chapters are written by scholars who have been where the action is—among the people. A good survey researcher knows that the effective management of a survey requires *experience*. By this he means that, without personally carrying through the process, one cannot imagine the complex relationships which develop, the problems which inevitably evolve, the need for extensive time, staff, and funds, the nuances of data processing and analysis—all of which are not taught in the textbooks or classrooms. He means that one must live the experience in order to gain knowledge and understanding of it. Yet this same researcher frequently views with suspicion, and sometimes shock, the subjectivity of the participant-observation process—of what anthropologists and some sociologists call "field work." The survey expert is unable to recognize that what he knows to be true of the survey research process is true of all human behavior: it cannot be properly understood until you have been there. The purpose of this volume is to take the reader among the people.

Encounters between the poor and agents of the larger society are often paternalistic, frequently exploitative, sometimes symbiotic, and occasionally conflict-laden. Rarely are they cooperative or mutually supportive. Seldom is there reciprocal respect or understanding. They are encounters between alien peoples, charged with suspicion and thinly veiled hostilities. Superficial efforts to involve "the poor" in the war on poverty reflect a vague awareness of the need for cooperative

2

attacks on a mutual problem. But the condescending attitude of middle-class citizens who assume the mantle of teachers of the poor does not sit well, even on those occasions when it is well intended. The good people find it difficult to teach the poor to behave right: that is, with appropriate restraint, cynicism, and hypocrisy, when engaged in face-to-face encounters. It is discouraging that the poor will not behave like gentlemen.

The contributors to this volume, having been among the people, are able to avoid some of the common palliatives. But there is no party line presented here. Thus, one author makes a plea for the "intercessor" as a middle-class agent who knows the ropes (and "learning the ropes" is the central theme of another chapter) and who can exercise influence on behalf of the poor, in the manner of the ward heeler in an earlier era of urban political machines. This is indeed one possible type of supportive relationship, but another author recommends providing the poor with their own organizational power—and warns against the dangers of the organizer being viewed as a "fixer." That both of these men have had some success in implementing their programs within the same public housing authority suggests that each may be an effective alternative. That this is the same public housing authority whose gatekeeping process is described in another chapter and in whose houses many of the people reside whose everyday lives are revealed in this book tells us something more about the pages which follow.

Most of the poor people whose lives and perspectives are reported here live in Syracuse, New York, an upstate industrial and commercial city with a population of about 250,000. In Part V, we are provided with a glimpse of how these people compare with the poor in such places as Shields, England, and San Juan, Puerto Rico. In Part IV, encounters with the medical and health systems are described in a rural North Carolina county and in the city of St. Louis, as well as in Syracuse. In other chapters, observations made in such places as Washington, D.C. and Boston appear.

Are the poor the same everywhere? Probably no, in the sense that no people are the same everywhere; probably yes, in the sense that all people are the same everywhere. The chapter "The Unemployables" should sensitize us to the fact that *in any place* there are several very different kinds of people who are thought of and think of themselves as "poor." And to be understood, these different kinds or types must be viewed separately, from both a sociological and a psychological per-

3

spective. It is true that poverty may have different faces in different parts of the world. For example, in some nations a majority of the population falls into the minority group of the poor, while a minority of the population forms the dominant middle or wealthy class. But in the more affluent societies, poverty is less a matter of exposure, starvation, and bare survival than it is a matter of relative deprivation. Although the Syracuse poor may be better off economically than the poor in the rest of the United States, and the Shields poor may be worse off than the rest of Britain, they all hurt. And although few of them die of starvation or exposure, they all suffer the indignities of the assistance offered by a "compassionate" society.

Whatever differences there may be among the poor either between nations or within cities, they must all find themselves confronting a system—an establishment—to which they are strangers and over which they exercise no influence or control. Although this is the special theme of Part II, it appears repeatedly throughout the book. Since that same system is, in fact, historically responsible for the condition of most types of poor people, its ameliorative and control efforts tend quite reasonably to be viewed with something less than confidence. It is also true that growing up poor, wherever one may live, presents youngsters and their parents with a peculiar set of problems. This is especially so when the vision of a prosperous world is flaunted on all sides. And this is the theme of Part III, but it, too, appears throughout the book.

With a few exceptions, the following chapters are reports based upon field work among the people as they go about their everyday lives. Among the exceptions is one survey, but it is a survey with a difference—one that compares the purported statistics of behavior with reports from the people who are doing the behaving. Another chapter demands a considerable stretch of the imagination if it is to be viewed as a "field study," since the "field" which is observed is constructed by the observers. Two other chapters are less reports of studies than commentaries by experienced and knowledgeable students.

Although a great variety of encounters between the poor and the rest of us are reported in this volume, it hardly begins to cover the range of critical meetings which have an impact on everyday life. Missing is the crucial commercial game: encounters between the poor and door-to-door salesmen, landlords, finance companies and banks, neighborhood shops, and downtown department stores. Although we fail to deal with this set of events in this volume, it has become increasingly apparent that the poor do indeed pay more—for everything. Also missing is any breadth of materials dealing with the ignominious everyday encounters and confidence games played between the poor and employers, public welfare agents, professional social workers, police, judges, and probation and parole officers, to mention only a few. And nowadays there is a new kind of confidence game deserving attention: that which brings "representatives" of the poor into contact with bland, self-controlled, and sometimes well-meaning "community leaders" on local poverty boards which purport to involve the poor in policy decisions. Such omissions, although unavoidable, are indeed regrettable.

In Chapter I we are introduced to what more pompous social scientists like to call an "indigenous leader"—meet Big Chino Garcia. Big Chino leads one kind of war on poverty. Slack doesn't tell us much about *that* war—only that it exists—and then abruptly takes us into the fortress of another order of crusaders, fighting another battle on another battlefield. But it's the same war—or is it? In this series of vignettes, we hop with Slack from one encounter to another: from the Lower East Side, to Montclair, to Trenton, to a luncheon in a posh midtown Manhattan club, and, finally, to a closing scene in Central Park—a fifteen-cent war on poverty.

1 • Encounters

CHARLES W. SLACK

It's FIVE O'CLOCK in the afternoon and Big Chino Garcia walks his block —6th Street between Avenue D and C. Big Chino has no foundation grant, no research committee, no theoretical orientation, no space. Having no degree, his formal status is low. Having no vocabulary, he has published hardly anything. Who is his supervisor or his father or, when it comes to that, his friend? But anyone can see that Big Chino is a very strong young man. He has been president of the Assassins and, before that, War Lord of the Junior Assassins. The gang-war days are over now and Big Chino doesn't particularly like to think about them, but the Junior Assassins, especially, were a great army and Big Chino led them in battle all over the lower half of Manhattan because he was so great. He has been a street leader since he was twelve. New York street-gang leaders are all remarkable people. They have to be. The competition is heavy and only the best survive. Today, Big Chino pictures in his mind exactly what he wants for himself and for his people. If he's inflexible or can't get around fast enough, he will lose it all. If, on the other hand, he does everything exactly right and is as great a leader in peace as in war, he thinks he can save them. Save us all, Big Chino—your whole gang— street kids and special detached workers, judges and junkies, save the chairman of the Department of Delinquency, spics, and project director.

Big Chino is very explicit about this. He feels he must create his own Great Society and social club in order to fight "Our Complex Society" right there on the Lower East Side of Manhattan. He needs space, a place "we can call our own." He wants an unstructured program, a

7

room to hold meetings and play bongos. A room without social workers and no skill-training activities, a place to hang around and do what you want. He thinks that if he can't get his society started, we will all die of an overload of heroin. The social workers have all the space in which to talk to each other. Chino thinks the social workers are as goofy as the junkies. Social science is the opiate of the professionals. Heroin is the religion of the masses. The old gang is useless now: there they are, whispering Spanish, girls and boys thinned to skeletons, gaping front teeth and red underlids from pot, arms black and blue—blue as only blue can be under a thin parchment of human skin. This is the rubble which lies, along with needles, in the chasm beneath the tightrope Chino walks gingerly, resolutely, his eye on his point, rarely excited and never self-centered, for that's but a step from selfishness, and from selfishness to a hole in the arm is hardly anything at all.

This is where Big Chino finds himself or where he worked to get. A human-relations consultant to dying spic children.

Now, I want all discussion of the issues stopped. No more papers published until this particular question is answered: Can he make it?

BIG CHINO IN MONTCLAIR

It's cocktail-party time and Big Chino is there along with a lieutenant in the Great Society named Angelo and the Junior League and their husbands. Big Chino seems to be carrying it off—so far. The Junior League is filled with inchoate longings. In his thick Spanish accent, Chino is telling how all the street gangs on the Lower East Side are going to bring an end to crime and poverty—are going to make a new frontier and create their own Great Society. Chino is eighteen, cold sober and full of practical ideas. One of the Junior Leaguers is flipping. She can hardly control herself. This is the first delinquent she ever met and he's not a delinquent.

She is a snap for Big Chino. Nothing to it. Everybody in the room can feel it. It's a small world but it's really marvelous, isn't it? The whole *image* of teen-agers is changing, simply marvelous. If they can do this, what next? If Big Chino says peace, prosperity, and brotherly love; if Big Chino says nobility, hard work, virtue, art, science, and fun. Then, I mean, well, what about everything you read in the newspapers? Big Chino says he doesn't read the newspapers (Big Chino can't read). The Junior League doesn't *want* to believe the newspapers. She wants to be convinced that Big Chino is right and, after all, he *looks* as if he might have been personally responsible for half the crime anyway. So there he is telling her and it all seems too easy.

But ho, up comes the husband. He has been listening like everybody else, even though they pretended not to be, saying little things to each other. So up steps Mr. Junior League, very much the young salesman, hard-nosed and positive-thinking, reading Ayn Rand and playing golf. This man has written them all off: "Let the lazy stew in their own juice . . . more cops and less welfare." He has five and one-half arguments and, in all seriousness, he's absolutely right. The liberal has no defense against these five and one-half arguments, absolutely none, except that overwhelming majority of the votes. Mr. Junior League is learning this. He was thinking seriously of moving to Australia, really serious. After Johnson was elected, it kept going around in his mind. Now he moves up to Big Chino about to ask *the* question. To put things in some, well, *perspective*. Pause. Mr. Junior League begins, "Well, this is all okay for you." He means he accepts Big Chino. I mean him, *personally*. "But what about the lazy ones? What about the ones who won't work? *You* seem to have get up and go but you can't tell me that all [he is polite] [pause] you—I mean all—people—well, let's face it, some—a—people are just plain lazy."

Big Chino listens seriously, very seriously, his big brown face angled down, looking somewhere at the Junior League vest. Then he throws his head up and goes "Ah-ha, ah-ha, ah-ha," half stuttering and half laughing. "I know what you mean. Let's say a kid is really lazy. Say he can't even find the floor he's supposed to wash." And suddenly Big Chino is acting for us. He has an imaginary broom in his hand, or a mop, and is describing how the laziest, stupidest spic you can imagine would fail to tackle the job of cleaning the floor. It's taking him hours. He doesn't want to do it. Mr. and Mrs. Junior League are laughing. Chino knows exactly what they mean. After the caricature is over, Chino says; "Now here is what I do. On the first day I let him do it as slow as he wants to, let him take all the time in the world. It takes him all morning to do one small floor. Let him take all morning. But make sure he finishes—that is the important thing. Then the next day, when he does the floor, he does it a little faster. Maybe you don't notice that it's a little faster, but it's a little faster. The next day it's faster still." Chino is acting again. His hands are on the mop, he's moving it across the oriental rug. He's wiping between Junior League's feet, is mopping rapidly under the card table. He gives the sides an extra fillip, all the time he's describing. "You see, he's got something to do this afternoon—maybe some girls he wants to see, so he works faster and faster. You can never tell," says Big Chino, "maybe he will be the best one. We win the war on poverty by starting with the worst and making them the best. That's the only way we can do it."

SKIRMISH

Trenton, New Jersey, nestled in a crook of the Delaware down there, home of pottery and poverty, sounds like a great place for the New Jersey Office of Economic Opportunity. Trenton *looks* like poverty. It's a flat, beat-up city. There are whole abandoned hotels there, big ones that used to ring with debutante parties—are there any debutantes in Trenton now at all?

Anyway, it was eight-thirty in the morning, and I was a half hour early for the meeting. I can't remember the name of the meeting, but it doesn't matter—it was a poverty meeting, and they're going on all the time, simultaneously. So I was early, sitting in this tiny, beat-up, kosher delicatessen having lox and eggs and being stared at by this friendly-looking street kid who asked me where I came from. It turned out he was poor and a school dropout, so I asked him if he wanted to work for me for the day. My idea was to take him to the meeting. I knew this would be the only time any poor street kid would ever get to one of those poverty meetings. So we went up together.

The Office of Economic Opportunity is located on the top floor of the Labor and Industries Building, and what a sight this building is! When first you see it you think it's not a building at all. It looks very much as if a rocket ship had landed and the urban renewal had just cut into the old wooden poverty buildings around it like a blast-off. In other words, "Labor and Industry" descended on Trenton—it just *landed* there.

The building was built wrong. Of course, and it was a cold day. When we walked in, the wind was whamming through the corridors and making all the bureaucrats shiver, including the woman behind the desk who gave out passes to make sure, I suppose, that nobody who didn't have real business there got in. I could tell by the way she looked at us that there never had been a poverty kid in that building before, at least not one who had any *business* there, so it seemed to be important for me to look casual, but straight into her eyes, with a kind of "you can be damn sure I do know what I am doing" air. We got in, and into the new elevators, and started riding up. Well, going up in that elevator was really a great beginning. The kid seemed so happy about it all. A fine ride, man. Maybe he had never been in an elevator before, certainly not one that went up twenty-two stories. Furthermore, it was a fabulous elevator, a Westinghouse Wurlitzer elevator, a silver-lamé elevator. You could just feel the poverty slipping away as you went up, as you left below all those beat-up wooden kosher delicatessens, those little, rubbly frame wooden houses, up, up, up to the top, to the *Office of Economic Opportunity*. It was thrilling. What an adventure! But of course one *could* be disappointed at the top. What would there be? I had my ideas. He must have had his, too.

When we arrived—lo, of lo . . . a penthouse—no, not a penthouse, a pent-barn. The Top of the Mark—glass, chromium, and cement buttresses winging free outside. It was the most magnificent top one can imagine to any building. Ugly, you understand, but what a restaurant it would make! The Trenton Office of Economic Opportunity. The kid's eyes really popped. You could stand there and see all the poverty, all of it. The horizon fairly curved with poverty. And of course, the usual people: those cute colored chicks with their auburn wigs and clicking heels, moving right along, but not giving you a tumble at all—very efficient, no poverty in them!—their new Falcons waiting downstairs to take them home to Mother.

The kid got the usual looks and then here came onto the scene our man—John Black, we'll call him—not casual he, hardly a touch of the academic, a real Washington pro, a pol, minor but genuine. His hand was out and it had mine. By golly, it did. He was just fine. And the kid, pause, well, why not—it would add a touch of . . . realism. "Gentlemen, if you will just wait for me here—I am sorry to say that the usual has happened—there are three meetings—I don't know exactly where they all are, but in good time, in good time." Black disappeared and we sat. There were no magazines, nothing to read. They hadn't been there long enough. Poverty was the latest thing, and it hadn't been around long enough to accumulate magazines. Just when I was beginning to get angry—I think we had been there for about twenty minutes—in came Black's head again. "Wait, wait, don't get discouraged," says the very crisp Mr. Black. Obviously he has said this before. "Things are getting organized—we're getting them organized. We will have you taken care of in a minute." Of course, it's all very Kafka. Everybody looks as though he knows what he's doing. I don't. All I received was an invitation to serve on a committee, a committee whose name I have forgotten by now, and anyway, it doesn't matter.

Why should I be taken care of? They're thinking in terms of my

11

needs. I can see it. I'm a client. So, let me be a client, me and the kid. You get the feeling that sitting is bad for your image. You're the kind of person they can afford to keep waiting as they hurry about getting things organized, setting up the lines of communication, the formal structure. We can't tackle problems until we have some kind of formal structure, guidelines, theoretical orientation, conceptual framework, desks in place, and water flowing in the urinals. Even here at the tippy-top of the lookout tower on poverty. Again Black's head: "Aha, now we're ready." He comes and stands before me, shakes his head sadly from side to side. "I'm terribly sorry, but I will be unable to attend this meeting. We're so busy here." I think to myself, "What meeting?" Perhaps I'm to talk to myself. Perhaps there are no others at all. It's not impossible. However, there is to be a group—"Aha, here they are—Dr. Jones, Dr. Slack. Mr. Thompson, Dr. Slack"—he looks at me, and I introduce Sammy. Sammy what? The kid, like so many other kids, doesn't say his last name, doesn't say a word. Now is the time for the confrontation. My joke. Anyway, they're not going to bat an eye, and they don't. So we go into the conference room and the meeting begins.

I can't tell you what we talked about, but it was unimportant. That much I remember. The War on Poverty was being lost minute by minute. Their stratagems, their plans, had all mounted to the same thing—hire more generals with or without Ph.D.'s, hire more troops. Not poverty-stricken troops, you understand. A man who is starving cannot fight the War on Poverty. Hire only healthy, well-fed troops, nice middle-class troops. The kind who have never missed a meal or a class, the kind who speak good English, present the proper image, the image of efficiency.

Through it all the kid sat there getting bored, occasionally standing up and walking and looking out the window, looking down, trying to find his house, maybe, or to see if he could see some other kid he knew. Nothing we said or did made any sense to him. My joke was not funny. He was getting bored. So finally I decided to start an argument. "I am against counseling." I said. "The poverty-stricken in the United States" (now I was getting noble) "have had enough counseling already." This was a shocker—to be against counseling! Imagine, what kind of note is this? So we started to argue, not real out-and-out arguing, you understand, but professional arguing. They began diagnosing me subtly. They began questioning my motives, all with kind understanding. I, meanwhile, defended the position that counseling was no good. It

12

could have been any position. I could have said psychiatry was no good, or that teachers didn't know how to teach the poverty-stricken— fire the teachers. It wouldn't matter. The point is that I was right and they knew it. It's easy to attack any middle-class professional in front of other middle-class professionals. It's no game, really. No sport in it. They all know they're no good. They know they're losing the war, but they try to pretend there is no war. They don't believe poverty can be eliminated. It's just not polite or professionally ethical to say so, that's all. But I always do. That's my joke.

Meanwhile, the kid sits there, not understanding, not saying any-thing, but beginning to be a little bit interested. He's seeing his parents quarrel. When the argument reaches a pitch, say, professionals should be fired and poor people hired—this is extreme, you understand—the kid speaks up. "May I ask a question?" he says in surprisingly good English—not "can," "may." Everybody sort of expected that he wouldn't be able to talk. You know, clients. His voice is rather resonant, as a matter of fact, and everything he says is perfectly understandable. Suddenly I know what is happening to everybody else in the room, because I'm feeling it in myself. Maybe he will really have something to say, and perhaps he'll put us all down. "Yes," says Jones, my op-ponent, who hates me by now, "Yes," and with a great display of not looking at me, he turns and looks directly at the kid. "It's obvious *we* have all been missing something here," says Jones—by "we" he means Slack. "We have been talking as if we knew what goes on in the minds of people. We have been making many assumptions. Now we can per-haps get them cleared up. Speak, young man—if Dr. Slack will give you a moment. I would like to hear what *you* have to say." Jones pauses . . . triumphant, looking at the others.

The kid looks at us all. The wheels are turning. There is a long pause. I begin to feel depressed—maybe the kid can't talk, after all, or maybe he has nothing to say. The pause is so long, in fact, that the argument is sort of forgotten. The kid decides to let it lie. He speaks: "Everybody— I mean all the people who work here," says the kid. "All youse, you go home from here five o'clock. Right?" Thompson lights up. He is very patient, very understanding, very professional. "Well, we go if we want to," he says, "but sometimes we have to work later. Last night I didn't get out of my office until nine-fifteen, but, generally speaking, people go home at five o'clock." "Then what happens?" says the kid. We all looked at him. The obvious question is, "What do you mean, what happens?" But nobody says it. There's just a pause. The kid speaks again: "I mean, what happens to this place—it just gets empty? Right?" Nobody says anything. "If it's just empty, why couldn't kids on this block . . . I mean neighborhood—they could come up here and . . . Why can't we use this for dances?"

THE DONOR'S CLUB

It's a meeting of the Council on Foundations, Inc. This is the circle in the circle-in-the-circle. I'm there because a guy took me, that's all. I certainly don't have any money to give away, but these philanthropists are all sitting around having a fairly good lunch and talking to each other about exciting things they've seen. To philanthropists the world is made up of the deserving and the undeserving. I suppose a philanthropist would *like* to view everybody as deserving, but nobody is that rich. The richer you are, the more requests you get, so that even the Ford Foundation has to sift out the deserving from the undeserving. This, of course, is the philanthropists' trap, for they cannot long sustain the policy of giving to the undeserving—at least not around *that* luncheon table where everyone is talking about putting money into good things and not putting money into bad, and everyone is secretly wondering whether the things *they* thought were "responsible" or "dynamic" were going to turn out "unstable" or "lifeless" in someone else's opinion, and whether or not they ought to mention them.

Giving money away gets right to the soul, no question about it. It's hardly possible to give away money without emotion, although some bureaucrats at Ford or Carnegie come close. The essential paradigm (and if you're not professional you have known this all along) is the case of the man who had fallen among thieves or fallen somewhere, or maybe he hadn't fallen but is just standing there nodding from too much glue or maybe he just stole your coat. Anyway, he is undeserving, or looks it. Now there are three things you can do. You can stop, give away the cloak, put him up in the best hospital, and have an emotional experience—unavoidable. But how about this part of the experience: after you've spent $150 trying to help this bum, what does your wife say when you get home? How do you justify it in terms of the children's education and what do you say under your breath about the government because the $150 is not deductible in April? The act of really giving real things like money to real people—not loans, you understand, but real gifts—is guaranteed to produce an experience, not altogether

14

pleasant, of course, but there's no denying it when it happens. On the other hand, walking right by and pretending that you didn't see the guy lying there, or even if you did, saying something like "We're better off if he's dead . . ." this, too, is an emotional experience—I mean if you really see the guy and decide to put him down, well, that's something.

The third thing is really what came to mind, however, and that's giving to the Community Chest, which is, as much as possible, set up to protect you from any emotional experience whatsoever. The closest thing you are going to get in the way of reaction if you give your money is a vague remembrance of the face of that kid in the commercial on the side of the stamp that doesn't have glue on it. Now when you give your money to the Community Chest, you somehow have the vague feeling that perhaps *they* (whoever *they* are) are going to know whether this person is deserving or not, or whether that kid is really crippled, and if so, what he really needs. After all, there *are* professionals, aren't there, and these professionals are *supposed* to know. The fact of the matter is that the professionals do not have emotional experiences either, for the simple reason that it's not their money—it's just their budget, and there's all the difference in the world, believe me, *all* the difference, between your *money* and your *budget*. Usually the professionals do not give it away at all, but pay the salaries of more professionals who in turn are supposed to give it away, and so on, until it is all used up and there is no more to give away anyhow.

Now, there is a real argument with real emotion behind it—I mean the kind of thing one can get upset about—that money should never be given away at all, but only invested. There is joy to investing, and one does know that the money is at least making a noise—I mean like toothbrushes or automobiles—and a profit, dividends four times a year. And this, as a by-product, creates jobs, and some of those jobs can go to bums—some even to undeserving bums. I know, because there are lots of undeserving people who work for large corporations, and if I were giving away money I wouldn't give it to them. But because they do their job, or a reasonable facsimile of it, they get paid by these corporations. And, as a matter of fact, there are some nice, deserving guys who are not doing their jobs, maybe because they are hung up on being a "real person" or something, or maybe they are frustrated artists. Anyway, they are not doing a good job, and even if they're nice guys, they get fired. Actually, corporations rarely fire anybody—they don't have to; people just sort of line up.

15

All of this was going on as I sat there eating that crosscut roast beef that comes in the little ovals *au jus,* and the broccoli spears. It seemed to me that anybody in his right mind would be able to see that the Foundation of Foundations divides itself into two groups. On the one hand, there are the rich people, one or two who made the money themselves and the rest whose fathers and grandfathers did. And then there are the professionals, the bureaucrat types who really don't think of themselves as philanthropists at all, but who "maintain identification with their disciplines." That is to say, they are really social scientists, which makes them very important and, in my opinion, very, very dangerous.

Some of the rich people who enjoy thinking about the results of their gifts are older folks. They command respect, what they say goes, they are not used to being said nay to; and although many of their thoughts are beautiful, many of them are just wacky. When the rich come out with some new idea—"Let's give the money to *so-and-so*"—the bureaucrats (who are trying to make their position secure even though as "professional scientists" they know that so-and-so is a kooky cult) still are not about to say "no." Consequently, the "real rich," as distinguished from the "budget rich," do have emotional experiences. As a matter of fact, some of them appear to be continually involved in a kind of orgy of redemption, their voices on the verge of cracking and their eyes kind of full, as they start to talk about the things they've done with their money. The professional budget guys, on the other hand, are as emotionless as you can imagine. The only way to get a rise out of them is to challenge their "disciplines," to make some statement like, "Why doesn't sociology ever create anything—all they do is analyze." If you can get these guys to imagine themselves having to come in contact with real people who, in real time, are actually suffering from something, then the social scientists begin to take on an emotion. But the emotion is fear—fear that somehow their discipline will get lost in the shuffle or that their job is not as secure as they thought it was. However you slice it, a bureaucrat is a bureaucrat.

The speaker at the luncheon (there always is a speaker) was just back from marching in Selma (one day down, one week marching, one day back) and told us all about the Role of Youth in Social Change. This guy was very smart, a first-rate, third-level politician. He spoke quickly and well, mentioning facts about the great things young people were doing, how Selma was really *their* march. One got the idea that

16

they were noble and great. On the other hand, "We mustn't romanticize them," he said; "we must be objective. We must realize . . ." and he went on to sew it all up with a quote from Gandhi and an allusion to Freud. When he had finished, he had made all of us in that room, rich man and sycophant alike, feel ten years older. When he talked about "we," he meant old folks. He left us no way except, of course, the one path that is *always* left to *all* people on all the foundations, the teller's window through which the money goes but through which people cannot pass. For what the smart politician told us all was, "Kids are great these days. Kids are wonderful. Kids are really *noble,* but we mustn't romanticize them. We must keep our heads and of course we must set up more subfoundations with more funds going to more bureaucrats, who will keep their heads, provide supervision and guidance . . ." and so on. In other words, "Don't *do* anything—just give 'support.'"

Suppose he said the opposite? Suppose he had told the people there that *they* were great, that *they* were noble, that *they* were responsible for the change in the world, that the money *they* had given had produced the change in youth, that the foundations *they* set up had helped to begin the Great Society. Suppose he told them, "Don't give any more money, just come out and be great yourself, since you are already so noble." This was what they wanted to hear, but they weren't going to hear it, at least not from a smart politician. So the meeting came to its quiet close with everybody thinking how great those kids were, how much they needed guidance and counseling, and how everybody should now set up another branch of their foundation with the special interests of youth in mind.

A FIFTEEN-CENT WAR ON POVERTY

I left the meeting, went out to 60th Street with John, the man who had invited me to attend in the first place, and we headed downtown for a meeting with Big Chino. On the way, however, we stopped off to fight some poverty. We did it on a budget of fifteen cents, and here's how it worked. It turns out that John is a musical-comedy singer as well as a philanthropist. I mean, he is just starting on his career. Actually, he thinks of himself as a student. If he thought of himself as a singer he would be one. And for a moment he did.

In Central Park there was an ice-cream man who was humming songs, along with a bearded guitar player and a student banging on the bottom of one of those cardboard five-gallon circular things. The five-

17

gallon thing had had pistachio in it which kept leaking on to his shoes as he held it like a bongo drum, but that didn't seem to matter. Anyway, he played that. His buddy played the guitar, and the ice-cream man was humming. It was all very soft and sort of sweet, and nobody was noticing at all. John and I walked up to this scene and he spotted the songfest at the same time as I spotted two kids with glue-soaked paper bags. They were lying half-hidden in some bushes there in Central Park. I know a lot about these things, and I can tell when youngsters are high on glue. These kids were not "there" yet. You could sort of see that they were going to try to get high. They looked to be about twelve or thirteen, and they were not Negro—maybe Irish. Anyway, they knew they were doing something bad and were looking at each other in that funny way, holding the paper bags behind their backs. Cops were all around, but that probably made it more fun. So this is the scene at this point: John spotting the ice-cream man with the guitar player and the bongo player, I spotting the two kids with the glue-soaked paper bags, and nobody else aware of anybody else's existence.

Now with fifteen cents John suddenly won a major battle against poverty. He walked up to the ice-cream salesman and bought himself a popsickle. The ice-cream man started to break up his act to go for the ice cream. John shook his head—"No, no," he said, "continue." So there they were, for two full acts, singing on the sidewalk right there in front of Central Park and 60th Street—rich John, the philanthropist who usually thinks of himself as studying to become a musical-comedy singer and who briefly in this moment became a real singer, the ice-cream man who was the best singer of all, and the accompaniment. For the first act John waved his fifteen cents around in time with the music. They did "Santa Lucia," "O Sole Mio," one third of the sextet from *Lucia di Lammermoor*. Then the man gave John the ice cream and for the second act he waved the popsickle, and then they got into what they really knew how to do, "Old Man River," "Danny Boy," and that kind of thing.

As the music grew louder and louder, the kids under the bush began to take interest and started to move toward us. They moved in close enough to become a real audience and sat on their heels that way during the second act. In order to do this they had to expose their backs, so they carefully tucked the paper bags with the glue in them behind the bushes. While they were watching the show I sneaked around into the bush and stole their paper bags, placing them way down at the bottom

18

of one of those "Don't Litter" bins. I watched the kids all the time I did this and I know they didn't see me. After the concert was over and we started to walk away, I was afraid to look back for fear that the kids might read my mind, or something like that. I never did find out what happened to them. But I know this much—you can get high just looking at some people.

Part II: The System

Editors' Introduction   In recent years, the rallying cry of indignant activists, whether in the civil-rights movement or in the universities, has been against something called "the establishment" or "the system." The concept is not without sociological foundations. Although there may *seldom* exist a monolithic, all-powerful, all-encompassing "system" controlled by a greedy and selfish oligarchy, there *always* exists a traditional *modus vivendi* which appears to those on top (and usually to those in the middle) to "work"—and work well.

The established ways of getting things done and of relating to others are comfortable, known, predictable phenomena. They provide the framework within which those who have obtained and achieved the most society has to offer can continue to operate under familiar rules with outcomes that can be anticipated within reasonable limits. For those on the bottom of the heap and for those who are "outsiders," the sacred quality of these systems is open to challenge. But how does a small minority of the population successfully challenge the power and authority which maintain the system? Especially when, unlike the revolutionary periods of world history, the great majority of the population perceives itself as having a vested interest in the status quo?

Part II consists of three excursions into situations in which the poor find themselves confronting one or another segment of "the system"; these excursions are sandwiched between opening and closing chapters which analyze the operations of the system from a broader perspective. Rose introduces us to the macro-system with a commentary on the national economy. He sketches, historically and in terms of their continuing impact on the working man, such large-scale changes as automation and economic depression. Rose hammers home one simple point: solutions to problems of unemployment and underemployment do not lie in primitive efforts to "stimulate the economy." He points out that there are several types of people who are thought of as "unemployables," including those who have the misfortune to live in the wrong place at the wrong time and those who are thought to be unqualified to work—unqualified by reason of age, education, ethnicity, or physical, mental, or moral characteristics. Clearly, different kinds of action are required if we are to deal effectively with these different types of "unemployables." Rose proceeds to spell out types of actions which can be taken to modify the system in ways that will convert each type of "unemployable" into an "employable."

The second chapter in this section takes us into one small segment of a system encountered by many (and studiously avoided by many more) of the urban poor—public housing. Low-income public housing was originally designed in the late 1930's for a relatively "deserving poor"—unemployed craftsmen and skilled workers without shops, college and high school graduates without jobs, schoolteachers without schools—people apparently trapped by a temporary defect in the economic system. These sudden and short-term poor were steeped in all of the accepted virtues and values of middle-class America. The Great Depression did indeed pass, but in the aftermath of the war which followed it, a new and possibly not so "deserving" poor knocked at the doors of these same public housing projects, requesting the same services and facilities. How does the system manage to minimize the potential threat in such a situation?

In this second chapter we meet a functionary whom the poor encounter frequently in all segments of their everyday life—the gatekeeper. This particular gatekeeper guards the public housing segments. By walking with her through her daily routines, we come to understand how the system is maintained and the problem which it poses for the poor. Other gatekeepers are making similar decisions in behalf of the system in public and private welfare, in the courts, in the clinics and hospitals, in the schools and colleges, and in local decisions concerning research, training, and demonstration projects that might have influence over the lives of the poor and the operation of the system.

In "Two Men and Their Families," Willie takes us through the looking glass, so that we no longer walk with the gatekeeper but now find ourselves viewing the system from the perspective of the people who pound on the gates. In describing the plight of two poor families, Willie builds a case for new kinds of encounters between the poor and knowledgeable, sympathetic agents of the middle-class society. He calls these agents who know the ropes "intercessors" and describes the manner in which they can facilitate the achievement of the American Dream for those whose lives are forever bordering on nightmare. As Willie states his case, "The story of two men and their families is the story of marginal earners in the nation's capital who are passed over by private agencies and turned away from public services because they have bread enough. Who cares if there's none to spare?"

Can the poor transform the world? Recognizing how the varieties of the poor (alluded to by Rose in Chapter 2) mitigate against successful organization—that "the poor are to be found in scattered, mutually hostile enclaves across the country"—Haggstrom begins his chapter with the observation that *all* solutions to poverty have failed. His purpose is to analyze the conditions under which the poor could organize effectively to transform the world and to consider whether such conditions can be met. Building from a solid base of theory combined with extensive personal experience in efforts to organize the poor and to train organizers, Haggstrom systematically formulates a program to effectively confront and alter the system.

Haggstrom is committed to the idea of self-realization for the poor. In contrast to Willie's proposed intercessor role, Haggstrom argues that the worst thing an organizer can do is to permit a definition of himself as a "fixer." People must define the problems which are important to them, must set the goals they hope to achieve, and must strive to attain these goals in their own manner. The organizer is little more than a technical assistant. He is a consultant on tactics and strategy, an architect who builds scaffolding rather than structure. For ultimately the organizer is an outsider. Haggstrom reminds us that although the world of the affluent is visible to and known to the poor, the reverse is not true. The middle and upper classes have only the foggiest notion of what it is like to be poor. In spite of our intent, it is unlikely that this volume will dissipate any significant amount of that fog. As social scientists, we belong to the other world; we are outsiders to what Haggstrom calls "that mysterious land of the poor."

With these "cases" behind us, Miller's indictment of the "credential society" provides an analysis of how the larger system operates—and why. Beginning with the observation that, contrary to the American Dream, the gap between the "haves" and the "have-nots" is widening, Miller knits together a chain of ideas resulting from his long-standing concern about poverty in America. Elsewhere in this volume, Pearl argues that poor youngsters are systematically excluded from school, and Rainwater and Higgins both show how the poor are excluded from health facilities and resources. In this chapter, Miller states that poor youngsters are increasingly and systematically excluded from the world of work. Our society, Miller observes, is more willing to spend money on welfare assistance for youth than to provide jobs for youth. "Youth and the Changing Society" spells out the problems confronting the system and our tendency to respond with sympathetic doles.

What can be done about the problems the system generates for the poor? Miller sees a need for preventive measures—measures which would require radical alterations in the perspectives of labor unions, helping professions, and, perhaps, the society as a whole. For one thing, he suggests that the poor need "fixers"—intercessors of the type proposed by Willie. But a major hope of Miller's is the politicalization of the poor. A prolegomena for the politicalization of the poor, a "how to do it" manual, is precisely what Haggstrom suggests in his contribution to this section.

Part II of this volume, then, reviews encounters between the poor and an assortment of outsiders acting on them, toward them, or in their behalf: gatekeepers, intercessors, and organizers.

2 • The "Unemployables"

ARNOLD M. ROSE

MOST OF THE GOVERNMENT efforts to cope with the high rate of unemployment that has developed since the late 1950's have been based on older conceptions of the causes of unemployment. Political and economic leaders have not fully grasped the fact that the causes of unemployment are more complex today than they have been in the past. Not that the older causes have disappeared and the older remedies are completely useless, but that additional problems have developed and new ideas are needed to cope with them. Unfortunately, even today there is an influential school of thought which advocates solution of the unemployment problem solely through stimulation of the economy. In this chapter, I shall emphasize conditions which demonstrate that such a policy, by itself, is inadequate.

Just as the United States seems to have learned to control cyclical unemployment ("depression unemployment") through government action, it has become faced with the serious re-emergence of a form of unemployment that was thought to have died with the nineteenth century—technological unemployment. The first Industrial Revolution had caused a considerable amount of displacement from traditional jobs as machines were discovered that could do the work of many men. The short-run consequences had been serious in the nineteenth century when there was no unemployment insurance or organized relief programs. Still, the technologically unemployed had been reabsorbed into the economy after short periods of personal hardship, for several reasons: (1) the economy and the country itself were rapidly expanding, and there was a constant demand for labor in the new industries; (2)

25

the frontier was open, and those dispossessed of their livelihoods in the older sections of the country could find a way of living in the wilderness; (3) the new industry, in contrast to the previous method of production, required a lower level of skills, so that while a man might not be able to get a job for which he was particularly qualified, he could find an opening which required *less* training or experience. Over the long run, the nineteenth century was a period of prosperity, in which population and productive capacity multiplied.

From the post-Civil War period to 1940, unemployment was increasingly associated with economic depressions, not with technological innovation. The 1930's saw the creation of two types of government policies to solve the problem. One was an elaborate program of work relief, intended to provide income for persons who had lost their regular jobs. The second was a program of "depression control" through increased government expenditures to absorb unemployment and increase purchasing power (the application of the Keynes theory). The periodic recessions since 1945 seem to have been controlled and adjusted to by means of these two policies.

Even in the best of times, however, there was a residue of unemployed persons. These were mainly considered unemployables: physically and mentally handicapped persons; old persons; youth who had little education; residents of depressed areas who did not move to other areas where jobs were available; and other persons considered poor risks for employment. To this list should be added members of certain minority groups—Negroes, Mexican-Americans, and Indians—who were discriminated against to some extent.

Since 1955 there has been a new major reason for unemployment: the reduced need for unskilled and marginal labor because of automation. This has expanded the number of "unemployables."

UNEMPLOYMENT: THE "EMPLOYABLES" AND THE "UNEMPLOYABLES"

In considering the unemployment resulting from automation and other technological changes, it will be useful to distinguish two categories of displaced workers: (1) those who are young or middle-aged and hence have many working years ahead of them, are basically educated, have good working habits, have no characteristics which handicap them on the labor market, are located where industry and commerce exist and are likely to grow along with the general growth of population and of

26

the economy; (2) those who lack one or more of the foregoing characteristics, and hence may be considered in some ways as unemployable
or underemployable. Most of the recent discussion of technological unemployment has concerned itself with the first category, whereas the
facts to date indicate that it is the second category who constitute the
victims of technological unemployment. The employable unemployed
in the first category need only retraining to get jobs, and both private
industry and government are now developing programs to provide
that. There is actually a *shortage* of properly trained labor, and there is
no other valid economic reason to believe that there will not be enough
jobs to go around. As the economist Leontief points out:

> The amount of capital needed for each unit of output has ac-
> tually been reduced in recent years, and the installation of
> automatic machinery will further reduce it. Therefore labor
> should be able to maintain or improve its relative share of the
> national income. The danger of technological unemployment
> should be even smaller in the foreseeable future than it was at
> the end of the 19th century, when capital requirements were
> rising.[1]

Of course, there is likely to be a period of temporary unemployment
whenever automation is introduced, but existing unemployment insurance and the developing paid training programs are capable of com-
pensating for that. The more serious problem of technological unemployment, I believe, is the growing number of persons in the second
category—persons who have some characteristics which prevent them
from fitting into the changing system of production, and hence may be
called unemployable.[2]

There can be little doubt that the number of "unemployable" persons
in the job-seeking population is increasing and that further technological advance will increase their number still more. The significant fact
seems to be that *technological unemployment today, as distinguished
from that which occurred in the nineteenth century, consists of unemployables.* In saying this, however, we must recognize that "unemployability" is not for the most part an absolute: it is purely relative to the
characteristics of the job-seeking population and to the jobs available.
A person who has characteristics which make him unemployable today
was not likely to have been so ten years ago, and need not be so next
year. In one sense, practically no one is intrinsically unemployable. If
the handicaps of the most unlikely person are adjusted and an appro-

27

priate niche can be found for him, the unemployable becomes employed. Still, in terms of existing personal characteristics and of existing job opportunities, it is useful to recognize that there is unemployability and that it is growing today largely because of technological advances.

Let us see what these characteristics are that currently make for unemployability, in a general way. One is residence in an area where the only major industry has sharply declined or has become automated. Major examples are cotton-growing areas of the South; some New England textile centers; coal-mining areas of West Virginia, Pennsylvania, and Kentucky; and iron-mining areas of northern Minnesota. The problem of these areas is not merely that the former industry has declined but that no new industry has arisen in them to take the place of the old. This problem is likely to increase as a reduction of tariffs cuts off the protected market for certain inefficient industries (such as textiles) located in regions where there are no other major industries. Within these regions are thousands of able-bodied potential workers, some even with skills that are in demand elsewhere.

A second category of unemployable is that of older persons—roughly fifty years of age and over—who are able-bodied but have been displaced from their jobs by automation and other technological advances and are not considered to have sufficient working years left to be "worth" retraining.

The third category consists of youth who, for one reason or another, have not finished high school and hence do not have enough basic education to be considered good risks for advanced training for skilled jobs which are available. The amount of basic education deemed necessary for giving specialized training to these youth, as well as the maximum age at which a displaced older person is deemed "worth retraining," is a function of the availability of other, "higher quality" labor.

A fourth category of unemployables consists of members of minority groups who, despite their good health, usable skills, and favorable age, are not hired because of racial prejudice on the part of employers, unions, or customers. Because of Fair Employment Practice laws in twenty states and forty cities of the North—which include practically all the areas where minority persons live in the North—most of this kind of unemployment now occurs in the South, but not all. In the North, the greatest discrimination is found in the building trades, where union rules governing apprenticeship, high initiation fees, seniority for advancement, and "recommendation" by present union members serve effectively to keep members of minority groups practically out of these trades.

A fifth category consists of persons with physical, mental, or moral handicaps (including alcoholics, drug addicts, hermits, "psychopaths," and "sociopaths") who seek work at least occasionally but are employed generally only in times of great labor shortage, such as in World War II or possibly again during the Vietnam conflict. This category is so heterogeneous that it might best be considered in terms of its component elements rather than as a group. The physically handicapped person who can be rehabilitated and trained for a specialized skill job should not properly be put into the same category as a person who has no real motivation to accept regular employment. Still, the policy considerations that apply to all these people are sufficiently similar to justify treating them as a single category. Also, perhaps needless to say, there is a certain amount of overlap among all five categories.

The usefulness of this classification lies in the consideration that *different* public policies are most appropriate for dealing with each category, and we shall shortly turn to a consideration of appropriate and feasible public policies. In suggesting a policy that will reduce unemployment in one category, it must be recognized that it could raise the number of unemployables in another category, although it will not necessarily do so. Some of the slackness of the economy is actually due to an insufficiency of qualified labor in the appropriate location, and government policy along lines already suggested could increase the total number of job opportunities. We are here limiting our consideration to the fact that the great technological advances of the current years have materially increased the number of persons who can be considered unemployables under present circumstances and that policies which we shall now discuss can reduce the number of unemployables.

Of course, once made employable, these persons will not necessarily get jobs, because of rigidities in the economy and because of recessions. A total government program practically to eliminate unemployment must be directed at expanding the economy, reducing its rigidities, and controlling recessions, as well as at reducing unemployability. Whether the economy will be expanded is a question of political feasibility which is beyond the scope of our analysis. Reducing the rigidity of the economy (that is, reducing restraints on trade and production) is also a question of political feasibility; the Kennedy-Johnson administrations' chief activity here has been along the lines of reducing tariffs. Controlling recessions does not seem to have been much of a problem for either Democratic or Republican administrations since 1940.

TOWARD THE EMPLOYMENT OF "UNEMPLOYABLES"

Type I: Dead Industries The federal act of 1961 to develop job opportunities in new private industries in areas which have suffered a major decline of their formerly sustaining industries is not likely to be very successful in the long run. State governments have already tried to attract new private industries to these areas, and while the resources of the federal government are greater, they are not likely to overcome a basic handicap. These areas—in the rural South, in the mountains of both East and West, and in northern Minnesota—are not favorable locations from the standpoint of transportation, raw materials, or markets. It is not economic (in the sense of efficient) to locate industries there, and while economic loss may be outweighed by human benefits, it is not to be ignored. Still, some minor successes have been scored by the government's Area Redevelopment Program, particularly in the Appalachian region.

Thus far, the government has done very little about a complementary policy—moving individuals and families to areas where jobs are available or where new industries can be more economically built. The historic lack of a "migration policy" by the United States government seems to be due to two sets of factors. One is the democratic postulate, and constitutional provision, that citizens must be allowed to live where they wish without interference by government. This does not explain, however, why the government has never aided people who might *want* to move, other things being equal, but who lacked the information and resources which would make migration feasible. The second barrier to a government policy of aiding migrants has been the "investments"—of both a private and public nature—which people have in their existing communities. There are homes, schools, churches, and other material facilities which it would be costly to abandon; there are also emotional attachments to family, friends, and community.

Still, some people have always been willing to give up these investments, for most migration—which has always been considerable in the United States—involves such losses. Public facilities in these old areas have already been mostly amortized, and there is no reason why the federal government could not buy out old homes of would-be migrants in certain areas, just as it now pays farmers to take land out of production. The main features of a migration policy would not be these, however. What is most needed is *information* about the location of specific kinds of job opportunities, about procedures to find housing in new communities, about the condition of schools, churches, cost of living, and so on, in new communities. Lack of information has always made a considerable amount of existing migration economically fruitless and personally tragic. An earlier study by Vance showed that, by five-year periods from 1920 to 1935, it took over 14,000,000, 18,000,000, and 13,000,000 total moves, respectively, in both directions to give *net* movements to cities of 3,300,000, 2,900,000, and 500,000.[3]

Also needed are better facilities for hiring over long distances, small loans to pay for transportation of families and household goods,[4] and other small material aids that will lessen the problems of long-distance migration. It would not be very costly for the United States Employment Service to become better integrated throughout the country, to expand its services to provide information about living conditions as well as about job opportunities, and to provide some of the small material aids suggested. There are now privately organized "Welcome Wagons" which provide local information and limited services for persons who have recently moved into a community. Perhaps they could be made somewhat more comprehensive, both in their organization in communities where they do not now exist and in the range of their services. This could be done either by voluntary associations or private businesses, as now, or as a new activity by United States employment offices, or a combination of both. Fear of the unknown is a major deterrent to migration, and it could readily and cheaply be reduced. At any rate, the United States government ought to consider that it has as great an obligation to native misplaced persons as it has to immigrant displaced persons. An aid-to-migration policy should not be a makeshift policy, as are so many other government policies; it would provide a long-run and self-liquidating solution to the problem of unemployability caused by the decline of traditional industries in certain areas.

Type II: Technological Displacement of Older Workers   Older workers displaced by automation and other technological advances cannot usually be economically retrained for the kinds of technical jobs available in the new kinds of industries. They can, however, be retrained for service occupations and part-time jobs which abound, and are continually expanding, in every American community. Those who have already

31

attained an age when they are eligible for social security or other retirement payments can be aided to spend their leisure time satisfyingly in recreational pursuits and voluntary association activities. Among the major problems of old age in our society are rolelessness and loneliness. Considerable success has been achieved in experimental programs to overcome them, and the White House Conference on Aging of 1961 recommended that the federal government help the states set up such programs systematically. It is very difficult under American culture to get people satisfied with a life of leisure, but there are good prospects for achieving this with older persons who have already put in a lifetime of productive labor.

The Older Americans Act of 1965 provided funds for state and local governments and private agencies to sponsor demonstration projects that would constructively utilize the free time of older persons in education, social service, and leisure. Already the Department of Health, Education, and Welfare and the Office of Employment Opportunity have under way two interesting projects on almost a nation-wide basis. One is the "foster grandparent" plan in which qualified older persons would serve in that role for underprivileged youth who lack natural grandparents. The other is Project Greenthumb, in which retired rural persons would participate in a program to beautify the highways and rural recreation areas. It remains to be seen whether these programs will be continued and, if so, what their long-range impact may be.

Type III: Undereducated Youth   The problem of undereducated youth is more serious, even though it probably does not affect so many individuals.[5] These youth face a whole life of underemployment and maladjustment to work. Some of them are of low intelligence, but others are merely immature, misguided, or misinformed. Some of them are in need of psychotherapy, in one degree or another; others are merely in need of vocational counseling and training. It is not a requirement of individualism, as John Stuart Mill long ago pointed out, that there be free enterprise in the education of youth. Failure to give some kind of reasonable opportunity to all young people to find some occupation mildly satisfying to themselves and useful to society marks one of the inexcusable failures of American society. That there are few effective state laws to prevent fraudulent trade schools represents a crime by our legislatures.

Failure to learn the rudiments of education is not only characteristic of those who drop out of high school. It is also found among a significant number of high school graduates in the United States. There are many reasons beside low native ability why pupils fail to learn basic reading, writing, and arithmetic skills in the elementary grades: personal and family problems; large classes; poor teaching; peer-group standards against learning; migration; and so on. The problem lies not so much in these early failures, because they are partially unavoidable, as in the practice of most American schools of advancing *all* students one full grade each year regardless of whether they have, or possibly could have, mastered the material of the preceding year. Programs of remedial reading, arithmetic, and composition are rudimentary in most American schools, and without them the schools push the children along from grade to grade without there being the slightest possibility that they can learn much in the grades to which they are advanced.

Remedial programs ought to begin by the third grade in elementary schools and be available at every grade thereafter. To make them effective, classes would have to be much smaller and teaching more individualized than in the regular classes. Until the remedial program is made thoroughly effective, so that slow-learning youngsters are caught almost as soon as their lag can be detected, the remedial classes might have to be very small to avoid having grown boys and girls in the same classes as third-grade youngsters. One solution for low-ability slow learners might be the ungraded schools with which some communities are now experimenting.

These and other adjustments to the problem of basically uneducated youngsters graduating from high school must be handled by local school administrations and boards of education, many of which do not see the problem at the present time. The federal government, aided by a distinguished committee of educators, needs to educate local school boards, administrations, and the public generally as to the deficiencies in the present American system of education. In saying this, we do not mean to imply that everything about the American system is bad or that the specific techniques of instruction are inadequate. There are many features of the American system that are so desirable that several European countries are now copying them, and we take no position with regard to the purely technical questions involved in methods of instruction. But it should be apparent by now that the American system does not do enough for the slow learner or for the gifted child. Adjustments must be made or the educational years will continue to be wasted and the slow learners will continue to add to the growing pool of underemployables.

President Johnson's anti-poverty program has been highly cognizant of the need to motivate youngsters to complete their schooling and to develop good work habits and attitudes. A great variety of local programs with these goals have been organized under the federal government's Neighborhood Youth Corps (within the community) and the Job Corps (outside the youth's home community). No over-all assessment of these programs has yet been made, but undoubtedly they will have varying success depending on the quality of the local sponsoring organization and its specific activity for the youth.

Type IV: Blocked Opportunities for Minorities   Little can be said about unemployability of some minority-group citizens because of racial prejudice that has not already been very adequately said over and over again. The Northern states are enforcing their Fair Employment Practice laws to a significant degree, and since 1961 the federal government's committee to enforce the non-discrimination clause in contracts between the government and private industry has taken some effective action, so that even Southern industry is becoming less discriminatory in employment. But the nation still has a way to go before a Negro, Indian, or Mexican-American youth will have the same material life chances as a white youth. Segregated education is unequal, specialized training is often closed to non-white youth, and job opportunities are not the same even for equally trained and equally able youth of different races. The federal Civil Rights Act of 1964, which provided that a federal F.E.P.C. be set up in 1965, is helping. The Negro unemployment rate has been falling in at least the same proportion as the white unemployment rate during 1965. In February 1966, it was down to about 7 per cent, while the white rate of unemployment was 3.5 per cent. Of course, this does not take into account the insufficient utilization of Negroes who are technically in the ranks of the employed.

In addition, there is the heritage of past discriminations. Under slavery and in the immediate post-slavery period, many Negroes had high vocational skills, but increasingly after 1870 they were not allowed to exercise them. For some thirty or forty years after 1890, the Southern state governments scarcely supported schools for Negroes. The result has been that most of the present adult generation of Negroes have grown up with inadequate basic education, practically no specialized

34

skill training, and no tradition of getting skill training, either formally through vocational schools or apprenticeship, or informally through father-to-son instruction. Thus, even though the present generation of young Negroes face much less economic discrimination than did their parents and grandparents, they cannot get from them the informed guidance and instruction that white parents are able to afford their youngsters. A special effort by government to provide vocational counseling, encouragement, and training for the youth of minority races can only partially compensate for the present damage caused by past discriminations. The damage done to the middle-aged and older generations of Negroes, Mexican-American, and Indians can never be repaired, but an effort to include these persons equally in vocational retraining programs by private industry and government would provide economic benefits through having able people able to produce at a level closer to their potential.

Type V: The Disabled   Those who have the various physical, mental, and moral disabilities which make them underemployable can be dealt with only under the various rehabilitation programs that have been developed by experts. Some of the programs—such as those for psychopathic and other mentally disturbed persons—are now receiving increasing attention from some state governments, but they need federal assistance. Others of these programs are more expensive to carry out than are the previously mentioned suggestions for government actions to reduce the other categories of unemployables. But they are the kinds of programs which have traditionally been carried out so well by voluntary associations. Perhaps a government program can be developed to stimulate and advise the relevant voluntary associations along these lines and to supplement their activities. Other Western nations—particularly the Scandinavian countries—do much more for their unemployables than does the United States.[6]

CONCLUSIONS

Not only do unemployability and underemployment create personal tragedies and economic waste. They are also a major source of other kinds of social problems—crime, family disorganization, mental disturbances, and others. Ours is not the kind of culture that permits its holders to relax under conditions of permanent unemployment.

Since large-scale unemployability in at least four of the five categories is increasing now with technological advance, even though temporarily camouflaged by general prosperity stimulated partly by the Vietnam war, the nation is faced with something that might be considered a *new* problem. Imaginative new programs by government, industry, and voluntary associations are called for. These should be based on careful study, to avoid such crackpot solutions as have already been experimented with, like cutting the working week of able-bodied skilled males down to twenty or twenty-five hours. None of the programs here is revolutionary, even though some are novel, and none is insuperably expensive for a rich nation. No nation can afford to have a growing body of permanently unemployed, and in the case of the leading capitalist nation, the failure to deal with the problem would indicate the failure of capitalism.

Some ideological reorientation of public opinion is perhaps needed to accustom the American people to accept some of the necessary new programs, but this is the usual educational function of politicians and intellectuals in a democracy. First, however, even the politicians and the intellectuals must understand that the major existing and planned programs to "stimulate the economy" will do little to wipe out most of the sources of unemployment discussed in this chapter.

Arnold M. Rose

Notes

NOTE: This chapter is a revision of parts of Arnold M. Rose's "The New Problem of Large-Scale Unemployability," *American Journal of Economics and Sociology,* XXIII (1964), 337–350. © 1964 by The American Journal of Economics and Sociology. Adapted by permission.

1. Wassily Leontief, "Machines and Man," *Scientific American,* CLXXXVII (September 1952), 156.

2. We shall use the term "unemployable" to include not only the totally unemployed because of these characteristics, but also the part-time or seasonally unemployed because of the same characteristics, who might more properly be called "underemployed."

3. Rupert B. Vance, "Research Memorandum on Population Redistribution Within the United States," *Social Science Research Council Bulletin,* XLII (1938), 105.

4. The present small-loan agencies may not be sufficient when the borrower has to leave the state and hence may be considered a high risk for collection purposes by the local lending agency.

5. Mary Conway Kohler and André Fontaine, "We Waste a Million Kids a Year," *The Saturday Evening Post,* March 10, 1962, pp. 15–22.

6. The programs in these nations are in the form of occupational and recreational therapy as well as the psychotherapy also found in the United States.

3 · The Gatekeeper in Public Housing

IRWIN DEUTSCHER

DURING THE EARLY YEARS of World War II, when he undertook the task of changing the food habits of the American family, Kurt Lewin[1] used the term "gatekeeper" to describe the person who makes the critical decision on whether an item is "in" or "out." The housewife, he discovered, was the gatekeeper in the long process which terminated with certain foods appearing on the American table and others being excluded. The gatekeeper, however, need not be one who has intimate knowledge of and concern for those whose gates she keeps; nor do the objects passing through (or blocked by) the gate need to be impersonal. Those objects can be, and often are, people.

In any society—primitive or modern, urban or rural—individuals encounter a series of gates as they move through the life cycle. And at each encounter the decision between in and out is made by the gatekeeper. It may be a foregone conclusion—a ritualistic decision; it may be one that is determined by tradition; it may be the whimsical result of a powerful and capricious individual. It is also possible for such decisions to be made according to formal rules and criteria—or, for that matter, according to informal rules and criteria.

As a society becomes more urbanized, more impersonal, more specialized, more governed by formal rules, so too does the gatekeeping process and the gatekeeper himself. In a bureaucratic world one should expect to confront bureaucratic gatekeepers. The common man, in particular, frequently finds himself compelled to seek access to mysterious regions. Whether he needs to approach the Veterans Administration, a hospital, a university,[2] or a public housing authority, he must encounter a gatekeeper who will determine just how far he will get and how long it will take him. He "must," that is, unless he has the power or the influence to circumvent the gatekeeper with a direct appeal to the throne, an alternative process which is discussed below. The fact remains that because of his ignorance of such specialized bureaucracies, the common man often finds himself at the mercy of the ubiquitous gatekeeper.

Although there is consistency in the function of the gatekeeper, there is variability in the manner in which this function is carried out. At one extreme is the rigid adherence to formal rules to such an extent that the goals of the organization become subverted to the means designed to achieve them. This is the mode of adaptation described by Merton as "ritualism." [3] At the opposite pole is the "debureaucratizing" type of gatekeeper, tentatively identified by Katz and Eisenstadt. They observed that in contacts between Israeli officials and newly arrived immigrants, the officials socialize immigrants with traditional familistic backgrounds to new role expectations such as factory worker, hospital patient, welfare client, and bus passenger. These gatekeepers assumed the role not only of teacher but of informal leader among groups of newly arrived immigrants.[4] Unlike the ritualist gatekeeper, who permits the goals of the organization to be subverted by the rules, these "debureaucratizing" gatekeepers may encourage subversion of the rules in order to facilitate achievement of the goals. In effect, they resemble Merton's "innovator." [5]

There are many variations to these themes. Some gatekeepers may simply apply the appropriate rubber stamps to the appropriate papers in the manner of customs inspectors, but others acquire a sense of personal commitment to and responsibility for the bureaucracy. They guard their gates with loyalty, and the force of their own belief in the system breathes vitality into the impersonal function. The gatekeeper becomes a person with a purpose, and each decision between in and out becomes one of personal importance. Such a bureaucratic gatekeeper is described here.

THE GATEKEEPER

The larger study for which the observations in this chapter were made is concerned with the flow of applicants and tenants through public housing projects. Early attention was focused on the region of the gate and the gatekeeping function in the housing projects to be studied. Preliminary explorations left the research staff with the impression that the application officer was the key person in tenant selection—the gate-keeper to public housing. This impression was supported by participant-observations made in her office. The analysis which follows derives from the observer's two weeks of experience in the application office of a municipal Public Housing Authority.

The observer sat at a small table in the corner of the application office, watching the intake procedure and assisting in it. The primary purpose of the observations was to learn enough about how the intake and assignment process works so that a system could be developed for randomizing future assignments with a minimum disruption of current procedures. Implied in this purpose was the need to establish a working relationship with the application officer. The application officer is the gatekeeper to public housing. She is the first contact a prospective applicant makes with the bureaucracy. Whether or not the prospective applicant becomes an eligible applicant, whether or not the eligible ap-plicant can hope to become a tenant, and in which project he is most likely to become a tenant—all of these depend, in large part, upon the impression he makes on the gatekeeper at the initial contact.

The gatekeeper whose functions are observed in this chapter is the daughter of a prominent local surgeon—a widow in her late fifties. She has been in the employ of the Housing Authority since its establishment over twenty years ago. She can be described as scrupulously honest, hewing carefully to the legal requirements of the job, courteous to the poorest and crudest of applicants, and exercising considerable flexibility in the interpretation of her function. Clearly she more nearly ap-proaches the innovating gatekeeper type than the ritualist type,[6] al-though certainly not to the extent of the Israeli officials described by Katz and Eisenstadt. Such flexibility derives from a secure knowledge of the formal rules of the game she plays, twenty years of experience, and an unwavering devotion to the ethical prescriptions of the urban middle class. She represents what has been described by students of the modern hospital as the "home guard"[7]—in her seniority, her informal power, her knowledge of the informal networks of the system, and her strong convictions of what is good and what is bad for the organization to which she has devoted a considerable part of her life.

THE DECISION BETWEEN "IN" OR "OUT":
SOURCES OF THE GATEKEEPER'S INITIATIVE

A potential applicant for public housing must make a personal appearance at the application office, where he is provided with a checklist of documents and items of information which will be required before a formal application can be made. On rare occasions, people are informed at this point of the futility of going any further with the application process. This may (but does not always) occur when the applicant is grossly over the legal income limits, when he does not meet residence requirements, or when his family is too large to be accommodated by existing units. The gatekeeper feels that she should always take applications from "desirable" families, regardless of current eligibility, because "you never can tell what will happen and I like to have good families in the files."

When the applicant returns for his appointment, the gatekeeper fills in the application as the prospective tenant answers her questions. Having supplied the necessary documents, completed his application, been declared eligible, and placed on the waiting list, the prospective tenant may feel that his greatest hurdle has been overcome—that now he needs only to wait until his name comes to the top of the list. Such a definition of the situation is, however, grossly inaccurate. Of the hundreds of eligible families in the files, few will ever get into public housing and fewer still will get in in the immediate future.

The gatekeeper has considerable initiative in determining which applicants will be selected to fill whatever vacancies appear. If an applicant does not have a unit offered to him within a month or two after applying, the probability of his ever getting into public housing drops rapidly. There may be, in fact, an inverse relationship between seniority on the waiting lists and likelihood for selection.

The gatekeeper's initiative in determining priority derives from two sources. The first source is the official policy of the Housing Authority regarding priority. That policy explicitly denies seniority as a basis for selection of prospective tenants. In place of seniority there are a number of criteria ranging from the highly objective and explicit event of having been a member of the armed forces during a specified time period to the highly subjective phenomenon of "need." [8]

The observer noted that the gatekeeper had a section in the front of her files labeled "priority," and that in seeking applicants to fill vacancies she would go through this group first. However, not all vacancies were filled from this group even when apparently appropriate families could be found in it. The observer suggested that this separation of "priority" families from others introduced a complicating factor in the sampling procedure he was attempting to develop and asked if the gatekeeper might have any ideas about how to handle this. Her response was: "Don't worry about priority, because nobody can check on whether or not you are putting priority families in first and I don't always do it anyway." It can be seen that considerable flexibility is introduced into the gatekeeper role by subjective *official* criteria which are open to a broad range of interpretation.

This flexibility is further enhanced by the second source from which the gatekeeper derives initiative in determining priority. This second source, for purposes of distinction, may be labeled the "unofficial." It consists largely of the esoteric knowledge of the gatekeeper, which is partly attributable to her seniority in the system. This esoteric knowledgeability has at least three distinct facets.

The first is the gatekeeper's influence on individual project managers and their office staffs. A public housing project manager traditionally has two primary concerns: (1) to obtain tenants who don't cause trouble and (2) to keep rental loss due to vacancies at a minimum. Without the active cooperation of the application office, his difficulties in both of these areas can spiral. The application officer selects the pool of applicants from which the manager must choose his tenants. Often this selection is discussed over the telephone with the manager or his assistant. The fact that the application officer has been with the Housing Authority longer than any project manager, that she has known each of these people since they began working with the Authority and is aware of their peculiarities, strengths, and weaknesses, manifests itself in a variety of subtle ways. These people are highly dependent upon her to assist them with their two primary concerns and she is well aware of her own power in this situation.

For example, when the observer asked the gatekeeper if one of the project managers and his assistant would complain about receiving "undesirable" tenants when the assignment process was randomized for the study, she replied: "Don't worry about Janet and Art. All Janet is really interested in is collecting the rent, and Art spends most of his time purchasing and apple-polishing. I can get anyone in any project that I want to." Although it rings of bravado and represents some exaggeration, this assertion is basically correct (this, incidentally, is a radical departure from the front put on by the gatekeeper during the early stages of observation, when she insisted that she was a mere functionary, routinely implementing a set of clear-cut rules).

The second facet of the gatekeeper's knowledgeability is her awareness of the unofficial feelings of officials. She is familiar with all of the members of the Authority as well as with the administrative staff and understands the points at which these people privately depart from stated public policy. This, in combination with her awareness of the nature of the political pressures which occasionally are brought to bear, accounts for a considerable amount of the flexibility which she is able to exercise in her role.

The third facet of the gatekeeper's knowledgeability can best be described as the "tricks of the trade" she has learned over the years. There are questions which one may or may not ask, depending on how "desirable" the prospective tenant appears to be. For those desirables who do not appear immediately eligible, there are devices which can be suggested in order to enhance their eligibility. For example, the most objective standard of "need" employed by the Housing Authority is the notion of "substandard housing." Unless an applicant can receive a relatively high score on a quantitative rating sheet, filled out by a housing inspector, he is unlikely to be declared eligible. During a quiet period in the office, the gatekeeper narrated a story about a highly desirable family which was eligible in every way except that it lived in a comfortable home. She solved this problem by hinting at the possibility of their moving into substandard housing for a short period of time, after which they would be declared eligible. Through a variety of such informal techniques, the gatekeeper may raise (or lower) an applicant's chances of becoming a tenant.

Mention has been made of the gatekeeper's distinction between "desirable" and "undesirable" applicants. Having indicated the opportunities she has for determining entré, let us turn to the criteria she employs in implementing these opportunities.

THE CRITERIA OF DESIRABILITY

The criteria of desirability are implicit in the gatekeeper's discussions of "desirable" and "undesirable" applicants. The following excerpt from the observer's notes provides a description of a "desirable" couple and the gatekeeper's reaction to them:

43

Both speech and dress of this couple reflect middle-class backgrounds and values. He described how he had started a small
business of his own and had gone bankrupt. They are presently
overwhelmed with bills, and he insists on paying off all of his
creditors even though not legally obligated to do so. He feels
that the only way he can manage this is by reducing his rent.
When he asked about priority, the application officer answered,
in a hopeful tone, "You will just have to keep your fingers
crossed." He commented that they were going to have to leave
their present apartment because of the new baby, and the application officer perked up her ears: "Well, *that's* priority," she
declared. "If you have to move through no fault of your own,
you let me know immediately!" When they left she said, "It's a
pity they aren't all like that," and indicated that she would get
them into her "best project." "We have one good project left
and we ought to keep it that way."

On the other side of the coin, the gatekeeper made the following
comment during the course of a conversation with the observer:
"Marge [social worker] asked me how I know who is desirable and
undesirable. Listen to this! [Waves an application.] This woman was
divorced in 1955. She has one child who is four, one who is two, and she
is pregnant now [1960]! Would you call *that* desirable?" At another
point, after a routine interview with a Negro woman, the application
officer checked her map and grumbled. The observer asked her what
the trouble was, and she replied, "I guess I will have to write 'Urban
Renewal Area' on this one, but I'm not really worried because even
with that top priority there won't be any three-bedroom units available."

On the basis of these and other value-laden remarks concerning applicants and tenants, it appears that there are three general criteria the
gatekeeper uses in judging prospective tenants: race, family constellation, and demeanor.

Race   The first of these three criteria is selective rather than excluding. Negroes are not undesirable *per se;* rather, they are undesirable for
certain housing projects which, according to the gatekeeper, ought to
remain primarily white. She feels that Negroes ought to live in the project located within the Negro ghetto. This feeling is accompanied by the
usual rationale of, "That is where they really want to go and where they

would be happier," "It would create trouble if large numbers of Negroes were assigned to projects in all-white residential areas," and "White people do not want to live in *that* part of town." [9]

The gatekeeper believes that these feelings are shared and supported by management and members of the Authority. The housing project in the Negro area of the city is rapidly becoming an all-Negro project, a phenomenon which everyone—gatekeeper, management, and Authority—deplores. The alternative, however, is seen as even more deplorable: large numbers of Negroes in all housing projects, including those in all-white residential areas. This reluctant resignation to the birth of an all-Negro housing project becomes, in effect, a self-fulfilling prophecy, leading to the acceleration of the process and the inevitability of the prediction of all-Negro occupancy coming true. It would appear that the process could be reversed only if the prophecy could first be altered.[10]

Family Constellation   Unlike race, family constellation operates as an exclusion criterion. The law does not permit families to be excluded from public housing on the basis of their constellation, but the filing system does. The gatekeeper (again with the assumed support of management) does not approve of families without fathers present. This becomes a categorically excluding criterion only in the case of unwed mothers whose applications are placed in the rear of the file drawer *and remain there*. The gatekeeper makes a careful check of children's birthdays as compared with dates of marriage, divorce, or separation and, after some finger-counting, determines which of the "married" applicants "belong" in the back of the file drawer with the other unwed mothers. Only once in recent history, according to the gatekeeper, has such a person been admitted to a housing project, and this was a special case in which her objections were overruled by higher authority. Otherwise these applicants have no hope of obtaining public housing.

Not quite so excluded are the "legitimate" families without fathers. These are filed alphabetically with others under the unit-size required. They are, however, described as "undesirable," and are admitted only when there is no desirable family available to fill a vacancy of the appropriate size. These mothers are not necessarily regarded as undesirable in themselves, but as a source of potential trouble in the projects. They are thought of as objects of possible temptation, both to fathers of other families in the project and to the maintenance crews. Both management and the maintenance staff themselves perpetuate a body of folklore concerning the sexual adventures of housing project maintenance men.[11]

Demeanor   The criterion of demeanor is more subjective than either race or family constellation. The gatekeeper assesses each prospective tenant at the time of application in terms of what Goffman has called "front." [12] The person's dress, speech, manners, attitudes, and whatever else he is able to present about himself during the interview situation are all taken into account by the gatekeeper in her determination of desirability. Her criteria are, of course, those of the dominant middle class: cleanliness, clarity of speech, appropriate clothing, self-assurance, integrity, and the like.

Although many items are actually recorded on the application form, others are recorded in the memory of the gatekeeper. She has an unerring recollection of every applicant whom she interviews and when she is pulling applications to be sent to project managers she employs both the recorded data and her recollections. Since there are no priority requirements in terms of time of application, the gatekeeper thumbs through the applications selecting those she prefers (largely on the basis of the criteria mentioned above) and passing over the "undesirables." Some formally eligible applicants have been systematically passed over in this manner for years.

COMPROMISES AND THE LIMITS OF AUTHORITY

To assume that the gatekeeper (or any bureaucratic functionary) has unlimited authority is as absurd as the assumption that persons in such positions are rigidly inflexible in the conduct of their occupational roles. A number of different types of constraints were observed. These include situational and political constraints, those related to the persistence of some applicants, and professionalization of staff.

Situational Constraints   Lewin has observed that the forces at work in the region of the gate vary considerably, not only in terms of who the gatekeeper happens to be, but also in terms of situational factors.[13] Thus, radical changes in the frequency of vacancies in the housing projects or shifts in administrative policy can, in turn, alter the functioning of the gatekeeper. For example, the concepts of "vacancy loss" and "undesirables" can be thought of as opposing forces operating on the gatekeeper in her consideration of applicants (this example is analogous to Lewin's case of the opposing forces of "expensiveness" and "desirability" in the housewife's decision on the purchase of food). The gates *tend* to be closed to undesirables, but should vacancy rates rise and continue persistently enough to be economically costly to the Housing Authority, a commensurate decline in the standards of the gatekeeper could be anticipated.

Political Constraints   The gatekeeper perceives ultimate power over the bureaucracy to lie outside of it—in the political realm. In addition, she is aware of the buffer function served by the appointed members of the Authority who stand between those external political forces and the bureaucracy itself. As a result, the greatest amount of variation in the operation of the gate can be found when the gatekeeper is under pressure from individuals whom she defines as holding political power, or, to only a slightly lesser degree, from members of the Authority whom she sees as reflecting such political pressures.

For example, a member of the Authority wandered into the gatekeeper's office one afternoon, exchanged a few amenities, and then mentioned an applicant by name. He described her as a "good woman" and suggested to the gatekeeper: "You should put a tab on that one." He was assured that the woman would get in. He then expressed interest in another family that he thought ought to be moved from a small unit to a larger one. At this point the gatekeeper "passed the buck" by explaining to him that he would have to discuss the family with the project manager since she herself had nothing to do with transfers.

When the Authority member left, the gatekeeper explained to the observer that she was frequently confronted with this sort of thing, but there was nothing to do done about it: "Some ward captain or assemblyman or some such probably called him about those people, so what else can he do? They can cause a lot of trouble or they can be a lot of help, so we play along with them when we can." She pointed out that such pressures often come to the executive director of the Authority, who then asks her to see what she can do for the people. Later that same day another member of the Authority telephoned and requested that the gatekeeper push through a certain application. At this point she began to grumble about the extent to which this sort of thing goes on, "but I guess there isn't much that can be done about it."

Applicant Persistence   The effective gatekeeper is not only sensitive to such external pressures as those discussed above, but is also responsive to certain kinds of pressure from applicants themselves. The frequently noted passivity or apathy of the poor[14] accounts in part for the ease with which such people can be manipulated by bureaucratic functionaries. When such people do assert themselves, the gatekeeper finds another limitation to her own authority. One method successfully employed by some applicants is "persistence." It may be possible to shoulder through any bureaucratic gate by the simple process of wearing out the gate-keeper.

One applicant was observed returning nearly every day to discuss the state of his application with the gatekeeper. About ten days after his application interview, this man appeared and informed the gatekeeper that one of the project managers would give him a two-bedroom unit if she would send over his folder. She expressed surprise and told him that there were no two-bedroom units available. After the applicant left she informed the observer that what he required was a three-bedroom unit and she immediately telephoned the project manager. Her opening gambit was: "Whose leg are you trying to pull; you know you don't have anything for that family!" The manager confessed that the man was wearing him down and that he had told him that if the application office would send over his folder, he would get him a two-bedroom unit. After concluding her telephone conversation, the application offi-cer turned to the observer, shrugged and said: "He's wearing me down, too. I'll just send the folder and let him [the manager] worry about it."

Professionalization of Staff   It has been suggested that the bureauc-racy bends under the weight of shifts in the situation, of influence, or of persistence. A fourth factor which penetrates the status quo appears to be the process of professionalization within the bureaucratic staff. The professional often brings to the organization a new ideology—a new rationale for its existence. In the case of public housing there has been a gradual shift away from the concept of a housing authority as primarily a landlord and toward the concept of the authority as a protective so-cial welfare agency. Along with this shift has come a changing orienta-tion toward the project resident, who is becoming more of a client and less of a tenant.

Such ideological change is personified locally by the addition of a

48

professional social worker to the Housing Authority staff. Working closely with the assistant director, the social worker moves to implement the new ideology. In doing so she inevitably clashes with the gatekeeper, who, it will be recalled, has held her position for over twenty years. With the formal power of the organization behind her, the professional is able to force the gate open for strategic cases over the open objections of the gatekeeper. In the case of situational shifts, political influence, or applicant persistence, the gatekeeper voluntarily compromises; in the case of professional pressure, she is overruled.

A case in point relates to the file of unwed mothers. It was stated earlier that these people never get into public housing. There are, however, exceptions. In the gatekeeper's words, "They never get in any more except when Marge [the social worker] interferes." The gatekeeper described one recent case to the observer and expressed indignation because she had "not even been consulted." According to her, this would "open the door to all of the unmarried colored people."

The system does bend and the gatekeeper and her cohorts do get overruled. Presumably the effective gatekeeper, being flexible, manages to avoid such situations, but the key issue in the present case is less the principle of tenant selection than the fact that the gatekeeper was "not even consulted." In effect, she was relieved of the gate—bypassed. The gatekeeper perceives the threat to her own position in the possibility of applicants gaining entry to public housing without her approval. It is imperative that applicants see her *first* and that she be instrumental in determining where they go from there.

The physical layout of the application office illustrates the nature of this jealously guarded prerogative. The application office is so arranged that prospective applicants coming in off the street can walk directly to the gatekeeper's desk, bypassing the receptionist, whose desk is slightly to one side of the entrance. After several days of observation, the observer naïvely made the sympathetic suggestion that if the receptionist's desk was moved in front of the door, people would be unable to walk into the application office indiscriminately. The gatekeeper met this suggestion with a glare and pointed out that the receptionist, like the social worker, "interferes"—"She gossips and gabs instead of sending the people in."

CONCLUSIONS

The gatekeeper is literally the "front man" in public housing and, as such, is in an extremely vulnerable position in spite of her seniority, knowledgeability, and feeling of support from the administration—or perhaps even *because* of these. Since she is the personification of public housing administration and policy as far as applicants are concerned, she is also the one who is *blamed* by the disappointed and the disgruntled. When they discuss their problems with social workers, landlords, the press, police, or anyone else, it is not unreasonable to expect that the gatekeeper's name is frequently mentioned. She is, after all, the only official whose name they know and with whom they have had contact.

She is also ideally located to serve as a scapegoat for administration and the Authority. Since many of the policies she carries out are based on unwritten (and sometimes even unspoken) understandings between herself and the policy makers, it is possible for the latter to deny such support publicly and, in effect, to leave the gatekeeper holding the bag. Although such deliberate treachery is unlikely, the same consequences may result from misunderstanding. And the probability of misunderstanding mounts rapidly during a period of official policy transition.

An ideological transition is now in process. The Authority itself is moving away from the older landlord concept of public housing toward more of a social welfare conception. To the extent that the gatekeeper has successfully internalized the earlier ideology and all of its concomitants and to the extent that she lags behind the Authority and its administration in the shift to a new ideology, she may expect to find herself pursuing an admission policy which no longer has the support from above which she assumes exists. The dangers inherent in such a situation are apparent. The region of the gate is a potential battleground during a period of institutional transition, and the gatekeeper becomes the most vulnerable warrior in the armies of the bureaucracy.

Notes

NOTE: This is a revised version of a paper read at the annual meeting of the Eastern Sociological Society, April 8, 1961. This paper is derived from a larger study of public housing and social mobility conducted under the co-direction of Seymour S. Bellin and Louis Kriesberg and supported, in part, by grants from the Ford Foundation and the Social Security Administration, United States Department of Health, Education, and Welfare. Publication has been delayed in order to protect the individuals and the organization concerned. Since the field work reported here was completed, the gatekeeper described has retired and there has been a complete administrative reorganization of the tenant-selection process in the public housing projects.

1. Kurt Lewin, "Frontiers in Group Dynamics: II. Channels of Group Life; Social Planning and Action Research," *Human Relations*, I (1947), 145. The gatekeeper concept has been employed in several analyses of news sources which indicate that the role of the desk editor is analogous to that of the intake person in any bureaucratic organization. See, for example, Roy E. Carter, Jr., "Newspaper 'Gatekeepers' and the Sources of News," *Public Opinion Quarterly*, XXII (1958), 133–144; David M. White, "The 'Gate Keeper,' a Case Study in the Selection of News," *Journalism Quarterly*, XXVII (1950), 283–290; and Walter Gieber, "Across the Desk: A Study of 16 Telegraph Editors," *Journalism Quarterly*, XXXIII (1956), 423–432.

2. Transcending the spatial limits of the campus, Riesman has employed the concept (in passing) in his discussion of the restraints imposed by disciplinary attachments. He refers to "gatekeepers insisting on tolls being paid to their fields." See David Riesman, *Constraint and Variety in American Education* (Lincoln: University of Nebraska Press, 1956), p. 105.

3. Robert K. Merton, "Social Structure and Anomie," in *Social Theory and Social Structure* (Glencoe, Ill.: The Free Press, 1957), pp. 149–153.

4. Elihu Katz and S. N. Eisenstadt, "Some Sociological Observations on the Response of Israeli Organizations to New Immigrants," *Administrative Science Quarterly*, V (1960), 113–133.

5. Merton, *op. cit.*, pp. 141–149.

6. A gatekeeper may, of course, be honest or dishonest, he may operate legally or illegally, he may be flexible or rigid, he may be courteous or rude, and he may tend toward ritualism or innovation.

7. Robert W. Habenstein and Edwin A. Christ, *Professionalizer, Traditionalizer, and Utilizer* (Columbia: University of Missouri Press, 1955), pp. 48–53ff.; Irwin Deutscher, "Nursing Service and Nursing Education: Some Observations on Intraprofessional Conflict," in *Roles and Relationships*

in Nursing Education (New York: National League for Nursing, 1959), pp. 106–115; and George K. Floro, "How to Get the Most from Old Guard Employees," *Hospitals*, October 16, 1958, pp. 43–44. The notion of the home guard, in the present sense, was probably introduced by Everett C. Hughes in "Discussion of the Bryan Report," in Lester Asheim, ed., *A Forum of the Public Library Inquiry* (New York: Columbia University Press, 1950), pp. 106–114.

8. Included among these official criteria are the following: (1) veterans of the Korean conflict have priority in state-financed projects; (2) persons displaced by public action have priority in both state and federal projects; (3) persons without housing through no fault of their own have priority in all projects; (4) generally, priority shall be determined by the urgency or need of the individual family in comparison with other applicants.

9. Stereotyped judgments such as these may in fact be partially correct, although not necessarily for the reasons assumed by the persons making the judgments. A sample survey of applicants on the waiting lists reveals that 73 per cent of Negro applicants do state a preference for the ghetto project. On the other hand, 73 per cent of white applicants reject that same project.

10. Merton, "The Self-Fulfilling Prophecy," in *Social Theory and Social Structure, op. cit.*, pp. 421–436. See especially pp. 434–436.

11. In spite of such exclusion policies, there are large numbers of unattached women residing in the public housing projects, partly because of desertions and divorces which take place after admission, partly as a result of occasional short supplies of "desirable" tenants, and partly because such women are more likely to remain in public housing as a result of diminished opportunities for residential mobility. The body of folklore surrounding these women is not dissimilar to that related to other sizable groups of unattached females. Tales of the sexual aggressiveness of such categories as college girls, W.A.C.'s, widows, and women in religious orders all reflect similar themes based on their supposed lust for gratification resulting from prolonged collective deprivation.

12. Erving Goffman, *Presentation of Self in Everyday Life* (Edinburgh: University of Edinburgh Social Sciences Research Centre, Monograph 2, 1956).

13. Lewin, *op. cit.*, p. 146.

14. See, for example, Genevieve Knupfer, "Portrait of the Underdog," *Public Opinion Quarterly*, I (1947), 103–114. It has been noted more recently that the poor are not necessarily apathetic and certainly need not be. See, for example, Chapter 5, by Warren C. Haggstrom.

4 • Two Men and Their Families

A story of marginal earners in
the nation's capital and
their need for intercessors

CHARLES V. WILLIE

ONE OF THE BASIC FACTS of social existence is that we are all interdependent. One person must do for another what the other cannot do for himself. But the needs of some may not be known, or, if known, others may not know how to respond. This, then, is the responsibility of an intercessor, a person who brings individuals and a community together so that they embrace each other in helpful response.

Compassion and justice seldom appear spontaneously; they are cultivated characteristics. The intercessor contributes to their cultivation by prodding the advantaged to assume responsibility for the disadvantaged and by pushing those who are considered outcasts into the mainstream of community life so that each may help and be helped by the other. Working in behalf of families of great need, the intercessor encourages the community to develop a retraining project, or to modify its educational system, or to revamp its welfare program, or to do any number of things that can contribute to the quality of life for the low-income citizen. It is expecting too much to ask the person or family in marginal circumstances to confront our gigantic bureaucracies alone.

One of the tragedies of modern life is that a disturbingly large number of families live out their time in closed and shuttered worlds. They are cut off from the larger community (often from their own neighborhood) and without an intercessor who could be both a prod and a link to the outside. This is the story of two such families, families with marginal resources and on the brink of difficulty. They are residents of Washington, D.C., citizens of the nation's capital. Sometimes these families have bread enough, but never any to spare.

53

The names used, of course, are fictitious, but the families and their problems are real. These are young families, hidden from the sight of the community at large, cut off from its compassion. Their plight has only recently come to public view through a community survey conducted by Washington Action for Youth, a federal-local delinquency prevention project sponsored by the President's Committee on Juvenile Delinquency and Youth Crime.

Armed with questionnaires, ten interviewers called on a random sample of 1,000 households in the Cardozo High School district, a four-square-mile area in the northwest section of Washington. The families of this area have diversified backgrounds, although most are low-income and Negro. During a two-month period in the summer of 1963, interviewers elicited confidential information about the way of life of family members, the organizations and associations to which they belonged, and their connections with the community at large, including public and private programs and services.

In a real sense, this survey has become a spokesman for unknown, hidden, and forgotten families whose problems and possibilities are ignored. The facts derived from the survey are the basis for several action programs for the benefit of poor youth in the community.

This, then, is the story of two families, their hopes, aspirations, and worries, and with some observations on their concrete problems and possibilities. Meeting these families, one is convinced immediately of their terrific push to make a go of it. But one also becomes aware of the community's responsibility to pull the family members along. This story is one of courageous push that has not yet found the compassionate pull.

THE PETER PAUL FAMILY

Both Mr. and Mrs. Paul are natives of Georgia. Though "just kids" when they were married—he was seventeen and she was fifteen—this was the second marriage for Mrs. Paul. It has been successful, however, and the couple recently celebrated their tenth anniversary. There are four Paul children, ranging in age from three to seven years. Mrs. Paul describes the family as "real close."

The Pauls moved to Washington two years after their marriage. Mr. Paul works as a cement finisher with a construction firm, earning about sixty-five dollars a week. The neighborhood in which the Pauls have lived for the past two years is "not as nice" as some of their former residences, but rental for their three-room apartment is only fifty dollars a month—all this family of six can afford. They have thought of moving to a larger dwelling in a residential section, since Mrs. Paul considers the neighborhood to be dangerous and the streets and buildings unclean. She knows there is some juvenile delinquency in the area. But finding housing elsewhere at a price the family can afford has not been possible, so Mrs. Paul has resigned herself to being "satisfied" with the neighborhood. Moreover, there is a "good back yard in which the children can play."

Mr. and Mrs. Paul share joint responsibility in disciplining the children. However, Mr. Paul is home very little because of his long working hours. He eats neither breakfast, lunch, nor dinner at home, and since he does not take his meals with the family, Mrs. Paul and the four children have no specific mealtime. Mrs. Paul does not work; she stays at home with the children. They appear to be well-behaved youngsters, but when questioned, Mrs. Paul has no advice on child-rearing methods that may help children to grow up without getting into trouble.

The Paul family members are engaged in a valiant effort to "make it" on their own. From time to time, however, they have had to turn to the Salvation Army for clothes and to the Welfare Department for surplus food. They have also attended clinics at the D.C. General Hospital and the Children's Hospital. Other than for occasional use of these facilities, the Paul family has depended little on the community for assistance.

Although Mr. Paul completed only nine years of school and Mrs. Paul has less than a fifth-grade education, both have high aspirations for their children. Mrs. Paul wants the children to work in a profession, such as nursing for the girls and law for the boys. But she has little idea of how much education is required to attain these lofty goals. An "average" education is what she thinks may be necessary. Inadequate information about requirements for these vocations is coupled with inadequate financial resources. According to Mrs. Paul, there is not enough money even now for the school needs of the children. The seven-year-old has never attended school, so is already one year behind.

Mrs. Paul, who is at home all day, knows from twenty to thirty persons in the neighborhood well enough to stop and chat. One of these, a housewife who lives next door, is her best friend, the person to whom Mrs. Paul would turn if she had a serious problem requiring outside help. In general, however, the Pauls have few connections with community organizations and associations, except for a neighborhood

Baptist church. The family attends Sunday School and morning and evening worship services, and Mrs. Paul sings in the choir. Going to church on Sunday is a family affair.

The Pauls have heard about one or two civic action groups, but do not participate in any. Mr. Paul does not hold membership in a union nor is he, his wife, or his children connected with any political, recreational, social, or fraternal organization. They have no contact with casework social services in the community, with character-building agencies, or with group-work programs. The family is connected to the community at large only through Mr. Paul's job, the church, the daily newspaper, and television.

In summary, one might describe the Pauls as a hard-working, God-fearing family that is hammering out an existence, a family that is stable but also highly vulnerable. With only a slight change in the circumstances of life, the Pauls could go under.

THE BERNARD BROWN FAMILY

Mr. and Mrs. Bernard Brown have been married five years and have two sons, aged two and three. Mr. Brown, twenty-five at the time of the survey, is a native of the District of Columbia; his wife, twenty-seven, was born in Mississippi. The family has lived in its present neighborhood, a low-income district near the downtown section of Washington, for more than four years. Mr. Brown is a gasoline service station attendant with an income of less than $3,500 a year.

The family would very much like to move to Maryland, near Mr. Brown's mother. It is "nicer back in Maryland" and "a better place to bring up the children," according to Mrs. Brown, who is "somewhat dissatisfied" with their present location. But the Browns continue to live in a three-room apartment; they know the owner, and the rent of $100 a month is normal for what they are receiving. These rental payments, however, are relatively high for Mr. Brown, taking 37 per cent of his monthly earnings. The family has thought about moving for more than a year, but cannot see how to follow through financially. Even though Mrs. Brown is unhappy with the present neighborhood, she doesn't quite know what ought to be changed. She does know that the steps in their apartment building are unsafe for children.

Obviously, money is a major problem for the Browns. Mr. Brown dropped out of school at the eighth grade and has no special vocational skills. His wife completed high school, but her job is to be at home with the children; Mr. Brown is the breadwinner. In the light of these circumstances, Mrs. Brown is uncertain about what the future holds for her two small boys and is unwilling to hazard a guess as to what they might do when they grow up. About all she can plan on, Mrs. Brown thinks, is to "teach the children right from wrong." She also wants to build some regularity into their lives. The family therefore has a regular mealtime, although the father cannot eat with his wife and children because of his work schedule. Mrs. Brown describes the family as "close" but not "real close."

A next-door neighbor is Mrs. Brown's best friend. Aside from this neighbor, Mrs. Brown does not know anyone in the community who can "really get things done," except the police. Moreover, she knows no one to whom her family could turn for help in improving neighborhood conditions, although she has a vague idea that "business people" could be of some assistance.

At home all day with the children, Mrs. Brown knows only five to ten persons in her neighborhood. And other than the bowling club in which Mr. Brown participates each week, none of the family members is involved in community organizations or activities. Though both husband and wife are Baptists, they seldom attend church. Sundays are devoted to visiting the grandmother in Maryland in the afternoon, having an early evening dinner, and watching television. Mrs. Brown has little, if any, knowledge of any civic action groups in the community and no contact with casework services. During the past year, some members of the family were "treated" at the D.C. General Hospital and the Washington Hospital Center. This is the only contact the family has had with the health and welfare services of the community, public or private. The Browns are connected to the "outside" only through the husband's job and bowling team, the television set, and one daily newspaper. There is no radio or telephone to extend family knowledge of the world.

In summary, the Brown family is one that is very much on its own, with small children, limited income, and a nagging sense of uncertainty. The Browns appear to be drifting in the present and afraid to plan for the future. Nevertheless, and in spite of several inadequacies, the family is making a go of it. But the present equilibrium will remain only if the future is unchanged from the past. To the extent that the future is different, this family may not survive.

COMMUNITY RESPONSIBILITY

The problems of the Bernard Browns and the Peter Pauls must be shared by the total community if such families are to be sustained at a self-supporting level and redeemed should they fall below it. Both the Browns and the Pauls stand on the brink of difficulty. The immediate, urgent challenge to the community is how to prevent these families from plummeting to the depths of disaster and settling down in perennial despair.

Race, some readers have undoubtedly noticed, has not been mentioned in this report. It is not important. But for those who need to know, one family is Negro and one is white—which one really doesn't matter. What does matter is that these are families who are passed over by private agencies and turned away from the public services because they have bread enough. Who cares if there is none to spare? The answer, of course, is that all of us must care. The Browns and the Pauls have the will; we in the larger community must provide the way.

Of all the lessons that can be learned from this story, three seem paramount. The community must (1) extend jobs and job training to unskilled men, (2) revise the administration of public welfare so that it becomes an instrument of prevention, and (3) provide new family services that seek out families in need of help rather than waiting for their services to be sought.

In an economic system increasingly dominated by technology, men and women need technical skills if they are to earn enough to meet the needs of their families. While both men in our story have jobs, they are unable to obtain better ones because of their limited education. These men should be candidates for retraining. They cannot teach themselves.

The community must provide new training experiences. Indeed, it has to be a community responsibility; for the community must subsidize retraining of the unskilled worker or subsidize his inadequate family income tomorrow. We are reminded of the testimony of Secretary of Labor Willard Wirtz in support of expanding the Manpower Training Program. He informed a Congressional committee that the average cost of training a person under the manpower program is one thousand dollars, as compared with a possible cost of one thousand dollars per year that the community may pay to support a family when the breadwinner is not trained for work that is in demand.[1] John W. Gardner, Secretary of Health, Education, and Welfare, suggests that men and women enroll in one or another kind of educational program throughout their lives—for example, to acquaint themselves with new technological developments. He recommends that this become an accepted practice.[2]

It is clear from the foregoing discussion that school dropouts must be considered a community problem as well as a personal tragedy. A recent three-year study of dropouts in the District of Columbia conducted by Washington Action for Youth revealed that one third of the high school youth who drop out of school do so to go to work. In a real sense, these youths may be classified as pushouts. They are pushed out of school by a community unwilling to provide a subsidy sufficient for them to remain in school until they have received the kind of training required in a technology-dominated economy. Also, they are pushed out of school by a system too rigid to modify itself to accommodate both part-time and full-time students.

The Manpower Development and Training Act provides an opportunity for communities to upgrade the skills of their workers through retraining. The community should insist, however, that these training programs be available for younger as well as older workers, and that training allowances be provided. What does it profit a community to provide training programs for older workers only when more than one fifth of its out-of-school youth are unemployed? What does it profit a community to establish elaborate training programs based upon assessments of community job needs, with no arrangement for financial compensation, when one third of the youngsters who leave high school do so because they need money?

This story of two men and their families also indicates a need for revamping local welfare regulations if public welfare is to prevent family disintegration. When the father in a family with marginal means becomes unemployed, the outlook is bleak. It is hard to save money for a rainy day when one earns less than sixty-five dollars a week. Yet with a father in the family, a household in the District of Columbia is ineligible to receive aid to families with dependent children to tide it over a "bout with bad weather." As pointed out by Senator Abraham Ribicoff, "We force men to desert their families so their wives and children can become eligible for help."[3] According to District of Columbia welfare regulations, aid to families with dependent children is provided if children are living with their mother and there is no father or substitute father living in or frequenting the home.[4] Reporter Bill Davidson has pointed out that this rule "does not distinguish between a man who will not work and a respectable husband who cannot get a job." [5] Peter Paul and Bernard Brown, for example, are respectable husbands devoted to their families. These are marginal earners who from time to time may need public assistance to tide them over minor difficulties. Such aid could prevent further dependency by keeping a family together.

The importance of keeping families together has been demonstrated by a study of the neighborhood distribution of juvenile delinquency in Washington conducted by the research staff of Washington Action for Youth. [6] A high relationship was found between the proportion of families without fathers and the rate of juvenile delinquency in a neighborhood. In the neighborhood with the highest juvenile delinquency rate (a neighborhood in which one out of every ten youngsters ten to seventeen years of age is referred to court each year), nearly half of the youth were growing up in households in which one parent was absent. Thus, public welfare could help promote family stability if families with fathers were eligible for assistance. Public welfare could even help prevent juvenile delinquency by facilitating the staying together of family members and discouraging their drifting apart. Public welfare could become a preventive service.

Finally, the story of two men and their families indicates the need for a comprehensive family service to help with practical, concrete problems. I have in mind a family service that provides homemaking consultants, helps with budgeting problems, gives information about health, welfare, educational, and legal resources, assists in finding housing for families in special circumstances, seeks out educational and job-training opportunities, and advises family members on the alternative ways to solve personal problems and refers them for specialized guidance. I have in mind a modified model of the Philadelphia Homemaking Consultants, who provide short- and long-term service ranging from two or three months to a year. The service proposed, however, should help fathers as well as mothers better meet the responsibilities of their roles. A generalized and comprehensive family service would be of particular help to marginal families out of contact with both public and private specialty agencies.

Existing family-service agencies have been oriented largely to solving psychological problems. The practical problems of living are sometimes overwhelming for marginal families. Where can they turn for help?

Where can they go for guidance? If the community has compassion for these families, it would appear to be in eclipse.

THE INTERCESSOR: A PRESENT HELP
IN TIME OF TROUBLE

The theoretical implication of this analysis for planners of community services is that the role of the intercessor must be extended and strengthened as an essential function in the community. Intercession is a marvelous concept. It has to do with "the act of interceding; mediation; prayer, petition or entreaty in behalf of another," according to *Webster's Seventh New Collegiate Dictionary.* In recent years, intercession has been limited largely to religious activity and has been viewed as a passive approach to problem solving. We think of intercession as prayer in behalf of another—an activity that does not involve direct confrontation with the oppressed or the oppressor, the victim or the victimizer. Because of this, intercession is seen as having little effect upon everyday problems; thus, it has fallen into disrepute in the minds of many as a useful method in community action.

Intercession, however, can be an active approach to problem solving. It can be an act of mediation between the oppressed and the oppressor, between the individual and the community; an experience of direct confrontation with all becoming involved with each other. In the case of the Brown and Paul families, an intercessor is needed to bring the burdens of these households to the attention of the total community and to engender within the community a sense of responsibility to share collectively what could become overwhelming for an individual or a single family.

The essential function of the intercessor was revealed in a research-demonstration study of problem families in a public housing project conducted between 1960 and 1962 in Syracuse, New York. A social worker was retained to give intensive help to half of the fifty-four households identified by the manager as being in need of immediate help. Since the social worker could handle only about twenty-two families on an intensive basis during the course of a year, the remaining households were observed as a control group. One goal was to determine whether the social worker (or family consultant, as she was called) had an effect upon the rent-paying patterns of problem families; that is, did she help these families pay their rent in full and on time each month?

When families are delinquent in paying their rent, they may be served an official precept, petition, or warrant. The findings of this study pertaining to the effect of the social worker are the following:

> . . . 41 per cent of the families in the study group and 52 per cent of the families in the control group received one or more precepts, petitions, or warrants during the study period. However, *none of the families seen by the worker was evicted* during this period. [Italics added.] Often she discussed their problems with representatives of the Housing Authority and of other agencies, and she succeeded in making special arrangements in behalf of her clients. Though at times the worker encouraged some families to make their own special arrangements in accordance with their unique situation, she often acted as an intercessor for them. Housing Authority personnel apparently reacted differently to families that had someone to speak in their behalf, and when the consultant acted as intercessor, they showed a willingness to continue working with families whose rent payment had been a problem.
>
> Families in the control group had to "go it alone." No one interpreted their situation to others or sought special help for them. No one supported them as they faced their daily problems. More than 20 per cent of these families were evicted or moved because of a threat of eviction when their rent-paying behavior, or some other behavior, became unacceptable to the management of the development.
>
> A specific test was made of the intercessory function of the worker. Without knowing that five families in the control group had been evicted or threatened with eviction, the worker was asked to identify the families in the study group that she judged would have been evicted if she had not intervened. She identified six families, almost the same number. The rent-paying patterns of the families that were saved from eviction and those that were evicted were very similar. . . . There is reason to conclude that the six families in the study group were retained in the housing project . . . because of the worker's intercession in their behalf. She interceded for them not only with the project manager but also with other agents of voluntary and public organizations, including the Department of Social Welfare.[7]

The study further revealed that the evicted families returned to unsound dwellings in the slums of the city. Thus, their condition of slum living was a function not only of their own actions but also of those of the Housing Authority, which, as a representative of the total community, evicted these families. The fortunate ones were those who had an intercessor; they remained in a clean and protected housing development. Standing alone before the Housing Authority, poor and marginal families are unable to resist its decisive judgments.

William Stringfellow, who practiced law for several years in the East Harlem slums of New York City, tells of his first case in court as a novice in law practice. The case involved four boys arrested on the charge of illegal possession of narcotics. As Stringfellow explains:

> . . . the amount was sufficient to warrant a felony charge if the "stuff" belonged to just one of the boys arrested. If, however, the four jointly and equally owned the drugs, then the charge against each would be only a misdemeanor. I interviewed all of the boys and was satisfied that they had all participated in the procurement of the drugs and were partners in its possession and intended use. But they had decided among themselves that it would be best if, as they put it, just one of them "took the weight." As they saw it, it was better for one to plead that the stuff was entirely his own and therefore be charged with a felony and risk a long prison sentence than for each of them to admit part ownership and each be charged with a misdemeanor, with the prospect of much shorter sentences for each. . . .
>
> On the day the case came up for pleadings, I left my tenement early. . . . I had decided, partly on the advice of another attorney, to go to court before it convened and discuss the case with the prosecutor and try to persuade him to reduce the charge, in exchange for a guilty plea. There were not any serious legal grounds for the district attorney to agree to this. . . .
>
> When I arrived at the court room, several other lawyers were standing in line, waiting to speak to the D.A. I overheard their discussions of other cases on the day's calendar. They were terse, to say the least, and seemed to me to be quite disinterested and even indifferent to the merits of the cases being negotiated. Finally my turn came. I identified myself to the district attorney, whom I had never met before, this being my first court case.
>
> I told him whom I represented, and then he said, "Well, counselor, what do you want?" "I want a misdemeanor," I replied. And then to my astonishment he said, "O.K. When the case is called, we'll talk to the judge."
>
> We did. The judge agreed to the guilty plea to a misde-

meanor, and the defendant was sentenced to seven months in prison. . . . I did not have to persuade anybody, either the D.A. or the court, that the charge should be reduced. I just had to go in and ask for it. It all seemed wrong—some great sham was being made of the law and of the legal system. Yet it all seemed right. . . . Maybe this is just the kind of world that is: upside down, broken, foolish, wasteful, and filled with irony. Maybe so.[8]

Maybe another boy has been arrested. Maybe he should have been tried for a misdemeanor but has been convicted for a felony. Maybe this has happened because no one interceded for him, because no one was there simply to ask that the charge be reduced. There is no justice for many in poor or marginal circumstances often because there is no one to intercede. As pointed out in one proposal for a legal service agency for the poor that was filed with the federal Office of Economic Opportunity. "The poor are seldom aware of their legal rights in relationship to governmental agencies, landlords, merchants and the like. Unchallenged procedures often create abuses which are accepted by the poor as part of life." [9] The poor or marginal person cannot challenge these procedures alone.

INTERCESSION PLUS SELF-HELP

At a time when self-help programs are being launched in many communities, it is important to highlight the continuing need for the intercessor—one who labors in behalf of another. There are some things none of us can do for ourselves. The intercessor role is not intended as a displacement of self-help programs. Actually, it is a necessary complement, with intercession preceding self-help. This sequential pattern is frequently forgotten. We want people to help themselves, but overlook the fact that the capacity to help oneself is a function of once having been helped. In 1964, in Syracuse, New York, for example, the Syracuse Community Development Association was established to help the poor organize to make their needs known to the community at large and to become participating members of that community. Essentially, this association was established to foster self-help programs among the poor and to enable them to identify their problems. Initial funds for the program, however, came from the Office of Economic Opportunity through the intercessory activity of Syracuse University. Representatives of the university prepared the original application in which the

Syracuse Community Development Association was described as a field-work extension of the university's Community Action Training Center. Although the Syracuse Community Development Association is no longer affiliated with the university, this self-help program of autonomous organizations of the poor needed an intercessor to come alive.

There is much that poor and marginal families such as the Bernard Browns and the Peter Pauls can do for themselves. But there is much that others must do in their behalf. While poor and marginal families may seize the opportunities that are available, only the community at large can provide the new and different opportunities that these families may need. Our inability to comprehend the role of the intercessor as a necessity in community life may be based in part upon our inability to deal effectively with dependency. As stated elsewhere, "Independency is not a virtue and dependency is not a vice. We all must experience both at some period in life. . . . It is time we acknowledged . . . that our feet are all caught up *together* (as Langston Hughes has put it) in 'the sweet flypaper of life.' All are sheep and all are shepherds. Each must minister and be ministered unto." [10]

Notes

1. *The Washington Post,* July 9, 1963.

2. John W. Gardner, "From High School to Job" (reprinted from the *Annual Report* of the Carnegie Corporation of New York, 1960), pp. 11–12.

3. Bill Davidson, "The Mess in Washington—A City in Trouble," *The Saturday Evening Post,* July 13, 1963, p. 22.

4. *Characteristics of State Public Assistance Plans Under the Social Security Administration,* Public Assistance Report No. 50 (Washington, D.C.: United States Government Printing Office, 1962).

5. Davidson, *op. cit.,* pp. 21–22.

6. Charles V. Willie *et al.,* "Race and Delinquency," *Phylon,* XXVI (Fall 1965), 245.

7. Charles V. Willie, Morton O. Wagenfeld, and Lee J. Cary, "Patterns of Rent Payment Among Problem Families," *Social Casework,* XLV (October 1964), 467–468.

8. William Stringfellow, *My People Is the Enemy* (New York: Holt, Rinehart and Winston, Inc., 1964), pp. 48–51. © 1964 by William Stringfellow. Reprinted by permission of Holt, Rinehart and Winston, Inc.

9. Crusade for Opportunity, "Legal Service Proposal for Syracuse, New York," 1965 (mimeo).

10. Charles V. Willie, "Our Changing Nation," in General Division of Women's Work of the Executive Council of the Episcopal Church, eds., *Knowing the Time* (New York: Episcopal Church Center, 1965), p. 38.

5 · Can the Poor Transform the World?

WARREN C. HAGGSTROM

THE IDEA OF ORGANIZING the poor in the United States has attracted much attention in recent years. One argument has been that the poor, through their own efforts, can organize to defeat slum landlords, incumbent politicians, discriminatory businessmen, and even government bureaucrats in order to attain the resources which would end poverty. The most ambitious variation of this idea has been the possibility that organizations of the poor can secure basic social change by violent or non-violent means which have been employed in the past by relatively small organizations. For example, in Russia and China organizations captured the state and used it to change society. In Asia and Africa tiny organizations gave leadership to successful nationalistic anti-colonial movements. The most modest variation of this idea has at least included the possibility that the poor could constitute a social force to support the efforts of government anti-poverty agencies and programs. The argument is that the agencies will be free to do what should be done when they are supported by a constituency, just as the Department of Labor and the Department of Agriculture have been supported by such constituencies. At a middle level of aspiration, organizations of the poor have been thought of as community-based analogues of labor unions.

On the face of it, however, it appears doubtful that the poor in the United States can secure an effective power base from which to organize to transform their relationships with the affluent society. In the first place, the poor are to be found in scattered, mutually hostile enclaves across the country. They include Mexican-American migratory farm

67

workers, Indians on reservations, rural black communities of small farmers, similar white communities, the urban black ghettos of unemployed and underemployed adults and their white or Puerto Rican counterparts, skid rows, elderly persons in institutions and scattered in homes, and many other groups. Populations so various, with so little sense of a common identity, so much in fear of one another, so widely scattered geographically, with no tradition of unity for a common struggle, and without even a common envisaged future, are not likely suddenly to be able to create a single social force of any consequence. This expectation is buttressed by history: organizations of the poor have usually been impotent singly, and they have also been incapable of uniting effectively for common action.

The objective situation of the poor leads one to a similar conclusion. No matter how one counts them, the poor are a minority in the United States. Of this minority, a large proportion of urban workers and rural farmers do not regard themselves as poor and would not at present join a movement of the poor. In any case, the poor lack connections with the levers of power. Workers can withdraw their labor and shut down an industry. Farmers can organize to sell their products selectively in order to maintain prices. The poor, however, produce little which the affluent community cannot do without. Consequently, the poor cannot easily compel the affluent community to begin bargaining.

Nor can we find much comfort from surveying past occasions in which organizations of the poor have been formed. Negroes organized politically after the Civil War and the new Negro leaders were used by white racists as symbols to panic Southern whites into initiating the terroristic prelude to decades of increasing oppression. Organizations which stress "self-help" have tended to provide excuses for inaction by the affluent without becoming agents of power for the poor. And the more militant organizations of the poor in the recent past have either disappeared, lost their militancy, or turned into sectarian forums in which rhetorical violence need not be contaminated by social reality.

At this point *all* solutions to poverty have failed. Public housing, public welfare, casework, job training, educational programs, the trickle down from affluence—all these have failed at least as dismally as the organizations of the poor to achieve their originally announced objectives. It may therefore be useful to attempt to analyze the conditions under which the poor could organize effectively to transform the world and to consider whether such conditions can be met. This chapter at-

68

tempts such an analysis. It begins with a portrayal of the relevant aspects of the nature of social reality, aspects which organizations of the poor must know about in order to secure substantial social change. Since the barriers to effective Negro organization are similar to the barriers to effective organization of the poor, this chapter also considers, with illustrations, the question of black power. Will "black power" remain only a verbal gesture, a phrase? Or can Negroes acquire black power through organization?

Sections 1, 2, and 3 of this chapter outline theoretical ideas which constitute one version of the "vision" which, it is suggested, must be held by a competent organizer. These sections can therefore be understood to delineate part of the role of the organizer. Other characteristics necessary to the role of the organizer are mentioned in Section 4. Finally, Section 5 relates the course of events which might occur when an organizer, fulfilling the requirements of appropriate roles, helps the poor organize successfully to transform the world.

In considering whether the poor can transform the world, I refer to the possibility of a decades-long process through which the poor would become organized and create coalitions with other acting populations. The organized poor would exercise primary leadership in such coalitions. The coalitions would have and use enough power to secure major social changes. The United States would emerge from such a long struggle transformed politically, economically, and socially into a good society in which poverty would have disappeared and in which many other basic changes would have been made. The following account is a somewhat abstract sketch, the subsequent expansion of which will describe in concrete detail levers of power which the poor must learn to use if they are to attain such an outcome. This chapter, therefore, is not a research report, does not grapple with several relevant and important questions which deserve answers, and only mentions many serious problems which will require further detailed discussion at another time.

1. THE NATURE OF SOCIAL REALITY

To be assigned a location in space and time is to be an object. A neighborhood, a marriage, a highway, a unicorn, and a mind are all objects. To make and carry out decisions is to be an actor. A person is an actor, as is a nation, a welfare agency, or a youth gang.[1]

Actors act on the basis of anticipated consequences to be secured through action. Therefore their action depends on the definitions of

69

objects in relation to which their action occurs. Actors define an object by placing it in one or more categories on the basis of how some characteristic attributed to the object relates to some criterion. For example, a person may define an object by placing it in the category of a chair on the basis of the fact that it was made only to be sat on and according to the criterion that we refer to any object which has been made only to be sat on as a chair. Or a community may define a group by placing the group in the category of inferior persons on the basis of their poverty and presumed lack of energy and according to the criterion that the value of any person depends on his relative success through striving.

An actor defines an object on the basis of characteristics which he attributes to it in accordance with criteria. For example, he may define an object as a hammer on the basis of its suitability for pounding nails, or as a weapon on the basis of other of its characteristics.

The definition which results may not be based on characteristics actually possessed by the object, since the object may not in fact possess the defining characteristics which an actor attributes to it. That is, the object defined as a friend on the basis of a presumed attitude toward the actor may actually be a hostile but devious rival. Even if an actor does define an object on the basis of characteristics which the object actually possesses, the actor selects only certain characteristics on which to base the definition. This selection depends on the anticipated relevance of various characteristics of an object to the course of action in which the actor is engaged. Thus, a social worker may place in the category of "client" the same person whom the detective places in the category of "suspect."

The *meaning* of an object to an actor is the anticipated relevance of the object to the course of action in which the actor is engaged. Meaning is acquired partly through definition. For example, an object defined as a tool will have a much different meaning from that of the same object defined as a weapon. A meaning is more or less positive or negative to an actor depending on the anticipated *returns* from the defined object for the actor.

From the above account it is clear that the meaning of an object to an actor can be changed in many different ways. Perhaps the most frequent occur through changes in characteristics of an object (as when a young girl becomes an old woman); through changes in the prominence with which characteristics are displayed (as when a former rake dons clerical garb); through changes in the relationship of object to actor (as when a person goes out of sight to get out of mind, or when a soldier begins to identify with his company); through changes in the course of action of an actor (as when food is no longer relevant to a man who has finished eating and is leaving for work); or through creation or revision of a consensus about properties which are presumed to be associated with the category in which the actor places the object (as when a stranger in a neighborhood acquires a reputation, or when a campaign of character assassination by a rival succeeds in changing the meaning of a person to his employer). The meaning of a situation to an actor is always in a process of change as a function of the shifting meanings of objects to the actor. As the meanings of objects shift, the meaning of the situation to the actor changes.

Communication occurs by means of physical objects (such as patches of ink like those on this page) or vocal gestures (as when a person speaks). Corresponding to the visible objects used for communication are parallel objects that are normally inaccessible to observation. For example, a physical portion of the nervous system corresponds to a statement made by a person. Analogously, sums produced externally by a calculator correspond to a physical object (possibly a set of gears in certain relationships with each other during a limited time period) in the calculator.

Therefore, objects necessarily involved in the communication process include (1) visible objects (the media of communication), and (2) parallel objects not normally visible (the communication base). Let us refer to both as *second-order objects.*

An actor fashions relationships among second-order objects (such as by creating sentences) which indicate actual or conceivable relationships among, or characteristics of, first-order objects. Objects are first-order by virtue of the fact that they are not second-order. Let us illustrate this point. When someone mentions that the street is wet, this verbal gesture indicates that the street has, in fact, the characteristic of wetness. The verbal gesture is second-order; the street and its wetness, first-order.

To place a first-order object in a category, to define it, is to assign a category of second-order objects to it. For example, for a social worker to define a colleague as egotistic is to assign to the colleague a class of objects which includes a form or type or kind of vocal gesture, a corresponding form of ink patch, and a nervous-system parallel.

71

An actor uses second-order objects to *define the situation,* that is, to anticipate characteristics of, and relationships among, first-order objects relevant to the course of action in which the actor is engaged. For example, a person may define his situation to some extent by reading a book in preparation for a trip in order to anticipate what he should take with him. The book displays second-order objects (ink patches) in various relationships which indicate a different order of relationships among, or indicate characteristics of, first-order objects (objects which the reader expects to encounter on his trip). Action continues on the basis of such definitions of the situation. To the extent that the outcome of the action is as anticipated, the definition on the basis of which the action proceeds is adhered to more firmly. On the other hand, surprises in outcomes may lead actors to revise their definitions, since surprises often accompany reduced returns to the actor.

As was mentioned above, to define a first-order object is to place it in a category of second-order objects. An actor defines his situation sequentially as he fashions relationships among the appropriate categories. In accordance with the rules which guide this definitional process, the category relationships are created by the formation of units which we will refer to as *elements* and which have a number of characteristics that deserve mention. For example, to the extent to which an actor anticipates that there is a first-order relationship such as is portrayed, the element may be regarded as *cognitive.* To the extent to which an actor does not anticipate that there is a first-order relationship such as is portrayed, but has an urge to create such a relationship from which returns can be anticipated, the element may be regarded as *imperative.* To the extent to which an actor has directions to create or avoid creating the first-order relationship, the element may be regarded as *directive.* To the extent to which the actor is willing and able to maintain the element for any period of time in spite of difficulties in doing so, we may regard the element as *weighted.* Directive elements which are very general in their application may be called *values;* imperative elements which are very general in their application may be called *interests.* To some extent, language reflects distinctions among kinds of elements. For example, a cognitive element might be, "The door is shut"; in the form of an imperative element it would be, "Shut the door." As a directive element it might be, "I ought to shut the door." A relevant interest might be stated: "It is our ambition to maintain personal privacy," or a relevant value, "One ought not to allow the rights to personal privacy to be violated."

72

The elements fashioned by an actor are themselves ordered in accordance with rules to produce an imperative element which, as the last
step in the process, is called a *decision*. A stream of decisions, each
derived from elements, directs a course of action.

Of the elements of self, some have been maintained from very early
in the history of an actor and will continue through wide variations in
situation. These constitute the residue self, much of which was created
through *primary socialization*. Other elements are also likely to be
maintained, but not so firmly, and have usually been fashioned more
recently. These constitute that portion of the self created by *secondary
socialization*. The remainder of the elements are more or less fashioned
and discarded in relation to the situation in which an actor is at any
time. This is the *situational* self.

Since actors may remain in similar situations over long periods of
time, and since observers see decisions more clearly than the elements
from which the decisions are derived, it is not easy to distinguish the
situational self from that created through socialization. Since observers
normally have little awareness of the social situation which an actor has
defined, they systematically tend to attribute to the socialized self characteristics which, in fact, are situational. The situational self consequently remains a relatively uncharted domain in the theory of action,
but a domain which is nevertheless crucial for the understanding of
action.

The situations of actors are normally occupied in part by other actors.
For example, a child in school is surrounded by other children, may
belong to a club, sees teachers and other school personnel, is within the
school system, and is oriented toward his family and to his neighborhood as well as to many other persons. Each of these persons and social
systems is an actor embarked on a course of action which more or less
affects the course of action of the child. There are also other actors
whom the child may not define (a city planner whose plans are resulting in disruption of the neighborhood, a city government which has
increased school appropriations), but whose actions have consequences
for the course of action of the child.

If we take the *power* of an actor to be its ability to overcome obstacles to the maximization of its returns, then it is apparent that the relative power of a social actor is a crucial variable for the analysis of its
course of action. An actor attempts to maximize returns to itself. A
powerful actor usually attempts to increase its returns through establishing control over powerless actors in the vicinity. The powerless actor

may be controlled by rewards or by punishments which increase or decrease returns to it in a fashion which ensures that returns are usually increased to the powerful actor. A powerless actor has few alternatives available to escape this trap. The control itself interferes with attempts to become powerful, and may also prevent withdrawal from the scene. For this reason, courses of action tend to fall under the direction of powerful actors.

When powerful actors define their situations, the situation tends to be created in accordance with the definition. When a slave owner defined Negroes as inferior, his power enabled him to prevent surprises by ensuring that his Negroes would not have access to opportunities to demonstrate superiority. Powerless actors, on the other hand, tend to be created by the situation. A slave is forced, in his definition of his situation, to appreciate how little the situation can be changed and how severe his punishment will be if he does not stay in "his place" (the place assigned by the owner). The human potential of a slave therefore declines; it is destroyed by his master. The situation creates the slave in such fashion that his inferiority is ensured and the definition of the master is thereby maintained.

A powerless actor must sensitively adjust its action to that of a powerful actor on which it is dependent. This adjustment would be more precise if the powerless actor could see the world as does the powerful. To some extent this can be accomplished through *identification*. The powerless actor increases its returns by fashioning in itself portions of the self which it perceives the powerful actor to have. But often identifications acquired at one time cannot simply be discarded when the situation which gave rise to them passes. Thus, some identifications forced on powerless actors may lead them to rigid and inappropriate courses of action at later times. On the other hand, some central identifications are situational and therefore are not rigidly adhered to. When a Negro family moves from a stigmatized slum into a destigmatized neighborhood with which it then identifies, the meaning of the move and of the subsequent identification may be such that the self-esteem of members of the family may rise very quickly.

Since powerless actors, in falling under the control of a powerful actor, increase the power of the latter, power tends to become ever more centralized in ever fewer actors. Exceptions to this rule occur when and to the extent to which powerless actors find new sources of power, including that which accrues to them if they unite to form an actor powerful enough to delay or reverse the process. Since the latter venture would be of uncertain outcome, the tendency is for power to centralize so long as powerful actors reward the powerless well enough for compliance. A powerful actor comes to have many powerless actors in its situation, all tending to identify with it. A powerful actor thereby maintains a consensus of many actors, with the result that the powerful actor and the powerless actors jointly define a common situation in which each acts to a large extent in ways which are comprehensible and predictable to the others.

Objects are assigned positions within or outside an actor as it defines its situation. The actor thereby creates an internal and an external world, each with spatial characteristics. When a number of actors jointly define a common situation, they similarly create a world which they inhabit together and in which they assign positions to objects. Any object is located, by *consensual validation,* within any one of the actors or outside them all. A definition which is inconsistent with one jointly held threatens the common world, and thereby threatens to reduce the returns generally available. A practical problem arises of how to maintain consensus in the face of such threats. Powerful actors may solve the problem by forcing the deviant actor to adhere to the consensus, by destroying the deviant actor, by expelling the deviant actor from the common situation, or by treating the deviant definition as itself an object which can be assigned a place within the deviant actor. This latter solution occurs, for example, in a school in which a child who disagrees with his teacher is dismissed as mentally retarded, as delusional, or as reflecting the superstitions of his parents. In all cases, treatment of the child's view as an object enables the teacher to avoid having to entertain a possibility which would disturb the consensus the teacher seeks to maintain.

Since some areas of action do not impinge on others, there may not then arise a consensual validation concerning such areas. In these cases, a definition may be regarded as an object and be assigned to the actor who has fashioned it. For example, if there is no aesthetic consensus, persons may each express varying opinions on the beauty of a sunset. However, if a consensus has formed, the general expression may be, "The sunset is beautiful tonight"; one who disagrees may treat his deviant view as an object and place it within him, saying, "It doesn't seem that way to me."

Because powerful actors maintain the consensual validation, they are not forced by the above process to treat parts of themselves as objects. Powerless actors, on the other hand, find that their selves are largely objects to other actors, except in areas in which they have incorporated other actors through identification. Further, the incorporation of other actors often assures that powerless actors draw into themselves their very treatment as objects, and come to agree with the consensus in regarding themselves largely as objects. Finally, in identifying with powerful actors, powerless actors reduce the extent to which they make independent decisions most appropriate to their unique situations. They end up engaging in activities which reflect the decision of powerful actors. Since the self as decision-process flourishes when decisions maximize returns and otherwise declines, all these conditions lead to a withering of the selves of powerless actors.

Actors are located within a common world maintained by consensual validation. Through action they move within the world. (They may be moved by other forces as well). Since the movements of actors have positive or negative outcomes for other actors, the common world includes paths along which movement is expected to occur. Powerless actors are forced to travel within such paths. A client of a social agency passes successively through intake, treatment, and termination. A person may enter a family as a baby and may travel from one family position to another until he leaves as a grandparent. People may follow career lines; travel from right to left in physical or political location; forge ahead or fall behind in physical races or social climbing; move from inside to outside a house or an in-group; go underground or into an underworld; make shopping trips or fishing trips or trips back and forth to work. Families, communities, agencies, nations, governments, and other social actors similarly make journeys. A group may create a social movement through which it begins a journey. Powerful actors, of course, may ignore or redefine previously existing paths.

Actors not only have relationships of power and dependency or of identification with one another. One actor may be a part of another (a police department of a city government) or a member of another (an organization which belongs to an organization of organizations). There may be *object* relationships (friendship, familial, neighbor, love), or *ecological* relationships (as when one city depends on another for coal or when the white population of an area is gradually replaced by a black population), or *communication* relationships. Actors may relate through *roles* which prescribe ways in which actors are expected to behave toward each other. A relationship normally has power-dependency, identification, object, role, communication, ecological, and other characteristics. We may refer to any actor which is not a person as a *social actor*. A social actor, such as a welfare department or a business, has an internal structure of social relationships. That is, a social actor is composed of a network of social relationships.

An actor moves along social paths through a framework of relationships into successive definitions of itself, each with consequences for itself. For example, a man in his career is redefined as he moves upward from position to position, changing his relationships with colleagues as he goes. The actor can move in various directions, advance or retreat, or go faster or slower; it can accept or attempt to reject definitions. An actor can originate definitions and seek to get them consensually validated. Or it can redefine and seek to get redefinitions consensually validated. An actor can also secure definitional changes of itself. For example, a politician acquires skill in using symbols, such as patriotism or religion, in order to get himself redefined positively when he would otherwise lose the support of his electorate. Thus, an actor not only is defined; it has some opportunities to define itself and its situation by creating relationships and characteristics in such fashion that certain meanings will be attributed to itself and to others.

As actors move about, they communicate with one another. Messages are exchanged between senders and receivers. In the communication process, the receiver fashions, or replicates in itself, elements indicated by the sender in accordance with rules shared by both sender and receiver. For example, when a boy compliments a girl, his statement is reproduced in the minds of everyone present. The message acquires additional meaning from the context in which it is sent and the context in which it is received, and may have meaning to bystanders different from that to the actors engaged in communication. When the boy offers to carry the books of a girl, the message may also mean sex (to the boy), status (to the girl), and puppy love (to a casual bystander).

2. SELF-REALIZATION OF THE POOR

If the poor in the United States are to attain self-realization, they will have to move from their present position to one in which they can greatly increase returns to themselves. They can deliberately undertake such a journey by creating their own social movement for that purpose. The nature of social reality provides the conditions which predetermine the possibility for such a movement to succeed.

An organization through which the poor can formulate the nature of their ideal world, and begin to move toward this world, must be a public place in which publicly expressed personal concerns of groups of members would motivate organization efforts to solve common problems. Since it is quickly apparent that the obstacles to movement are actors, rather than mere conditions of existence, the organization's pressure would simultaneously transmute common problems into public issues to be resolved in a struggle with opponents whose privileged positions lead them to oppose the movement of the poor. With this revelation, the beginning movement develops into an extended struggle which must be won if the movement of the poor is not to end.

In the very beginning, the poor might only understand that they were embarking on a difficult journey which would, if successful, result in the world which they most want. However, with the onset of the struggle, they now also have to acquire a practical understanding of the world of opponents, including an awareness of how opponents see and use the poor. They must also acquire the skill necessary to vanquish their clearly revealed enemies. The early enthusiasm may at this point give way to a time of doubt and confusion as it becomes apparent that the conflict will last for years or decades, if it can be won at all. The question is then posed for everyone: How can a minority with virtually no power confront and overcome the determined opposition of powerful and entrenched opponents who seem to represent the majority population? The organizational effort may stall. The poor may decide to settle for limited benefits while remaining in their present position, or they may retreat into sectarian militancy, hurling rhetoric at opponents rather than seeking practically to push aside the opposition to their movement.

On the other hand, it is not impossible *a priori* for the poor to develop a successful course of action. They would have to learn how to isolate their opponents from the majority population and from each other. Isolated opponents cannot so easily maintain the social reality which degrades and stigmatizes the poor. In a long struggle, if they were able to undertake one, the poor could gradually develop organizational skill, become proficient in the use of strategies and tactics, and attain ability to recruit large numbers of members to their organization. There would also be other possibilities. The poor could win allies from within the major population, and could render some opponents indecisive, ambivalent, or cause them to retire from the fray. It would be important that the organized poor seize the initiative in determining

78

the times and kinds of encounters with carefully selected opponents. The poor would redefine themselves and their opponents, and thereby transform to their advantage the world in which the conflict took place.

In other words, a social movement by the poor would have a better chance of success if oriented not only to opponents, but also to the symbols, myths, assumptions, traditions, and underlying values and interests of the majority population. The poor could succeed if their movement became a part of the development of the majority community, which then would seek to create a better world and assist the poor in order to realize its own values for its own self-interest. Opponents would fail. They would find they were fighting losing battles on behalf of objectives widely understood to be illegitimately interfering with the development of the majority community.

Action by the organization of the poor should be evaluated on the basis of its outcome in *organizational mileage* for the poor. For example, a demonstration at City Hall would not be evaluated on the basis of whether concessions were wrung from the city government. It would be judged on the basis of whether the organization had more power after the demonstration, and therefore had moved some distance toward a better world. The organization would have logged mileage only if it did not decline after having won the concession. Although a mass membership would eventually be essential for a powerful organization of the poor, one cannot assume that organizational mileage automatically results from expansion in membership. New members could cripple the organization if they entered it as a clique determined to capture control in order to enhance their own political fortunes.

On the other hand, apparent disasters may, under some circumstances, result in organizational mileage. For example, a dramatic and sudden decline in active membership may lead to increased analysis by the leadership and eventually to beneficial internal changes in the organization. A crushing defeat may become a symbol around which people rally for a more strenuous and determined struggle. A series of defeats by a powerful opponent may each result in organizational mileage. This would happen if the membership were to gain in self-confidence during the first encounter through the realization that their organization had survived an attack by such a powerful opponent. From the knowledge and skill acquired in subsequent unsuccessful encounters with the opponent, the organization may each time be able to make victory for the opponent more difficult. The morale of the members would rise as they began to understand that the opponent could not be victorious many more times.

Even organizational activities apparently irrelevant to movement may result in organizational mileage. The elderly ladies who constitute an inactive committee on lawn beautification may thereby acquire enough identification with an organization to vote for organization-approved candidates in the city elections. An organization which sponsors a chest X-ray drive may be acquiring an identity and building a structure which will prove invaluable in later campaigns against opponents.

Organizational mileage is a subtle and complex criterion of action. It can be used only by those who clearly understand where the organization, if successful, would go. Organizational mileage is mileage in the direction of a distant and fundamental goal; movement by an organization often does not add up to organizational mileage. It would, therefore, be important for the membership of an organization of the poor to acquire as rapidly as possible a sophisticated understanding of the journey which they are attempting. To some extent they must learn social geography[2] and fashion a map based on that discipline in order properly to guide their organization in the direction of their goal.

No matter how sophisticated the members were to become, they would not, however, be able to anticipate or to prescribe in advance details of the course along which the organization would move. The organization resembles an army which has to traverse vaguely charted territory in order to capture an enemy fort. The present position and nature of the army, the position and nature of the fort, and the general direction in which the army has to move may all be clearly known to its commander. But the details of the journey will depend on such unknown factors as the nature of the intervening terrain, the strength and deployment of enemy forces, and vicissitudes of the weather, all calling for improvisation during the march.

The minority and initially powerless status of the poor makes it necessary for them to present themselves as acting on behalf of the values (the underlying assumptions of what is good or right) as well as the interests of the majority population. In this way, the poor seek to enlist the majority to their support or at least stave off majority intervention against them. But this also requires a climate in which it is possible for the poor to communicate with the majority. It is necessary, therefore, to limit the conflict to methods and actions which do not irrevocably violate majority sentiments. However, at some point there may be more organizational mileage in proceeding counter to majority opinion in order to win some advantage, provided the majority antipathy would not result in intervention to undo the gains of the poor. Thus, rent strikes may sometimes be appropriate weapons to use against slum landlords, even though public opinion may be whipped up against the striking tenants.

Because the struggle would be long and the outcome distant and uncertain, and because the poor would not have financial, status-ascribing, or other resources in the abundance normally available in the society to elicit effort, the major problem is to create an organization which would motivate a low-income population to begin and to continue its arduous journey. This problem becomes solvable in principle when it is recognized that the nature of social reality provides conditions which can be used to develop motivation. The poor receive few returns in their present situation because of a lack of power and resources and because they are imprisoned by a stigma which they have partly internalized through identification. The world which they could envisage building contrasts dramatically and fundamentally with their present condition. The problem of motivation could be resolved if the organization were vividly to contrast the two worlds and illuminate a path which the poor can reasonably hope to use in passing from a dreary present into a creative future.

An illustration may clarify this possibility to some extent. Let us suppose that an organization of Negroes, after many defeats, eventually gets jobs for its unemployed men, even over the violent resistance of an entrenched union which opposes racial equality in employment. In such a case, the violent attacks on Negroes would make it difficult for them to conceal from themselves the deprivation of their present situation. To have at last overcome the resistance of the union would mean that the Negroes have the considerable power necessary to make progress against even such a formidable opponent. The interpretation of the victory as one step in securing a fundamental longer-term change central to the aspirations of the membership would then connect the oppressive present world to a vividly contrasting future.

It would be a tougher problem for the organization to sustain its struggle in the face of successive defeats. Even this, however, would not be impossible if the members were to be clear about ways in which defeats can result in organizational mileage. The members could then develop strategies based on the criterion of organizational mileage.

The *violent* resistance of the union would be widely regarded as illegitimate. The union would realize this and try to conceal the violence from public scrutiny. The organization of Negroes would be able to exploit this need of the union for secrecy by arranging for accurate, dramatic, public portrayals of unjustified violence directed against its members. At the same time, the Negroes should publicly demonstrate their own moral superiority to the union and their own affiliation to basic values and symbols to which the majority adhere.

Other possible strategies follow from other needs of the union as well as from resources available to the organization of Negroes. The latter perhaps could secure training for members and create a rival union through which employers at less expense could secure trained workmen. The Negroes possibly could form a work group which could contract to do entire sections of some work process, a strategy which has been used in some European countries. There might be mass picketing of work sites, together with public exposure of employers and others associated with the segregated union. Prior to entering the conflict, the Negroes could have developed economic enterprises and other devices to bring income that would, however meager, be sufficient and secure enough to ensure the possibility of a long campaign. Political power could be organized, including both voter registration and thorough voter education. This would result in the ability of the organization to deliver a large number of votes along lines recommended by the organization and thereby prevent the entrenched union from effectively using its political power to defend its segregationist policies. The Negro organization could research the opponent union meticulously, and publicly expose many other ways in which it engages in, or is associated with, activities which are widely regarded as illegitimate. With reflection and analysis, these broad strategies could be replaced with others, more effective, more carefully outlined, leading to tactics more likely to assure success.

In developing power, the organization of the poor would sometimes choose to make alliances even with enemies to secure limited objectives at certain periods of time. For example, a mayor who generally opposes the poor may nevertheless work with an organization of the poor to improve police protection if he believes that the prevalence of crime is hurting his chances for re-election. It may be reasonable for the organization to join such an effort, provided the meaning of cooperation with the mayor does not make the organization vulnerable to attacks that it has sold out to the mayor. Since the organization would have to take into account how the consequences of cooperation with the mayor would affect the continuation of support by the poor and by its usual allies, the theory of strategy and tactics can be seen to be heavily dependent on the theory of the meanings of objects to actors. In particular, it is often useful to analyze the meanings which the organization has for any actor to which it is relevant and to consider ways in which the organization might alter that meaning in one direction or another.[3]

3. THE ROLE OF THE ORGANIZATION OF THE POOR

The preceding account of the nature of social reality was designed to state and illustrate some of the requirements necessary to an organization of the poor which could transform the world. Let us now pay closer attention to the characteristics which such an organization would have.

The positions, roles, symbols, rituals, procedures, and other aspects of the structure of an organization of the poor should be devised on the basis of their outcomes for organizational mileage. Since many of the poor have little organizational experience, the structure should usually be clearly defined, clearly understood by the membership, and not too complex. For example, members of a political organization may be able to divide up organizational work and jointly carry it out with little formal structure, since they are used to working together and know what needs to be done. The poor are equally adept at maintaining informal organization in areas in which they have relevant experience. However, an organization that is building power would constantly require the performance of tasks for which skills have not been developed, and would also require division of tasks among people who have had little experience in acting together (as distinct from only associating with one another). Under such circumstances, clear lines of authority and communication, plus clear assignment of responsibilities, in a structure which is not too complex to understand, would be a prerequisite for collective action beyond the most primitive kind. Further, the heterogeneity of the poor would make integration of the membership of their organization a serious problem which would be more easily solved if common, highly visible symbols and procedures were adopted by the organization.

Along with the development of explicit structure, there would arise a distinction between (1) behaviors which constitute the action of the organization, and (2) portions of the lives of members which clearly lie

83

outside responses to expectations associated with organizational roles. In other words, members would begin to participate *segmentally* in their organization. When this segmental participation is legitimated and publicly recognized, members become able to act as parts of the organization and to see themselves as creating and carrying out decisions of the organization. Designated members then become able to *represent* their organization and to understand that they are acting for the organization. When representation is legitimated and publicly recognized, the representatives are no longer treated merely as informal leaders of the poor. The organization directs and controls its representatives. For this reason, the development of an explicit structure would be a precondition for an organization to be able to negotiate with allies or opponents, or to participate in forums or on boards or committees, or to participate as a member of an organization-of-organizations.

The *aim* of the organization in relation to opponents would be to exercise power in order to control or affect them. This is possible since the exercise of power does not require total control. It should be apparent, for example, that an organization can have power even over a community "power structure" without the organization itself having to engage in the day-to-day running of a community, just as corporations may have power over a community which is not expressed through the routine control of community decisions. Power is complex. The power of the poor need not look like the power of the affluent in order to have impact on the community processes which affect the poor. On the other hand, there is a difference between exercising power over a power structure and merely shaking it up. The latter is characteristic of expressive protest groups which provide group therapy for members and occasionally thereby unite and strengthen their opponents. For example, a militant organization which publicly celebrates violence may enable its opponents to unite the majority population against the presumed menace, while at the same time the public expressions selected primarily for shock value would also drain off the hostility of its members and substitute for deeds.

Although the poor need not control opponents in order to change them, the development of enough power for this more limited objective would remain a very difficult task for the poor. For that reason, the organization of the poor would have to be based on all possible sources of power, including that stemming from knowledge and skill superior to that of opponents. The power base for the organization would also have to be as extensive as possible. The organization would have to acquire mass memberships from black and white, urban and rural populations, and other groups of the poor as well. The organization of groups with various identities would have to be accomplished without threatening, for example, racial or ethnic identifications, but by building on such identities as resources for the development of a common effort by all the poor. Clear organizational structure and superior knowledge and skill in the context of a serious thrust for power will enable the organization to mobilize a large membership and direct its energies to carry out members' wishes.

The organization itself also becomes institutionalized, and begins to be viewed as an object independent of the individuals who occupy positions within it. This object is an actor that increasingly is able to redefine the world within and around it. If the organization is effective, it will increasingly redefine the poor as subjects, no longer merely as stigmatized objects, and will become an instrument through which they express their subjectivity. Powerful opponents will no longer be taken primarily as subjects. They will become objects as well, no longer entirely free from the definitions of those they define.

Since the organization is an object of continual definition and redefinition by the actors within and around it, it selects its visible acts not only on the basis of right or good or honest intention, but also for the meaning of the acts to the relevant actors. The meaning of an action for opponents, for the majority population, and for the poor should be considered, even though the same act may have a different meaning to each of these groups.

When the poor are held away from resources as a group, one meaning of this oppression is their inferiority. The responding efforts by the organization of the poor carry their own meaning to the poor, a meaning which varies by context. When an organization has just been formed, militancy may be feared by many members as meaning danger of reprisal, loss of employment, and so forth. Later, the same degree of militancy may also mean that an injustice is being removed. Finally, when the movement of the poor through their organization has been considerable, the danger associated with militancy will virtually disappear. On the other hand, opponents of the organization may regard early militancy by the poor as inexplicable ingratitude demonstrating incredible naïveté and probably provoked by outside agitators. Later, it may mean that the organization is threatening established values and ways of doing things. At a late stage in the organized movement of the poor, opponents may simply see themselves fighting in their own self-interest in an essentially amoral world. This occurs when the organization has gradually captured the weapon of legitimation from its opponents and has used it to enlist the support of the majority population, which can, through its institutions, decisively intervene on behalf of the poor. A clearly illegitimate attack on the organization at a late stage also is likely to rally the poor to the defense of their organization. The attack is therefore apt to build and strengthen the organization more quickly than several organizers could do without it.

The organization grows and becomes powerful partly through engaging in hundreds of actions and campaigns. Several may be conducted simultaneously. The organization also mobilizes churches, businesses, youth groups, and other existing structures of the poor, and draws them into a unified effort intended to attain a single distant goal. The organization is deliberately inclusive of the population in areas of poverty and the institutions which that population regards as belonging to it. So far as possible, potential members would be considered as part of the organization regardless of whether they appeared to satisfy pre-existing stereotypes of "the poor." Neighborhood institutions would be counted in regardless of whether or not they had previously demonstrated a social consciousness. The organization would take care not to become defined by the poor as relevant only to one kind of problem or issue; that is, it would not become simply a welfare organization or an organization concerned only with employment or police brutality.

By coming to represent the poor, the organization not only acquires resources for the struggle with opponents but also acquires the ability to send communications to the majority community on behalf of the poor. It then dramatizes the struggle in which it is engaged. It rehearses prior to a public confrontation with opponents, then ensures that an accurate account of the confrontation is transmitted throughout the community, and afterward analyzes the strengths and weaknesses of the performance. There is, of course, no advance script, and the public event develops in accordance with its own internal rules. Over time, the organization becomes increasingly able, through such dramatic presentations, to educate the majority population and to raise doubts about assumptions concerning the poor which were once regarded as unquestionable.

Initially, the most powerful weapon of opponents of the organization of the poor is the capacity to control consensual validation and treat the divergent views of the organization as if they resulted from personality defects of its members or leaders. Thus, one hears of the "collective paranoia" or "hostility" of poor persons. This projection onto the poor of problems resulting from relationships between the poor and powerful others allows the causative power-dependency relationships to be concealed. Social workers, psychologists, and psychiatrists have made scapegoats of the poor, and thus all have played the role of defense mechanisms for the community, held in place through the provision of money and the ascription of status by opponents of the organization of the poor. Through these collective defense mechanisms the majority population can avoid considering an area of social reality which they would otherwise find painful to view. The helping professions have often been agents of collective repression as well as of oppression and have compounded their role by unconsciously misrepresenting to themselves and others the forces which they actually serve.

The first theoretical defensive objective of the organization of the poor would be to divest its opponents of the power of consensual validation, and to rally enough support so that the orientations of the organization would be received by the majority population with as much credence as are those of opponents. The organization would attempt to shake the confidence of the majority population in their world, and thereby would stimulate in the majority a desire to redefine the situation and to create an alternative and more secure world. In view of the sources of doubt, this alternative world evaluates the communications of the organization of the poor as seriously as it does the communications of opponents. At this point, opponents can no longer control the orientations of the organization of the poor as objects, and the initial struggle of the poor to enter the world as subjects has been won. The struggle continues in a world which is more fluid than before. Now drastic shifts can occur in any of a number of directions. If the organization of the poor does not capitalize on its new advantage, it may find itself again moved into a hopeless position, as were Negroes after Reconstruction or the American left in the 1950's.

To say that the poor have been controlled as objects by opponents is to say that the poor have been living in an *underworld*, in a collective unconscious, kept out of sight of the majority population except in distorted and virtually unrecognizable representations. Like other groups held in the collective unconscious, the poor as a force are disguised, appearing in forms as strange as those impulses which appear from the personal unconscious in the form of dreams, symptoms, or humor. (For that reason, Freud's *The Interpretation of Dreams* is also relevant to interpretation of the reality which is excluded from the collective unconscious.)

Just as the poor can be said to live in an underworld, we may also designate the place in which most people live as an *overworld*, the world of collective consciousness. Persons inhabiting the underworld (Negroes, the poor, the mentally ill, narcotics addicts, criminals) usually have lacked legitimate power within the overworld, but need resources from it. For this purpose, members of the underworld typically create a *cover* which enables them to enter the overworld with disguises necessary for participation in it. Underworlders legitimate themselves in the overworld. Thus, the poor *are* normally invisible. Of course, they may appear as poor before a welfare worker[4] or an employer, but become legitimated as the "worthy poor" by being docile and cheerful. Otherwise, the poor tend to appear in disguise *outside* the "role of the poor," as consumers or as citizens or in other overworld roles. In any case, appearance in the overworld requires cover. The poor may become attached to their cover and be dependent on praise, money, and even the modest status which accrues to them through cover. For this reason, the poor are often reluctant to endanger their benefits by becoming associated with an organization of the poor. The poor in the overworld therefore appear in roles which they did not fashion and which are not central to their actual lives. Through the attachment to cover, some of the poor have given up their rights to valid or authentic existence in return for certain benefits. The poor who individually appear in the overworld manipulate the actors relevant to their overworld roles, since there is no jointly held basis for mutually honest action because the poor are not valid members of the overworld.

The structure of the social world ensures that the poor, in the underworld, will be closest to the overworld groups (alienated and marginal) at the bottom of the overworld. The overworld groups nearest to the poor would appear objectively to be their natural allies in the overworld. In practice, the opposite often appears to occur. Members of wealthy families sponsor "social legislation" while the nearly poor flee from the poor and cling to symbols of their precarious status. On the other hand, the powerful beneficiaries of the overworld seek to help the poor only through changes which do not jeopardize their own power. Since the alternatives which the powerful allow are thus severely limited, it is usually to the advantage of the organization of the poor not to be controlled by initiatives of the benevolent powerful. Rather, the organization of the poor should enter the overworld only on its terms, making alliances with all actors which further its objectives. Over a longer time, an alliance of the organization of the poor with marginal and alienated overworlders on the basis of mutual interest is likely to be more enduring than attempts to maintain coalitions with already powerful, self-proclaimed friends of the poor.

Actors primarily in the underworld are free to observe the overworld, but the reverse is not true. Because of their use of cover with overworlders, the poor are seldom perceived by overworlders with much clarity. A position in the underworld, therefore, allows more scientific objectivity than is otherwise easily possible, even though studies are constantly being made by overworld social scientists of the mysterious land of the poor. The resulting knowledge bonus can be put to good use by the organization of the poor: the presentation to overworlders in undeniable form of aspects of reality which they seek to expel from consciousness coerces a revision in overworld assumptions. For example, the collective denial in fantasy by members of an overworld of relationships actually existing between Southern whites and Negroes may be tackled by techniques which range all the way from conventional agitation (through ridicule, sarcasm, or moral superiority) to the televised portrayal of Negroes who, when attempting to register to vote, are attacked with clubs, cattle prods, and dogs. The organization of the poor has the permanent advantage of the ambush: while largely in concealment itself, it can attack on the basis of a nearly complete awareness of overworld opponents and the terrain in which the opponents are situated.

An organization of the poor has also a direct interest in reducing the disparity in power between its opponents and other actors in the overworld. It therefore should support the development of social movements of overworlders, even when such movements develop around issues not directly relevant to poverty. Overworlder social movements, when they occur, interfere with the tendency of the overworld to become managed by experts employed in the bureaucratic organizations of opponents. The decline of social movement, the end of ideology, the decline of democracy, all these accompany a hardening of the overworld on the basis of naïve assumptions which place powerless actors at a disadvantage in acting to secure social change.[5]

In some respects, the conflict between an organization of the poor and its opponents would resemble a game played by several actors. The difference would lie not only in the seriousness of the organizational undertaking but also in the fact that many of the rules are ill-defined, and that the rules can be changed in the middle of an encounter. An organization of the poor would attempt therefore to set the rules in its own interest. At one point, the organization may seek to limit the range of conflict, perhaps to disputation alone or to non-violent conflict relationships. At another point, it may withdraw from an encounter temporarily to end the conflict altogether. By virtue of its structure and situation, an organization of the poor would have certain moves theoretically available to it, moves which make up its repertory. Opponents, by their structures and situations, have different repertories available to them. If an organization of the poor could maintain the initiative in determining the course of the conflict, it could limit the conflict to places, times, and methods most appropriate to moves in its repertory, moves which require responses not in the repertories of opponents. For example, it may be effective to encourage persons in opponent structures to act in alliance with the poor, to change sides, and thus to dramatize the vulnerability of the opponents to desertion. In some instances, organizations of clients have formed alliances with welfare workers in united action for common objectives. On the other hand, an organization must be clear about its goals or it will not be able to discover its best moves. If an organization personalizes opponents and does not regard them tactically, if it does not clearly set out to transform a social system rather than to punish bad people, it is not likely to make the best use of the possibilities for alliances.

In estimating the progress of the conflict, an organization of the poor would often be tempted to mistake verbal gestures of opponents for actual concessions. For example, the mayor would appoint a Human Rights Commission; the urban-renewal agency would agree to more citizen involvement in relocation of people from the demolition area; the state legislature would pass a resolution setting forth state policy on housing-code enforcement; the public education system would announce classes for adult poor; trade unions would state that they no longer exclude anyone from apprenticeship programs on racial grounds; a war would be announced on poverty; public welfare publicly would decide no longer to support the slum landlords by paying rent for welfare recipients in slum housing; the police chief would assure the organization that there is now a new complaint process to which he pays personal attention, and so forth. All these would be *promissory notes,* issued under pressure. An organization of the poor must not accept them at face value without being certain that they would be converted into the legal tender of actual changes in practice to benefit the poor. Securing the conversion into practice at full value will usually be far more difficult than eliciting the original verbal gestures.

Certain long-term trends of the overworld can be utilized by the poor. In an industrial society, technology develops more rapidly than definitions can be collectively elaborated. For example, language to describe computer information retrieval enters the common-sense world long after computers have been used for retrieving information. Between the introduction of a technological innovation and the later time at which a suitable language describing the innovation is in lay use, the innovation remains outside the consciousness of all but computer experts. Technology therefore tends to threaten the prevalent consensus by making events inexplicable within it.

The role of technology, however, is not merely to create undefined areas in the overworld. We can illustrate its further role as follows. In one rural locality, there was a system of exchange labor such that each farmer helped the others in threshing small grain. At the end of the season, no farmer owed another labor, since each had contributed an equal amount to the collective effort. Then one farmer invented a machine which meant that he could do the work of all the rest put together. But the others did not understand the new machine and its impact, although they quickly saw that they would end each threshing season owing work to the inventor. They promptly defended their traditional practice (and reduced their profits) by bitterly excluding the inventor from their labor-exchange arrangement. They could have— but did not—acquired and used the new invention collectively.

The underworld is a place in which objects are kept which would threaten the overworld consensual validation. Many of these objects, including the poor, press toward admittance to the overworld and are therefore social forces which the overworld opposes. Individual innovations are often not threatening to the overworld. A corporation can sponsor and profit from many inventions. However, although the sum total of new technology has economic value and is desired, it also threatens existing overworld social arrangements and is feared. For example, the contraceptive pill has been eagerly sought by women but it

91

is regarded as a threat by the Catholic Church. The total of technological innovations shakes the entire overworld. Since technological innovation is a collectively feared but undefined force which tends to be
pushed out until it can be incorporated without threatening the overworld, we may regard it as another underworld social force.

Underworlders, of course, may also oppose technological innovation.
However, they have no vested interest in maintaining the overworld
assumptions, and therefore seek social change and are free to learn how
to use technological innovations. In this sense, although overworld in-
ventors create technological innovations, to a large extent technology
itself makes its appearance from the underworld and can be best appreciated and used from underworld perspectives.

Further, the centralization of power in bureaucratic organizations of
increasing size tends to place the overworld in the hands of a few powerful social actors, thus reducing returns for powerless actors inside or
outside the overworld. The tendency to replace self-realization by
system-realization may eventually force system change. An organization of the poor may thus find it easier over time to acquire allies in the
overworld.

Because of its roots in the underworld, an organization of the poor is
threatening to the majority population. This is the source of the power
of Negroes to induce panic behavior in white persons who flee their
neighborhoods, and is the reason behind some contributions of large
sums of money to civil-rights organizations. For similar reasons, white
persons may compulsively support symbolic gestures which reaffirm in
civil-rights legislation the virtue of the present world, or descend en
masse on black neighborhoods to arrest, injure, or destroy Negroes "in
self-defense." The organization of the poor would have to try to create
only those panic reactions which would assist the movement of the
poor. It should avoid becoming the dreaded object of attack by a
hysterical majority swept into action by unscrupulous opponents of the
poor. The organization of the poor must therefore know when and how
to present interpretations of itself which effectively reassure the pan-
icky overworld. It must learn to interpret its actions in careful relation
to the basic values and interests of the majority population, principles
which provide common ground from which the poor and the majority
can together perceive, judge, and control the course of events which
would otherwise fall under the direction of opponents of the poor.

The kind of problem which this process poses for organizations of the poor can be illustrated by considering the dispute among civil-rights leaders on whether to adopt the slogan, "black power." Since no disputant disagrees that Negroes should have more power, the dispute is over strategy, not principle. It is a dispute about the consequences for Negroes of adopting such a symbol.

The argument for the use of this slogan is most plausible when one remembers that the stigma attached to black skin color has necessarily also been drawn to some extent into the Negro personality, leading to a self-devaluating immobilization which is the outcome of identification with a powerful aggressor. To free black people, then, requires that black be transvaluated, that black skin color become a positive symbol. The anger of white toward black, introjected by Negroes, can then be re-projected outward to become part of the motivating force in a struggle for black self-realization. In a sense, the force of oppression would itself have been turned back on the oppressor, enhancing the prospects for Negroes to enter the overworld on a reasonable basis. In such a process, black-white relationships would be transformed through many stages:

1. complete oppression of Negroes;
2. individual violence by Negroes (usually personal and directed against Negroes);
3. collective action by Negroes against white opponents, strengthened by slogans which include "black power," and a reduction in anti-Negro action by Negroes; and
4. social movement either to leave the white society or to enter it only when it assures black self-realization.

The strategy of opponents of black self-realization will be partly to seize such a slogan as "black power," to give it a meaning which will alienate the majority population from Negroes, and to lead the majority into action to ensure that Negroes cannot enter the overworld except on terms provided by their opponents. Thus, opponents may seek to employ black agitators and to use the communications media to equate black power with organized and deliberate black violence against white persons. Negroes may accept such a trap laid for them by opponents, a trap leading to a latter-day suicidal analogue of the celebrated Charge of the Light Brigade. If Negroes use a slogan whose meaning has been fixed by opponents, the outcome may be disastrous even without violence. The slogan may remain conspicuous and effective in rallying the white majority against Negroes. At the same time, militant Negroes may embody the slogan in expressive sectarian, safety-value institutions which drain off black discontent. Such institutions would be analogues of the otherworldly religious sects also to be found among oppressed peoples. The black-power sects would bear witness to injustice while propping it up.

The question of whether it is advantageous for Negroes to use black power as a slogan must be answered by their analysis of their situation, since Negroes know their situation better than does anyone else. It may turn out to be useful in some circumstances and not in others. But it cannot be useful if its meaning is controlled by opponents of Negro militancy or without rational consideration of the consequences of its use for Negroes. In view of the pressures exerted against organizations which attempt to secure social change, perceptual distortions by the leadership will result in unforeseen disasters if devices and techniques to ensure rationality are not employed.

4. THE ROLE OF THE ORGANIZER

The preceding sections discuss the characteristics that an organization of the poor should have if it is to transform the world. This knowledge can also be understood to constitute part of the theoretical apparatus which should be known by an organizer who aspires to help create that organization. In this sense, the preceding sections have outlined part of the role of the organizer. Let us now consider further characteristics of that role.

The theoretical ideas (or vision) of an organizer are a framework through which he defines his situation and notes those features of the world which are relevant to the creation of an organization. The organizer has a vision of how the poor can channel present discontents and longings into an effort which has some reasonable chance for success. He helps to create an instrument by which the poor can move into a world which they desire. An organizer introduces that vision into an area of poverty.

Introduction of the vision would begin with agitation by the organizer in areas of poverty. As he firmly and conspicuously believes in and acts to create a new world, the present world becomes discredited to the poor, who themselves soon begin to talk and act in a way closer to that of the good world which they are beginning to create.

94

Agitation has been given a bad reputation by newspapers, schools, and other institutions which defend the stability of the world of common sense. Except for defenders of the status quo, however, that reputation is undeserved. Gandhi was a great agitator. His lifework was to raise doubt about the comparatively sordid, common-sense world. Socrates was primarily an agitator who used disputation to challenge the ideas which held together the world of his time. Jesus Christ combined an account of a better world to come (after death) with a life which illustrated aspects of the good world of the future, and through conversations in the language of the people drew them away from the old world and toward the new. The parables of Christ illustrate the language of the agitator: through the use of concrete metaphors, Christ captured and redirected the attention of those about Him. In the United States, Frederick Douglass, Mary Ellen Lease, the senior Robert La Follette, Malcolm X, and Saul Alinsky have illustrated the power and varieties of agitation to begin movements to secure a better world. Danilo Dolci has demonstrated in Sicily that agitation can have considerable influence in spite of apparently overwhelming opposition and apparently insurmountable difficulties.

The agitator throws people off-balance, asking them to move outside their customary routines. Instead of the normal conversations about baseball or sex or children, the agitator initiates conversations about what is to be done by neighborhood people working together. Instead of the passivity of watching television, he elicits action which, by its very nature, is new and outside routines.

The agitator takes advantage of the fact that people realize that they do not live up to their ideals for themselves. Normally, people conceal this discrepancy from one another by presenting themselves in face-saving ways. The agitator, however, displays the discrepancy for all to see. He may use ridicule, as did Voltaire and others, in piercing hypocrisy. In any case, his language must incorporate concrete, highly visible imagery which transmits with impact the contrast between people as they are and their ideals for themselves. He may act as others would ideally act and thus place them in a bad light, as did various saints and martyrs. The agitator humiliates others in order to make their present situation painful. Humiliation will motivate their efforts to escape their present situation in which the painful comparison is publicly displayed.

Since the agitator lacks power but humiliates others, it is natural for those who have been humiliated to attack their tormentor. Agitators who cannot avoid such attacks may suddenly find themselves persecuted, imprisoned, banished, or they may be murdered. The agitator therefore not only humiliates others, but he also redefines the situation so that agitated people will not attack him. He seeks to get the hostility projected onto the opponents of the poor and away from himself. He helps people to begin to see organization as a vehicle by which they can in the future live up to their ideals for themselves in a good world.

Opponents of the poor, of course, attempt to keep the poor in their place by turning the aroused anger of the poor away from themselves and onto the agitator. The past success of opponents is indicated by the bad reputation of agitators (dangerous, emotional troublemakers from outside) and by the precarious lives which many agitators have led.

The organizer of the poor should be an agitator. Over time, however, his purely agitational role would decrease as he devoted more time to building and maintaining the organization of the poor and to their movement into a better world. From the very beginning, the organizer would help develop an alternative account of the world in the organization. He might tell and retell the story of how this leader stood right up to the Commissioner and told him the truth, or how that demonstration led to an increase in police protection, or how the voting power of the organization has the council passing ordinances which they never considered before. The action of the organization becomes fixed in a positive account which creates a clear context whereby people can gain self-esteem through action, whether or not individual employment or other opportunities are open to them. The neighborhood loses part of its stigma for its members, who are thereby released into more effective activity. A positive collective identity becomes rooted in the past and is no longer subject to the vicissitudes of the uncertain present. This identity would be publicly known; it could be revived at any time to bolster self-esteem in contemporary actors.

From the above account, it is clear that an organization of the poor would be of psychological value to its members. It would also be of psychological value to the overworld. In helping the poor to organize, the organizer would release energies throughout society which would otherwise be bottled up and withheld from socially valuable expression. The organizer would help the poor to become therapists for society, uncovering paralyzing internal conflicts and releasing society from them.

The most problematic aspect of the role of an organizer arises from

96

the meaning which he has to the people with whom he works. Initially, an organizer tends to be inappropriately defined by the poor on the basis of their previous experience with the world as they have always known it. An organizer may be seen as a hero, as a fool, as making a fast buck, as a saint, or as an ineffective and obnoxious do-gooder. But the organizer cannot accept such definitions of himself. For example, if the poor define the organizer as a fixer and rely on him to do things for them, then it would end the prospects for organization if the organizer began, in fact, to respond as a fixer.[6] The organizer therefore works out with the poor a clear understanding of his rights and responsibilities in relation to them and of their rights and responsibilities in relation to him.

Normally, the organizer makes his expertise available to the members of the organization and helps them acquire the skills and knowledge necessary to maintain the organization. The president of the organization may use this resource in learning how to conduct a meeting or how to make suitable appointments to committee chairmanships. Another member may learn how to produce a monthly newsletter. The strategy committee may consult with the organizer on ways in which a proposed action might succeed (or fail).

In some cases, the lack of organizational experience of members leads them into courses of action which would destroy the possibility of the organization attaining its fundamental goals. It is the responsibility of the organizer to oppose such courses of action. He will try to prevent the organization from becoming the instrument of any one person or faction. He will try to prevent the decline into an inactive status group or an ineffective sect. He will oppose making scapegoats of dissenting members or minorities and work to prevent any tendency to have as members only welfare recipients, or only Negroes, or only women. The organizer must sometimes assert vigorous leadership and, in addition, he may have to fill roles which the members have not yet learned to fill. Very early, however, the members themselves should be expected to be responsible for the maintenance and functioning of their organization. On the other hand, the organizer should not be a member of the organization, should not vote, should not become an officer, and should not allow his personal problems or feelings to influence the organization.

The organizer should be legitimated only to act to ensure that conditions are met which make possible the eventual success of the organization. When he goes beyond this point, he would illegitimately be exceeding his responsibility. For this difficult task the organizer has as resources (1) his understanding of the nature of social reality and (2) his skill in altering social reality from a beginning position without power (such as the ability to create and maintain consensual validation through conversation and the creation of relationships). These are relatively modest resources and they can be mobilized only within a very limited role. For this reason, an organizer cannot be assured that his efforts, no matter how determined, informed, and skillful, will lead to success. He can only believe that, if he fulfills his responsibilities as well as possible, and if the members of the organization fulfill theirs, the organization will eventually be successful.

The membership should have the primary responsibility for maintenance and direction of the organization. The organizer, by virtue of his unique role, would be uniquely treated by the membership. He would be different from the members engaged with him in a joint effort on the basis of an assumed equality. Thus, the organizer would neither idolize the poor nor accept their adulation of him. He would criticize and praise members to the extent to which they carry out their responsibilities and expect them similarly to praise and criticize him. On both sides of this relationship explicit expectations would be clearly stated; on both sides there would be critical evaluation (within a generally supportive context) of the way in which these legitimate expectations have been met. If the joint effort of organizer and membership is to succeed, each person engaged in it must be able to rely on the others, to count on their having carried out the responsibilities which they have accepted. The organizer would therefore be a partner in a mutual effort with the membership, a partner to be dealt with openly and honestly, neither manipulating the members as objects nor being an object manipulated by them. As an equal partner, the organizer would insist that his rights be observed—for example, the right to attend meetings and to talk in them. Members who did not carry out responsibilities and who had no good excuse could be candidly asked by the organizer, "How important is the organization to you?" The members, on the other hand, would similarly insist that the organizer not run their organization. The organizer would not become a servant for the members, nor they for him.

The need for honesty, explicitness, and equality in the organizer-member relationship follows from temptations inherent in the role of the organizer. For example, it would seem natural for an organizer to exaggerate the importance, and possibility, of an early success in order to draw additional people into the action effort. Unfortunately, a sense of failure is destined to follow almost any outcome of such a beginning, and members would then lose their confidence in the organizer. It would seem equally natural for a member to agree to attend a meeting only after the organizer has provided him with transportation downtown. But this kind of (often unspoken) bargain needlessly wastes organizer time and leads people to attend meetings in which they do not wish to participate. It would seem natural, at first glance, for an organizer to be as agreeable as possible to members in the hope that he will then become popular and better able to organize. But the consequences of such agreeableness are that the organizer becomes an object to use, abuse, and blame for failures, and may be regarded by members as "our" organizer in the same sense in which other groups may refer to "our" Negroes.

Many of the characteristics of the role of the organizer are specifically related to meanings which would otherwise interfere with the organizer-member relationship. Equality ensures that neither the organizer nor the members become dependent on the other and thus prevents the appearance of new stigma. Explicit mutual expectations help clearly to define the situation in such fashion that the complex course of action can be coordinated and carried out. The absence of such expectations would result in immobilization except in the performance of simple tasks, since there would be no clarity about who should accept what individual responsibilities. The long time perspective assumed by his theory of organization would allow the organizer to avoid both (1) the demoralization which would otherwise accompany the inevitable failure to achieve major objectives quickly, and (2) the reduction of aspirations to a trivial level which could never result in the attainment of power. The recognition that an organizer cannot ensure success, that he is responsible only for carrying out his own duties, protects him from demoralization due to member irresponsibility or other forces which could not be anticipated or controlled. The requirement of mutual honesty and rational analysis of the course of events adjusts the expectations of the organizer and of members appropriately to the present situation and gradually works to develop more adequate definitions of the situation. (Without these bulwarks against perceptual distortion, the organizer may elaborate a dream world of brilliant rhetoric which is far from the reality of building a powerful organization.) In general, careful explication of the role of the organizer tends to support his effective action to an extent which would not otherwise be possible.

Within this general framework, a number of special points about the task of the organizer deserves mention.

First, the organizer starts by helping the poor unite to solve what they had initially regarded as personal problems. As the struggle develops in a public arena, the many personal problems become transformed into public issues between the organization of the poor and its opponents. It is therefore a task of the organizer to transform the personal problems of the poor into public issues to be resolved by changes in social policy or program, rather than by idiosyncratic application of present policies to individuals.

Second, when the organizer enters the area which he seeks to organize, he discovers that the relationships in which the poor are involved are primarily (a) friendship, familial, or neighbor relationships, all object relationships with persons within the area, and (b) ecological dependency relationships with persons and institutions outside the area. In the beginning, people simply shift to some extent their dependency from other persons and institutions to organizers. When an organizer first appears, he is interpreted within the context of the usual ways of relating. He is an outsider on whom people depend for the provision of skills and resources. He is also like a friend. Therefore, at first, he is likely to be loved, and at the same time hated, deferred to, and depended on. Because he is valued for what he does, he cannot easily transfer responsibilities to others. People find it difficult to accept a substitute for him. One task of the organizer is to transform this personal relationship into a role relationship in a structure with which people identify. He is successful (a) to the extent that members value him as a resource, but in relationships of interdependence in which members make the important decisions and do much of the work; (b) to the extent to which members want an organizer without needing a specific organizer; and (c) to the extent to which members value him for his contribution to the organization rather than for the broad range of his unique personality characteristics. In other words, the relationship of an organizer to the organization becomes gradually depersonalized and egalitarian from a beginning point of personalization and dependency.

Third, for people to be able to act through a structure, it must be democratic. Any large number of people can act together democratically in complex activities only when the rules for their participation are

100

clearly stated and equally applied to all members. Complex activities also require specialization of roles (the spokesman, the chairman, the secretary, the committee member) and a clear definition of the relationships among the roles. Thus, rules must be explicit and generally accepted, allowing the members of the organization to have an equal opportunity to participate in decisions and to occupy various positions. The organizer's responsibility is to see that such a structure develops and that formal equality is reflected as far as possible in actual practice. Since many low-income people are learning for the first time to maintain organizational roles, these structural requirements must be communicated and legitimated more vividly than would be necessary with memberships with more organizational experience.

Fourth, an organization of the poor acts toward the poor as well as toward external forces. For example, the members may act through their organization to create services for themselves. Provided the services are of good quality and efficiently maintained, members who receive them are not thereby stigmatized as they would be if they were dependent on services extended by agencies rooted in the majority community. It is a task of the organizer to ensure that actions of the organization toward the poor accelerate the social movement of the poor.

Fifth, it is a task of the organizer to arouse the poor from their bad dream (which includes an underlying fear of their own weakness and inferiority) by pointing out and describing the changes which are taking place even outside the areas of concrete actions by the organization. The organizer must go beyond the creation of an account of neighborhood action by helping the people in the organization create an alternative and more accurate view of their world and of their position in it. For example, the assumption that Negroes are excluded from an apprenticeship training program may be generally believed and, although no longer true, may be important for the behavior of young Negro men. The assumption that the barriers to professional education are fixed and unchangeable may be important if people act on these assumptions, even though they are no longer accurate. The organizer helps the poor to discard assumptions which impede movement.

Sixth, the organizer can fail in three ways: (1) the organization does not attain its objectives; (2) it attains its objectives, but someone other than the members of the organization is seen as responsible for the result; and (3) the organization attains its objectives and then declines into a bureaucratic skeleton going through routine motions while the poor sink back to their previous position. Because the criterion of success is the self-realization of the poor, the organizer must ensure that success is achieved, is known to have been achieved, and is maintained through the collective efforts of the poor. When the organizer has ensured that these conditions are met, he has also succeeded as an adult educator: through participation, the poor will have learned many skills and acquired much knowledge; and since the poor will then have demonstrated their ability, they will also have provided crucial data so that planners in the larger society will no longer create public housing and other institutions on the basis of assumptions which make it more difficult for low-income populations to exercise responsibility.

From among the assumptions implicit in the preceding analysis let us consider here those which most centrally determine the ways in which an organizer of the poor carries out his professional task.

It is assumed that, because the organizer can take nothing for granted in creating uniquely new social entities, he lives in a tentative world in which half-perceived and complex structures constantly dissolve and re-form before him. He therefore must act on the basis of inadequate knowledge, and his action must often result in failure. As a result, his fundamental orientation is to basic principles and values as they relate to his practice over a long period of time, rather than to explicit recipes for quick success.

It is assumed that the physical structure and location of a low-income area carry collectively held meanings to the people of the area, meanings which mediate the relevance of the physical context to their lives. The social situation in low-income areas, determined by such collectively held meanings, can vary widely around any physical environment. Thus, the organizer must also orient himself to the social situation, being sensitive to it as well as to his own meaning as a stranger in the neighborhood. He begins his work where he and the poor are, in a social situation which only gradually becomes intelligible to him.

It is assumed that, in addition to change through primary and secondary socialization, personality also changes immediately with changes in the situation of a person. For example, the self-esteem of a person may rise or fall with his perception of success or failure in a vital enterprise which is said to "separate the men from the boys." The organizer also must orient himself to the possibilities for direct enhancement of personal self-realization of the poor through helping them move into more nurturant situations.

It is assumed that power is the ability to overcome obstacles. The organizer must be able to distinguish clearly the power of the poor from a rhetoric which merely celebrates a nonexistent power, and must continually orient himself to the enhancement of the power of the organization with which he is associated.

5. HOW THE POOR MIGHT ORGANIZE TO TRANSFORM THE WORLD

The preceding sections outline a set of criteria which, it is proposed, should be met if the poor are to transform the world on their own behalf. These may not, of course, be criteria which would ensure the success of the poor if they were met. But assuming that the criteria are adequate, there remains the question of whether the poor can organize to meet the criteria.

The answer to this question is not provided by pointing out that present or past organizations of the poor do not meet these criteria, since the poor have not yet collectively attempted to meet a previously formulated set of conditions which would enable them to transform the world. The answer will only be furnished by the poor, and only if they consciously make various attempts to organize to change the world. It would be impossible, of course, to describe in advance the course which would be taken by such organizational efforts. However, it may be useful to descend briefly from the clouds of abstraction in order to imagine one way in which such an effort might proceed.

The organizer will select, or will be invited into, a suitable area of poverty. He then will seek legitimation for his work in that area from persons and organizations respected and approved by the poor. Legitimation for the beginning of his work may take weeks or months, since it requires that the organizer first discover which persons and organizations can provide legitimations. This will be a difficult task in an area in which the "leaders" visible to outsiders may be "Uncle Toms" or else may be only public relations ambassadors to the outside world who lack general respect from and support by the poor. When an organizer does discover legitimators, he has then to communicate to them his vision of how they can enter a better world and, so far as possible, win their support for it. If he is successful, the legitimators will understand how the organizational effort will realize their interests and values as well as those of most people in the area.

Concurrently, the organizer will acquire as much organizationally relevant knowledge as possible about the area and its relationships to the surrounding community. He will become acquainted with the structures and perspectives of political organizations, businesses, schools, labor unions, youth gangs, churches, and other social actors with roots in the area. He will also become acquainted with the public welfare agency, the public housing authority, and other actors based outside the area which often become opponents of organizations of the poor. Concerning these, he will carefully select information relevant to the possible course of organizational work and ignore the rest. He will begin to analyze the ways in which an organization of the poor might eventually overcome such opponents. Thus, his vision of a movement of the poor will acquire substance as it incorporates unique and concrete aspects of the area of poverty which is now to be organized.

The organizer next will begin to relate the newly concretized vision to the problems and grievances of the poor. He may seek invitations to informal "house meetings." At each he will begin the discussion by briefly describing his work to a small group of neighbors, friends, or relatives of the hosts, using illustrations of the accomplishments of the organized poor in other places. He mentions the legitimators who will have agreed to vouch for him. Very early the organizer attempts to elicit from persons at the meeting their ideas of what needs to be done and which could possibly be done through collective action. To begin this phase the organizer may say: "At a meeting last night people wanted to do something about landlords who won't fix up their buildings. Is that a problem around here, too?" Or, "Father ——[a legitimator] told me that there are practically no good jobs open to people around here. Is that true?" Or (with people on public welfare), "Did people around here get the clothing allowance for their children this fall?" (The organizer knows that people are entitled to, but probably have not gotten, this allowance.) These are *agitational* questions, since they raise the possibility of doing something about aspects of reality which are normally regarded fatalistically.

When the people at a house meeting begin to describe their problems, the organizer listens carefully and then asks questions or makes comments which make it clear that he identifies with the people in the neighborhood and is on their side. The organizer does not, however, simply agree with what the people say, and may express opinions contrary to theirs. For example, when people at a house meeting say that nothing can be done about urban renewal, or that the people in this

104

neighborhood just don't care, the organizer may respond with an illustration of an action by an organization of the poor which changed urban renewal. He may mention his experience that other people in similar neighborhoods do care and often eventually unite in action. The organizer at a house meeting also is careful to inquire about a wide range of problems (public welfare, housing, police protection or brutality, garbage collection, jobs, public transportation, quality of schools, availability of medical care, traffic dangers) and he may seek volunteers to work immediately on committees to handle the most urgent and common of such problems. It is important that everyone understand that this will be a multi-purpose organization that will work on all major problems which plague people in the neighborhood.

At the end of a house meeting the organizer gets the names, addresses, and telephone numbers of those persons attending, and seeks invitations from them to hold other house meetings in their homes with other guests present. In this way an organizer works along informal lines of communication in the area to begin a redefinition of the situation and to develop a first awareness of the possibility of forming an organization of the poor. Even if he works at top speed, attending two or more house meetings each day, it will take many weeks for the organizer to talk with the largest possible number of people in the area. In the meantime, the house-meeting drive may have run into many hitches. For example, persons who agree to have a house meeting may change their minds and the organizer will find no one at home when he arrives. In some cases, enemies of organization will spread rumors which frighten people away from the idea that they can organize. The drive may need to be interrupted if an incident occurs which demands immediate action (a boy is beaten by police, people on welfare are harassed by investigators, and so forth).

The house-meeting drive may be supplemented by visits to the homes of people who otherwise would not be reached. Meetings of various interest groups (beauticians, barbers, union members, the clergy) may be developed. Churches or other respected organizations may sponsor large public meetings in which people begin to express their grievances and volunteer for work. During this early period (as throughout his work), the organizer will place great stress on analysis of his successes and his failures, learning gradually the approach most appropriate for him to use in his present situation.

At the time which seems most favorable, a meeting will be held to

105

which everyone in the area has been invited. At this meeting the poor will officially begin to form their organization. Through an analogous process, and working over a larger area in which there are enough existing organizations with mass support, the organizer will later bind together many organizations of the poor into an organization-of-organizations.

Only a small minority of the poor will continue indefinitely as active members of their organization; a much larger number will be only sporadically active. However, the organizer will attempt to develop active participation by as many of the poor as possible. He will also attempt to develop the organization as an actor with which most poor people identify, so that inactive members or non-members in the area will support the efforts of the organization at crucial times (such as elections) and in crucial ways (such as supporting economic enterprises sponsored by the organization).

At this point of expansion we must take into account not merely an organizer working alone but a number of organizers working together. Even building an organization-of-organizations in one locality will require organizer teams. With the idea of teams of organizers there arises the problem of the social structure of such a team and the relationship of the team (as an actor) to the developing organizations of the poor. In our hypothetical world, these problems will be solved as follows.

An institute will be created which will train and employ organizers and make organizational services available to areas of poverty. The organizer described above will have been employed not by the poor but by this institute. The institute will provide competent organizers who will serve the poor within the limited, legitimated, and explicitly described role of an organizer. It will be the mutual and contractual responsibility of the institute and of the organization of the poor to ensure that the organizers, as well as the poor, meet their role expectations.

The institute will begin in an area on a very small scale while perfecting its ability to help the poor organize. After three or four years it will begin to expand at an accelerating rate by helping new organizations of the poor to develop in nearby urban and rural localities. By the end of two decades the majority of the poor will have organizations through which they can act effectively. By the end of three decades the poor will have transformed the world. The poor will have joined together across the United States in a loose confederation of organizations which

106

will act so effectively that their power will then ensure the basic social changes demanded by them.

The success of this venture will depend upon the institute being able to train organizers with a high level of competence rapidly enough to meet the schedule for expansion. The training program will start very gradually until the ability to train competent organizers has been perfected. Then the program will be rapidly expanded. An organizer will receive two years of intensive training which will provide him with organizational theory and the skill to use it in field practice. Because of the rate of expansion, new staff will always be needed. When any organizer graduates, he will be assured of a career on the staff of the institute.

Recruitment of organizers into the training program will be a more subtle problem, since a large proportion of those who seek to become organizers will not be successful and since there are many potentially successful organizers who are not now interested in this vocation. The perfect candidate for training (of which there will be, of course, no real-life examples) would have the following characteristics:

1. He would value, respect, and be honest with people in general, including himself, and be concerned with helping persons even at the expense of social systems (but not the reverse), no matter what situation he finds himself in.
2. He would flexibly strive to help create a better world, and would be groping and undogmatic, learning as he went. He would be responsible in his relations with others, ensuring that his own duties were carried out competently, in detail, and with self-discipline, being satisfied with movement toward that better world without himself having to take credit for the movement.
3. He would understand and be able to build and flexibly use social structures on behalf of people, and would intuitively be aware of the extent to which social reality can be transformed.
4. He would be able to think abstractly enough to acquire the vision of the organizer and think creatively enough to apply that vision to his practice in various neighborhoods.
5. He would be able to identify with the poor and view the world as they view it, without losing his identity as an organizer or his ability to understand the powerful.
6. He would not instinctively rebel against or instinctively identify

with authority, and would be able to work autonomously. Lacking a history of alienation or *ressentiment,* he would have acquired past satisfaction through action and therefore would be able to channel his anger and emotions into ending injustice, and not merely into bearing witness to it.

The institute, of course, will be an object of attack by opponents of the organization of the poor. The usual recourse of such opponents would be to place the institute in a power bind by threatening to reduce or end its source of funds. The institute will avoid the threat by securing funds solely from the poor, who will pay the costs associated with their movement because the movement will be regarded by the poor as effective and important enough to be worth the expense.

SUMMARY

The question was asked whether, in view of their present powerlessness, the poor can organize seriously to effect social change on their own behalf. A set of criteria was formulated. It was then proposed that, if the poor could organize in accordance with these criteria, they could transform the world. Finally, one possible course of events was described in which the poor could successfully build an organization which meets these criteria.

Notes

NOTE: The content of this chapter stems primarily from my own organizational experience. I am particularly indebted to Fred Ross for helpful reactions to many of these ideas, and have also benefited from conversations with Saul Alinsky and Tom Gaudette.

The theoretical basis for this chapter has been sharpened by conversations with Danny Foss and Jeanne Davis. Several key points were re-examined and clarified in response to a general critique of a earlier draft which was prepared by Lois Olkin, who also made a number of valuable suggestions concerning the training and recruitment of organizers. The orientations of Foss, Davis, and Olkin will be presented in papers to be included in the final research report of the Community Action Training Center of Syracuse University.

1. Since an actor is not necessarily a person, I will frequently use the pronoun "it," rather than "he," in referring to an actor in the following pages.

2. A term for a discipline which does not yet officially exist but which consists in demarcation of the social turf which is fought over and along which people make social journeys.

3. A struggle between an organization of the poor and its opponent can also be interpreted more abstractly than the above account suggests. In a society, many systems of elements are mutually inconsistent. However, these do not lead to conflict if such systems are segregated from each other, or when one is powerless in relation to the other. In either case, the over-all returns to the two systems are reduced by the inconsistency as it relates to the systems. The waste involved in holding groups of people in segregated areas (Indians on reservations, prisoners in jail, Negroes in black ghettos, the poor in unemployment and underemployment, the mentally ill in institutions) is obvious and immense. By and large, if the same groups could be brought into a conflict process which would end with unity, the general increase in returns would be substantial. In such a realistic conflict, the inconsistent systems would each be transformed through a derivation process which would end the inconsistency by relating both systems to common values and underlying mutual interests. It is this kind of conflict which creates depth and integration in a society that would otherwise be superficial and without meaning. In the relationship between a mutually inconsistent, powerful actor and a powerless one, the organizer helps to enhance the power of the latter in order to initiate a process of derivation which will end with advantage to both actors and more generally contribute to the richness of the broader social reality. This ever-deepening process of derivation I refer to as the *generic* process. It will be precisely described elsewhere, together with its implications for professional intervention in social reality.

4. The use of cover by welfare clients makes case work with adults in such a relationship virtually impossible, even from the point of view of the welfare workers. The client is responding to the expectations of the welfare worker, rather than expressing himself. He therefore cannot easily participate in a deep relationship because of the meaning that the worker has acquired as a representative of the welfare agency.

5. It is no accident that the poor are skeptical of experts sent to study or help them. Such experts can be helpful to the poor primarily as the experts of the poor, working from underworld perspectives on behalf of the long-range basic values and interests of the entire population. They are of little use to the poor as agents of the overworld come to invite the poor to become absorbed into the overworld through their cover: in effect, an invitation to symbolic genocide.

6. Since the collective unconscious is reflected in the individual personalities of members, or of those identified with the collectivity in question, it follows that the personal unconscious is partly situational, that the situational unconscious of persons can be diagnosed by analyzing the social situation of the person, and that it can be altered by an alteration of the social situation of the person. Theory and research in the sociology of knowledge and in perceptual distortion provide the extant literature most relevant to the personal situational unconscious.

Since it is normally the role of the agitator to uncover elements of the collective unconscious, it is not accidental that the language of many individual therapists is agitational, especially during stages when "movement" is not occurring. Unfortunately, the agitation of personal therapists is often ineffective except in relation to elements idiosyncratic to the client or patient, since the situational unconscious is held in place from outside and therefore more accessible to the organizer functioning as agitator.

6 · Youth and the Changing Society

S. M. MILLER

THE UNITED STATES is in a watershed period, with many different streams of development pooling together. Our successes and failures in resolving the resulting problems will have a long-term impact upon American society. "Urban renewal" and suburban sprawl have been changing the anatomy and character of metropolises, affecting where people (especially the poor of our semi-affluent society) live, under what conditions, and in what relationship to potential workplaces. Efforts to obtain full equality for Negroes, Puerto Ricans, Mexican-Americans, and others are uneven and jerky. Whether these minority Americans become and feel themselves a part of the mainstream of American life will depend to a large extent on the events of the next years. The dual economy—the growing segmentation within the economy insulating the affluence of the main sector from the poverty of the marginal sector—emerges as our dominant economic problem. Schools are in transition, and it is still unclear if they will make a serious rather than a symbolic effort to deal effectively with the varied kinds and growing numbers of youth.

These issues have great import for all youth—but they are particularly important for those not born into or unable to gain entry into the more affluent sections of American society. The recent rediscovery of the poor has led to the awareness that one of every five Americans lives as an outsider, frequently invisible to mainstream Americans. It is shocking to learn that in 1963 over half of all non-white children were in poverty families! It may well be that one of every ten Americans has had to rely on welfare aid at some point in his life.

111

The great changes taking place impinge most upon youth as they enter the labor market. The problems of obtaining and keeping employment are difficult for many youth; they are especially acute for the children of the poor, many of whom also suffer from the double handicap of ethnic and racial discrimination. We cannot adequately understand the processes of youth development and the future of youth without understanding the economic, political, and social systems which structure their experiences. It is the purpose of this chapter to provide some general background for the understanding of problems of youth born into low-income families.

THE WEIGHT OF UNCERTAINTY

The labor force is changing rapidly and probably will be changing even more rapidly. Several factors are affecting its composition. Basic *economic* changes are driving many from the land into cities, where, in contrast with the past, they no longer find a demand for their labor. Service industries are growing, swelling the number of white-collar workers, while agriculture continues to decline as a furnisher of jobs. Within manufacturing, a major reshuffle seems to be occurring; once-important industries are dying while new ones are reaching their apogee. Many established communities are losing their economic base as outmoded plants and declining firms are closed. Paralleling the changing nature of economic activity are the changing *technological* demands within both new and old industries, due to the introduction of various kinds of machinery and procedures. In many industries, the occupational mix is shifting so that the percentage of white-collar workers, especially the technical and professional salaried, is increasing. Many of these changes have been crudely subsumed under the term "automation," covering all types of technological changes as well as the more limited cases of the introduction of self-regulatory processes. Despite confident statements about the skill impact of automation, narrowly defined, a clear and consistent picture of increased demand for high-level skills has not emerged. It seems to be premature to make firm predictions about automation skill demands, particularly since automation installations vary enormously. What does seem to be definite is that many of today's jobs will soon not be in demand, while many new jobs —at what skill level is still unclear—will appear.

In this situation, the young jobholder has to face the prospect over his working lifetime of not only changing employers but, more importantly, changing skills. Apprenticeships, in the form of graded training for specific skills, will decline even further; indeed, it is not much of an exaggeration to contend that apprenticeships exist mainly in occupations which have been able to insulate themselves from technological innovations and thereby maintain old craft skills. Outside of apprenticeable occupations, the flow of occupational movement is not clear and predictable. Though it is customary to speak of "entry" jobs for young workers, it is unclear what they enter into except the general domain of paid work. While there is a pyramid of wage scales, systematic and graded progression within it is limited.

Dahrendorf has contended that for much of British industry the unskilled category is a temporary occupation which people work at during relatively short periods of crisis (beginning job, after loss of long-term job, in old age).[1] In the United States, it seems that for many, especially those in service occupations and for ethnic groups affected by strong discrimination, the unskilled category—an omnibus classification—is not a temporary refuge but a permanent level. The relative demand for unskilled labor is declining, and intermittent or chronic unemployment may become even more important in this group. At the same time, those in skilled and semi-skilled occupations may also face more frequent or more prolonged unemployment as technological and economic changes redirect labor demand.

The need is for a "training in versatility," but the low-income group that needs it most is least likely to have this kind of training and the requisites for rapid adjustment to new training.[2] Those who are in a risk situation in regard to one job may not be the most rapid in moving to another job which may have more long-run but not short-run stability.

Clearly, the demand for versatility is in conflict at many points with the demand for security. The latter, the overriding demand of workers, requires seniority and long-term service in today's industrial structure. Job versatility and flexibility—which may yield more security over the long run—may require giving up a present job for a future possibility. Irving Bluestone, Special Assistant to Walter Reuther, President of the United Automobile Workers, has recognized these problems and has suggested that long-service workers may be benefited if they are laid off first rather than the traditional last in case of labor-force reductions by defense industries. An early release would give them a better chance to get jobs in other industries. If they used their seniority to

113

keep jobs as long as possible in declining defense industries, then their chances of relocating might be reduced. Such a suggestion is unlikely to be institutionalized, however, as traditional methods are maintained in changed circumstances.

It is not only that short-run and long-run security may be in conflict, but that the unpredictability of events is pronounced. In these circumstances, the possibility of building walls of protection is limited. Those who recognize the precariousness of their situation become anxious.

Youth, faced with this uncharted and choppy sea of expectations, may figure that not having an emotional investment in work is the best protection. One of the few certainties for youth in the coming days is that if they are not selected into certain kinds of white-collar jobs, they face the likelihood of repeated crises of unemployment.[3]

THE CREDENTIAL SOCIETY

There is increasing stress on credentials rather than performance in American society. Emphasis is on the possession of formal qualifications as certified by diplomas, rather than on the evidence of the ability to perform at a particular level. Those who can do a satisfactory job but who do not possess educational credentials are ruled out of consideration for certain jobs. At dramatic levels, an Admiral Rickover or an Einstein would have been barred from teaching in a public school because he did not have required courses in pedagogy or in his "specialty." At less spectacular but more important levels, those who cannot make it on the educational track are barred from a whole host of jobs by virtue of their lack of a satisfactory educational credential.

Education increasingly becomes the route for social advance. In doing so it forces youth to perform satisfactorily in school in order to be eligible for a whole host of jobs. As Abromovitz has said:

> . . . if one side of the coin of industrialization is the greater opportunity which is afforded to skill and education, the reverse is the barrier it sets up against the employment and advancement of young people who are deprived of formal training. . . . [The extension of training] has aggravated the disabilities imposed on the substantial fractions of our youth who may be deprived of a chance to gain all the formal training from which they are able to benefit.[4]

Many youth who do poorly in school are able to perform well in many jobs. Nonetheless, they cannot obtain these jobs. Higher demands are

114

being placed on students at the same time that educational achievement becomes more important. The effects are to retard advance for those who are not able to fit readily into the school mold.

The variety of routes to social and economic advance which once existed in American life has been narrowed down to mainly one, the educational route. Consequently, the character of social stratification in the United States will be sharply attuned to the pattern of educational selection. If schools are unable to operate so that more children from low-income families stay in schools and benefit from educational processes, then the pool of long-term problems of American society will deepen.

GROWING INCOME DIFFERENTIATION

Income data by level of education show the advantage of increasing education. The break in the income statistics is between, in Vance Packard's phrase, the "diploma elite" of college graduates and all the others. The former are distinctly advantaged, and the gap is widening.

Consequently, we are facing the likelihood in the United States of increasing income differentiation. The long-term decline in wage differentials between skilled and unskilled blue-collar workers has been reversed in the last decade and the spread is increasing. The narrowing of the gap between white- and blue-collar workers has also been stopped. The income advantage of high-level white-collar workers over low-level white-collar workers is also increasing. These occurrences may be temporary reversals of the 1900–1944 equalization trend, but the likelihood is that they are harbingers of long-term developments which will accentuate income inequality in the United States.

While there has been a pronounced general shoring up of income levels in the United States, high-income and especially middle-income families are improving more rapidly than low-income families. Relative deprivation may become, therefore, even more accentuated.[5]

THE WASTAGE

American society is suffering an enormous under-utilization of labor. John Miner, in a neglected book, has estimated that 85 per cent of all those in unskilled labor have the capacity to do high-level work.[6] William V. Lockwood gauged Baltimore high school students' occupational expectations against their occupational potentials, as judged by three knowledgeable judges. The surprising conclusions were that only 5 per

115

cent of the students were unduly optimistic, while 37 per cent were aiming below their potential.[7] At least one third of all youth do not complete high school. These data suggest the wastage in American society. In addition, the skills of most women are unutilized or under-utilized. Changing the job prospects and possibilities of many low-income youth requires action at both national and community levels.

THE TYPES OF WELFARE STATES

In Britain, Titmuss and his associates have written of "the casualties of the welfare state," those who are getting inadequate help from the government to meet their needs.[8] In this country, the recent rediscovery of "the other America" has shocked many into a recognition that our welfare state is not operating very effectively. While we have a substantial number of poor people, they are no longer a majority as they were in industrial life a century ago. Nonetheless, they are not now rapidly declining in numbers, nor is their plight adequately handled by the war on poverty or the older assistance schemes. Indeed, "the other America" —Harrington's counterpart to Disraeli's depiction in the last century of the "two nations," divided by class, that comprised England—raises severe doubts about whether we have a welfare state except in slogan.

The concept of welfare state is an amorphous one. It has been used to refer to a wide variety of nations and conditions, and carries an equally wide variety of implications. To some, it seems to mean that poverty, as defined by a particular society, has been eliminated; to others, the stress is on the willingness of the government to assume responsibility to alleviate the economic distress by providing funds and/ or social services. To the extent that we can speak of the United States as having a welfare state, it is that we have a limited commitment to do something about the impact of the market economy. Our welfare state does not attempt to regulate in great detail the operations of the private economy. The welfare-state apparatus primarily cleans and clears up some of the social debris produced by the operation of the private economy, rather than preventing such debris from being created.

POLITICAL DIRECTIONS

The likelihood of a large-scale redirection of national economic policy depends, to a large extent, on whether low-income groups become politically effective in insisting on change. The politicalization of the low-income population in the United States is a real possibility.[9] Racial and ethnic factors are important among the poor, interweaving class

116

(economic) issues of poverty with ethnic and racial issues. The inter-meshing of these concerns may lead to the wider political mobilization of the poor. Mexican-Americans are becoming politically active and winning office; Negroes, a rapidly growing segment of the urban poor, are likely to be demanding more effective political citizenship rights. If political movements of the poor grow and are more sharply related to class as well as to ethnic issues, then the economic environment in which youth operate may change drastically.

YOUTH-EMPLOYMENT PROGRAMS

Obviously, job opportunities must increase if youth are to be employed, but an increase does not automatically ensure that jobs will be available for low-skilled, minority youth. With the changing occupational mix of industry and the diminution of jobs for the low-skilled, the prospect may be that even a general over-all increase in production will not bring about more jobs for youth of little skill. The existence of openings for skilled workers at the same time that many are unemployed underlines the absence of a rational, organized labor market. If those presently employed at limited jobs below their skill potential (as is true of a great variety of individuals in mass production and other industries) were to move up and obtain the more skilled jobs, then the jobs they vacated might be available for the young unskilled. But this is unlikely to hap-pen because of the Balkanization of labor markets, the absence of or-ganized, structured recruitment and promotion procedures, the invest-ment in accumulated seniority, the limited outlooks of employment, and a host of other factors.

It may consequently be necessary to develop more work programs specifically beamed at providing employment for low-skilled youth. These programs should be coupled with training, so that these youth have a chance to break out of the cycle of low-education, low-level, insecure jobs breeding low income with all of its consequences. The war-on-poverty training programs (Job Corps, Neighborhood Youth Corps) are too short-term, provide very limited training, and serve more as certifying agencies than as skill-producing enterprises.

VARIATION AMONG YOUTH

The variability among low-income youth is enormous, and it is impor-tant to avoid stereotyping all of them into "hard-core unemployables." Many school dropouts of low skill are able to obtain fairly good jobs without any help; others, even though they find jobs or are placed in jobs by agencies, are unable to keep them. Our studies in Syracuse, New York, suggest that the difficulty of these hard-to-employ youth is not that they have values of anti-authority and anti-restraint which bar them from working smoothly in many places; indeed, they recognize that authority and punctuality are important. Their difficulties seem to come in dealing with issues at a concrete level. For example, they concede that a boss may have to criticize, but they may find it difficult in practice to accept such criticism, for it frequently seems to be a personal indictment or perhaps an indication of weakness to accept criticism without a strong response.[10] Various kinds of training and sheltered experiences may be necessary in order to make some low-income youth more permanently employable.

Robert Schrank has pointed out that many of the problems of low-income youth are age problems, that if they could be "aged" to twenty-five, many of their difficulties in employment would be eliminated; employers would be more willing to hire them, and the youth themselves would be more accepting of the routine and demands of working. Is there a functional equivalent of aging that can be developed? Can youth learn to accept work more easily? And be more easily accepted for work?

THE LIMITS OF PROFESSIONALISM

One implication of the foregoing analysis is that the traditional operations of the professions oriented to youth are inadequate. Existing services have the danger of "cooling out the mark" if they continue to operate as though they are of substantial help when, in actuality, they may be able to accomplish little or are effective with only very limited numbers of their clientele. This stricture applies to vocational guidance personnel, school officials and teachers, psychologists offering therapy, and the like.

Occupations have gained professional status by an interwoven process of expansion and concentration—expansion to claim that certain tasks are theirs exclusively, concentration by focusing on certain activities as central to the professional role. We are at a point where an expansion is needed in professional focus. Today, in many professions it is necessary to recognize how the matrix of the larger society is affecting (and frequently limiting) the operation of the profession. If one is concerned, for example, with improving guidance for low-income youth, one must be concerned with the limited opportunities that many

118

face. The profession as a profession should be in the forefront of active (including political) concern about these issues, just as many are about licensure provisions affecting the status of the members of the profession.

What seems to have happened in many professions that are presumably beamed at a clientele with many difficulties is that the profession has dealt less and less with those in greatest difficulty. Rather, the concentration is upon "the cream"—those who are already in more advantaged circumstances or those disadvantaged who have extremely good chances of moving into middle-class styles. (Recently, there does seem to be a counter-movement aiming at working with those in the most dire straits, e.g., the hard-to-reach, multi-problem, hard-core cases. In some situations, however, this movement seems to reflect a new "glamor" group and activity for the professional and ignores the wide range of youth and of the poor who are not in the worst circumstances but who need help.) In general, the emphasis on the techniques and methods of the profession has led away from working with the disadvantaged. This is not because of repugnance to the disadvantaged (though for some professionals that may be a problem), but because the changes in the American economy and society have frequently limited or destroyed the effectiveness of these professional approaches and techniques for the disadvantaged. It is a tragedy that the improvement in the quality of professional work has not directed the professions toward those who most need help. For the professions to be more effective with the disadvantaged, important changes must take place in American life. And the professions as professional pressure groups should have a significant role in trying to promote action that would enhance the possibilities and opportunities of the disadvantaged.

Professionalism is having a negative role in another regard. The so-called "helping professions" are in great demand at the same time that shortages of personnel are acute and growing. What is the response of many professions to this demand for more trained personnel? All too frequently, it is to upgrade standards of entrance into training and requirements for completion of training. The result is frequently to increase even further the shortage of skilled personnel. Obviously, one cannot argue against having highly qualified people in professions. If the more highly trained people functioned so as to make it possible for more people to operate at some level in providing the services which concern the profession, then the improved training could meet the so-

119

cial need for increased personnel. Such a step would involve a finer graduation of activities, so that the professional task is broken down into a series of non-professional tasks which less-trained people could perform under the supervision of the more highly trained. But this is frequently not the case. The primary task of the highly trained today is to make it possible for the less trained to work effectively.

Another effect of the increased training is that it leads many professionals to want to respond to the prestige status of tasks as defined by the profession, rather than to the social needs as defined by society. For example, as psychotherapy became treasured by social workers, fewer social workers became available for other kinds of tasks which did not involve this activity. The possibilities of recruiting staff mainly concerned with the needs of wide numbers of people continue to decline.

Further, if only highly trained people are available, they are unwilling to perform the variety of tasks which may be important for youth. For example, a special experimental employment program had social workers who were in close contact with potential dropout students. One social worker reported that a girl was flunking out of school because of her deficient performance in shorthand classes. The supervisor inquired if the social worker knew shorthand. She did, but sharply and immediately refused the suggestion that she help the girl. It would be "unprofessional" to provide this kind of direct aid. It may well be that such aid would have been undesirable, but the important thing is that there was not even consideration of the possibilities of direct aid in this particular case.

Frequently, highly trained professionals may not be willing to act as intercessors, as "fixers" and advocates to help youth over the bureaucratic hurdles, when they have the training and capacity to do more subtle and sensitive operations.

Professions are in tension between their internal needs and development and the needs and demands of the community. Acceding automatically to the demands of communities can be extremely detrimental to the effective development and behavior of a profession. Responding mainly or exclusively to the exigencies of the profession's internal development and codes may lead to its becoming irrelevant and self-seeking. At various points, one side or the other of the tension has been accentuated. In the postwar years, the emphasis has been by and large on internal professional development, with limited concern for changing social needs. Less and less attention was paid in our semi-affluent soci-

120

ety to those below the poverty line. Recently there has been criticism within many professions of the lack of attention to broader community problems, especially the inappropriateness or non-usefulness of many professional tactics and strategy for the other America of the poor. This tendency needs strengthening, particularly in terms of changing professional strategy and tactics so that the professions become more directly aimed at the target population of the poor.

CONCLUSION

Melvin Herman has told me of a revealing incident: The work programs of Mobilization for Youth obtained work uniforms for neighborhood youth employed in various projects. The uniforms were too large for the sixteen- and seventeen-year-old boys, since it is impossible to obtain such uniforms in the small sizes which fit youth.

Our society does not have a clear-cut role for those who have been pushed or have pulled themselves out of school—they are frequently "too old for school, too young for work." If strong attempts are not made to train youth more effectively and to find or make work for them, the changes taking place in our society are likely to worsen the relative position of these youth. Public policy must be geared more effectively than it has been to aid those young people who are outsiders in the affluent society.

Notes

NOTE: Research at the Syracuse University Youth Development Center on school dropouts and their prospects (supported by the Social Security Administration and the New York State Division for Youth) and on the problems of poverty (supported by the Stern Family Fund and the Ford Foundation) has been a springboard for many of the conclusions reported. The work of my former colleagues, Betty Saleem and Ira Harrison, has been particularly stimulating. Some of the ideas presented here were developed in my role as a consultant to Mobilization for Youth, where I had intensive discussions with the heads of its World of Work programs—Melvin Herman, Robert Schrank, and Martin Moed. I am indebted to Pamela A. Roby for comments. I am, of course, alone responsible for the formulations of the present chapter.

1. Ralf Dahrendorf, "Unskilled Labor in British Industry" (unpublished Ph.D. dissertation, Department of Sociology, London School of Economics, 1956).

2. The age at which adjustments have to be made may be important, though the notion of the decline with age of versatility or flexibility undoubtedly has been overstressed.

3. Harold Wilensky has analyzed work lives and concluded that professionals have less time for leisure than do blue-collar workers. Among other reasons, he argues that workers are frequently unemployed (not working) during their work careers, while professionals are continuously employed. Nels Anderson in *Work and Leisure* (New York: The Free Press of Glencoe, 1961) has suggested that not working because one is unemployed is not the same thing as having leisure time above and beyond the work time.

4. Moses Abromovitz, "Growing Up in an Affluent Society," in Eli Ginzberg, ed., *The Nation's Children*, Vol. I: *The Family and Social Change* (New York: Columbia University Press, 1960), pp. 164, 167.

5. The analysis of trends in income inequality is discussed more fully in S. M. Miller and Martin Rein, "Poverty, Inequality and Policy," in Howard S. Becker, ed., *Social Problems* (New York: John Wiley & Sons, 1966).

6. John Miner, *Intelligence in the United States* (New York: Springer Publishing Company, 1957).

7. William V. Lockwood, "Realism in Vocational Choice" (unpublished Ph.D. dissertation, the Johns Hopkins University).

8. Richard Titmuss, *Essays on "The Welfare State"* (London: George Allen Unwin, 1958).

9. S. M. Miller, "Poverty, Race and Politics," in Irving L. Horowitz, ed., *The New Sociology* (New York: Oxford University Press, 1964).

10. See S. M. Miller and Ira Harrison, "Types of Dropouts: 'The Unemployables,'" in Arthur B. Shostak and William Gomberg, eds., *Blue-Collar World* (Englewood Cliffs, N.J.: Prentice-Hall, Inc., 1965).

Part III: Trying to Grow Up

Editors' Introduction   A child is largely the creation of a child's world, and for the contemporary American child that world, like all Gaul, is divided mainly into three parts: the world of home and family; the world of school; and the world of the street and his peers. Growing up in a modern industrial world is not an easy process even under the best of conditions. The process may be no more difficult for poor than for privileged youngsters, but it is certainly a different one. And when poor youngsters happen to be Negroes, the problems become compounded. This fact is documented all too clearly in the second chapter of this section which provides evidence that, although race differences in delinquency "suspect rates" are large, differences in actual violations between the races are not significant.

Hardt's analysis of delinquency and social class is methodologically unique for this volume. It is the only chapter which is based on survey research methods—but with a difference. This is no "attitude" study derived from a population for whom the issues have no salience. The author asks youngsters about their own behavior and shows us how these self-reports compare with official records. Criminologists have long observed that crime rates are in part a function of criminal behavior and in part a function of police diligence. Hardt provides evidence concerning the extent to which differences in apparent delinquency rates among different segments of our young population may be attributed to each of these two factors.

Those who remain unconvinced that the public housing gatekeeper described in the previous section is a typical agent of the System should

125

note that the criteria employed by the police in disposing of cases are identical to those employed by the housing official in disposing of applicants. As suggested in that chapter, the rules for dealing with poor people are in fact not idiosyncratic; rather, they reflect the line officers' notions of the values of those who occupy the seats of power in the community.

The Cummings move us from Hardt's disturbing general statistics to an inside look at the specifics of the everyday life of poor kids, at home and on the streets. In "The Everyday Life of Delinquent Boys" we have a play within a play. David Cumming observes himself and the boys with whom he participates, while Elaine Cumming provides a generational perspective in her participant-observations of David in the process of observing. Where David contrasts his middle-class adolescent existence with that of his lower-class associates and searches for differences, Elaine identifies commonalities.

This middle-class boy is shocked not by the behavior of lower-class boys but by the behavior of middle-class adults toward himself when he is identified with these boys. He discovers an unaccustomed quality in these encounters with the storekeeper, the housewife, and the policeman. In spite of the title he gives his chapter, Cumming eventually decides that there are more accurate terms than "delinquent" to describe his companions. He suggests "poor," or "deprived," or "adolescent"—and his co-author is inclined to emphasize the latter. The boys' code of morality has a pungent clarity and simplicity reminiscent of the legal interpretations of an ancient Talmudic rabbi: "Stealing money from strangers is all right, but stealing money from people you know is rotten."

Perhaps because the Cummings were both legitimate participants in as well as observers of the enterprises they describe, we find none of the self-conscious ethical qualms related to the conduct of the participant-observer role, such as those which disturbed Melvin Weiss (see Cassetta's chapter in Part IV) or Blanche Geer and her colleagues.

Having caught a glimpse of that small segment of a youngster's life that is with the family and the large segment that is with his peers and on the streets, let us see what the remaining third looks like—life at school.

As the title, "School Versus Kids," of Pearl's angry polemic suggests, he views schools and poor kids as protagonists in a constant battle which the schools always win and which the kids always lose—along with the rest of society. Like Miller, Pearl takes aim at the "credential society" which locks out the poor and, by labeling their children "dropouts," effectively fixes responsibility on the kids while simultaneously absolving the schools. In this attack on the "snob" and in his defense of the "slob," Pearl takes the position that school may be a destructive influence on children and that the new compensatory programs are no more than appendages which increase its destructiveness. Children don't drop out, they are driven out!

Pearl's suggestion of a systematic exclusion of the poor from education anticipates the documentation in Part IV of the systematic exclusion of the poor from health facilities. It is probably safe to assume that the poor reciprocate by rejecting education as irrelevant, just as they are shown to reject health facilities. Like Rainwater and Haggstrom, Pearl zeroes in on the problem of identity and self-esteem among the poor and, through this avenue, offers some solutions. But it is left to the reporting of Beker and his colleagues to document the sources of Pearl's indignation. Both observe essentially the same phenomena, see essentially the same things, and reach essentially the same conclusions.

Beker takes us among the people into the classrooms and, with him, we encounter the teacher face to face. "School Days" provides contrasting profiles, not only between poor urban and poor rural school children and schoolteachers, but also between them and their more affluent suburban counterparts. Sitting in these classrooms with the observers, we achieve some insight into the variations to be found among American schools and their teachers and pupils. Among the many contrasts he draws, Beker shows us the manner in which a deliberate effort is made in the poor urban school to coerce children into viewing the world as the teacher defines it, regardless of inconsistencies with other worlds: "Thus, truth and knowledge are not the goals. Success is to perceive the dichotomy between the classroom and the rest of the world."

In the poor urban school we find most children building their own systems of survival and resistance to learning. In the poor rural school we find an apathetic absorption of misinformation. Only in the suburban school do pupils exercise a relative degree of autonomy and freedom to think and to dissent and, possibly, even to learn. But while Beker presents contrasting profiles of the business of education, Geer and her colleagues illuminate a process which must be common to all. There may not be much that the poor have in common with the affluent or with those in-between, but, whether beggars or kings, all must "learn the ropes" if they are to succeed in occupying an occupational slot.

Though the theme of "Learning the Ropes" relates to various modes of teaching and learning, in this chapter we do catch glimpses of some of that motley crew customarily referred to as the poor—for example, both among the pupils of a barber school and among the clientele that comes to the school for haircuts. To "make out" in a complex society is difficult enough under any conditions. The process can be considerably eased if one is fortunate enough to encounter a helpful gatekeeper, intercessor, or organizer, as these roles have been described in Part II. But in the long run it may be more efficient to learn the ropes for oneself. And this requires close association with those who already know them.

In this final chapter of "Trying to Grow Up" we learn something of the introduction to work at high and low levels of the occupational ladder. Among sociologists like Geer and her associates, who "go into the field and talk to the people they study," knowledge is derived from a series of encounters. What can be learned about human behavior from encounter analyses that cannot be learned from tabulation of computer output is illustrated in this venture among the people. Let's forget, for a moment, about "input" and "output" and sneak a peek inside the little black box.

By way of introduction, "Trying to Grow Up" is launched with a poetic vignette by Joseph Gelman, who isn't a professional social scientist at all. Gelman expresses himself in a style which probably comes easiest when one is twelve years old and wants people to understand what it feels like to be sent to a strange place. In his introductory comments, Beker sets the stage for a poetic essay on an encounter with an exotic world.

7 · The Rural Life of the Urban Poor
A vignette

JEROME BEKER AND JOSEPH GELMAN

PEOPLE WHO LIVE in city slums, particularly the children, often lead lives as restricted geographically as in other dimensions. It is easy, in such neighborhoods, to meet pre-adolescents who have never been farther than a few blocks from their homes. But the setting for the story of the urban poor cannot be confined to the slum or even to the city, because society and the law decree otherwise.

Traditionally, the poor have been left alone in their own neighborhoods except when they impinge on the larger community. Confinements of various kinds are arranged to isolate poor people whose condition or behavior creates problems for others. For example, we typically institutionalize those with long-term, communicable physical illnesses such as tuberculosis, or disturbing mental malfunctions such as some forms of psychosis and retardation. We do the same with alcoholics, drug addicts, and criminals. The institutions involved are usually located in rural areas, conveniently removed from the activity and visibility of urban life. Even youngsters—"juvenile delinquents," for example —are removed from the urban environments which they know and to which they will probably ultimately have to adapt.

Thus, there are many youngsters whose only escape from the slum is to be "sent away" to an institution. For some, perhaps, home and neighborhood are so stifling as to make the prospect of any change a relief. For others, institutionalization is a calamity to be avoided at almost any price. But for most institutionalized youngsters whose homes are in the slums, the usually rural setting is new, strange, and perhaps even frightening. Not only is the setting alien, but also the rigidity and strictness so often characteristic of institutional life.[1] Our picture of the urban poor cannot be complete if we forget the many thousands of their representatives who are "out of sight" in a variety of residential institutions.

An institution must present a confusing caricature of the outside world to youngsters who find themselves uprooted from their homes, neighborhoods, and familiar peers, and kept "inside." Those who work with children in such settings are often sensitive to the seemingly intrinsic conflicts and contradictions, but few find either the time or the eloquence to express them. The artificiality is "funny"—strange—yet "not as funny as it seems," since human life and interaction have commonalities whatever the setting.

An institution is heterogeneous—like the world outside—but it is homogeneous and tightly structured at the same time. It is home to the youngsters who live there, but it is hard to imagine a less "homey" home. Small as it is, the institution is large for a family—large enough for a child to get lost. We know many do not survive as people, but we also know of youngsters who seem to have been "saved" by institutions. This morass of contradiction has baffled practitioners, theoreticians, and researchers alike.

When "experts" fail, our society often turns to its poets, and who knows our institutions better than their wards? We offer the following, produced by a twelve-year-old resident at one of our best-known institutions. Perhaps he has something to tell us.

"WHAT I THINK OF SHORT HILLS"

(A Creative Poem)

Short Hills is a funny place, full of people,
From every race, from every country, from every state,
Every type and every weight.

It is called the Hills, it is like a town,
With people white, with people brown,
With people tan and even green.
It is not as funny as it seems.

It is much unlike the outside world,
Where children play and grown-ups work,
You go to school and come back (home),
It is like as follows, it is in a poem.

130

It is called a cottage, it is pretty
                  (BIG!!!)
With trees and leaves and falling twigs.

It is in one (cottage), 14 children,
How we survive it is just bewildren HELP!!!

But all these things make Short Hills great,
Because it helps to change your fate.

Note

1. So-called "military" or "prep" schools may provide similar experiences for youngsters, similarly unwanted, whose access to material resources is greater.

8 · Delinquency and Social Class
Bad kids or good cops?

ROBERT H. HARDT

USUALLY when we think of delinquency, we have in mind the law-violating behavior of youngsters. But whether such behavior is designated as delinquency is dependent upon the response of the police and the attitudes of the general community. In this chapter, we shall explore the extent to which apparent differences in rates of delinquency between poor kids and those who are better off reflect the behavior of youngsters or the behavior of the police.

Almost all analyses of official police and court statistics have revealed a marked socioeconomic gradient in crime and delinquency rates.[1] Berelson even includes the following proposition in his recent inventory of generalizations in social science: "The lower classes presumably violate the law more frequently that the upper classes." Then he immediately qualifies this by adding, "in any case they are more likely to get caught and punished," and, finally, after noting the possibility of recording bias, Berelson admits that "it is not at all clear what the fact is." [2] Nevertheless, in listing the facts that a delinquency theory must fit, Cohen concludes that "almost all statistical analyses of juvenile delinquency agree that delinquency *in general* is predominantly a working-class phenomenon." [3] However, two types of evidence accumulating in recent years challenge the notion that social-class differentials in delinquency violations are as great as suggested by official statistics.

A growing number of studies reveal that at various stages of the criminal-justice process, lower-class youngsters are more likely to be referred for further or more serious types of official treatment. According to these studies, the social-class level of a youngster tends to be a selective factor influencing:

132

1. whether a youngster with a police contact is booked;[4]
2. whether a youngster who is booked is referred to juvenile court;[5]
3. whether a youngster referred to court receives an official or un-official hearing;[6] and
4. the type of disposition recommended for adjudicated delinquents in pre-sentence investigations.[7]

A second type of evidence is provided by questionnaire and interview studies conducted among general community samples of youth.[8] These investigations have disclosed that relatively few delinquent-type acts result in police apprehension and that social-class differences in self-reported delinquent acts are minimal.

These two sets of findings raise a serious question as to whether the two procedures, official records and self-reports, produce indicators of delinquent involvement which are "interchangeable." [9] We shall examine whether the two delinquency measures show similar associations with certain social structural variables frequently employed by sociologists in delinquency research. Specifically, how does each delinquency indicator relate to neighborhood status, family status, family composition, and race? To the extent that a different pattern emerges for each indicator, how much of the lack of correspondence may be attributed to the selectivity of the police referral process?

PROCEDURES

The present analysis is based on one segment of data collected during 1963 within a community embarking upon a neighborhood-based delinquency prevention program. The city has a population of slightly under 250,000 and is the center of one of the major metropolitan areas in a Middle Atlantic state.

Selected for initial study were those sections of the city which had consistently recorded the highest official delinquency and school dropout rates over recent years. This procedure identified three contiguous low-income areas: a predominantly Negro section adjacent to the center of the city (Area A) and two predominantly white areas which differ from each other in ethnic composition. For this analysis, the two white low-income areas have been combined and are designated as Area B. For purposes of comparison, a middle-income section of the community was selected which has had low delinquency and dropout rates, and is designated as Area O.

During June 1963, questionnaires were administered to seventh-, eighth-, and ninth-grade pupils attending one parochial and four public junior high schools located in the study areas. A special team of test monitors provided the pupils with standard explanations and instructions. Pupils were assured of the confidentiality of their answers and were asked not to sign their names. Students were allotted approximately 100 minutes (two classroom periods) to complete the questionnaire. In addition to the section on reported behavior, the questionnaire sought to obtain information on a variety of other topics, such as the pupils' educational and occupational aspirations and their perceptions of schools, neighborhoods, police, and community agencies.

The introduction to the questionnaire section on reported behavior and the nineteen reported-behavior items are presented in Figure 8–1. Among the nineteen are three items (3, 10, 17) dealing with the juvenile's contact with the police and court. These items have been used for checking the extent of police surveillance and the validity of the self reports. Two items (5, 19) refer to approved or positively valued behaviors in order to reduce response set tendencies and to minimize objections about investigations emphasizing "bad behavior."

As is indicated in Figure 8–1, several items were included from such specific delinquency domains as theft, fighting, wayward behaviors, and vandalism. Brief three-item scales were formed in the first three of these domains, as well as a two-item vandalism scale. In this chapter, the analysis will be limited to boys and will be concerned with lifetime involvement: responses of "never" to each item are given zero weight, while admission of involvement is scored "one" regardless of the recency of the act.

As may be seen in Table 8–1, the four delinquency subscales show high positive correlations with each other as well as with an omnibus scale based on all eleven items included in the subscales.[10] The omnibus violation-scale score has been used to define violator status. Those boys with scores of six and above are considered "high violators," those with scores of two and below as "low violators," and those with intermediate scores as "medium violators." [11] Not only do "high violators" participate in a wider range of delinquent behaviors, but they are also likely to be involved more recently in each type of behavior. This latter finding suggests that the high violators are more likely to be frequent or heavy violators.

The information used to classify the juvenile population as "suspects" or "alleged delinquents" was obtained from the Central Registry of Ju-

Figure 8–1

REPORTED BEHAVIOR

Young people do lots of things that are good—BUT ONCE IN AWHILE THEY BREAK SOME RULES. SOME OF OUR MOST FAMOUS PEOPLE SAID THEY BROKE QUITE A FEW RULES WHEN THEY WERE GROWING UP.

WE WANT TO GET A CLEAR PICTURE OF THE THINGS YOUNG PEOPLE DO. THE WAY YOU CAN HELP IS BY GIVING A TRUE PICTURE OF HOW YOUNG PEOPLE ACT.

DON'T WORRY ABOUT LOOKING GOOD—OR LOOKING BAD.

WHEN WAS THE LAST TIME THAT YOU DID EACH OF THE FOLLOWING THINGS? IN THE LAST 7 DAYS? IN THE LAST 12 MONTHS? OVER A YEAR AGO? NEVER?

1(W)	I SMOKED A CIGARETTE
2(V)	I BROKE STREET LIGHTS OR WINDOWS IN A BUILDING.
3	I WAS SENT TO COURT.
4(T)	I TOOK SOMETHING WORTH MORE THAN 50¢ FROM A STORE.
5	I HELPED MY PARENTS AROUND THE HOUSE.
6(V)	I DAMAGED OR MESSED UP SOMETHING IN A SCHOOL OR SOME OTHER BUILDING.
7(W)	I STAYED OUT ALL NIGHT AND DIDN'T TELL MY PARENTS WHERE I WAS.
8(T)	I BROKE INTO A PARKING METER.
9(W)	I DRANK SOME BEER, WINE, OR LIQUOR WITHOUT MY PARENTS KNOWING ABOUT IT.
10	I WAS WARNED OR QUESTIONED BY A POLICEMAN.
11	I TOOK PART IN A FIGHT WHERE OUR GROUP OF KIDS FOUGHT A DIFFERENT GROUP.
12(F)	I HELPED TO JUMP SOMEBODY AND BEAT THEM UP.
*13(W)	I TRIED TO GET KICKS FROM SMOKING REEFER CIGARETTES, TAKING PEP PILLS OR SNIFFING GLUE.
*14(W)	I RAN AROUND WITH SOME KIDS WHO HAD A BAD REPUTATION.
*15(T)	I TOOK SOMETHING WHICH DIDN'T BELONG TO ME WHICH WAS WORTH MORE THAN $2.
16(F)	I TOOK PART IN A FIGHT WHERE KNIVES OR OTHER WEAPONS WERE USED.
17	I WAS GIVEN A TICKET OR WAS ARRESTED BY THE POLICE.
18(T)	I WENT FOR A RIDE IN A CAR TAKEN WITHOUT THE OWNER'S PERMISSION.
19	I LET A FRIEND BORROW A LITTLE OF MY OWN MONEY.

NOTE: Letters in parentheses which follow the item numbers indicate the subscale to which item was assigned. Items designated by asterisks were not included in the scoring of subscales or the omnibus scale. *F*—Fighting; *T*—Theft; *W*—Wayward Acts; *V*—Vandalism

TABLE 8–1

INTERCORRELATIONS (GAMMA) OF
SELF-REPORT SUBSCALES (N = 914)

Scale	Fighting	Wayward	Vandalism	Omnibus
Theft	.77	.75	.74	.91
Fighting	—	.68	.84	.87
Wayward	—	—	.61	.89
Vandalism	—	—	—	.85

venile Police Contacts. The registry provides a centralized confidential registration of juveniles alleged to be delinquent by any of the nineteen police units which operate in the county. The files are virtually complete from 1957 until the present.

A moderately high correlation exists between the self-report violation scores and official suspect status, gamma = .55. However, a more detailed analysis reveals that while most suspects tend to be high violators, most high violators are not suspects (officially recorded delinquents). Thus, despite the high correlation between the two measures, a possibility exists that independent variables may show substantially different relationships with the two dependent variables.

FINDINGS

In Table 8–2, data are presented on the number of police contacts registered for boys living in the three neighborhoods. Findings are presented separately for the twelve-to-thirteen- and fourteen-to-fifteen-year age groups, since age increases the risk of delinquent involvement and the age distributions in the areas differ somewhat. In each age group, Area A boys have the highest rate of suspects and Area O boys the lowest rate. In Area A, one third of younger boys and over one half of older boys have had at least one police contact. In Area O, only one out of sixteen younger boys and one out of eight older boys are listed as suspects. The degree of association between neighborhood rank and number of contacts is quite high and of similar magnitude for each age group.

The major findings in regard to area differences in self-reported violation status are presented in Table 8–3. Among the younger age group, there is no significant relationship between the social rank of an area and the incidence of self-reported delinquent activity. Among older boys, self-reported violation scores are somewhat higher in low-income

136

TABLE 8–2

NUMBER OF POLICE APPREHENSIONS
BY AREA AND AGE GROUP

Age Group	No. of Contacts		Area O	Area B	Area A	
12–13 yrs.	3+		.0%	2.0%	8.8%	
	2		.0	3.3	11.8	
	1		6.2	10.7	16.8	
	0		93.8	84.0	63.2	gamma = −.59
		100% =	(161)	(150)	(68)	
14–15 yrs.	3+		1.3	5.0	16.5	
	2		1.3	6.1	10.6	
	1		5.4	12.2	23.5	
	0		92.0	76.7	49.4	gamma = −.60
		100% =	(149)	(180)	(85)	

neighborhoods. This age group shows a particularly marked upward progression of high-violator rates from Area O to Area B to Area A. Even in this case, however, the over-all association of −.20 is much less than the corresponding value of −.60 for police-contact rates.

TABLE 8–3

SELF-REPORT VIOLATION SCORES BY
AREA AND AGE GROUP

Age Group	Violation Category		Area O	Area B	Area A	
12–13 yrs.	High		15.2%	9.2%	22.5%	
	Medium		28.7	32.9	31.0	
	Low		56.1	57.9	46.5	gamma = −.07
		100% =	(164)	(152)	(71)	
14–15 yrs.	High		16.8	27.9	43.2	
	Medium		39.6	35.8	20.5	
	Low		43.6	36.3	36.4	gamma = −.20
		100% =	(149)	(190)	(88)	

The discrepancy between the incidence of police suspects and self-reported violators in certain categories may be demonstrated by another procedure. In the total sample, the suspect rate is 19.8 per cent and the high-violator rate is 22.6 per cent. The suspect rate is .86 of the high-violator rate. If suspect rates for different categories merely reflected violator rates, we would expect the suspect (arrest) rates to be .86 of the high-violator rates. If the ratio were higher, it would reflect an over-representation of arrests, and if it were lower, it would be an under-representation. In order to make numerical comparisons simpler, the "expected ratio" of suspects to high violators has been adjusted from .86 to 1.00. Thus, for any given category of boys, the index of representativeness (I.R.) equals the suspect rate for that category divided by the high-violator rate for that category, with the ratio divided by .86.

$$\text{I.R.} = \frac{\text{Suspect Rate}}{\text{High Violator Rate}} \times \frac{1}{.86}$$

Table 8–4 presents the I.R. values derived from the findings in Tables 8–2 and 8–3. The index values depart considerably from the expected value of 1.00. For the older age group, Area O has a police-suspect rate only about half that expected, while Area A has a suspect rate one third above that expected. Among the younger boys, both Areas A and B have suspect rates nearly double that expected, while Area O has a rate less than half of that expected. Thus, these findings suggest that accurate inferences about the relative incidence of boys involved in extensive delinquency behaviors in low- and middle-status neighborhoods cannot be made from official records.

TABLE 8–4

INDEX OF REPRESENTATIVENESS OF ARREST RATES
BY AREA AND AGE GROUP

Age Group	I.R. Values		
	Area O	Area B	Area A
12–13 yrs.	.46	1.98	1.86
14–15 yrs.	.54	.95	1.33

Only in Area A is there a sufficient number of whites and non-whites to permit the computation of suspect and violation rates by race. The findings presented in Table 8–5 indicate that non-white youth tend to have a higher number of police contacts. The two racial groups are quite similar, however, in their self-reports of delinquency activity. The pair of I.R. values reflect a marked under-representation of police contacts among whites (.56) and a heavy over-representation of suspects among non-whites (1.81).

Finally, an examination was made of two facets of the household

TABLE 8–5

RACE DIFFERENCES IN SUSPECT
AND VIOLATION RATES, BOYS AGED 12–15, AREA A

		White %	Non-White %	
Suspect experience:				
3+ contacts		3.6	15.2	
2 contacts		3.6	13.6	
1 contact		10.7	24.0	
0 contact		82.1	47.2	gamma = −.63
	100% =	(28)	(125)	
Violation status:				
High		36.7	33.3	
Medium		13.3	27.9	
Low		50.0	38.8	gamma = −.08
	100% =	(30)	(129)	
I.R. values:		.56	1.81	

context in which the boys lived. First, households were divided into those headed by a male and those headed by a female. Households headed by a male were then subdivided on the basis of the occupational status of the head into white-collar and blue-collar groups.

In the total sample, approximately 23 per cent of the boys lived in households headed by white-collar males, and a similar percentage lived in female-based households. The majority of boys had blue-collar fathers. However, the areas differed substantially in the distribution of types of households. Since area variations in arrest rates proved to be considerable, it was decided to examine the impact of household context within each area.

Suspect and violation rates were computed for the three household contexts for each of the three neighborhoods. The I.R. values based on the ratio of the two rates are presented in Table 8–6. The basic findings may be summarized as follows:

1. In all three neighborhoods, boys from female-based households have both the highest police-suspect and self-report violation rates. However, in the two predominantly white areas, the I.R. values indicate that boys from female-based households show an appreciable degree of over-representation in the police-suspect rates when compared with boys from other types of households.
2. In the two low-income areas, boys with blue-collar fathers have

higher suspect and violation rates than sons of white-collar fathers; the I.R. values suggest that some over-representation of blue-collar sons may take place in all three neighborhoods.

3. In general, it appears that police selectivity shows a closer link to neighborhood status than to the varying types of household contexts.

TABLE 8–6

SELECTIVITY OF POLICE TICKETING (I.R. VALUES)
BY NEIGHBORHOOD AND HOUSEHOLD CONTEXT

Household Context	Area O	Area B	Area A	All Areas
Male Heads				
White-Collar	.43	.85	1.14	.52
Blue-Collar	.57	.94	1.40	1.01
Female Heads	.82	1.50	1.42	1.31

INTERPRETATION AND DISCUSSION

What accounts for these neighborhood variations in I.R. values? At what stage of the detection and referral process do these selective factors begin to operate? One possibility is that delinquents from middle-income neighborhoods are less likely to be detected or, at least, less likely to be referred to or apprehended by the police. There is accumulating evidence, however, that a powerful source of the selectivity of official records occurs as a result of the discretionary authority of the police officer.

On the basis of observations and interviews with ninety policemen in four Pennsylvania communities, Goldman discovered that "Parents holding responsible positions in business, industry, or in politics were usually spared the official registration of their children's delinquencies." [12] In a large scale survey of police opinions,[13] a majority of police agreed to the statement that: "In most cases involving lower-class, underprivileged, slum type juveniles, strong police and court action are necessary because the families of these offenders are incapable of exercising proper control." In addition, one third agreed that, "Most middle- or upper-class juveniles come from families of responsible people who are able to take the necessary corrective action, thus making strong police and court action less necessary." In an observational study of police officers' contacts with juveniles, Piliavin and Briar found that in deciding about disposition, police employed such cues as "the youth's group affiliations, age, race, grooming, dress, and demeanor." [14]

Some supplementary data collected on the self-report scale provide further evidence about the impact of differential disposition. On item 10, boys were asked to indicate whether they had been warned or questioned by the police, and on item 17 they were asked to report police ticketing or arrests. Table 8–7 summarizes the replies made to these items by boys who live in the three neighborhoods.

The percentages of boys who admit having received a warning differ little among the three neighborhoods. Such contact is reported by 54 per cent of Area O boys, 59 per cent of Area A boys, and 62 per cent of Area B boys. In contrast, substantial area differences are found in the rates of ticketing, ranging from a low of 13 per cent in Area O to a high of 40 per cent in Area A. The percentage of questioned boys who received tickets is reported in the third column of Table 8–7. In Area A, two out of every three questioned boys received tickets. At the other extreme, in Area O, only one out of four questioned boys received a ticket.

TABLE 8–7

REPORTS OF POLICE QUESTIONING
AND TICKETING BY NEIGHBORHOOD

	Area O	Area B	Area A
% Reporting Questioning	53.9	62.1	58.5
% Reporting Ticketing	13.2	21.6	39.8
Ticketing/Questioning Ratio	24.5	34.8	68.0

This interesting finding was subjected to more detailed scrutiny. Could the findings of Table 8–7 be accounted for by area differences in violation status? To examine this possibility, an analysis similar to that presented in Table 8–7 was conducted separately for three subgroups: boys who are high, medium, and low violators.

In each neighborhood, boys with greater involvement in delinquency activity are more likely to report that they have been questioned by the police. Police questioning is admitted by nearly nine out of ten high violators, two out of three medium violators, and one out of three low violators. These rates differ only slightly among the three neighborhoods.

141

The ticketing rate is also highly related to violation status, but within each category of violators the risk of ticketing shows a strong linkage to the boy's area of residence. For example, among high violators the rate of ticketing is 69 per cent in Area A, 52 per cent in Area B, and 36 per cent in Area O.

The discrepancy in ticketing rates among areas, together with the relative similarity of the incidence of questioning in the three areas, produces sharp gradients in the ticketing-to-questioning ratios. Among high violators who have been questioned by the police, 83 per cent in Area A have been ticketed, but only 40 per cent in Area O. Among low violators who have been questioned, 47 per cent in Area A have been ticketed, but only 9 per cent in Area O. In Area A, low violators who are questioned have a greater chance of receiving a ticket than Area O high violators who have been questioned.

In summary, both suspect rates and violator rates tend to be somewhat higher in the lowest socioeconomic neighborhood. However, the magnitude of area variations is much greater for suspect rates than for violator rates. Race differences in suspect rates are large, but in violation status the race differences are not significant. Boys living in female-based households tend to have higher suspect and violator rates than other boys living in the same neighborhood. Again, suspect rates show much greater variation between household types than violator rates.

The percentage of boys who report police questioning shows little variation among neighborhoods. However, marked area variations are found in the percentage of ticketed boys and in the percentage of questioned boys who are ticketed. It appears that *one of the prime factors accounting for area variations in official delinquency rates is the differential disposition of juvenile cases which is made by the police. Police questioning or warning of boys from low-income areas is much more likely to be followed by the issuing of a ticket than in the case of boys from middle-income neighborhoods.*[15]

These findings tend to reinforce the reminder furnished by Piliavin and Briar that "the official delinquent, as distinguished from the juvenile who commits a delinquent act, is the product of a social judgment, in this case, a judgment made by the police." [16] The results of the present study raise a serious question as to whether official statistics can be counted upon to reflect variations in the incidence of delinquent youth. It was ten years ago that Merton cautioned a group of delinquency researchers "to acknowledge the brutal hard fact with which we must

142

cope—that often the data which are at hand on a large scale happen not to be the data which are needed." [17] Our findings suggest that delinquency theories, prevention programs, or evaluation studies which place heavy reliance on the readily available official data are subject to serious challenge.

Notes

NOTE: The original data were collected with funds made available by the President's Committee on Juvenile Delinquency and Youth Crime. George Bodine, Sandra Peterson, and Linda Morrow Cohen made substantial contributions to the survey design and analysis. At an early stage, Mel Weiss conducted lengthy intensive interviews with local teen-agers which provided important leads for this study.

1. For example, see Robert J. Havighurst *et al.*, *Growing Up in River City* (New York: John Wiley and Sons, Inc., 1962), p. 68; or George E. Bodine, *A Delinquency Profile of Syracuse and Onondaga County, N.Y., 1962* (Syracuse, N.Y.: Syracuse University Youth Development Center, 1964), p. 17.

2. Bernard Berelson and Gary Steiner, *Human Behavior: An Inventory of Scientific Findings* (New York: Harcourt, Brace, and World, Inc., 1964), p. 488.

3. Albert K. Cohen, *Delinquent Boys: The Culture of the Gang* (Glencoe, Ill.: The Free Press, 1955), p. 37.

4. Martin Gold, *Status Forces in Delinquent Boys* (Ann Arbor: Institute for Social Research, University of Michigan, 1963), pp. 9–11.

5. George E. Bodine, "Factors Related to Police Dispositions of Juvenile Offenders." Paper presented at the annual meetings of the American Sociological Association, Montreal, August 1964.

6. Albert J. Reiss and Albert L. Rhodes, "The Measurement of Delinquency," *A Socio-Psychological Study of Conforming and Deviating Behavior Among Adolescents*. A final report of research under contract project 507 (8133), A Cooperative Research Project of the United States Office of Education and the State University of Iowa, 1959, Chapter 8, p. 52.

7. Yona Cohen, "Criteria for the Probation Officer's Recommendations to the Juvenile Court Judge," *Crime and Delinquency*, IX (1963), 269.

8. For a review of these studies, see Robert H. Hardt and George E. Bodine, *Development of Self-Report Instruments in Delinquency Research: A Conference Report* (Syracuse, N.Y.: Syracuse University Youth Development Center, 1965).

9. Two indicators may be considered "interchangeable" to the extent that they show associations of similar magnitude when linked to other variables. Lazarsfeld cites several instances of cases in which two indicators of a concept, although not perfectly related to each other, show similar associations when linked to outside variables. Paul F. Lazarsfeld, "Problems in Methodology," in Robert K. Merton, Leonard Broom, and Leonard S. Cottrell, eds., *Sociology Today* (New York: Basic Books, Inc., 1959), p. 63.

10. Neighborhood variation in subscale scores has been presented in Robert H. Hardt and Sandra J. Peterson, "Neighborhood Status and Delinquent Activity as Indexed by Police Records and a Self-Report Survey." Paper presented at the annual meetings of the Eastern Sociological Society, Boston, 1964.

11. The mean score on the omnibus scale is 3.5, with a standard deviation of 2.9. An index of internal consistency, Kuder-Richardson Formula 20, yields a value of .82, indicating moderately high homogeneity of the eleven-item scale. See Helen M. Walker and Joseph Lev, *Statistical Inference* (New York: Henry Holt, 1953), p. 312. The validity of the self-reported offenses is believed to be moderately high. For a discussion of this issue, see Robert H. Hardt and Sandra J. Peterson, "How Valid Are Self-Report Measures of Delinquent Behavior?" Paper presented at the annual meetings of the Eastern Sociological Society, Philadelphia, 1966.

12. Nathan Goldman, *The Differential Selection of Juvenile Offenders for Court Appearance* (New York: National Council on Crime and Delinquency, 1963), pp. 3–4.

13. George W. O'Connor and Nelson A. Watson, *Juvenile Delinquency and Youth Crime: The Police Role* (Washington: International Association of Chiefs of Police, 1964), p. 134.

14. Irving Piliavin and Scott Briar, "Police Encounters with Juveniles," *American Journal of Sociology*, LXX (1964), 210.

15. We would caution against inferring that most of the differential treatment by the police is discriminatory in its intent or in its eventual consequences for youth from over-represented groups. Police claim that in exercising their discretionary powers they attempt to assess the preventive (or rehabilitative) and the deterrent effects of various actions. As in most other areas of social intervention, the accuracy of such differential diagnoses and the relative effectiveness of various remedies have not been formally evaluated.

16. Piliavin and Briar, *op. cit.*, p. 214.

17. Helen Witmer and Ruth Kotinsky, eds., *New Perspectives for Research on Juvenile Delinquency* (Washington: United States Government Printing Office, 1956), p. 31.

9 · The Everyday Life of Delinquent Boys

DAVID CUMMING AND ELAINE CUMMING

PART I
by David Cumming

THE BOYS AND THEIR NEIGHBORHOOD

IN THE SUMMER of 1962, I was a participant-observer among a group of ten boys who lived in and around a public housing project. The boys ranged in age from about fifteen to twenty, but most were closer to fifteen. I was eighteen. All but one of the boys were white, and all but one (other than myself) came from poor families. This one boy, Ted,[1] was from a nearby middle-class neighborhood and his father owned a supermarket. None of the boys had police records at the time that I worked with them, but all freely admitted to illegal acts. During the summer I saw a number of acts that were technically criminal, and on this basis I will refer to these boys as delinquent. I have been told that since that summer, four of the ten have acquired police records.

I approached the group through two boys I had met the previous summer while observing smaller children in city playgrounds. The group was not particularly tight knit, and there was really never any question of "acceptance"; I was there and the boys didn't seem to mind my being there. They never openly questioned my purposes in being among them—I was simply part of the environment. In a situation where information about who and what you are is required only in minimal quantities, it was very easy to become a part of such a loose and nebulous group. No one ever asked me for more information about myself than my phone number, which the boys wanted in case they might wish to get in touch with me. It was about two weeks after I started wandering around with them that they figured out where I lived. I mention all this to dispel any illusion that this was an organized

146

gang that I was observing. The word "gang" brings to mind cohesion, structure, control, and group boundaries—all things that these boys had only in a diffuse way. Although they were, of course, not without norms, their norms did not have the structure and clarity of Whyte's older street-corner boys.[2] Nor did they seem to have the clearly "lower-class culture" that Miller describes.[3]

The neighborhood in which the ten boys lived is heterogeneous. The housing project in which half of them lived is located between a working-class and an upper-middle-class neighborhood. For this reason, most of the contacts the boys had with adults outside of their own families were with people geared to serving the upper middle class.

EXPECTATIONS

At least according to their report, most of the boys were "flunkies" in school; by this they meant that they were the pet whipping boys of the teacher, who, through her dislike for them, would fail them. I have no way of knowing how true this was. It is true, however, that the cashiers in the local supermarkets treated the boys with an attitude which was, at best, condescending. On one occasion, Jack and I went to the store because his mother had sent him to buy a bag of potatoes and a watermelon. His mother had found the prices in the newspaper and had given him one cent more than he needed to buy them. He picked out both the potatoes and the watermelon with great care, and while he carried the potatoes to the check-out counter, I carried the watermelon. Jack put down the sack of potatoes and the money (a dollar bill and change), and I put down the watermelon. The cashier picked up the dollar bill, took fifty-nine cents out of it, handed him the change, and turned to me. At this point Jack said:

"Hey, I'm buying that watermelon, too." (He extends his handful of change.)

Cashier: "You don't have enough. Those cost seventy-nine cents."

Jack: "Yeah?"

Cashier: "Yeah."

Jack: "I got eighty cents."

Cashier: "Count it."

Jack counted out the seventy-nine cents for the cashier, showing her the extra penny. She picked up the money, counted it again, rang it up, handed him his second receipt, and both of us walked out of the store. On the way back to Jack's apartment, he complained a little about stu-

147

pid cashiers, but it did not seem to strike him as being out of the ordinary that he should have to demonstrate that he had enough money before buying a watermelon.

This example illustrates some of the expectations, or rather, lack of expectations, which these boys faced. Recently, in thinking about writing this piece, I took a walk through the area in which the boys live. I did not meet any of them, but one incident recalled a great deal about what it is like to be on that street. As I walked, a large, rather new car pulled up to the curb and a lady stuck her head out of the window. "Hey, boy," she said, "which way is Thornden Park?" When I had told her, she thanked me and drove off. I am never addressed "Hey, boy" in my own neighborhood. I do not mean to imply by these examples that these boys are expected to be rude, abusive, or delinquent. But neither are they expected to be polite. Had I replied to the lady in the car with an obscenity, she would probably have been shocked but not surprised.

On a more memorable occasion, I was with three or four of the boys in my father's car. I was in the driver's seat, although we were just sitting, not moving. A couple of the boys catcalled at a squad car driving by and the policeman stopped, came over, and proceeded to check the car for violations. I was the only one he could hold responsible, so I ended up on the front seat of the squad car while he lectured me. He explained that I could be just as "wise" as I wanted, but that it would cost me every time. He seemed to interpret my rather frightened denials of any wrong intent as further impudence. When he found that I was not carrying a registration for the car, he used his radio to check on its ownership. While he waited for the plate numbers to be traced, he wrote out tickets for the violations he had found (no registration, light out above rear license plate, no brake lights—the brake lights were in working order but I had forgotten, in my agitation, to turn on the ignition). His radio then gave him the information on the ownership of the car. He asked if the Dr. Cumming who owned the car was my father. I told him that he was, and his tone toward me changed very quickly. He was not really impressed, but he wanted to know what a nice kid like me was doing with a bunch of punks like that. He asked what my father would say if he knew the kind of things I was doing. I do not know if the policeman would have done anything at all to me if he hadn't already written tickets. He said he didn't like to do this kind of thing, gave me the tickets, and drove away. I am not saying that the policeman had prejudged the kind of boy he thought I was; he was judging an action—the catcalls. I am saying, however, that he prejudged the kind of boy I was when he found that my father was a doctor. From me he expected more.

IDENTITY

To some extent, all adolescents are in a state of limbo when they wander streets where no housewife knows their names. But most adolescents do not spend as much time on the streets, or in playgrounds, or in swimming pools as do these boys; very often, they are away from home as much as eighteen hours a day, getting meals when and where they can. Several times during the summer I ate meals in the apartments of boys whose parents were out. Occasionally, someone's mother would feed me. When this first happened, I wondered whether the mother in question had any idea of who I was. I found out later that she was one of two mothers who regularly fed a number of boys. Later in the summer I ate there again; at the same time, two boys who had run away from a local orphanage and seemed to be strangers to the boys I knew were also eating there. These two boys slept in the halls of the housing project and were given meals by mothers who neither knew nor cared who they were. If this source failed, the two runaways would shoplift food or steal small change to buy potato chips rather than go back to the orphanage.

This episode of the runaway boys is a good example of the independence from their parents all the boys were able to maintain. The two runaways were living in approximately the same pattern as the boys I was with, and they were able to keep themselves alive and undetected for three or four days. During that time, the boys in the housing project helped them find food and gave them money—both of them went to a dance on Friday night, and Carl even shoplifted cigarettes for them.

By such methods, all of the boys managed to stay away from parents and other adults for most of every day during the summer. I could not say what their pattern would be like during the winter, when they are at school. I would suspect that it would be similar but not so pronounced, mostly because they do not have enough time during the day to beg, borrow, or steal money or food in order to remain away from home.

DEPRIVATIONS

In observing these boys, I was especially interested in those things that contrasted most sharply with the kind of life I had led as an adolescent and was still leading at that time. Delinquency was not one of the star-

149

tling differences. After all, delinquency in young boys appears to be to social development what the Oedipal phase is said to be to psychic development—entirely normal and inevitable.[4] What was startling to me was that these boys managed to live with what seemed to be a kind of deprivation. They lacked parents, knowledge, clearly defined expectations, and organization and control. What struck me most during that summer was this deprivation and the boys' method of adapting to it.

Of the ten boys with whom I had reasonably close contact, four had fathers who were living at home and were employed, two had unemployed fathers, and four were living with their mothers, who worked. All but one of the families, as I have said, were poor. From my vantage point, the boys seemed to be acquiring from their parents many diffuse, negative, and self-defeating attitudes. At one time during the summer, Jack was invited to spend a week at a summer place on Lake Ontario with Ted (whose father owned the supermarket). At this point, my field notes say:

> Went over to the project unaware that Jack had gone to the lake for a week. [Jack's] father was there. Father wanted to talk to me. Said that he had heard that I had given Jack a ten-dollar bill. Jack's older brother had told his mother who had told him. I assured him that I had done no such thing and that I had trouble enough coming by ten-dollar bills myself. He laughed and said he had the same trouble. Said he just wanted to find out where Jack got the bill . . . (pause). "My boys aren't angels." I responded, "Who is?" He laughed again. About this point, he loosened up a bit and talked. Told me about Jack's going away Sunday. Ted had asked if Jack could go but he [the father] insisted on having Ted's parents ask . . . "You let kids go off like that and they may go where they say and they may go anywhere else too . . . I don't want any cops coming to that door . . . The farther I keep from the cops the better." Finished up by explaining he just wanted to check [about the money] because he had no idea where he or Jack could ever get ten to pay back if I had lent it. Parting remark [in the tone of an accomplice], "If you find out where he got that ten, tell me, next time I may split it with him."

That Jack's father's attitudes were negative, I think, is fairly plain. The major emphasis was never on valued actions but on *what not to do*—most importantly, not to become involved with the police. At the

150

same time he seemed to sanction the behavior that in the end *does* bring the police to the door (as in his parting remark to me).

An incident the previous week, in which the boys had stolen some records and money, illustrates some of the boys' attitudes about things that are *not done*. Greg and I had gone over to the house of a girl I did not know to find Jack and Tom. When we got there, Tom was in a bedroom with the girl and Jack was in the living room picking out things to steal. Jack came away with fifteen phonograph records and $1.90 in dimes. Tom had managed to take twenty-five cents, an identification bracelet, and a ring. I was told as we walked back over to the project that the girl's mother gives her the support check received from her father so it is therefore all right to steal from her. Greg was not entirely sure about that. Stealing money from strangers is all right, but stealing money from people you know is "rotten." To quote him, "Money isn't the same as records. You can always get more records." The other boys seemed to feel that this statement was generally true, and that only the fact of the support check made it all right to steal this particular money. Later the same day the boys stole some goggles and fins that were lying on the grass near a municipal swimming pool. None of them seemed to have any hesitation about doing that.

I do not mean to say that the boys had no positive attitudes. They had quite strong expectations of friendship. Money passed among them with no accounting that I was aware of. Those who had it gave it to those who didn't. This kind of pattern was quite essential to a group of boys who often had no money but who stayed away from home for as long as they did. What I am saying is that many of their attitudes were inconsistent within themselves as well as with the law. They did not seem to have what I would call a delinquent subculture however; their culture seemed to me to be more correctly described by words like "poor," "deprived," and "adolescent" than by the word "delinquent."

SPECIALIZED KNOWLEDGE, AND LACK OF IT

None of these boys had any real idea of how to go about getting a job, other than by walking down a street and applying everywhere. They knew nothing at all about such middle-class things as scholarships. What they did seem to know in great detail were the processes involved in such things as collecting insurance and suing for damages. While it is common for adolescent boys to become interested in what they can "sue for," these boys had more information on the subject than I had ever come across. It may have been totally incorrect, but it was the kind of information for which they felt a need, and was regarded as a money-making skill—a racket that everyone could get in on.

In general, however, the boys' knowledge, like their experience, was extremely narrow in scope, and what knowledge they had was often associated with coping with the chaotic lives they led. They knew the schedules of the bus that took them to the record hops on Friday night. They knew (or thought they knew) what policemen could and couldn't do to you. They did not know and were not very much interested in knowledge that did not have this kind of immediate practical value to them. Since they did not read for pleasure, their acquisition of knowledge was limited to word-of-mouth communication and whatever the schools tried to teach them. Most of the information they had was obtained from parents and friends. Neither source was very reliable.

As I have mentioned, these boys suffered from what I considered to be a chronic lack of organization. I was most impressed by three areas that I had assumed to be rather well defined for everyone: money, time, and names and addresses.

Money was something the boys came by in irregular ways and at unforeseen times. None of them had what might be termed an allowance. One had the income from a paper route; one worked as a packer in his father's grocery store; one occasionally received money from an older married sister. The others shifted as best they could. Their parents seldom gave them money. In general, money came as a windfall and was regarded as something special; that is, it was not simply a means of transferring goods and services. At the time, I asked them questions about money, but they were either unable or unwilling to state their thoughts about it very clearly. I suspect that money represented everything besides money that they did not have (to the rather limited extent that they felt they lacked anything but money).

Whatever money meant to them, the boys never kept it very long. When they had money, they stopped stealing and started spending. Very often they bought things they did not need, and sometimes things they did not want. They would perhaps plan in rather meticulous detail how much money they would save for what, but the money seldom lasted long enough to be spent even the next day. The one clear exception to this pattern was the behavior of the boy who had a paper route. Although he spent most of the money he made, he also saved some. I believe he had saved for and bought football equipment the previous year. This boy was the only one who seemed to be able to believe in the future sufficiently to plan for it.

During the summer, the boys "borrowed" small sums of money from me when they needed it for something specific. I believe that it was clearly understood by everyone that "borrowed" money was never returned. On one occasion, one of the boys asked if I would lend him a dollar to go to a record hop the next night. I told him that I probably would. He then asked if I would lend it to him on the spot. I told him that if I gave him a dollar, then he would probably only have a dime of it left for the next day. He grinned and asked what I thought he would be keeping the dime for.

The above example says as much about the boys' organization of time as it does about their organization of money. I have mentioned that the boys did not organize their day around anything in particular. In the summer the week had only one focus—the Friday-night record hop—and at that, they did not organize very well. Their day cannot be said to be split into morning and afternoon. They did not have watches and they did not go home for lunch. There was no effective way, and no reason, for them to know the time of day.

The smallest unit of time that had real meaning for the boys during the summer was a day. Some days they spent with each other, others not. They had no way of meeting at any specific time, or even "after lunch." If they found each other, they usually spent the rest of the day together. Because of this diffuseness of time, the first part of every day was taken up with looking for other members of the group. (This is why the only thing they asked about me was my phone number.)

Another thing I found disconcerting about the boys was the small amount of information they had about each other. I had grown up with boys who knew a great deal about each other and each other's families —whose father made his living at what, where they lived, and where they had come from. When I first asked the boys about these things, I found that it was not information they had about each other nor the kind they were willing to give about themselves. When they were asked, they didn't answer; they asked why you wanted to know. When they were asked about their friends, they knew very little. At first I thought that this was only distrust of me. Later on, I became convinced that this was simply not the kind of thing that they found out about each other. I arrived at this conviction after asking Jack for the last name of another boy. He was willing to tell me and said that he had known the name at one time but could not remember it. After trying out a number of names which were similar to each other, he came up with one that he was sure was correct and which I later discovered to be correct. These two boys had lived in the same public housing project for eleven or twelve years, and they must have started school together. Their occasional recollections of previous years suggest that they must have been friends for at least three or four years. If Jack had never remembered the name, I would have strongly suspected that he simply did not want to tell me, but since he did finally remember it, I conclude that he really *did not* remember at first. Another aspect of this voluntary anonymity was the fact that, unlike the boys I had grown up with, this group never referred to each other by their surnames. By the time these boys reached fifteen they rarely identified each other with their families. At the time, I thought this sensitivity about vital information reflected the interest that policemen and other unfriendly adults take in it. At any rate, their public identity included only their given names.

These are only examples of what seemed to me to be unstructured lives. While my impression of these boys is one of deprivation, I do not mean to imply that they are alienated from society's goals because they have no means of reaching them. It is rather that they lack the kind of attitudes and knowledge necessary to imagine and choose the means. That they *have* a choice and that there *are* means is illustrated by the fact that Reggie had been delivering newspapers for some time. He chose to deliver newspapers; some of the others chose to steal. These boys knew that stealing is bad and working is good, and they knew that there *are* ways of achieving what the world calls success. They wanted to succeed, but they didn't know how. In the meantime, they were not convinced that it is so bad to "beat the system," and they did not have the competence to find work. In brief, rather than saying that these boys had no means of achieving major goals, I would say that the lack of structure in their lives made them unable to make effective choices among these means.

ACTIVITIES

A typical day began for these boys with one going to find another. Two of them sought out a third, and then a fourth, and so on. Often two groups would meet during this process, both groups looking for the members of the other. Just as often, they missed each other, and the process of looking was protracted for an hour or so until a reasonable group was formed or until they gave up trying to form one (they seemed to be positively uncomfortable in groups smaller than four).

During the time I spent with them, the boys swam at least once a day and very often twice, except when they had been expelled by the guards from the swimming pool for a few days. They did not swim or dive well; they preferred jumping off the diving board onto one another's heads. When they were not at the swimming pool, they sat around or simply wandered. Occasionally they would go to visit girls, but this was a major project because they did not associate with neighborhood girls so much as with girls they met at the Friday-night dances. Going to see these girls was often a matter of walking two or three miles each way. Between such activities, they would think about ways of getting meals without going home. In the evening they sometimes sat on the front porch of one of the boys who did not live in the housing project. (His mother was one of those who fed all-comers.) Neither of his parents took much interest in what was going on on the porch and this may have been the reason that this was the only set of parents the boys spent any considerable time around during their waking hours. I cannot, however, be sure, since my contact with the other parents was extremely slight.

At other times, not so frequent, they sat around in the local dairy bar or sat in the swings of the local playground. During all of these activities, there were very long periods of utter silence. Very often the boys would sit against a wall for a couple of hours at a time carrying on a desultory conversation, sweating in the sunlight, idly trying to trip smaller children, and smoking cigarettes. Their ordinary day in the summer was excruciatingly boring. They knew that there were other ways to spend the day—some of them had gone at one time or another to some of the recreation centers that are available. The boys I was with did not like these centers. They did not like to be told what to do. They especially did not like to be asked questions. When I asked them why they didn't go to the centers, they made derogatory remarks about "social workers." Later in the summer I formed the impression that "social worker" meant any adult who asked questions and who was not a policeman or a teacher—but just as bad. "Social workers" included recreation leaders, social scientists, school psychologists, psychiatrists, and so on. To avoid "social workers," the boys kept away from the centers and were thrown entirely on their own resources for amusement. They were not what I would call resourceful.

The major exception was the Friday-night record hop. Almost all of the boys managed to gather enough money to go. The extraordinarily loud music at this affair was supplied by local groups or by records. Most of the boys could do ten or twelve different dances, and some of them danced very well. At these record hops, groups of boys characteristically settled upon one area of the dance floor and stayed there. The girls milled about on another part of the floor. At the beginning of each dance, the boys went across the floor and brought girls back to their group. At the end of the dance, the girls rejoined their own girl friends. After an hour or so of this, the girls sometimes stayed in the boys' area between dances. All of the boys seemed to enjoy these dances. Very often all of Friday would be devoted to raising enough money to go. At one of the record hops, a fight started over a girl, but it was broken up by the boys themselves before the four or five policemen who were always standing along the walls could intervene. Other than that, the record hops were uneventful.

I have described what I saw of the life these boys led. If I had relied on the stories they told, the picture would have been much gaudier. At one time, the boys claimed to have broken into a local car dealer's garage and stolen some parts. I never saw the parts. At another time, one of them claimed to have "wrapped up a four-speed Pontiac." He said he would have to go to court. When I asked him about the incident a week later, he said that his lawyer had managed to "get him off light" with a ten-dollar fine. These and other stories always lacked corroboration, and I never believed them. It is possible that they were exaggerations of real incidents, but I doubt it. They seemed to be descriptions of the life the boys would like to lead.

CONCLUSIONS

The boys lacked a great deal. Many had lost a parent. They didn't have anything to do, and nobody required much of them. They had weakly formed goals, little information, and almost no money. I believe they chose to steal not so much because they knew no differently as because they did not know how to go about choosing other ways effectively. They stole when they needed or wanted something, not because they were unaware of work as an alternative, but because their weakly structured lives lessened their ability to make a real choice. When I describe these boys as disorganized, I do not mean the kind of frenetic chaos the word can suggest. Chaos might, of course, have resulted from a major effort at organized activity, but I never saw them make one. My point is rather that the lives of "juvenile delinquents" are not exciting or interesting. They are dull and, above all, frustrating, because when these boys try to deal with the general society they are trying to do so without adequate knowledge and skill. What is more debilitating is that they do not know that they lack this knowledge and skill. As far as they are concerned, they lack only money. I do not think they know why they have difficulty dealing with the world; they consider it to be the normal state of existence.

Toward the end of the summer, one of the boys suddenly announced that he was going to get a job the next summer. I asked him why, and he said, "To make money." "For what?" I asked. "Just to have it around," he said. "How are you going to get the job?" I asked. "I don't know yet," he answered.

PART II
by Elaine Cumming

The disconcerting thing about this account is the combination of naïve judgment and detached comment. I think that this is because most participant-observers are equipped with a frame of reference out of which they observe; David was not. He entered this group of boys as one of them, divided from them not by a theory he had in his head but by his social class. When he came to write this account, three years later, he had to cast it into some framework; as a result, he wavers in a discomforting way between slightly disapproving participant and wise, detached observer. But this aside, three questions came to me as I read this description. First, how does the long idle summer of these boys differ from the many superficially similar summers of the boy who was observing them? Indeed, for that matter how do they differ from the even more unstructured summers of my own childhood? Second—and this is an easier question—are these boys any more delinquent than other boys? And third, what kinds of lives are such summers preparing them for?

There seems to be only one important difference between the diffuse and languid days described here and the ones I had seen my son spend so recently. That one difference seems, however, to be the key to why he found these boys so "excruciatingly boring"; it is the different kind of

157

organization of both facilities and time. Although I had seen David himself read and loaf for days in what seemed to me a miasma of inaction, I have also seen him, together with his friend Mike, spend days digging out a cave, putting a solid roof on it, and installing some kind of cooking apparatus, only to abandon it and spend further days renovating a Model T Ford in order to drive it bumpily around a field. David's sloth, when it came upon him, had a volitional quality, and David's comments betray a kind of impatience with boys who let idleness just happen to them. Indeed, at eighteen, he seems to have mistaken for disorganization a less complex and more diffuse organization than the one to which he was accustomed.

When I think further back, to my own childhood, I can remember even idler days: days of riding aimlessly around on a bicycle, of loafing and reading, and of many, many days spent at the swimming pool jumping off the board rather than learning to dive. But again there is a difference: for some part of the time I was feverishly busy with friends building a clubhouse or making things to sell in a bazaar or putting up a lemonade stand. My idlest summer days never seemed to have bored me, perhaps because I also chose them.

Finally, neither David nor I was ever permitted to escape from the inflexible family ritual of three meals a day at our own tables. For this reason alone, it seems to me that the answer to my question is that from a middle-class child both a minimal level of observable order and a regular reaffirmation of family values are expected.

My question as to whether these boys were more delinquent than any others is easier to answer. In spite of the fact that four of them have managed to accumulate police records, I think they were not. On top of their lack of structure, both personal and social, is the expectation on the part of the policeman that they will break the law, and his willingness to pick them up and charge them when they do so. The fact that they have higher rates of delinquency at this particular age seems to me to be an artifact of the class system, and, of course, this has been noted by many others. Today, unfortunately, most adults are fearful and mistrustful of adolescent boys and try to avoid them.[5] These friends of David's are taking the brunt of an intergenerational tension that has somehow been built into all of our lives.

When I ask myself my final and most difficult question—what kinds of lives are these boys being prepared for?—I come closer to understanding the bewilderment revealed by David in his account of this

158

summer. A middle-class boy knows that eventually he must learn to string his life out in some orderly way. To find people who neither know nor care about the time of day is disturbing to a youth who is learning to allocate time effectively. (Perhaps it arouses a doubt in him as to whether this difficult task is worth while.) Many of the boys described here are going to end up working in unskilled jobs—service jobs, laboring jobs. They are not going to want or need a keen sense of time to do that. Nor for that matter are they going to want too clear a view of too many goals. Perhaps they are going to need stoicism—the ability to carry on as if time were standing still. Such a quality is not much help to ambitious people, but it may be essential equipment for those who are going to do routine jobs. Perhaps some of the "disorganization" of these boys' lives is really an adumbration of their futures.

What finally strikes me is the beginning of an emergence of some boys who are organizing themselves toward a different and more highly differentiated way of life. The boy with the paper route and the boy who worked in his father's grocery store look as though they were heading toward a more organized type of life than the others, and yet there is no evidence that David saw any great difference between them and the others at that time. Certainly there is no suggestion that they were any less delinquent. The future of the remainder of the boys is an enigma, and in thinking of them, I end with a question: How can you train a boy to become a man who is able to bear the monotony and drudgery of a laborer's life without imbuing *all* of his life with the diffuse, unstructured quality that this summer suggests? This is a harder question to answer than the other two.

Notes

NOTE: These data were collected under the auspices of the Syracuse University Youth Development Center. The authors thank Helen Icken Safa and Irwin Deutscher for releasing them.

1. All names are fictitious.

2. William F. Whyte, *Street Corner Society* (Chicago: University of Chicago Press, 1943).

3. William C. Kvaraceus, Walter B. Miller, *et al., Delinquent Behavior: Culture and the Individual* (Washington: National Education Association of the United States, 1959).

4. Nils Christie, Johs. Andenaes, and Sigurd Skirbekk, "A Study of Self-Reported Crime," in *Scandinavian Studies in Criminology*, I (Oslo: Universitetsforlaget, 1965), pp. 86–116.

5. Frank Musgrove, *Youth and the Social Order* (Bloomington: Indiana University Press, 1965).

10 · Schools versus Kids

ARTHUR PEARL

PREMATURE WITHDRAWAL from school has been euphemistically dubbed "dropping out" with good reason. The label implies that such youth leave school voluntarily, thus neatly absolving schools and schoolmen of responsibility. Although a perennial phenomenon, dropping out has only recently gained the status of recognition as a social problem. As with all phenomena which achieve such status, the compelling question is, "Whose problem?" Schooling has become a necessity for adequate adjustment to a technologically sophisticated world. It would be false to suggest that the requirement of years of formal education exists because schools instill skills, sensitivities, and breadth of knowledge in students; it is closer to the truth to suggest that education has become a necessity with the emergence of the "credential society." The credential society is a bureaucratic system which insists upon ritualistic license awarded only to those who have been exposed to years of school routine. The credential society, coupled with the obsolescence of traditional absorption systems (agricultural pursuits, unskilled labor in service and products-producing industries, and entrepreneurial enterprise with limited capital), tends effectively to lock the poor out of participation in society.

If education were merely a luxury, then a high incidence of early school-leaving would be a minor problem. For some, lack of education is only an inconvenience. The relatively affluent, for example, may find that an adequate education is not a necessity. If a family is sufficiently wealthy to have a controlling interest in a department store, and if one of the children is unwilling or unable to complete a college or even a high school education, that family can find something for its undereducated scion to do around the store. Such alternatives are not available to the poor. They have but one way out—through education—and they are not getting that education.

The credential society holds forth most persuasively in the largest and fastest-growing industries of our country—the industries of health, education, and welfare.[1] The credential demanded for any career with potential upward mobility in these fields requires, at the very least, four years of college. The poor cannot get a toehold in these industries because they are hard pressed to obtain a high school education. The main argument advanced in this chapter is that the poor fail to get an education because they are not given a chance to get an education. They are not educated in school. On the contrary, they are humiliated and degraded, subjected to meaningless gibberish, told that they are inferior and intolerably deviant, and frustrated in their need for a sense of competence or a feeling of value to others. They are rendered powerless.

Much of what passes for theory in social science or education ends up placing the onus for educational failure on those who do poorly in school. It is proclaimed that schools are plagued because they are given shoddy material to work with—children who are damaged because they are constitutionally inferior, inadequately socialized, or subjected to accumulated environmental deficits.

A variety of nostrums for education is being wholesaled to the public. The greatest emphasis is on providing some compensatory service to the reluctant learner. A regular smorgasbord of service would be offered to the disadvantaged, including pre-school programs, specialized training for teachers, seducements for "good" teachers to work in "bad" neighborhoods, sortings into homogeneous learning groups, addition of social workers to school staff, a marked increase in counseling and other pupil personnel services, and tutoring and other remedial activities. Taken individually, or even collectively, these solutions fail to deal with the alternative that the school as presently constituted is a destructive influence on children and that any appendages to it may only increase its destructiveness. It is important to examine the attributes of schooling which could conceivably be driving youth out of education.

In one sense, all youth are exiles from the establishment. All youth are held in extended periods of dependency. Not very many years ago

162

it was possible for young people to assert a measure of independence and to assume adult roles. Now, because of the accent on prolonged education, most persons must live almost a quarter of a century before they are liberated.

Those who do not undergo the ritual of education may live their entire lives in dependency (as may their children and their children's children). Adolescence thus becomes a period of ambiguity and frustration. It is not surprising that some youth react in defiance against their overlords. But the rebel, despite all the publicity given him, is a relatively rare phenomenon. More prevalent, and thus more distressing, is the defeated conformist. Society, unable to find a place for its adolescents, seems to mobilize its energies to destroy the spirit and the initiative of its youth. When the power of the most powerful nation is arrayed against its youth, knuckling under is the only possible accommodation. One particularly perceptive observer laments the surrender of youth to the imperious authority of teachers and other representatives of the adult establishment:

> Students, I find, do not resent this; that is the tragedy. All weakness tends to corrupt, and impotence corrupts absolutely. Identifying, as the weak must, with the more powerful and frustrating of the forces that impinge upon them, they accept school as the way life is and close their minds against the anxiety of alternatives.[2]

To some extent the school militates against all youth. But the nature of the problem shifts dramatically in different socio-economic settings. Schools are much more difficult to negotiate if students have chosen poor, uneducated Negroes to be their parents. The major thesis offered in this chapter is that the school gives much less than its best to these students and in effect drives them out of education.

The alienation of youth from school is a many-faceted phenomenon. Some of the components of alienation which tend to exclude disadvantaged youth from the benefits of education are: (1) the school's inability to tolerate differences; (2) the powerlessness imposed on students; (3) the meaninglessness of curriculum; (4) the lack of connection between school and other systems of society; and (5) the humiliation and degradation of students in the classroom.

TOLERANCE FOR DEVIANCE

Schools are irrational in their determination of tolerable behavior. The schools enter into areas where they have neither right nor competence. The school dares to determine clothing and hair style and then attempts a ludicrous defense of its high-handed action. There is not a smidgen of evidence to support the contention that long hair interferes with the learning process, yet boys face expulsion from school if they are not groomed according to the teacher's or the principal's prejudices. Mini-skirts draw adverse rulings from principals who not so many years ago ogled the sweater girls of a prior generation. Tolerance for deviance is negatively correlated with social class. Almost without exception, authorities in schools which cater to middle-class youth are more relaxed about youth behavior than is the administration of a slum school, where control is the major emphasis.

Tolerance for deviance is influenced by xenophobia. Teachers fear and distrust youth with backgrounds and styles different from their own. As a consequence, an aura of dislike and distrust is exuded and students respond in kind. Schooling functions quickly deteriorate as relationships become distorted and antagonisms fester. The inevitable consequence of such exacerbating conditions is an invidious definition of the persons who are taught. They no longer are considered to operate according to the rules. The teacher cannot empathize or identify with them. They are not made of stuff with which the teacher is familiar. They take on humanoid qualities. They are *the* enemy. Here is how one noted educator, Max Rafferty, superintendent of public instruction in California, describes the deviant, whom he characterizes as the "Slob." The Slob is readily detected by superficial differences such as dress. His "trousers are slick denim . . . boots are standard Slob attire as is the cheap leather jacket with 'GENTS' or 'ROADRUNNERS' blazoned luridly upon its back." He is also known by his talk, which "is a modern thieves' jargon relying strongly upon scarcely disguised obscenity." The Slob lacks appropriate social values. He is obsessed with violence, which is reflected in his "ubiquitous switch-blade knife, normally used to force terrorized quiescence upon the victim of a mass rape . . . the bicycle chain . . . the zip gun which lends a deadly note to gang rumbles." [3] The Slob is not tolerable in an educational process because "it has been truly said that his sole interests are sadism, sex and speed, in that order." [4] And thus the solution reduces simply to the proposition that

164

"the Slob must go . . . he must be excluded from our schools as socially uneducable." [5]

According to the above authority, "slobbism" is the result of too much tolerance for deviance. The sin of modern education is its emphasis on permissiveness. If this is true, it certainly hasn't been communicated to students confined to slum schools. Certainly they have not regarded the school as a sanctuary. To the contrary, almost unanimously they contend that the school is repressive, that the teachers are hostile, and that the operation from start to finish is a conspiracy against them. True, the theme that teachers are weak runs through many youth commentaries about school. However, when a youth places a value on physical strength, it is not necessarily indicative of his lack of amenability to education. It is more likely the response to the only attribute which the school values. It is the school that continually emphasizes its power to inflict punishment, and physical punishment is by no means excluded in the school's repertory of retributions. I would offer the hypothesis that the dysfunctional behavior of youth is caused by the behavior and attitudes of persons with approaches similar to Mr. Rafferty's.

The Cult of the Snob   The threat to education is not the cult of the Slob (I doubt if such a cult exists). The real threat is in the cult of the *Snob*. The Snob is the self-proclaimed conscience of the community. He decides what is good for all of us. He lays claim to intellectual prowess, but can offer no evidence for his claim. He never documents his positions with facts. His analysis falls short of minimal standards of acceptable scholarship.

The Snob demands special privileges. He reads books too pornographic to be reviewed by the commoner. The Snob reneges on his responsibility and then castigates those whom he has betrayed. The Snob derives pleasure from the bullying of those less powerful than himself. The Snob projects his lust and sadism on others and then torments those whom he accuses of misdeeds or evil thoughts. The Snob is the incarnation of the inquisitor and the witchburner, citing as support for the palpable righteousness of his cause the present scarcity of witches.

The Snob insists that he alone knows what is right. He is the sole judge of beauty, culture, and style. It is he who determines custom, and he denigrates all who will not accept his definition. The Snob is the enemy of education because he limits education to those who will agree with him.

A Special Form of Intolerance—Ability Grouping   Intolerance for difference takes many forms. The most sensational guise attacks such superficialities as deportment or bearing, while a more virulent type attacks the deviant learner. Many teachers, unable to establish contact with students whose learning differs significantly from theirs in style or tempo, judge such children to be intellectually inferior.[6] On such judgments a life career is seriously affected. Nowhere does the self-fulfilling prophecy operate as viciously as it does in education. Some students are labeled minimally educable; as a consequence they are educated minimally and then they grow up minimally educated. The institutional procedures used to bring about this undesired effect have varied trappings, but all can be reduced to a prejudgment of learning ability.

The current vogue in education is to group children together if they are deemed to be similar in intellectual ability. The justification for homogeneous grouping is simple and at first blush seemingly incontestable. When children of allegedly similar ability are grouped, curriculum and teaching can be tailored to the capacities of the students. It is further argued that lower-ability children will be especially benefited by the grouping because they will not have to compete against persons of superior abilities and will therefore be protected against the ego wounds which come with defeat.

Unfortunately, it doesn't work like that. Although there are few carefully designed evaluations of the impact of homogeneous grouping, these few do not appear to support ability groupings. For example, in England (where homogeneous grouping is called "streaming") there is some evidence indicating the undesirability of grouping by alleged capacities:

> A recent study compared children at unstreamed junior schools with children of similar intellectual ability from streamed schools; the unstreamed children drew ahead of the streamed children in tests of intelligence and of school subjects and there was a suggestion that the backward benefited more from non-streaming than the brighter children.[7]

It is not too difficult to explain the negative results in ability grouping. The segregation of low ability worsens rather than enhances self-

166

esteem. The students are aware that they are being stigmatized as stupid, despite the clumsy efforts at camouflage (such as the practice of giving groups such euphemistic titles as "bluebirds").

Ability grouping leads to low-level achievement because teachers expect little from "low capacity" students. Thus it should come as no surprise that there is a high correlation between appraised ability and social background. The poor, and particularly the Negro poor, are shunted out of the mainstream of education. The schools in Washington, D.C., are only one example of a universal phenomenon. In the public high school in the nation's capital attended by the affluent (almost 100 per cent white; median income of parents in excess of $10,000) 92 per cent of the students are on college-bound tracks. In the high school attended by the poor (almost exclusively Negro; median income of parents less than $4,000) 15 per cent of the students are assigned to college-preparatory programs.[8] If the intolerance for deviance in learning style and speed was uniformly distributed it would be bad enough, but when those sorted out of meaningful education are precisely those who need it the most, the results are calamitous. Such action relegates literally millions of people to society's junk heap.

Segregating the Deviant Out   A narrow span of tolerable deviance is accompanied by irrationality in attending to activities judged intolerable. Much punishment in the schools is *ad hoc,* an impulsive judgment by a teacher which must now be legitimated by the entire system. A teacher becomes angry (often at behavior which at other times is ignored or even enjoyed), punishes a student, and then, to maintain an illusion of superhumanity, insists that the principal and other administrators back his hand. The administration, following its canon of "loyal up—loyal down," inevitably does just that.

Very often a minor infraction can become a serious problem because of teacher-inspired escalation. The following is a sequence of events as described by teachers: Two pupils in the seventh-grade class were leaning back in their chairs. The teacher, concerned about their safety, ordered them to return all four legs of the chair to the floor. The students were sluggish in obeying the order, and the teacher then demanded that both students immediately kneel in a praying position in front of his desk. One student complied; the other refused—and the teacher ordered him to report to the principal. The boy refused on the grounds that he had done nothing to necessitate removal from the classroom,

167

whereupon the teacher "had to" forcibly remove the student. Certainly there was greater possibility of injury in the tussling of student and teacher than in the original act that started the chain of events. Holding the youth up to ridicule and humiliation could serve no useful purpose. And to cap it off, the teacher relented and did not bring the boy to confront the principal because he didn't wish the youth to be suspended from school.

A school will continue to default on its responsibilities to youth as long as that school is unable to generate rational and consistent regulations that are based on sound educational principles. Given the present state of the arts (to paraphrase Thomas Jefferson), the school which regulates least, educates best.

POWERLESSNESS, IRRELEVANCE, AND DEGRADATION

Edgar Friedenberg and Paul Goodman are two celebrated critics of public education.[9] They rail, in particular, against the totalitarian nature of schools. The public school student is hardly in a position of power. No matter how regarded, the student lacks potency. He has no guaranteed *rights,* he has little latitude or choice in any activity, nor is he empowered to change his state by delegated representatives. Student government is a fraud. Reduced to its essentials, student government is the right awarded students to agree with the administration. Even in the trivial matters allowed to student councils, woe be to those who happen to run counter to the established authority. Inevitably, such action leads forthwith to the end of the student council. The student from a disadvantaged background, either economic or academic, is particularly handicapped. He is unrepresented on student councils. He lacks even the limited expressions of freedom awarded his more favored counterparts.

The lack of freedom of students is most strongly felt by those who run afoul of the rules. The student has no legal protection. There is no machinery for redress of grievances. He is at the tender mercies of the system. If he is an inadequate student, he is much more likely to be put upon because the school, like a huge bird of prey, feasts upon the defenseless. The good student will find champions in the system. But there is no lonelier soul than the academic non-achiever who has dared to violate the rules. He is regarded as an interloper and, given the chance to remove him, those in control of the system rarely hesitate. The economically advantaged student does have alternatives and thus

168

some measure of power. He can, with the aid of his parents, obtain outside assistance—tutors, psychologists, or lawyers—and he can escape to a private school. No alternatives for outside resources are available to the poor! The supreme irony of all this is that a major goal of education is to prepare youth for citizenship in a democratic society.

Meaninglessness of Curriculum   Almost everything that goes on in a classroom is, by all standards, drivel. Most lessons are given without fire or conviction, presented in a language and style to repel even the ardent student. Subject material which is intrinsically exciting is diluted to produce tedium. English is a routine of rules. Mathematics is a jumble of confused symbols. History is desecrated distortions, consisting almost exclusively of pasteboard heroes emerging victorious from battle. And science? Science is a clutter of formulae, definitions, laws, and alleged experimentation. The so-called experiments, however, lack the basic ingredients of experimentation, since there is little self-initiation or sense of discovery. Schoolwork is an endless stream of assignments without time for reflection or conceptualization.

Disadvantaged youth, in particular, suffer from meaningless curriculum. Unlike the advantaged, they have no one close at hand to translate material into comprehensible language or to fill in gaps in lecture or text. Once disadvantaged youth fall behind in class, there are no procedures to allow them to catch up. A tragedy about school is that a student may feel hopelessly lost because he is merely without a simple rule or a connecting concept. It is no wonder that disadvantaged youth in disproportionate numbers are labeled incorrigible or uneducable. They are driven to relieve boredom by outrageous behavior or by a retreat into passive disinterest.

Teachers argue that they, too, lack freedom of choice. They insist that they are forced into a routine because of the large numbers of students assigned to them. It is their opinion that it is beyond the capacity of humans to teach effectively the twenty-five to thirty different kinds of youth that they encounter hourly. Such assertions are based on an assumption that education must be packaged as education has always been packaged; that classroom organization is fixed and immutable and that the process of teacher actively emitting and student passively absorbing is the proper way to stimulate learning. None of these assumptions is tenable.

To a large extent, education is showmanship and salesmanship. It is possible to interest a large number of students if the product is attractively presented. English, history, science, and math are exciting in their own right but lose appeal because teachers either refuse or do not know how to push the product. It is also possible to alter radically the organization of the class. Students can be more "social" in their learning by engaging in "team learning." Older students can contribute to education by teaching younger students. Spontaneity can be introduced into the classroom through student-initiated inquiry if the teacher role is reshaped to include consultation and if the relationship between student and teacher changes accordingly. Education can and must be fun. However, much too little is being done to make it so.

Lack of Linkage   The school is not "with" anything that is "happening" for disadvantaged youth. Little that occurs in the classroom relates to either the present or the future. Youth from privileged circumstances may suffer discomfiture in the classroom, they may protest the rules, their helplessness, and the thin gruel which is offered for intellectual digestion, but they can endure it. They are on a path leading somewhere. If they stay with it, there is a place for them. They will obtain the credential which is a visa to the more prestigious sectors of the world of work. School fits into the home life of the advantaged student—the language, the subject material, and the tempo of the school are compatible with the situation at home. None of this is true for disadvantaged youth. They cannot comprehend why they are "forced" to go to school. They see no earthly value in geometry, grammar, biology, or American history. How will such "courses" help them, since they have no plans to go on to college? And if such students are relegated to non-college tracks, their resentment is only increased. They are righteously indignant about the "Mickey Mouse" curricula because these excuses for education are also dead-ending: successful completion of the programs will not lead to marketable skills. Vocational education is a cruel sham—much of what takes place in vocational education is obsolete training with obsolete equipment leading to obsolete skills. Much more of vocational education is offered without any consideration of the "informal credentialing" (appropriate friends and relatives) demanded by unions, and thus the program is a worthless endeavor. Apparently, everyone but the educator is aware of the lack of connection between the school program and the world of work. Small wonder disadvantaged youth become disaffected with school!

170

The school system, by some weird, convoluted reasoning of those in control, expects youth to expend energy in education (and suffer frustration and humiliation in the process) without promising *anything* in return. Very few persons in their senses would be party to a contract where they must risk all to gain nothing. And yet the school demands investment with negligible prospects for profit. In this impossible situation, teachers decry the "lack of motivation" in students and place blame on outside influences (home, subculture, and prior failure) without even giving cursory consideration to the proposition that lack of motivation is best explained by the hopeless situation of the student.

It is the obligation of the schools to *guarantee* to *every* student that expenditure of effort will bring a favorable result—employment with assurance of security and upward mobility, social acceptance within the mainstream of the society, entrance into higher education with the wherewithal for matriculation. Until such a guarantee can be given, the school system is derelict in its responsibility to the youth it pretends to serve.

Daily Humiliation and Degradation   Humans, by and large, are not overly consumed by future concerns. Life's gratifications have to take place in the here and now, yet most youth derive little pleasure from their school experiences. Many go to school to be told, *every day,* that they are worthless, stupid, lazy, and evil.

Only a few children are able to derive gratification from school. Some are able to obtain a sense of competence and thus a favorable identity as part of the establishment. These, by and large, are the "brains," the "athletes," and the "sociables" (who are able to exploit physical attractiveness or financial means to obtain popularity). All others are exiled into the "hoods," the "fringies," the "surfers," the "greasers," or, even worse, those who are forced to experience the loneliness of non-acceptance by anybody. The passive role of student precludes any opportunity for contributing to the world. There is none of the gratification that comes from helping others.[10]

The poor have the least chance of obtaining gratification from encounters in the school. They are most likely to be categorized as of low ability, inadequately socialized, and cognitively understimulated. All of these labels carry a stigma, causing the student to lose self-esteem and associate the wounds to self with the school.[11] There is no way that the poor student can maintain a positive self-image if so much of school

171

progress is gauged by competition which is inherently unfair. The poor cannot compete equally with the rich. Those with deviant styles or tempos cannot compete equally with those whose learning systems correspond with the narrow band understood or appreciated by the teacher. The non-achieving, the minimally achieving, and even the moderately able students are denied a true sense of competence. They are not credited with value and cannot thus attain the impetus to growth that goes to those rare few who are acknowledged as leaders.[12]

In the place of competence, students are placated with patronizing attitudes and token rewards for non-achievement. Such bogus blandishments continue to spoil the image of youth and add to their feelings of resentment. Thus, much of compensatory education not only fails to help youth but, by lowering expectations and by segregating students into special categories and labeling them "different," has just the opposite effect.

CONCLUSION

In a world in which education has become the single highway to the "good life," the school is an atavistic monstrosity. Students become disengaged from education for the very best of reasons—they are forced out. They are buffeted by authoritarian rules. They have no political power and little freedom of choice. They are faced with subject matter that is dull and irrelevant. Worst of all, the very process of going to school robs students of their dignity and self-esteem.

If the Marquis de Sade could have invented education as it is now, he would probably have given up beating women.

Notes

1. For a more complete exposition of the changing nature of society and its impact on the economy, see Arthur Pearl and Frank Riessman, *New Careers for the Poor* (New York: The Free Press, 1965).

2. Edgar Z. Friedenberg, *Coming of Age in America* (New York: Random House, 1965), pp. 47–48.

3. Max Rafferty, "The Cult of the Slob," *Phi Delta Kappan,* XXX (November, 1958), 56.

4. *Ibid.,* p. 58.

5. *Ibid.,* p. 59.

6. For a discussion of differences in learning style associated with class factors, see Frank Riessman, *The Culturally Deprived Child* (New York: Harper & Row Publishers, 1962).

7. J. W. B. Douglas, "Streaming by Ability," *New Society* (February 6, 1964), p. 6.

8. Elias Blake, "The Track System in Washington, D.C.," *Integrated Education,* III, 2 (1965), 27–34.

9. See Friedenberg, *op. cit.,* and Paul Goodman, *Compulsory Miseducation* (New York: Horizon Press, 1964).

10. The concept of the helper principle developed by Frank Riessman has relevance here and is elaborated in Pearl and Riessman, *op. cit.*

11. For an explanation in depth of the spoiled self-image, see Erving Goffman, *Stigma: Notes on the Management of Spoiled Identity* (Englewood Cliffs, N.J.: Prentice-Hall, Inc., 1963).

12. Robert W. White, "Motivation Reconsidered: The Concept of Competence," *Psychological Review,* LXVI (1959), 297–333.

11 · School Days

JEROME BEKER, JAMES B. VICTOR, AND LINDA F. SEIDEL

AMONG THE REQUIREMENTS imposed on young people in our society is formal education, usually through the public schools. Such phrases as "universal free education" may obscure the fact that school is often a different experience in different classrooms, schools, and areas. Common sense and our own educational experience confirm the existence of such differences on an idiosyncratic basis. One teacher may seem "harder," "nicer," or "better" than another. Some schools appear more friendly and relaxed than others, some school systems maintain higher academic standards than others, and the like.

We might also expect to find characteristics that tend to be common to inner-city or slum schools in contrast to schools in more "privileged" urban or suburban neighborhoods, and rural schools seem likely to be different from both. Many observations have, in fact, been made to the effect that slum schools tend to be dirty, overcrowded, largely custodial institutions where most pupils "do their time" without learning much. Suburban schools are frequently characterized as tense and highly competitive. The movement toward consolidation of rural schools reflects the observation that they tend to be too small to provide adequate educational resources and stimulation. It seems worth asking whether such apparent differences are real, and, real or not, the extent to which they are reflected in the ways teachers and pupils alike perceive school and its expectations. Some recent, tentative findings in this area are reported below, along with hypotheses about possible consequences for youngsters in school.

The project was undertaken as an observational pilot study of one

174

first- and one sixth-grade class at each of three schools serving an "inner city," a suburban and a rural district, respectively. The discussion that follows is based on preliminary work in the sixth-grade classes only. For several months, the two participant observers made frequent, independent visits to the classrooms involved and recorded their observations in depth. In addition, it was felt that an indication of how pupils and teachers perceived the setting and its demands could be obtained from their own descriptions of a (real or imaginary) "ideal pupil" in their classrooms. Therefore, each student in the sixth-grade classes studied was asked to respond in writing to the following five questions about his concept of the ideal or "perfect" student in his class:

1. What kind of student is he or she? How does he act?
2. If he learns well, tell me what he does in the classroom that helps him do this.
3. Is he liked by most other students? If so, why? If not, why?
4. Do you think he was this way when school started this year, or has he improved as the year has gone along? Explain.
5. How many students in this class are like the student you are describing, if any?

The teachers responded, also in writing, to questions that were essentially similar but with appropriate differences in wording. These "essays," along with the observational data and background material from school records, provided the basis for this chapter.[1]

Downtown Elementary and Briar Hill Elementary (all names are pseudonyms) are both part of the same medium-sized urban school system. Downtown, however, is many years old and serves a predominantly lower-class, inner-city population, while Briar Hill is almost new and serves an affluent neighborhood on the edge of the city. Brookville Elementary School is located about thirty miles away in a small, rural community. Of course, since only one classroom representing each "condition" was studied, idiosyncratic factors related to school or classroom may have influenced the results. It was felt, however, that this exploratory effort was warranted to help guide future study of the situations faced by pupils and teachers in inner-city, suburban, and rural school settings.

Information available from school records demonstrates that pupils' backgrounds, apparent ability, and achievement differed predictably in the three schools.[2] Table 11–1 summarizes available data on age, intelligence-test scores, achievement-test scores, and parental education and occupation. Gross differences between Briar Hill and the other two

TABLE 11–1

BACKGROUND DATA ON PUPILS BY SCHOOL AND CLASS—
SIXTH GRADES

Variable	Measure	Downtown School	Brookville School	Briar Hill Class Studied	Briar Hill Class Not Studied	All Briar Hill Sixth Grade
Age	N	38	22	28	28	56
	Median	11–2	11–3	10–7	10–6.5	10–7
	I.Q.R.[5]	13.5 mo.	16 mo.	5 mo.	9 mo.	8 mo.
I.Q.[1]	N	31	23	27	28	55
	Median	90	97	131	109	122
	I.Q.R.[5]	29.5	21.75	10.5	18	23
Achievement[2]	N	28	23	25	27	52
	Median	5.4	6.3	8.3	7.4	7.8
	I.Q.R.[5]	2.2	1.84	.64	3.64	1.2
Parents' Education (Years)[3]	N	34	12	28	25	53
	Median	12	11	16	16	16
	I.Q.R.[5]	4	4	0	4	4
Parents' Occupation Score[4]	N	28	21	25	27	52
	Median	18.5	8	78	51	68
	I.Q.R.[5]	17	22.75	35.75	37	37

NOTE: No significance figures have been computed because it is not intended that the data presented be generalized beyond the particular populations studied. See Robert K. Merton, G. G. Reader, and Patricia L. Kendall, eds., *The Student Physician: Introductory Studies in the Sociology of Medical Education* (Cambridge, Mass.: Harvard University Press, 1957), pp. 301–305; and H. C. Selvin, "A Critique of Tests of Significance in Survey Research," *American Sociological Review,* XXII (1957), 519–527.

1. Intelligence test scores were obtained from the California Test of Mental Maturity at Downtown and Briar Hill schools and from the Henmon-Nelson Test of Mental Ability at Brookville School.

2. Iowa Test of Basic Skills for all schools; however, the tests were administered in the fall at Downtown and Briar Hill schools and the following spring at Brookville School, so it may be assumed that the Brookville scores are artificially inflated relative to the other two. Composite scores are presented here; only minor variations were noted in the score patterns on sub-tests.

3. Years of education for the parent with more education.

4. For the parent with the higher-status occupation. Parental occupations were scored according to the Socioeconomic Index developed by Otis Dudley Duncan and presented in Albert J. Reiss, Jr., *Occupations and Social Status* (New York: The Free Press of Glencoe, 1961).

5. Inter-Quartile Range.

schools are immediately evident.[3] It seems apparent that pupils at Downtown and Brookville are less able, or are being educated less effectively, or both, at least in terms of the goals implicit in the test scores reported. Further attention will be given to the apparent goals and motivations of schools and pupils as well as to questions of pupil ability and educational effectiveness. Finally, there were no non-white pupils in the class studied at Brookville, one at Briar Hill, and about six (under 20 per cent) at Downtown.

Based in part on the observers' impressions, it was anticipated that the inner-city school, Downtown, would be the most heterogeneous, but this expectation was not fully supported for the variables reported in Table 11–1. Most striking, perhaps, is the homogeneity within the class studied at Briar Hill, which apparently reflects the school's grouping practices. The composite scores for the two sixth grades at Briar Hill give a better picture of the children the school serves, but the particularly high-achieving, homogeneous class is the one to which reference is made in the remainder of this chapter. There does seem to be a tendency for the two lower-income schools to serve not only older sixth-graders but also a wider age range. Intelligence and achievement scores also seem to reflect somewhat greater variability at Downtown than at the other two schools. The apparent heterogeneity in occupational status at Briar Hill may be partly a function of differential discrimination at the high and low ends of the scale, but it seems also to suggest that suburbia may be less homogeneous than some have thought.[4]

The atmosphere of each school is described below and illustrated with edited and sometimes condensed excerpts from the observers' field recordings. The excerpts were selected as much to convey the tone and feel of each school as to document the points that are made, and space does not permit specific documentation of every statement. Rather, the material is viewed as providing a basis for the selection of dimensions and the building of hypotheses for more systematic study. In the final section of the chapter, an attempt is made to draw the material together and to suggest some possible directions for subsequent work in the same area.

DOWNTOWN ELEMENTARY SCHOOL

On the edge of the center-city business district, excavations mark the route of the unfinished section of an interstate highway through the city. Just beyond is an old neighborhood where large frame houses, many of them dull and dingy-looking, are packed closely together. The area seems to be a relatively stable, largely Italian, working-class section, with a few Negro families who may be newcomers from the nearby ghetto. The school—a large, dirty, overcrowded, old building—appears, in contrast to most of its surroundings, to be in good repair. Most of the pupils come to school on foot. They are usually greeted with little enthusiasm by teachers who seem to know what will happen today because it happened last week, last year, and the year before that. To the teacher, life is not very exciting—even boring, perhaps—but work is never fun and teaching does carry some prestige in addition to almost a living wage. These attitudes are reflected physically in the antiseptically clean hallways and relatively messy and colorless classrooms. The atmosphere is gloomy, almost institutional, seemingly unchanging.

The observers seem to be a threat, but inescapable: they have the approval of the central administration. To resist them actively might make waves "upstairs"—probably better to live with them. Although the teachers seem concerned at first lest they be evaluated, perhaps a deeper worry is that such projects may eventually lead to change. In any case, the prevailing apathy soon overcomes anxiety and the observers seem to be largely ignored.

A basic dichotomy appears quickly. The teacher establishes the "official" rules and the youngsters respond. Many of the youngsters observe a conflicting set of unofficial "rules," and the teacher perceives his response to these as one of his major functions. Hardly a cooperative venture, education in this classroom proceeds largely through teacher-pupil competition, except at clearly contrasting "social" times. The pervading feeling is one of negativism and even belligerence, and not on the part of the youngsters alone.

Among the forty-one pupils (later thirty-five) in the class, three behavioral groupings seem to emerge. Some youngsters tend to be non-participants, apparently passively rejecting the situation by spending the school day slouching, looking out the window, and occasionally sleeping. The teacher usually ignores these children, as they do him, and rarely calls on any of them. If they are asked to respond, they tend to do so poorly, if at all, but no one seems to mind:

> During a math lesson, Mr. Howard called on one girl with the comment, "I haven't had you to the board in five years." He handed her a piece of chalk and indicated in a friendly way

that she should put the next example on the board. When she got to the front of the room, she returned to her desk to look at her book again. The teacher said, "Take a good look," but he stopped her when she attempted to bring her book with her to the board. She looked at the page again, and many of her classmates began to snicker. "Give her a chance," the teacher said, and he helped her put the problem on the board. She was not able to complete it, however, and another child was called to come up and finish.

Other youngsters are busily engaged in a variety of seemingly extraneous and often disruptive activities. One may be writing on his arm, some are playing with toys or their pens, a few communicating with one another in various ways, and so forth. The teacher feels he must control them and show them who is "in charge" by stopping the "bad" behavior, using open-ended or indefinite threats as his sanctions:

> During a social studies test, Mr. Howard read a question that the class apparently had not expected. They groaned and began to protest, but he replied, "Don't tell me you haven't heard of this before because I know that you have, and you'd better write an answer!"

> The teacher said, "Go back and do the bulletin board. The first time you make a mistake and talk . . ." and he snapped his fingers.

This teacher feels that it is his duty to students to "adjust them socially," and the use of the active voice conveys the approach:

> The teacher chided the children about their demonstrated inability to wait their turn during the previous day's art lesson. He told them that they might as well learn to wait now because they would be spending a large percentage of their lives waiting—in restaurants, theaters, and places like that.

> Mr. Howard told the children to sit up straight, for if they continued to slouch, he would have to walk around the room and "sit them up straight."

> While Mr. Howard was doing a math problem at the board, he noticed that some children were not paying attention "as if their lives depended on it." He told them that their lives may depend on math some day, especially the girls. He explained that the girls could not be housewives for the rest of their lives; "they work nowadays, you know."

The teacher told the class that the reason children quit school at sixteen was because they were lazy and couldn't study. "They may give other excuses for dropping out, but laziness is the real reason behind it," he said. He also warned the children not to get into the habit of making excuses for themselves and blaming others for things they did.

Mr. Howard was talking about the draft and told the boys that the Army would not take them without a high school diploma. He explained that the Army wasn't going to "trust any numbskull" with weapons, trucks, or ammunition if he didn't have a high school education. "And," he continued, "if you can't serve your country, you get a very empty feeling inside."

When control attempts seem ineffective, the teacher ignores the same behavior; there is little else he can do to save face, an important consideration to him. Nor can he allow the youngsters to feel that they are flouting his authority, since once youngsters like these get the upper hand . . . Better to survive to fight them another day:

After he walked down the aisles inspecting their papers, Mr. Howard asked if everyone was ready. Then he showed the children the exact position in which he wanted them to hold their papers on their desks. One girl raised her hand and said, "Mr. Howard, I can't keep my paper that way 'cause I can't write with this hand." "Why not?" he asked. "What's wrong with your hand?" She replied, "Nothing. I write with this [left] one." Peals of laughter filled the room as the teacher disregarded her and went on with the directions.

Miss Stewart, the student teacher, asked the class, "Who would like to live in the Sahara Desert?" and Joe raised his hand. The regular teacher then interrupted to ask Joe, "Why?" Joe said nothing at first, but the teacher questioned him further, and the class began to laugh. He asserted that "This is not funny" and that he wanted to know why Joe would like to live there. Joe finally replied that he "just likes the desert," at which the teacher dropped the issue. He walked over to the observer and commented quietly, "I thought I could pin him down, but I couldn't."

Meanwhile, there is a curriculum to be taught to those who will listen. A third group of children do "listen." They stay "with" the teacher, they race each other to get their hands in the air, and they respond

180

vibrantly and efficiently to questions. The "official" rules are their rules; little justification is required in terms of the value, the relevance, or even the accuracy of what they are learning. In this context, they are motivated, competitive, and achievement-oriented; in many ways, they are not unlike the children at Briar Hill. But they seem a bit out of place and unsure of themselves, and they would be less likely to debate a point with their teacher. Six of these children were to be reassigned around mid-year to a fifth-grade class, which would then become a combined fifth and sixth grade. This was done because the school authorities felt that the atmosphere of the sixth-grade class was too disruptive to their learning. For the most part, the teaching seems to be directed at them. The teacher sticks to the formal curriculum, however; there is little effort to expand horizons or the realm of inquiry. Rote learning is emphasized, and drill seems to be the method of choice. The higher achievers tend to be rewarded by the teacher but rejected by their peers:

> Mr. Howard gave out the spelling papers from the previous day and told the children to write the words that they had missed twenty times each. He told them not to complain and tell him that they didn't have time to do it, because he knew that they did.

> "Who doesn't know what democracy means?" asked Mr. Howard. One girl raised her hand, and he said, "Are you kidding?" "No," she replied. Mr. Howard became annoyed and told her to write the word one hundred times and then to recite it twenty-five times orally.

> Jimmy was working by himself on a special project in the back of the room and, when the teacher stepped out for a few minutes, several children told him rather angrily to go back to his seat.

The three types of youngsters described (the apathetic non-participants, the disruptive non-participants, and the "go along" students) emerge clearly, as do the differential teacher responses. In addition, the range of ability levels represented in the class is noteworthy, but the underlying commonalities are of interest as well. The appearance and behavior of the youngsters suggest common stereotypes associated with low-income, urban youth. Despite the apparently wide range of intelligence, verbal skills tend to be low. Even the pupils who are successful by the teacher's standards often appear to be "serving time" rather than becoming academically oriented and involved. It is as if the three groups differentiated above have chosen three ways of coping with an irrelevant but compulsory experience. Some actively reject it, some essentially ignore it, and the "good pupils" knuckle under, learn the rules, and "play the game" without it seeming to have much meaning for them. Whichever their predominant mode of operation, most of the youngsters seem to have a strong capacity for survival in spite of, rather than facilitated by, their school experience.

This is not to say that the youngsters are passive in their classroom behavior. They are lively and colorful, far from placid or bland. They may compete fiercely to be called on to answer the teacher's questions, but many seem to care little whether their responses are correct. Perhaps the attention is more important to them, or the opportunity to affect (and sometimes disrupt) the class. Social factors such as these are apparently the motivators, with academic considerations usually in the background.

It seems apparent that the pupils have not learned how to function effectively without the teacher. When he is present, the situation is rigidly structured and authoritarian; there is no doubt about who is in charge. But when he leaves the room, the children's spontaneity erupts as negativistic, rebellious misbehavior:

> During the health lesson being taught by Miss Stewart, the regular teacher left the room for a few minutes. As soon as he was out the door, the boys began to kick one another and to throw spitballs and other paper objects around the room.

> The teacher took a small reading group to one corner of the room and told them that they could pick a story for their reading lesson. "I really shouldn't let you make the choice," he said, "but I will this once." There was a great deal of confusion about which to choose and, when the teacher finally suggested one, they promptly began to read it.

In a sense, some of the children recognize that they are largely dependent on external control:

> Miss Stewart was trying to conduct a lesson on letter writing while the regular teacher was out of the classroom. The class was very disorganized, there was a great deal of noise and extraneous movement, and only a few children were paying any

attention to her. A boy and a girl were working by themselves on a new bulletin board, but the rest of the class was in a state of disturbance. Miss Stewart battled for about five minutes, trying to continue the lesson and to get her point across; the class was going its own way. After a while, she gave up and assigned written work to be collected in fifteen minutes. The class became quieter except for a series of disruptive incidents involving one or a few children at a time. . . . The regular teacher then walked into the room, and the class came to order almost instantly. One girl breathed what seemed to be a sigh of relief and said, "Oh, Mr. Howard, you're back."

The teacher is a disciplinarian first and a teacher second, and he perceives himself with pride as being among a small, informal fraternity of teachers who can work effectively with "this kind of child." He has his own approach, one not necessarily approved by educational "authorities." Since he feels that the majority of teachers cannot handle this type of teaching assignment, he enjoys a special subjective status even though teaching at Downtown carries low status in the school system as a whole. His assignment at Downtown is seen as a hard and honorable calling that requires the teacher always to be the boss. The youngsters cannot be permitted to get the upper hand, so the teacher must pose as omniscient, rarely acknowledging that he has been wrong about something, or that he doesn't know:

> During a lesson on syllabification, a girl raised her hand to tell Mr. Howard that he had made a mistake in one of the words he had written on the board. Mr. Howard did not check to see if she was right (which she was) and dismissed the mistake by saying, "I'm sorry. That's the way English is. You can't argue with that." Soon afterward, he made the same mistake again. When he realized, he told the class that he had done it intentionally to see if anyone would catch his mistake.

Pupils are not expected to take much initiative and seem to do little work on their own; they accept the teacher's authority and seldom attempt to correct him. There are many "special rules" they must learn and observe concerning classroom behavior:

> Mr. Howard noticed one boy chewing without permission and ordered him to "swallow whatever is in your mouth, even if it is an eraser, and eat it." (On another occasion, a boy had asked

183

Mr. Howard if he could chew gum that afternoon, and Mr. Howard had given him permission.)

Mr. Howard surveyed the room and said, "Susan, do you have studying to do?" Susan's reply was, "Yes." Mr. Howard said, "Yes, Mr. Howard," and the girl repeated, "Yes, Mr. Howard." Some of the rules almost seem contrived to minimize the need and opportunity for pupil-teacher interaction and confrontation.

Many children had their hands raised after completing an English assignment. Those with one finger in the air were allowed to sharpen their pencils, those with three were permitted to go to the lavatory, while those with five were visited by Mr. Howard. (Two fingers is a request to get a library book from the back of the room.)

When the last lesson of the morning ended, Mr. Howard told those on patrol to get their coats. A number of boys and girls got out of their seats and began walking toward the closet. Suddenly, Mr. Howard shouted, "Freeze!" and everyone "froze" in the positions they were in at the time. Mr. Howard told them that no one should be out of his seat unless he was going on patrol or talking to the student teacher. Then he called, "Unfreeze!" and the children scattered toward the closet to get their coats or toward their seats.

The teacher stresses that things should be done "his way" in school even if they are done differently elsewhere. Answers are expected to reflect what is taught this year in this classroom, whether or not it contradicts what was learned last year or in the "outside world":

Mr. Howard then wrote the number 3914 on the board and called on individual pupils to read it. One boy said, "Three thousand, nine hundred and fourteen." Many of the children responded with excited "Oohs" and "Aahs," indicating that he had made a mistake. Mr. Howard called on two others who offered the same (apparently incorrect) answer. The fourth respondent said, "Three thousand, nine hundred, fourteen," the response desired. Then Mr. Howard had the entire class chant the number that way several times: "Three thousand, nine hundred, fourteen." He told them that when they inserted the word "and," he would put a decimal there and call them wrong.

Thus, truth and knowledge are not the goals. Success is to perceive the dichotomy between the classroom and the rest of the world and to respond as is appropriate and expected in each situation. Not only potentially constructive motivation and initiative but also the development of personal integrity and identity may be retarded by these requirements and the over-all teacher-centered atmosphere:

> During the project, the children responded anonymously in writing to several essay questions about their concept of the "ideal pupil." A few weeks later, it was decided that the papers should be identified to permit comparative analyses with aptitude, achievement, and other scores. Therefore, the children were asked to identify their papers, and they agreed. Several of the children were unable to do so, however, either by handwriting or by content. Two pupils selected the papers of other pupils as theirs. (In the two other sixth grades studied, the children were able to identify their papers quickly and accurately.)

> When Mr. Johnson asked for the meaning of a word, several children called out the answer. He told them that he would not talk above them; there was room for only one talker in the room and that was he. He said that he loved to hear himself talk and that the children "hate" to hear themselves talk. "Isn't that right?" he asked. The children nodded in agreement, and the lesson continued.

The teacher's basically condescending approach must be reflected to the youngsters and seems prone to reinforce their alienation from school and the larger, adult society it supposedly represents, encouraging further suppression by the teacher in a continuing cycle. Despite his efforts at self-justification, it seems apparent that the teacher in such a situation must be "serving time" along with his pupils:

> Miss Stewart was having a particularly difficult time trying to control and teach the class. Mr. Howard turned to the observer and told her never to become a teacher.

> While the boys were at gym, a number of the girls came up to Mr. Howard's desk and gave him work that they had completed. He seemed rather disgusted as he commented to the observer that he had already made up the marks and the children were still handing in work.

It should not be inferred that this teacher is always remote and disinterested or that his pupils dislike him. He often plays the "showman,"

185

using a variety of gimmicks to arouse and stimulate the class when he wants to get a point across:

> While giving the test, the teacher read the questions slowly and with exaggerated precision, emphasizing key points, in an effort to keep the attention of the class.

> The teacher tried mumbling to get the attention of the class. The children began to call out, "What? What did you say?" His mumbling gone, the teacher responded, "See, I could get your attention by speaking Greek, but when I speak English, you don't listen. Next time you *listen* when I speak English."

> The teacher called the children to attention by telling them, "Look at me, because I'm the best-looking person in the room."

> While reading about ancient Egypt, the class encountered a date labeled, "B.C." "Quick," asked Mr. Howard, "tell me how many years ago that was." After a slight pause, he continued, "Well, what is the first thing you have to remember? Quick!" The class began to get excited. Someone said that negative numbers were needed, and Mr. Howard continued to fire rapid questions. Finally, a boy gave the answers sought, and the excitement dissipated.

The teacher is well liked and frequently, at relaxed times, he socializes and jokes with the children, although he attempts not to let the reins become too loose:

> One boy asked the teacher how long the social studies test would be. He replied, "Three or four hours, or maybe a few days."

> The class was discussing components of the Greek diet, and someone mentioned "kids." The teacher said, "Oh, that's good. Now I can get rid of some of you kids." Several children called out to correct him. "No, no. Kid means goat!" In a disappointed tone, the teacher responded, "Oh. I was hoping I could get rid of you. I was saying 'Hooray' already!"

> During "chorus time," when half of the class was out of the room, the teacher began to hum rather loudly and deliberately, apparently very much aware of what he was doing. When the children began to laugh, the humming became even louder and more flowery. One boy called out that "Someone better close the door." The teacher then walked to the front of the room

186

and suddenly clapped his hands together. The children came to attention immediately, then relaxed when they realized that this, too, was part of the fun.

A girl approached the teacher and asked him whether he would like to hear a joke. He was smiling, but she told him to be "very serious," and he immediately changed to a serious expression. She said, "Do you think Mickey Mouse could ever be a rat?" to which he did not respond at all. "That's the joke, you stupid nut!" she exclaimed. He said nothing more to her but turned to the observer soon after she had taken her seat, indicating that he "really shouldn't tease these kids" but that because of the relaxed classroom atmosphere now, it was all right. He also indicated that this type of interaction had to be controlled, particularly with the girls. The teacher then turned to the class and said that "talking time is over" and that they were supposed to study now.

The teacher's behavior seems to stimulate cooperation and enthusiasm but action still seems to be in the service of the "right answers." In large measure, the teacher operates as he pleases within the classroom, even when this is in conflict with officially approved practices. He is open about this with the children—perhaps using it in part as a device with which to enlist their loyalty—so they seem able to dissociate him from the "system" he supposedly represents and which they reject just as he does. To an extent, then, the children and their teacher are allies, united against a system whose nominal goals and methods they perceive as alien:

> The teacher told the children that the school would have an "open house" for parents instead of individual parent conferences as in the past. He said that he did not approve of the change, that he had told this to the Board of Education, and that he liked talking with the parents. He went on to say that he might chat informally with parents during the open house and "No one will ever know about it."

> During a discussion of the concept of infinity, one of the pupils referred to "way back before Christ was born, when the earth began." The teacher said that he did not want to discuss religion but that he would sneak it in now and then. "I'd rather not get reported," he said, "but I've been in trouble before, and it's all right to continue." He then indicated that theologians

believe the world was created in 4004 B.C. "But if you believe in evolution," he continued, "you can just rip up your Bibles and not believe this date either."

Fundamentally, this teacher seems able to turn "teacher behavior" on and off at will, just as he expects his pupils to differentiate academia from the "real world," with minimal interaction between the two. It seems that he, too, is in this sense rejecting the concept and the substance of school. Perhaps he is helping to create the socially disadvantaged, anti-intellectual, working-class adults of tomorrow.

BRIAR HILL ELEMENTARY SCHOOL

One of the city's four high schools, located in the Briar Hill section near the city limits, is reputed to serve primarily the intellectually elite; an overwhelming majority of its graduates go on to college. This school and its neighbor, Briar Hill Elementary, share a large, rolling site surrounded by modern, ranch-type homes with ample lawns. Both buildings are new and of similar light brick construction. Landscaped school grounds and playing fields enhance an already attractive setting. The halls and classrooms at Briar Hill are bright, clean, and excitingly adorned with children's work and information on current events and study units. The children greet their teachers and each other with an air of expectancy, and the teachers seem to know that they need to be "on their toes," at least in an intellectual sense. There appears to be an undercurrent of concern about the observers among the faculty, although some teachers quickly begin to converse with them almost as colleagues. Beyond social pleasantries and amenities, the children pay relatively little attention to them. The classroom atmosphere reflects the teacher's general informality:

> As one boy was presenting a report on the population of Argentina, Mr. Allen was returning homework papers to others in the class.

> The teacher sat at his desk eating candy as a boy gave a science report.

> The teacher came to the observer's seat and told her a joke during an oral report.

> While the children and the teacher were working quietly at their desks, a girl took a book she had received from her sister to the front of the room to show the teacher. They discussed it

188

for a few minutes, and he suggested others that she might be interested in reading. She then went back to her work and he to his.

The twenty-six pupils move around freely as they do their work, rarely disturbing their classmates. All seem concerned with both learning and grades, and most work seriously and competitively to achieve. Concern with college admission is already visible. Frequently, such pressures find overt expression in the classroom:

> At the conclusion of her report, one girl produced a large scroll of paper which she unwound with the help of two classmates to show various pictures of countries in Latin America. Mr. Allen seemed impressed and commented that he enjoyed her originality. At this, many boys and girls in the class called out with apparent distaste that she had done the same type of thing in the fifth grade.

> After a self-graded social studies test, the children were requested to call out their marks when their names were called. A few children refused to do this and walked up to the teacher's desk to show him their papers instead.

> After Mr. Allen graded a notebook and the pupil returned with it to his desk, classmates in the immediate area turned to ask him what grade he had received.

Despite this concern for achievement, the youngsters are usually good-natured and enthusiastic. They are attractively dressed, well groomed, and bright-looking, and many have a keen, although often sarcastic, sense of humor. Most tend to be highly verbal and relate almost as comfortably to adults as to each other:

> After giving his report, one boy told the class that he wanted to give another teacher in the school (whom he named) credit for its title, "The Economy of Argentina." He explained that he was about to title it "The Agriculture of Argentina," but that Mrs. S. had suggested the word "economy" when he discussed his report with her.

> While discussing Chile, the teacher mentioned that the Chilean government had a naval station near Cape Horn. The children tried to determine why Chile needed a navy and suggested that they might look for lost Antarctic explorers or catch penguins.

189

> Someone made a joke about smoking Kools, and then they moved to a new topic.

Little "traditional" teaching occurs. The teacher serves more often as a group leader than as the "boss," and can and does admit when he has been wrong. He provides the class with a flexible framework for learning in a particular content area, but most of the actual learning is a joint effort involving pupils and teacher together:

> As the class proceeded from one person to another, with each spelling a given word, pupils often raised their hands to challenge particular answers. The teacher's responses were often challenged along with the rest.

> During a lesson on diagramming sentences, the teacher sent two boys to the board to illustrate the method. They did the first two sentences correctly but were unable to do the third. He told them that they were "mixed up" and said, "Let's start at the beginning." Then they all went over the sentence step by step, analyzing and diagramming each part together.

Although the classroom structure is loose and learning tasks are often ambiguous, the youngsters can and do provide their own structure when the teacher does not. They take a great deal of initiative and responsibility and are largely self-directing, self-disciplined, and self-sufficient:

> As one boy began his oral report, a girl raised her hand and asked the teacher if they should take notes. He replied, "Well, make up your own minds and do whatever you think is best." Nearly all of the pupils took out their notebooks and began taking notes.

> During a library period, a few of the girls asked the teacher whether they would be required to write individual reports about Chile. He indicated that they would. They then wanted to know if there would be assigned topics. The teacher told them that topics would not be assigned and that if they found a topic they would like to research, they should consult him for approval.

> The teacher stepped out of the room for a few minutes while the children read silently from their texts. There was absolute quiet as they read and, as each child finished the story, he began working on something else or walked to the class library to browse.

190

The boys left for gym, and the girls immediately put their books away. One girl went to the class library at the back of the room and began to call the rows, asking girls to bring back borrowed books. When this procedure was completed, she called the rows again, asking those who would like to borrow books to do so. This period lasted one-half hour, during which the girls talked quietly and joked sporadically but were primarily engaged in reading their books. The teacher busied himself with his own work, apparently paying very little attention to the class proceedings.

The youngsters often become involved in and excited about their work to the point of disruption, the most frequent cause of intervention by the teacher. He is more apt to intervene with subtle or direct "reminders" or good-humored sarcasm than with direct threats or punishment, whether to control behavior or to stimulate improved academic performance:

While testbooks were being collected, the children began to talk rather loudly to one another about their workbook answers. The teacher rang a bell at his desk and asked those who had questions to come up front and talk with him. The class quieted down quickly and about ten pupils came to him with questions. While checking one girl's science notebook, the teacher pointed out a number of spelling errors and told her that her book was of generally poor quality. He reminded her that she would not get a very good science mark if she did not improve.

Mr. Allen checked one boy's notebook and told him he would accept it if this was the best work the boy could do, but that he had a feeling that this was not the boy's best effort; the boy agreed that it was not. Mr. Allen then said that he would not accept anything less than the boy's best and that the boy should not accept less either.

The teacher told the children that he would soon collect and grade their notebooks. One boy asked if he could re-copy his in order to get a better grade. Mr. Allen replied, "No. You did that in the fourth and fifth grades; this is graduate school, man!"

Frequently, members of the class use similar techniques to improve performance and to restore order themselves before the teacher does— apparently, in some cases, to court his favor. This is another manifestation of the importance with which school success is regarded by Briar Hill pupils. On occasion, there may be hurt feelings when the more sensitive youngsters find themselves the targets of virtually unconscious ridicule to which their teacher as well as their classmates may contribute. In most cases, however, the children do not seem to react overtly even to rather biting taunts:

> At one o'clock, pupils began drifting in from patrols or from lunch, and most worked quietly at their desks while some browsed in the library area at the rear of the room. One boy began to tell jokes, thus interrupting the quiet atmosphere, and others started to talk more loudly as well. The children soon became quiet again of their own accord. A few minutes later, when someone else raised his voice, a boy said, "You're not supposed to talk now." The class quieted down again, and work and whispering continued until the teacher returned at 1:15 P.M.

> The teacher chided a boy for writing too small, commenting that the boy wrote everything too small. Another youngster across the room called out, "Someone made *him* too small," referring to the latter's small stature. The class laughed.

> The teacher called two boys up to his desk and asked them if they were competing for last place in the class.

> Mr. Allen asked someone to volunteer to read a paragraph in the encyclopedia. When no one responded, he asked for his "pushcart peddler who sells fish." The boy he was referring to stepped forward and began to read in a loud, penetrating voice.

> As the class was preparing for an arithmetic lesson, one boy dropped several things underneath his desk. The teacher said, "Having a problem, Walker? Do you need to be changed or something?"

> A pupil mispronounced many Spanish words while delivering his report on the economy of Argentina. At one point, when he mispronounced *Buenos Aires,* the teacher repeated the mispronunciation and made fun of it. Soon after this, another Spanish noun was mispronounced, and a boy sitting in the back of the room began to snicker.

> A girl made several mistakes while putting an arithmetic example on the blackboard, and the teacher's comments elicited laughter from her classmates. Finally, he took her hand and led her closer to the board, saying, "Let me take you where you can see it." The class laughed uproariously.

Much of the time, there is an active exchange of verbal humor and sarcasm between pupils and teacher; occasionally, the teacher seems to be beyond his depth:

> Before giving her report, a girl told the teacher that she could not find much information about the clothing of Argentina. He said, "What? You mean they don't use too much clothing in Argentina?" The class burst out in laughter. Then she tried to explain that she could not find out very much about Argentinian food either. Mr. Allen replied, "Doesn't everyone eat hamburgers? There is so much meat down there, they must eat hamburgers."

> One of the exercises the children were to do involved using as many new vocabulary words as possible in sentences. One girl had a particularly ludicrous, though correct, sentence in which she had squeezed in as many words as she could. Apparently tongue in cheek, Mr. Allen told her that it was "very good" and that he could "hardly wait to hear another one." The girl began to giggle, but Mr. Allen became angry and abruptly told her to read.

> The teacher commented that George Washington Carver had thought up "thousands of uses for peanuts." One boy quipped, "Oh, then he worked for peanuts." Mr. Allen's unsmiling response was, "It is not even a nut, but a bean."

The youngsters also challenge their teacher on the content of what he teaches, and they capitulate, if at all, only in the face of evidence that he is right. Rarely can they be browbeaten into agreement, nor does the teacher try. These students are already concerned about grades for college entrance, but given a choice, most prefer to be right—particularly if they can show the teacher that he is wrong:

> While the teacher was criticizing the class for doing less well on a test than he had expected, Steve interrupted to say that he could prove right an answer that had been marked wrong. The teacher listened to Steve's explanation, then explained his own, different point of view. Steve then agreed that the answer his teacher had preferred was better than his own.

> In going over the social studies test, the teacher read question one and gave the answer he thought was correct. He then asked if there was any difference of opinion, and many people raised their hands to offer alternate suggestions. The

teacher agreed that some of the other answers suggested might be just as correct as his and accepted them for credit.

Most Briar Hill youngsters, at least those in this particular class, have had a relatively wide range of "educational" advantages, perhaps even more than their teacher, outside the school. They have the support of family traditions and peer standards which reinforce the value their teachers and the schools place on academic learning. Perhaps these students represent the "haves" in our society; they are in tune with it, and they are enjoying its rewards. Their school may not, however, be giving them a picture of the broader spectrum of the changing world of today, but rather an echo of the cultural encapsulation that they may experience at home as well.

BROOKVILLE ELEMENTARY SCHOOL

A new interstate highway provides the most direct route from the city to the Brookville vicinity. The twenty-minute drive from the highway to Brookville itself winds through an area of small, hilly farms. Most of the houses that dot the countryside are modest, old, and in varying states of disrepair. The dilapidation becomes more frequent as one approaches town, where the new building that is Brookville School looks almost out of place. It is a small school, with but one class in each of the seven elementary grades, including kindergarten. The sixth-grade teacher serves as principal ("head teacher") as well, and is supervised by a district principal who is responsible for several schools in the area. Many of the children arrive by bus from the surrounding countryside. No one seems to be in much of a hurry, and the presence of observers appears to arouse more curiosity than anxiety. The teachers seem almost flattered, though hard put to understand why anyone interested in studying education would choose their school to observe. The over-all atmosphere is reflected in the relaxed, non-restrictive acceptance of the observers, although it sometimes seems that a teacher is making a special effort to impress the observer in the classroom:

> The teacher asked the children if they would like to change the class schedule for the day. She explained that they might very easily get into a rut, so they should talk about science this morning, since the observers were in the room.
>
> During an experiment, Mrs. Drake said to the class, "If you can't see, come over and gather in a circle." She then looked

194

back at the observer and said, "Out of the way, please; make a clearing for the observer." The children then made a gap in the circle to give the observer a better view.

The girls were giving their answers to homework questions in arithmetic. Each time one of the responses was wrong, the teacher looked at the observer and smiled.

Don's seat is on the left side of the room, and it was necessary for him to pass the observer on his way to and from the closet where he picked up an object for the science display. The teacher was giving a class assignment as he did this but stopped to approach Don as he reached the science table. She leaned over to say something to him, and then he returned to his seat. After a few minutes, the teacher said, "Don, will you now go do what I spoke to you about?" Don left his seat, came closer to the observer, and said, "Excuse me for walking in front of you."

Most of the twenty-four youngsters in the sixth-grade class at Brookville seem to be not only poor in the economic sense but also socially limited. They appear shabby and colorless, almost lifeless. Even the girls seem little concerned with their appearance. Many are overweight as well as unkempt, poorly groomed, and poorly dressed. In general, they are downtrodden-looking children, and their school behavior does little to dispel this impression. They are apathetic, docile, submissive, even self-deprecating. Negativism in any form seems not to be in their behavioral repertory. They do what they are told, they seem to believe unquestioningly what they are taught, and they have relatively little interaction with their peers. There is an absence of classroom "play"— no paper folding, passing of notes, making paper airplanes, drawing pictures on notebooks, or chuckling together about a playground incident after lunch. Nor does the school situation promote play opportunities, since many of the youngsters must leave on the bus soon after the school day ends.

Spontaneity seems to be lacking as well. The children rarely initiate contacts even with such frequent visitors as the observers, as sixth-graders are wont to do. They know the observers' names, but use them mainly in "Hello" situations in the hall or in prompting a teacher who has forgotten. There is no excitement, no enthusiasm, no "brilliance" to their relationships. Individuality is lacking, and the students hardly seem to differentiate themselves clearly from each other. They give the impression of being inferior and that the world is beyond their ken, to be coped with only by listening to whatever they are told and keeping out of the way.

This pattern fits comfortably with the "homey" approach and needs of their teacher, who appears in many ways to be one of them. She often draws on her personal experience to illustrate concretely, somewhat dramatically, and on the children's level what she is trying to teach:

> While discussing the concept of fear, the teacher told of her childhood reputation as a tomboy. She added that she is now very frightened of some of the same things she did so easily as a child.

> Mrs. Drake asked the children if they had seen any old movies where a man used a long funnel in his ear to hear better. She described this horn-like device used by the deaf to funnel in more sound and talked about its use as a hearing aid. Then Mrs. Drake went on to imitate an old, New England-type farmer with his funnel in his ear, the characterization being complete with walk, regional accent, and "By cracky" interjections. The children seemed quite amused.

In general, the Brookville teachers do not seem particularly well educated in their profession and may be unaware that some of their methods are outdated at best. No one seems particularly defensive, nor is there much concern about the possibly more advanced and more effective educational practices in the city.

What interaction occurs in the classroom tends to be teacher-centered; group discussion appears to be unheard of. Communication flows from the teacher to the class or to an individual. Rote learning, memory, rules, and drill are emphasized, and results are tested primarily through questions-and-answers and oral recitation:

> The teacher called on a number of people to give the successive steps in problem solving but found that only one girl knew them. She scolded the class, saying that they had all copied the steps down but probably had never even looked at them. That was the reason, she said, that they had so much trouble with arithmetic.

> Mrs. Drake asked one of the girls to go to the board and write the first "thing" (step) of problem solving. The girl did this, writing "Read Carefully" on the board. Another girl was asked

196

to write the second step, but she did not know it. Mrs. Drake said, "It just goes to show you," and indicated that the girl had a number of answers wrong because she did not know the rules.

Much of the time, the class responds on cue, in unison:

> The teacher was reviewing a list of nouns that the textbook had described as "things that cannot be seen." Discussing the word "idea," for example, she asked, "Can you see an idea?" The class responded, "No." "Can you feel an idea?" "No."

> Mrs. Drake asked the children how they could make sure that their arithmetic answers were right, and they all called out, "Check it." The teacher told the class how they could construct a diorama for display during the school's Open House for parents. She said it was a very good way to present their work and asked if they liked the idea. Everyone replied, "Yes." She then asked if they would like to break up into committees and again the children responded with a unanimous "Yes."

> Mrs. Drake wanted the class to tell her the last step in problem solving. She said they might as well learn it now because it was going to be required "over there," referring to the junior high school. She said, "Class?" and they answered, "Label."

The teacher's histrionics and the group responses of the class sometimes combine to create an atmosphere almost like that of a revival meeting:

> The teacher then went back to her desk, retrieved a *National Geographic* magazine, and said, "One of our new states, what?" The class responded in unison, "Alaska." She went on to tell the children that here were some pictures of the Alaskan earthquake. In a dramatic voice, she said, "That's what happened— the earth cracked right there and dropped to nothing. Houses, stores, everything tipped like this (illustrating with her hands that the earth had changed position), hanging. Then the water comes in like this," she continued, showing the children a flooded area that was illustrated in the magazine. She then said to the children, "Have you ever had a truck passing by that shook the schoolroom like in our old school building?" The children responded in unison, "Yes." Then she said, "Does our earth's surface change?" And the children responded in unison, "Yes." The teacher then said, "It surely does."

That the children seem to acquiesce in this teacher's approach is illustrated by their apparently blind acceptance of what she says as truth, at

197

least for classroom purposes. Erroneous or misleading material is frequently presented and accepted:

> The teacher began a lesson on prehistoric man by explaining that these men lived on the earth "billions and billions of years ago."

> The teacher was asking the children to give causes for changes in the earth's surface while she listed them on the blackboard. She said that she would accept only distinctly different causes, but at the end of the session she had included both "erosion" and "water carrying the soil away" on her list.

> Mrs. Drake told the youngsters that those with sixth-grade readers were to begin the story of Pecos Bill. She asked the children if they knew anything about Pecos Bill stories, and one boy replied that the stories were non-fiction. Mrs. Drake agreed with this answer and asked for a definition of "non-fiction"; she finally accepted the answer that "not an ounce of it is true."

> After being told, "You use some words to describe what you name and some to join other words together," the class was asked to give an example of a word used to join other words together. One child suggested the word "grandmother," which the teacher apparently accepted, for she continued with the next part of the grammar lesson.

> The teacher asked, "What are the three essentials for man's life?" Someone answered, "food"; another, "clothing." A girl then raised her hand and said, "oxygen." The teacher seemed a bit surprised, but she dismissed the answer almost immediately by saying that they were "not discussing that now." After a while, the third desired response, "shelter," was given and accepted.

> Mrs. Drake asked the class what cave men looked like, and one boy responded that they were "hunched over." Asked to explain further, he said, "Sort of like apes." The teacher then explained that, while cave men were hunched over, "We certainly don't want to say that they came from apes." The discussion was then dropped.

Sometimes things that are obviously incorrect, seemingly even to the children, are accepted by them nonetheless—almost as if the teacher's

198

role is to define what is fact and what is not. In part, "school" consists of learning the teacher's idiosyncrasies and expected answers, and honoring them. It also includes learning incorrect information. The children seem to exert a great deal of effort in these directions, apparently in an attempt to please their teacher, and they rarely argue a point even if they think they are right.

Classroom discipline in the usual sense seems to be absent; it is as if no one would even think of "misbehaving." Pupils and teacher alike emphasize learning—even if the material communicated is false—and little else seems to happen at school. The over-all submissive climate is further illustrated by the apparent absence of negativism among both pupils and teachers. Perhaps "resignation" or "fatalism" best describes the general attitude. At the same time, there seems to be a feeling of closeness between pupils and teacher which may have some elements of an "in-group" mutuality and which apparently reflects a general nurturance of and concern for the children. This may be related to the absence of visible negativism, but it may also render the children more vulnerable to misinformation communicated by their teachers as well as to distorted and inadequate social stimulation.

Although the school climate seems tightly structured, the teaching process is poorly organized and tends to present assorted facts rather than coherent "units":

> The girls finished their paper correction about ten minutes before the boys were scheduled to return from the gym. The teacher started a new formal lesson which continued until the boys returned and was then dropped in the middle.

> Mrs. Drake asked the class to list various causes of changes in the earth's surface. One boy answered "lightning," and was asked to "explain your thinking." He responded by saying, "Fire or rotting," and used the example of a tree falling and decaying, thereby changing the earth's surface. Mrs. Drake seemed to consider this answer wrong, and tried to give several concrete examples illustrating the difference between his response and a "correct" one. She then told him that a tree's rotting was not enough of a phenomenon to bring about a change in the earth's surface and that the process of decay took a long time. She went into a lengthy discussion of volcanic action, told an anecdote about a volcano erupting on a cornfield, drew pictures of cornstalks on the blackboard, and illustrated a

199

statement about rock stratification. She then returned to the boy and asked, "Do you understand now?" The boy responded, "Yes."

The teacher drew something on the board and told the class that it was a pie. "Pies have layers," she said, "and they also have a—what?" Several children responded, "crust." She went on to tell the class that the earth has topsoil with "the good stuff in it." Next, she described the process of digging a well near her house: "Over at our place, we have hardpan and, when they tried to dig a well, they ran into that stuff—what?" (no response) ". . . can't build—what?—what am I thinking of?—quicksand. They hit a cross vein where there was plenty of H_2O. They used one of those divining rods and, right where the pull was the greatest, they went through the layers to the water." She talked a little more about the layers of earth, then said, "Coal, what are you burning when you burn coal?" One of the children responded, "Wood." The teacher said, "Paper."

There is much apparently random and undirected activity, except when there are specific facts to be regurgitated. The structure that does exist provides a seemingly rigid, authoritarian environment:

The teacher asked Linda to divide a square into fourths. Linda did so, but her dividing lines were not exactly straight, so the teacher erased them and drew them herself. She then asked Linda what each part was called. Linda replied, "Fourths," but the teacher said, "No, no. *Each* part." Linda seemed puzzled and could not respond. The teacher spent the next twenty minutes giving concrete examples (which Linda understood mathematically) before Linda "caught on" and could give the desired response, "*One* fourth."

Much of what is taught appears to be inappropriate to the needs, interests, and abilities of the youngsters.

Despite the teacher's enthusiasm, spontaneity, and apparent concern for the children, she seems to have neither the educational skills nor the sensitivity to stimulate them out of their general lethargy and to provide them with a fertile educational experience. Barring outside influence, Brookville School seems destined to continue on its present undefined course, with its most gifted graduates going on to college to qualify to teach in the Brookville Schools of the future.

Jerome Beker · James B. Victor · Linda F. Seidel

CONCLUSIONS

Three classrooms have just been described. While they may not be typical or representative of anything beyond themselves, they may reflect more general practices in inner-city, suburban, and rural schools. In any case, it seems appropriate to examine the similarities and contrasts to see what they may be able to teach us. Many hypotheses emerge, and readers are encouraged to develop and examine their own. A few are presented here in an effort to draw the material together, to suggest some ways in which it may "make sense" as a whole, and to imply a few directions for subsequent, more systematic study and program development.

It seems clear that each of the classrooms can be, and sometimes is, a negative, perhaps damaging environment for children. In this context, it is important to emphasize that each of the three classroom teachers is doing the best job he or she knows how to do. None of the teachers is attempting to hurt or short-change any child, and all are committed to their work. Their failures reflect particular personalities and value orientations, deficits of knowledge and skill, and limitations consciously or unconsciously imposed by the schools, rather than willfully negative or apathetic behavior.

This is at once both a most hopeful and a most discouraging conclusion. It is hopeful because we have seen teachers who care, teachers who want to give children something of themselves and something of value. It is discouraging because we have seen that the same teachers, restricted by their personal and professional limitations and sometimes by the organization of the schools themselves, frequently cannot do so. The inner-city teacher who openly resists authority yet severely restricts autonomy in his own classroom is, in effect, teaching disadvantaged children how to be disadvantaged. The rural teacher, apparently with a limited conception of the "outside world" herself, is able to do little to help her pupils realize new vistas and seems, instead, to be rewarding passivity. The suburban teacher seems to accept and even to reinforce the competitive, sometimes hostile values of his talented class, making little effort to introduce new perspectives. And these appear to be three of our better teachers. It seems once more evident that grassroots educational change will not come easily even if we can agree on the directions it should take.

All three settings show structural and organizational similarities; all

201

are readily recognizable as "school." The "system" in all three schools tends to demand behavioral conformity and academic achievement, although in different proportions. Still, marked differences among the schools appeared from the beginning of the study. Principals and teachers at both Downtown and Briar Hill were somewhat suspicious and defensive when the project was proposed. At Brookville, on the other hand, school personnel seemed almost naïvely flattered to learn that someone, particularly someone with the status of "researcher," wanted to observe them. The predominant pupil attitude at Downtown is one of opposition or negativism; at Briar Hill, it is participation and achievement; and at Brookville, it is passive acceptance.

Briar Hill pupils both conform and learn, although it seems that less conformity is externally imposed on them than is expected at the other two schools. They "buy" the system which, in many ways, seems to be made for them. Brookville sixth-graders conform even more, but do not seem able to learn a great deal in the academic sphere. The youngsters at Downtown seem to reject the system itself: they learn poorly, if at all, what their teacher is attempting to teach, and they do not conform to his behavioral expectations. To attempt to teach them in a school context is to be constantly and actively concerned with control. It is not surprising to find the Briar Hill youngsters already worried about college, the Downtown class negative and resistive, and the Brookville children submissive and passive. What is surprising is the extent to which these stereotypes are reflected in reality at the three schools. It suggests that further study may demonstrate that the three schools are, after all, not atypical of the kinds of schools they represent.

The children's own descriptions of the "ideal student" reflect the same kinds of variation reported by the observers. Youngsters at Briar Hill frequently describe the ideal student favorably: he is seen as honest, friendly, and a hard worker, but within a normal range; they feel that he should not be "too good." A different twist appears frequently among the youngsters from Downtown. The ideal student is often characterized as one who "acts too big" or is "stupid," "creepy," or "mean," in addition to being a hard worker. Apparently, anti-intellectualism runs deep and starts early among some of our people. Brookville provides yet another contrast: relatively colorless descriptions and apparently limited verbal facility. Brookville youngsters seem to write less about classroom behavior and more of learning performance as determining the ideal student than do youngsters at either of the other schools. Their relative poverty of expression provides another view of these students as relatively passive and colorless. Although the Downtown youngsters are also verbally limited, they are able to communicate their message loud and clear.

The form in which the responses were made also reflects what seem to be significant differences between the classes. For example, responses of Downtown pupils to all five questions average a total of sixty words; those of Brookville pupils average eighty-six. Briar Hill pupils, on the other hand, average 164 words in response to the five questions. Three per cent of the words used by Downtown and Brookville pupils consist of three syllables or more, but the total for Briar Hill is only 4 per cent, so the difference is slight. A count was also made of errors—spelling, punctuation, and grammar—and the percentage of errors to total words was computed. The figures are 18 per cent for Downtown—about one error per six words—14 per cent for Brookville, and 5 per cent for Briar Hill. Of course, these differences tend to parallel the intelligence and achievement scores reported earlier; nonetheless, they are real differences. Unfortunately, there was not enough overlap in intelligence or achievement scores to permit comparisons with those factors controlled, but an attempt to do so is planned for the future. The situation is further complicated by the ambiguity surrounding what an intelligence test measures in such disparate settings.

It is harder to draw conclusions based on the teachers' "ideal pupil" descriptions, largely because only one teacher representing each of the three schools was involved. In addition, it was only after repeated requests that a response was obtained from the sixth-grade teacher at Downtown School, who claimed that he had previously responded to the same questions. Wherever the slip-up occurred, the description finally obtained seems almost as perfunctory as those of his students. In the first question, for example, the three teachers were asked to "Describe the kind of behavior you would like your ideal students to display." Their responses, by school, follow, just as they appeared:

    A. Downtown School:
        1. Well manner (curteous) [sic]
        2. Willing to accept the total environment of the classroom (rules, etc.)
    B. Briar Hill School:
        a. First and foremost, EMOTIONAL BALANCE.
        b. A degree of SELF-ANALYSIS whereby he or she might have certain self-correcting abilities.
        c. PROGRESSIVE PARTICIPATION that permits him to con-

> tribute without dominating, accept correction without withdrawing, admit inability without shame, or regret, and the sense to value the worth of someone else's contribution or analysis when it is worthwhile.
>
> d. The ability to ANTICIPATE RESPONSIBILITY, listen carefully and carry out directions intelligently.
> e. Cheerfulness and zest.
> f. Charity.

C. Brookville School:

> I am one who believes that the ideal student should be friendly, but not overbearing, courteous, and willing to take helpful criticism.
>
> This student should have the want to learn more about any subject we may have in our daily schedule and not be content with the minimum of knowledge.
>
> Also, this student should be one whom I could feel free to trust at any time, any place.

While it would be rash to attempt to generalize on this basis, it seems apparent that the teachers are in tune with their pupils, as is suggested in the observers' reports as well. Still open to question—and an important question—is the source of the similarity. Do teachers tend to make pupils become more like the teachers? Do children "seduce" their teachers to support and reinforce, often unconsciously, the children's own developing behavioral orientations? Do teachers gravitate toward schools with which their own personalities are in harmony? These possibilities and others, as well as their implications, will be subjected to further study.

Of the many contrasts among the three classes, only a few can be noted here. It is informative to consider class size—around forty at Downtown and under thirty at Briar Hill and Brookville. Presumably, the size of a class at Brookville is determined by happenstance—the number of children at a given grade level in the district. At Downtown, when it became apparent that the class provided an unwieldy learning environment, it was the high achievers who were removed and placed in a makeshift, combined fifth- and sixth-grade class. While this reflects the school's concern for the welfare of its better learners, it may also indicate the predominance of children whom the school is unable and/or unwilling to help. As can be inferred from Table 11-1, even school records are less complete at Downtown and at Brookville than at Briar Hill. Perhaps this provides additional evidence of a relative lack of concern for individual pupils and their needs.

Jerome Beker · *James B. Victor* · *Linda F. Seidel*

The subject of evolution arose at both Downtown and Brookville during the course of our observations. In each case, the teacher at least implied a rather strong distaste for the idea. Little, if any, interpretation is warranted, but neither should this interesting coincidence go unnoticed.

The chaos at Downtown School when the teacher leaves the room seems highly significant, especially when contrasted with Brookville (where pupils tend to do what they are told and may have little to say to one another anyway) and with Briar Hill (where internal controls are relatively strong and pupils seem to be too busy learning to get into much trouble). Accumulating evidence supports the notion that people who are trained to function with tight external control tend to become dependent on it for effective behavior, and the present work seems to point in the same direction. This also points up a serious dilemma. The assertion is frequently made, particularly by inner-city educators, that disadvantaged children need tightly structured programs. Certainly we have seen that they cannot function well when the structuring force is gone. Taken alone, however, this approach tends to perpetuate the very dependence on external control that may be a major component of a possible "disadvantaged syndrome." Consequently, what is needed is not only structure but also a planned attempt to help youngsters learn to operate with less and less of it. Such findings as those of Hunt and Dopyera that there seem to be particularly wide developmental variations within lower-class populations should also be considered in this context.[5]

It is relevant, although not new, to point out that even the rebelliousness of these children may be an expression of their dependence on external attention and limits and of their lack of developing identity— as reflected in the inability of some of them to recognize their own handwriting and words. These tend to be low-status children, and they know it; and they will be helped little to feel better about themselves, or to achieve, by continued suppression, although this may be the only way in which the school as now constituted can deal with them at all. Reference has already been made to what may be the teacher's techniques for minimizing or avoiding meaningful confrontation with his pupils.

The observations at Briar Hill, it should be remembered, turned out to involve an atypically high-achieving, high-status class, although the other sixth grade there also tended to be high achieving and of high status when compared with sixth-grade classes in the other two schools.

Despite the fact that the observers entered the situation "cold," not having seen any pupil records in advance, it quickly became evident that the class being observed was too "good" to be the whole story. Suburban children do have problems and suburban schools do have low achievers. In this case, as we subsequently learned, grouping was homogeneous—the "problems" were virtually all in the other class. Little else can be said about this here, except that the situation clearly points up the need for further study of suburban schools, the kinds of problems they face, and how they deal with them. It should also be noted that, despite the apparent acceptance of the hostile sarcasm so evident in the class observed at Briar Hill, it may be a source of pain to at least some of the children. This could be the message of their description of the "ideal pupil" as one who is "modest" and not "too good," "perfect," "haughty," "snobby," or "boastful."

The apparent absence of stimulation and excitement at Brookville is reflected in many ways, one of which may be that a sampling of the observers' notes showed them to be shorter and sparser than those from either of the other two schools. Perhaps less "happens" at Brookville; it certainly does not seem to be "where the action is." The children's passivity, authority-orientation, and lack of visible negativism in almost any form seem to render them more vulnerable to the adults in their lives. Apparently, these are adults who are often wrong to the extent of teaching incorrect information and who are ill-prepared to introduce the students to horizons much beyond their own rural community. This is not to say that the teacher is a bad one. She is a nurturing and skillful teacher, but her own knowledge and experience seem limited; she can only give the children what she has. Nor is she particularly authoritarian—the situation seems to be an authoritarian one primarily because the children's passivity makes it so. Certainly this is a setting where more could be done, but it seems unlikely that many people except "home-grown" products would, in the present situation, choose to teach there.

The implicit goals of the three schools represent, perhaps, the most overriding contrast of all, within which the other differences make a kind of sense. Downtown School seems to be largely a custodial institution, a place where poor children can, perhaps, be trained at least for social acceptability. Briar Hill, on the other hand, is more like a "prep school"—the orientation is toward bigger and better things in the future. Brookville School seems fairly clearly to be educating its pupils for life in Brookville. Perhaps these goals are not unrealistic, but some may believe that what seems realistic today is not enough. By plan or happenstance, the schools are moving in particular directions, and it seems more intelligent to make sure that movement occurs by plan.

Other questions arise, of course, and three appear particularly worthy of note here for future reference. First, the first-grade classes in the same three schools proved much harder to differentiate, perhaps due in part to the more subtle and complex and more frequently non-verbal nature of the transactions. It seems likely that first-graders, being closer to infancy, tend to behave more instinctively and less on the basis of learned patterns. Therefore, perhaps, the first-graders in the three schools appear more similar than do sixth-graders. Also, teachers may treat them more like they treat babies—instinctively and, therefore, more similarly. The critical question, however, concerns what happens to children between grade one and grade six to convert apparently similar learning environments and pupil responses to the vast differences observed on the sixth-grade level.

Second, the observers reported many outside interruptions for special classes, notices, and other reasons throughout the school day. The impact of this on teaching continuity and effectiveness needs careful attention. Finally, more systematic study of the reciprocal impact of school environments and how they are perceived by their participants might shed new light on effective strategies for change.

It seems likely that the teachers observed would feel that they have been falsely portrayed if they were to read the observers' recordings of their classrooms. This suggests that such a technique might be of value in training and supervising classroom teachers, since they rarely have the benefit of such a mirror in which to examine their own behavior. Observations followed by group or one-to-one discussions should be explored as a means for enhancing teacher insight and effectiveness.

It bears emphasizing that this report may make the schools look worse—and in some ways, perhaps, better—than they really are, since the written word carries particular impact. Our purpose is to identify the baseline—where we are—and the challenge. The settings observed may be idiosyncratic in some aspects, but they are probably not atypical in others. Therefore, a first task is to determine the extent to which they represent prototypes and to build more precise models of inner-city, suburban, and rural school environments. This can lead to new perspectives on the changes needed and ways to achieve them.

Notes

NOTE: The research reported herein was performed pursuant to a contract with the United States Office of Education, Department of Health, Education, and Welfare, under the provisions of the Cooperative Research Program.

1. More extensive and systematic reports of these data will be made later.

2. It is interesting to note that pupil records at Briar Hill are virtually complete, while there are numerous gaps at both Downtown and Brookville. If one can assume that the gaps tend to represent less favorable scores (more frequent absences, inadequate information from the home, and the like), then the real differences may be greater than those reflected in Table 11–1.

3. While Downtown and Brookville each had only one sixth-grade class, there were two sixth grades at Briar Hill. The class available for study turned out to represent a generally higher-achieving group than did the other sixth grade, although there was some overlap. In view of this difference, background characteristics such as test scores and parental occupations presented in Table 11–1 are computed for each sixth grade separately as well as for all sixth-graders. Conclusions should be drawn separately for the total group of suburban sixth-graders and for the apparently gifted group that was studied. Unfortunately, essays and observational data were not available for the second sixth-grade class at Briar Hill.

4. Parental occupations were scored according to the Socioeconomic Index developed by Otis Dudley Duncan and presented in Albert J. Reiss, Jr., *Occupations and Social Status* (New York: The Free Press of Glencoe, 1961).

5. David E. Hunt and John Dopyera, "Personality Variation in Lower-Class Children," *Journal of Psychology*, LXII (1966), 47–54.

12 · Learning the Ropes

Situational learning in four occupational training programs

BLANCHE GEER, JACK HAAS, CHARLES VI VONA,
STEPHEN J. MILLER, CLYDE WOODS, AND HOWARD S.
BECKER

SOCIOLOGISTS who go into the field and talk to the people they study sometimes get a bonus in the form of a colloquial phrase which points up a complex process worthy of sociological analysis. This happened to us in our studies of occupational training when we heard trainees use the phrase, "learning the ropes," to describe their experiences as they began training. You can't expect a new man to know what's what right away, we were told; even if he's had some experience, it takes time to learn the ropes.

The phrase alerted us to the process of initial learning by the new-comer in any social situation—his attempts to master where things and people are, the niceties of rank and privilege, who expects him to do what, at what time, for how long; what the rules are—which ones can or must be broken, which followed to the letter.

The process is one we seldom dignify by the term "learning." Educators and others in authority may cover it in brief orientation programs but, from their point of view, it is inevitably an adjustment to the organization expected of everyone; newcomers who fail at it are more apt to receive attention than those who succeed.

Inevitably, sociologists take a more abstract view, and have long been interested in successful situational learning, usually in the broader context of adult socialization. Situational learning has been studied in such diverse settings as an industrial plant, a mental hospital, and the prison,[1] but as yet no one has reported on comparative studies of the process in more than one organization. When both similar and dramatically divergent patterns of initial situational learning began to emerge

209

in four of our studies of occupational training, we began to ask ourselves such questions as: what are the ropes the newcomer learns, how are they learned, do they differ from one training situation to another, and who teaches them? This chapter reports some preliminary comparisons of initial learning in a business-machine school, a barber school, a training course for nursing assistants, and a medical internship.[2]

Our approach has its theoretical origins in the symbolic interactionism of George Herbert Mead, which suggested that we interact with the trainees we were studying in order to understand the situational symbols they use to construct courses of action,[3] and in a sociology which focuses on the continuing interaction of social structure and group process in occupations and educational institutions.[4] Our methods have included the use of documents, interviews, and questionnaires but, because we have been most interested in following the training process as trainees experienced it, our chief technique has been participant observation.[5]

The observer in the twelve-month intern program remained in the field for two years in order to see more than one group of trainees. In the other programs, since trainees entered at irregular intervals, a period of several months sufficed for observers to interact with new and old students as well as staff. They watched trainees at work, sat in on their classes, talked with them during the day at coffee breaks and meals, and occasionally followed them home.

We found the four programs strikingly different. They prepare people for office work, a unionized trade, relatively menial care of hospital patients, and an honored profession. In two of the programs, trainees are homogeneous in background. In the two others, in contrast to most school populations, students vary widely in age, education, and experience. The number of trainees in a program at a given time varies from one to fifty.

Of the four groups, only the interns begin together; the rest enter training one by one or in very small groups. The business-machine school alone approaches the traditional classroom structure; the barber school is unique in having an examination set by outsiders; the program for nursing assistants combines classwork with on-the-job training; only the interns have a program of fixed duration.

Whatever the differences in the programs, trainees in each of them must successfully negotiate the process of initial learning in order to continue in training. We have been most interested in searching out, if only in preliminary fashion, relationships between the structure of a program and the process trainees go through in learning its ropes. Broadly speaking, we have found four structural variants: a program in which trainees learn the ropes almost entirely from their classroom instructor; one in which they learn them from peers; a third, from clients or subordinates; and a fourth in which they selectively use several different groups as teachers.

THE BUSINESS-MACHINE SCHOOL

Our first training program, the Kard Business Machine School,[6] is a small, privately owned organization that gives training in office practice and in the operation of calculators and other business machines. Most of its students are recent high school graduates, many have come into the city from rural areas to attend the school, and women outnumber men. A large number of students attend part time, and have jobs as waitresses or store clerks. Since the course lasts only three months and there are no extracurricular activities, the school takes up a relatively small portion of students' time and non-school groups play a major role in their lives. Unlike high school and college students, people do not identify them (nor do they identify themselves) as students outside the classroom.

Although they sign up for three months, the management permits students to continue in school free of charge until they have completed the course. They may enroll on any Monday; from one to eight students usually start in a given week, joining a group which varies in size from ten to fifty. Using self-instructional manuals, students proceed at their own rate in a daily routine of individual work and timed class drills.

The staff consists of the owner-manager, a public relations man, a secretary-receptionist, and two teachers. New students interact chiefly with the teacher in charge of instruction on calculating machines. He supervises their work, sets schedules, gives drills and tests, and releases them for coffee breaks and lunch.

On his first day of school, a student fills out a short registration form. The secretary-receptionist provides a list of rules on tardiness, absences, smoking, using the telephone, and returning report cards. She introduces Mr. Stevens, the instructor for the first half of the course, who assigns desks. If more than one student enters on the same day, he usually seats them together:

> Mr. Stevens then brought the new girl to a seat; he had taken with him one of the calculator books. He said, "This is the red

211

book." He opened it up to the page showing pictures of the various comptometer machines. "These are the various comptometers: Bell, Fund, and Fund-Duplex—that is because it has two dials."

The teacher has introduced the student to the most important elements in the course: himself, the calculator, and the workbook:

He then pointed to a picture of a woman sitting at a comptometer. Mr. Stevens said, "Notice the correct posture. The machine is always to your right at an angle." As he said this, he moved her machine about an inch . . . and firmly stationed it. He then asked Betty if she was right-handed and she said she was. He said, "Good. Your pencil goes under your thumb." As he said this he turned his hand palm up and put the pencil under his thumb. He said, "You always hold your pencil."

Having described the proper physical relationship to the machine, Mr. Stevens explains how to use it:

"Now this is your keyboard: you always use the first two fingers. Now we draw an imaginary line above the 'five' keys . . . don't use the numbers above the number five. If you have to, use, for example, when you want the number seven: four and three; nine: five and four; six: three and three. Never use the numbers above five for addition. Now—the one, three, and five are hollow; the two and four are flat. That way you can feel the difference. The one, three, and five are concave; they are hollow." Then he showed her the decimal indicators and the clear button.

Instruction proceeds rapidly from *how* to *what* and in *what sequence:*

He then showed her the drills [in the workbook] which were a series of two column additions . . . he said, "This is the first lesson. Add these numbers up as I told you, then go on to the next page . . . don't go on to Lesson Two until you see me and I check these."

The entering student has been told to do the first assignment, what to do next, and how to deal with the teacher. Mr. Stevens amplified the last point for another beginner:

Do the first lesson and when you get done, bring it up to me before you go on. If you have any questions, don't yell: come up to my desk.

212

As they work in the same room, the newcomer sees this request obeyed by more advanced students. There can be no doubt in his mind as to what the teacher wants.[7]

The workbook is equally clear. Easy things come first and procedure is outlined step by step:

> 1. Clear the machine. All dials must register "0" before starting a problem.
> 2. Add the numbers in Problem (1). Start at the top of the column and proceed as follows:
>   a. Place the index finger on the 30 key, fully depress key and release it . . .[8]

Assignments in the workbook and on tests are mathematical; there is only one correct answer. The student is graded on two easily discerned and objective factors: speed and accuracy on the machine.

Things go so smoothly at first for new students that we might conclude that learning the ropes is only a matter of following the directions given by teacher and workbook. This is not quite the case. The newcomer finds that there are things to be learned about the school and classwork which the teacher does not tell him, and, in this situation, he makes teachers of his fellow students.

New students change their style of dress to conform to that of their peers, and imitate them in such matters as leaving in the middle of class for the washroom or to sharpen a pencil. It is difficult to talk over the clatter of the machines, but during coffee breaks and lunch students exchange information about successful excuses for cutting class and ways of doing assignments.

Although the teacher emphasizes that developing speed and accuracy (something each student must do by himself) is more important for graduation than one's score on a particular test in the workbook, newcomers ask more advanced students about the next examination:

> Sandy Long pointed to one of the problems in her book . . . she said, "Is this on the test?" Annie said, "Yes, there is one of those." Sandy groaned, "Oh" . . . Annie then pointed to Sandy's book and said, "They also have one of those. I got it wrong. But it's really very easy . . . I made a foolish mistake and didn't use the small o's on the keyboard."

Understandably perhaps, teachers seldom see providing information about what will be on a test as part of their duty. For students, if there is no penalty for cheating, the information is a practical solution to the problem of making a good record. They are less likely to consider it wrong if, as the instructor says, examinations are relatively unimportant for graduation.

In addition to his instructor and the peers who act as teachers, a Kard student has a teacher in his machine. In a very real sense, the machine is a perfectionist. It punishes mistakes promptly and exacts a penalty which often angers its would-be master:

> Jill said, "This work is frustrating." I asked her why. She said, "I am doing my work and I get down to the last number and ready to write the answer when the machine gets stuck. You can tell when you've made a mistake. And then I have to start all over again." Evelyn said, "I could tell that this morning. You really slammed your hands against the keyboard."

Although the Kard newcomer learns some of the ropes of his school situation from fellow students and others from the machine itself, he learns most of them from his teacher. The teacher is nearly always present in the classroom and in control of it. As school goes on, it is he who appraises the student's progress in speed and accuracy, grades him, and recommends him to employers. From the outset, the teacher structures the student's time, establishes sequences of action with workbook and machine, and specifies proper modes of interaction between student and teacher at the end of each sequence. He leaves the student relatively few opportunities to make choices among alternative courses of action; few problems to solve. He provides so much information about what to do, when to do it, and how to do it that the student turns to his peers as supplementary teachers in only a few instances. When one person, the instructor himself, teaches them to the newcomer, learning the ropes can be relatively easy.

THE BARBER COLLEGE

The Pacific Barber College is both a school and a barbershop. Located in the skid-row section of a large Western city, its clients include derelicts, winos, and pensioners. The heterogeneous student body is composed of men and several Negro women from seventeen to sixty years of age. There are recent high school graduates and dropouts, and a large number who have held one or more unskilled or semi-skilled jobs. In ethnic background whites predominate, but Negroes, Mexicans, Filipinos, and Orientals are represented. All students must have a ninth-grade education or its equivalent to be admitted to the school.

The staff includes a manager, two instructors, and a janitor. Students may begin the course at any time, choosing one of two shifts and attending six days a week. The 1,250-hour course can be completed in six months, and must be completed within one year. It includes 100 hours of classroom instruction and 1,025 hours of practical application. In addition, students must learn the barber theory presented in lectures and textbooks. At the end of the training period, they are examined by a state board to qualify as licensed apprentices.

On his first day, the student receives a brief orientation from the manager, who assigns chapters in the textbook on shaving, haircutting, and the care of tools. There is a wooden dummy for practicing shaves.

The new student begins to learn the ropes when he recognizes that he faces three problems and seeks to solve them. His first and most pressing problem is the relative absence of ordinary teaching. Accustomed to the structured patterns of other schools, he finds that in barber college—aside from the daily lecture, which consists chiefly of going over materials in the text—there are no prescribed sequences of study. The teachers do not tell him what to do or when to do it and, although he may ask them for help, they are not always readily available.

State law requires one instructor for each twenty students, but the manager spends the greater part of his time in the office and the other two instructors have lectures to give and papers to grade. With three practice rooms operating twelve hours a day and only two instructors, adequate coverage is difficult if not impossible. Newcomers typically define the situation as follows:

> I guess we're supposed to be pretty much on our own, just to go around and watch and study . . . I guess they just give you your tools when they figure you're ready and then you go ahead, but I don't know too much about it . . .

On the second or third day of school (rarely later), newcomers get their tools and join other beginning barber students in a shop that provides free services to clients of the school. The situation is a bewildering one for the newcomer. Students do not take customers in rotation, and barber chairs are not assigned. When a chair is available, the student sets up his tools, puts his license on the mirror, and accepts a customer.

He usually gives his first shave or haircut without help from the instructor:

> Boy, I just don't know what's going on around here. You come in and you get some scissors and a razor and then you start to work and nobody tells you nothing. I just don't know what's going on.

He makes mistakes, sometimes bad ones:

> Well, I was a little nervous about everything . . . the first time I shaved a guy I cut him from here to here (he put one finger at the ear lobe and the other almost to the point of the chin) and that was the first stroke of the razor. After that I wouldn't pick up a razor for three months.

As no one urges them to take customers, newcomers deal with their fears in different ways. A few return to practicing on the dummy, some read the text, others loaf; still others begin to teach themselves:

> I finally just accepted the way it was and decided to do it by myself. I'll try something one time one way and the next time I'll try it a different way and that way I learn something. You just have to figure you're not going to get any teaching here . . .

Although a few students continue on their own, most learn to combine trial-and-error methods of self-teaching with getting help from other students. They ignore the school regulation posted on the wall which forbids such practices:

> I go to guys who I think know more than I do. I watch them and if I figure they are better than I am then I can ask them [for help] but a lot of times they come up and volunteer information.

Once he has learned the ropes sufficiently to break the rule against help from his peers, the student finds that this solution to his first problem—how to get instruction—generates other problems.

Fellow students help him in a number of ways. They demonstrate technique, give advice on how to deal with different kinds of hair, and provide tips on what the state examiners want. But not all student teachers are skilled enough or knowledgeable enough to teach well.

> You know, I appreciate it when somebody helps me, but that guy really screwed up the haircut. He left a big patch on the

216

> side and there's no way to get rid of it now . . . I really do ap-
> preciate it and I guess the guy was trying to help, but he sure
> fouled me up. Hell, even the instructor couldn't straighten it
> out after he got through.

Since there are no such devices as grades to rank students' barbering
skills publicly during the course, the student has to appraise his own
progress in relation to others' skills in order to know which fellow students to ask for help. How to avoid volunteered help of the kind that
does more harm than good poses still another problem.

Analysis of our data has not proceeded far enough to establish clearly
whether students become increasingly capable of evading poor teaching from peers. It is clear, however, that the relative absence of schedule left students with free time, which many spent in apparently aim-
less horseplay with each other.[9] We can interpret the half-serious blows
and verbal joking simply as ways of passing time and relieving tension.
But it is probable that they also help newcomers to learn the "pecking
order" of the group, and provide concrete knowledge of the strengths
and weaknesses of others. The man who backs away from rough joking
may have to accept inexpert help; the tough guy may establish a prece-
dent that enables him to protect himself:

> I noticed Dan talking to Richard as he was cutting a twelve- or
> thirteen-year-old boy's hair. Dan was saying, "See that line
> around the back of his head? You've got to get that off. You've
> got to taper that more." Richard tapered the hair a little bit
> more and smoothed it down and then said to Dan and me,
> "You see, it's just because his hair is so fine. It won't lay down
> no matter what you do." Dan said, "I'll fix it," and with this he
> wet his fingers and slicked down the kid's hair in the back . . .
> Richard said, in a very nasty tone, "You didn't have to do that."

While securing help in learning to barber is the major problem of the
new student, he has two other problems to solve in the process of becoming a successful barber student. With an average of eleven years of
formal schooling behind him, such topics as the skin and the epidemiology of syphilis discussed in lectures and the textbook appear formidable. Learning the ropes includes learning that this is an inescapable
part of one's training:

> . . . and this book stuff. I didn't know it was going to be like
> this. I thought you just got your tools and learned how to cut
> hair and practiced this practical stuff. I didn't think you had to

217

have all this book stuff. You have to be part doctor and part dentist and part everything else. You have to learn all about cells and genes and tissue and all that stuff.

For many students, getting used to clients presents a third problem:

> One of the things that really shook me was the low class of people that come into the [beginners'] room . . . I'd never had any contact with that kind before. I remember one guy. He was an Indian with one leg who came in and he had to spit so he just picked up his shirt at the neck and spit down on his chest and then closed up his shirt again. I couldn't believe it.

The newcomer learns by watching his fellow students handle such clients. He may also discover that if he can spot troublesome customers as they enter the shop, he can often hang back and let less observant (or more eager) students serve them.[10] As in the case of his major problem (securing teaching), the student solves his problems with clients, at least in part, by observing his fellow students and interacting with them.

It should be clear that the barber college and the business-machine school have a number of common elements. Both have only a few instructors and texts and students who begin the course at irregular intervals. At both Kard and Pacific, newcomers work in open rooms where they can see more advanced students. If the barber student must learn the peculiarities of his clients, the business-machine student must learn the way of his calculator. But here the similarities end.

The barber college does not establish the sequences of students' training. The teacher is often not even in the room, and outsiders give the final examination which determines whether a student will become a licensed apprentice. In this situation, students learn the ropes (and barbering as well) from teaching peers.

THE TRAINING PROGRAM FOR NURSING ASSISTANTS

Our next example is not a school, but a hospital training program for nursing assistants.[11] The hospital hires trainees on a probationary basis when it needs new workers, and a small group (two to five persons) usually takes the program together. Trainees are carefully selected, but vary considerably in age, education, background, and experience. They are required to take the program even though they have had previous hospital experience.

During the first ten to twelve weeks, trainees have two one-hour

218

classes daily, taught by a nurse in charge of training. For the rest of the day, they work as nursing assistants on a training floor of the hospital—bathing patients, making beds, cleaning rooms, and serving trays of food. The nurse in charge assigns patients to trainees just as she does to others on her staff. The trainee is much on his own; in some cases, he is the only nursing assistant on the floor. Nominally, the charge nurse supervises his work; the teaching nurse, his learning.[12]

The trainee's problems in learning the ropes of the classroom situation are similar to those students face in ordinary schools. He must discover what the teacher wants him to learn and how to demonstrate his learning. The process is one of gradual discrimination. He relies on what the teacher herself says she wants, and supplements this information with such other cues as the amount of time devoted to various types of instruction and the emphasis put upon them by techniques the teacher uses in class.[13] The instructor's unscheduled visits to the training floors provide further insight into her wishes.

In class, the teaching nurse presents information on procedures, diseases, and relationships with patients and other personnel on the floor. Her instruction in procedures is consistently detailed and thorough:

> Then Miss Thomas [instructor] went to the blackboard and drew the outline of another kind of binder. She drew a "T" on the board, with a split down the bottom part of the "T." "This," she explained, "is known as a 'T' binder as is used for patients who have had rectal surgery." She turned to her desk and while demonstrating the folding of the binder around the patient, she said . . . "Take the two straps and wrap them around the waist and then take each one of these end pieces and bring them up through the legs, cross them, and pin them on to the middle section. This holds the dressing in place for the patient." She continued, "Well, I think we'll be able to put this on Mr. Stone [dummy patient]. We have time and it will be good practice."

Organizing the material into a series of steps, the teacher describes, explains, demonstrates, and offers time for practice. Although it is impossible for her to check each procedure performed on the training floor and trainees know this, they quickly learn that she often uses her visits to check their work closely. Things which trainees do every day—making beds and keeping patients clean—are especially easy to check.

Classroom instruction about disease includes discussion, but does not receive the emphasis of extended and meticulous presentation accorded to procedures:

> Miss Thomas started out by asking what kind of infectious diseases they might encounter in the hospital. Mrs. Smith [trainee] said, "T.B." Miss Thomas wrote T.B. on the board and asked for the Latin name. Both Al and Mrs. Smith [trainees] had difficulty pronouncing the name, but after several tries Mrs. Smith finally blurted out, "Tubercula bacillus," which Miss Thomas wrote on the board. Then Miss Thomas asked, "What is tubercula bacillus?" Al said, "It's a germ." Miss Thomas wrote "germ" after "Tubercula bacillus" and then asked, "How's it contracted?" Mrs. Smith responded, "It's passed through the air, it's airborne, you know, like coughing or sneezing, or sputum."

Trainees learn the names of diseases and how to pronounce them, and a little about their causes and how they are contracted. It is information the trainee seldom uses in his work; failure to use it does not leave evidence of a sort the instructor can easily observe.

The third and least concrete type of instruction the teaching nurse offers—information about relationships with others—receives still less emphasis, as we suspect it does in most training programs and schools. Rarely explicit, the instructor hints at the complexities of the trainee's situation on the floor—a situation in which she herself is involved, since a trainee's performance reflects her teaching:

> I [instructor] want you to know how to do these neatly and accurately, so that the nurses will never be able to say, if they do have you do these, that you didn't do them right.

At work on a training floor, the trainee discovers that the order of emphasis in the classroom—procedures come first in importance, medical information second, and interaction with others third—is virtually reversed. Learning the ropes is a matter of interpreting new priorities and defining in action the responsibilities his work entails. The trainee does this in a situation which provides little teaching in the conventional sense, but many subtle clues which guide his developing understanding of what people on the floor, both staff and patients, expect of him.

The priorities of the job are among the first things the trainee learns. He has to decide whether being a trainee makes him primarily a student responsible to the teaching nurse or a worker responsible for getting things done:[14]

> Al said, "What really fouls me up is when Miss Thomas comes up and checks my work. She is a very complete and thorough woman and expects you to spend a half an hour with each patient. If I did this, I would never finish my work." He gave me an example, "She expects you to do a bed unit in about a half an hour and then she comes in and checks it very carefully. She even goes to the extent of taking a fingernail file and scrapes the frame of the bed to see if there is any dirt. The best I can do is make sure that there is no dust around."

Although he knows that the teaching nurse makes reports on his progress, the trainee has also learned that the head nurse wants a smoothly running floor with all patients cared for and all tasks somehow done, and he tries to do it.

Since classwork follows its own schedule of topics, trainees must sometimes decide whether to do things they have not yet been taught in class. Aware of this possibility, the instructor warns them to call her for assistance, but the request often goes unheeded:

> [In this example, the trainee was turning a patient on a stryker frame, an extremely complicated and dangerous maneuver which requires, by hospital rule, two persons to execute it.]

> I asked Al, "Have you done this in class already?" He said, "Oh no, we haven't come to this yet." I asked him how he learned about it, and he said, "Well, I guess it's OJT [on-the-job training]. I just watch someone and pick it up that way." He continued, "You know there is supposed to be two people doing this anyway."

In this instance, the trainee not only puts getting his work done ahead of obeying a hospital rule, he also defines learning as something he must do on his own when his work demands it.

He learns that his relationship with patients is an important part of his job.[15] In a sense, they are his teachers on the floor: they define the situation and know from experience how things should be done. They tell the trainee what to do,

> Al placed the tray of food on the stand but the patient complained, "How do you expect me to reach the food? Hand me my meat loaf." Al gave the patient his meat loaf, the patient ate

221

it out of his hand and then said, "Gimme my tools [meaning knife and fork] so I can eat the rest of this."

but make completing his work more difficult by unpredictably undoing it:

> The heavy-set nurse entered and said to Al, "That Mr. Teller made a mess, he spit up all his water. I wonder if when you get a free minute, whether you could give me a hand." Al fumbled a little, then replied that he would.

Pressed for time and repeatedly interrupted, the trainee learns to bargain with others, even his superiors whom he is trying to satisfy, in order to get his work done:

> [The head nurse and male attendant from physical therapy] both entered the room. The nurse said, "Tom, Mr. Smith [patient] has to go to P.T. today. Mr. Weeks is here to take him down." Tom said, "Sorry, but Mr. Smith is not finished yet." The nurse then asked, "How long will it be?" Tom replied, "About five minutes more." The head nurse said to Tom, "Well, you finish him up and see if you can get a patient to take Mr. Smith downstairs."

The willingness of the nurses to bargain with him provides the trainee with evidence that they share his definition of the situation. Finishing the assigned tasks has first priority.

As in the barber school, the student's problems in the nursing-assistant training program are the interactional ones so seldom classified as things to be taught in school. The trainee learns the ropes—how to solve his initial problems—as he perceives and uses a set of situational rules which govern the interaction of staff and patients on the training floor. He learns that, although there is seldom time enough to complete assigned tasks, getting them done comes first. Once he has defined his situation in this way, the trainee can make decisions about whose orders to follow and even take orders from patients. He knows when to ask for help and who can help him when he needs it.

In the absence of peers in his immediate situation, the trainee shares his definition of his responsibilities with the floor nurses, and puts himself in a position to bargain with them. The divided line of authority over him may well encourage the trainee to interact with other personnel on the floor, nominally his superiors, almost as if they were peers.

Unlike the barber student, who learns relatively little from his brief interaction with his clients, the nursing assistant in training learns from his patients how to do his work. Because they are people to whom trainees do things, and in this sense are temporarily subordinated clients, patients seem to us poorly cast as teachers of the ropes. But many of them are residents of the hospital before the trainee arrives on the scene and, under the hospital's system of rotating employees, may have dealt with several nursing assistants. They know how his job should be done. Teaching him to do it properly can only add to their comfort.

The high standards of performance taught him in class can seldom be reached on the job, but the disjunction presents a less disorienting problem for the trainee than one might expect, since class and work go on at the same time and the demands of the job (if only because they fill most of his day) have priority from the beginning. Classes are brief, and the trainee sees relatively little of his classmates afterward. Since they usually work on separate floors, the fact that their experiences are similar affects trainees less than the exigencies of their immediate situation on the floor. Learning the ropes is a matter of learning to get work done in ways both charge nurse and patients will approve.

THE MEDICAL INTERNSHIP

Our last training program is a situation even more complicated in structure than that of the nursing assistants. It is a hospital setting once again, but this time we examine the learning problems of young physicians beginning their year as interns on the Harvard Medical Services at Boston City Hospital.

The intern begins the year more familiar with the environment he enters than do newcomers to our other training programs. As a medical student, he has spent years in a hospital and has had opportunities to observe interns at their work. He comes to his new duties with the confidence of the good record in medical school which led to his acceptance in the Harvard program and the newly acquired authority of a medical degree.

The new intern enters a highly differentiated hierarchy of medical and hospital personnel, each group a potential source of situational learning. In the hospital as a whole, he does not begin at the bottom, as so often happens in a career transition from one organization to another, but immediately fills the central position accorded a physician. Students, nurses, and other hospital personnel are his subordinates; patients, in his immediate care. In the hierarchy of physicians, however, the intern ranks beneath the assistant resident who supervises his work and was himself an intern before the new man arrived. Above the assistant residents are senior residents, a chief resident, the program director, and research and consulting physicians.

The intern has a clearly identifiable peer group. The sixteen admitted to the program each year make a small group in comparison to the large number of their superiors in medical authority and experience. Yet they have the advantage of being a cohort or class of people who pass through a career stage together. Their identity as new interns is not blurred by the policy of irregular admission used for the business-machine and barber students or the nursing assistants.[16] Furthermore, they rotate in groups from one ward to another, and the men see each other frequently during rounds, in the laboratory, and at conferences and meals.

From the outset, his superiors encourage the intern to define his situation as one in which his chief responsibility is to get his work done,[17] and in this he is like the nursing assistant. His work is the care of patients, but getting it done is not just a matter of performing a series of tasks. He must diagnose disease on the basis of information provided by other hospital personnel as well as what he himself discovers, and the treatment he prescribes may be carried out by still other groups. He must secure the cooperation of others in running tests, taking X-rays, and obtaining medical consultation. In many respects, his job is administrative, and the ropes he must learn are ways of so managing people that events proceed rapidly and in proper sequence.

At the beginning of his internship, the new man faces a number of problems, some of which result from the ambiguity of being both the physician in charge and a neophyte with much to learn. In the overlapping system of authority characteristic of the teaching hospital, he carries out his responsibility for the care of patients under the eyes of the assistant resident and other physicians who also see the patient—men whose good opinion he needs if he is to continue to progress in the elite medical world he has entered by interning in the Harvard program.

At the same time, the intern is in the somewhat uncomfortable position of having to learn from students, nurses, and other staff who lack the authority of a degree in medicine, but who know the ropes at B.C.H.:[18]

> Field said, "On my ward, I'd be lost without my student. He just took over. There I was. I didn't even know what forms to

fill out, but he did. He didn't have to but he filled the forms out . . . and really helped me out. I wouldn't know what the hell to do if it wasn't for the students on the floor."

Where forms are kept, which ones to use, and the niceties of filling them out are administrative details the intern must learn if his work is to go smoothly. Nevertheless, they are details—not the kind of information a man wants to bother his superiors for, and the student makes a convenient source.[19]

Nurses teach other kinds of ropes, often ones crucial for the care of the patients:

> [The patient's] feet were uncovered, they were horribly scaled, dirty, the nails had been allowed to grow and became twisted and gnarled. Andrew turned to me and said, "That's the way witches must look," . . . when looking at the feet, "I think it's just dirt and failure to cut those nails. We'll have to have someone look at it. It's interesting though." . . . We returned to the [ward] kitchen. Andrew mentioned the woman's feet to the nurse. In response to Andrew's question about scissors with which to cut the toenails, the nurse said, "Oh, no. Don't do that . . . Put in for a consult with Dr. B. in the diabetic clinic. He's the foot man. The only one around. He'll come and use a saw."

In this incident, a nurse saves the intern from possible error, and also provides him with two sorts of situational learning. First, he learns the limits of his responsibility in cases of this kind: in this hospital, interns need not perform a procedure which entails risk of infection for the diabetic patient. Second, to the growing fund of administrative facts which help him to manage his work, he adds a name (Dr. B.), a place (the diabetic clinic), and a procedural arrangement (consultation).

The intern, however, does not always define nurses as helpful teachers of the ropes. As he continues his search for ways of controlling people and events, he begins to recognize how much he depends on nurses to carry out the treatment he orders for his patients:

> I heard Andrew say to Holt [another intern], "I'll tell you, the nurses can make your internship hell." I asked, "How?" Andrew replied, "Well, they just won't do things for you if you don't handle them right. You have to flirt a little, never appear heavy-handed, and just jolly them along." I asked, "Do you mean that if you don't do this, they won't do the things they have to for

you?" Heath [medical student] said, "I think they just won't do anything for you." Holt nodded his head. Andrew said, "That's right. If you want to make things easy on yourself, you have to get the nurse on your side."

For these interns at least, learning to manage nurses is part of learning the ropes.

The intern also learns the ropes from his immediate superior, the assistant resident who administers the ward. Like the teacher in the business-machine school, he makes himself almost continuously available. During rounds when they are together at the bedside, he tells interns about important policy on the treatment of disease customarily practiced on the service. He provides reasons for the policy, and outlines the steps to follow in carrying it out.

> The next patient . . . was a myocardial infarct. Wilson [assistant resident] turned to Bud [intern] at the bedside and said, "We keep them three weeks right in bed, up in the chair the early part of the fourth week, and discharged at about the fifth week." Bud said, "No kidding? Really?" Wilson said, "That's what we do here." Bud said, "What do you think of that?" Wilson remarked, "I like it. Obviously, if we're doing it here on the ward, I like it. What do you think?" Bud said, "It's so different from what I'm used to. We usually had them up at thirty-six hours. Do you have any trouble with phlebitis?" Wilson said, "We have had some, but we have to watch for it. We could do it [get them up earlier] if we had the equipment. If we had the special chairs and all that. But we don't have them. If we did, your way would be easier. Here, this way is the best."

In informing the intern about medical policy on the service, the assistant resident is tactfully careful to respect the intern's knowledge of good practice elsewhere. His job is to persuade the new man to Harvard ways, but the difference in experience between an assistant resident and an intern is not great: he himself was a new intern full of his medical knowledge only the year before.[20]

It is the assistant resident who tells the intern how to integrate sequences of medical treatment with administrative rules in order to avoid delays:

> The first patient . . . had been admitted in coma. Andrew had stayed up with her most of the night. Wilson [assistant resident] said, "I think she's coming around. When she does come around all the way, I see no need for the IV. You can start her

eating . . . When she is eating, just call the executive office and take her off the danger list. You can't discharge them right from the danger list. If it's at night, call the main desk and let them know."

Thinking ahead so that medical contingencies and hospital regulations do not conflict is one of the important things an intern must master if he is to succeed in the management of his patients.

He makes more progress toward control of his work by a process interns refer to as "running around":

Rodney said, "Let's go over to X-ray and see if we can't squeeze these pictures in." We walked across the roofs . . . and entered the basement of the building. Rodney had two requests: . . . a gall bladder and . . . a GI series. [Joe] a fellow in a lab coat, . . . asked, "Is it an emergency? Do you want the pictures right away?" Rodney said, "I'd like to get them as soon as possible, but it's not an emergency." [Joe] said, "Well, follow me, you have to put it in the book then. If it's something you want done right away or it's an emergency then either see the nurse or myself." He then led us around the corner, where two officious looking young men in white shirts with ties and dark trousers were seated with a pile of ledgers between them . . . The fellow behind the desk asked, "Is that right? Is that the way you want it done? The GI first, then the gall bladder?" Rodney said, "That's not my preference. I just want to get the pictures taken as soon as possible." The fellow behind the desk said, "Well, that's the way it's usually done. We do the GI first and then the gall bladder." . . . He began thumbing through his ledgers. He assigned the GI for [the next day. Joe] said, "Well, maybe you'll be able to get the bladder done [the day after]. Good luck." He left. The fellow behind the desk said, . . . "I don't know about the gall bladder. . . ." Rodney asked, "What about the next day, isn't it free?" The fellow thumbed through the ledger again, never letting us see the date, and said, "No, there is no way of getting her in. We are just booked solid. There is no other time before [next week]. The barium doesn't clear out that quickly anyway." Rodney shrugged his shoulders and agreed to the dates. We left, and he said, "There is a hell of a lot of running around you have to do here."

In this incident, hospital employees make clear how much work they have on hand and teach the intern their schedules and rules. By encouraging him to follow certain courses of action, they train him in what, in their view, is the proper performance of his duties.[21] In time, the intern learns to handle these attempts at control:

> "In the beginning," Bud told me, "you think you really have to do things that way and you do everything [hospital employees] tell you to. How the hell do you know what's what? But now, I think I know how to get what I want."

By understanding work which lies outside his area of responsibility but is necessary to his diagnosis and treatment of patients, he increases the possibility of controlling the sequences of his own work.

The intern masters his new situation in a relatively short time. Although he could turn to his immediate superior, the assistant resident, for all the information he needs, he accepts teaching from each group in the hospital whose work intersects with his. In coming to understand their work at first hand, he builds personal relationships which facilitate his work. For the intern, learning the ropes is a complex matter of achieving a measure of control over people and events.

DISCUSSION

At the beginning of this chapter, we asked several questions about situational learning, or learning the ropes. These were: (1) what are the ropes? (2) how are they learned? (3) do they differ from one training situation to another? (4) who teaches them? and (5) what is the relation of the structure of a training program to the process of situational learning in trainees? Perhaps we are now in a position to advance tentative answers to these questions.

It should be clear that ropes are facts about persons, places, and things which the trainee thinks relevant to mastering his situation. To learn the ropes is not only to become aware of these facts; it is also a matter of learning how to deal with them to advantage.

If we think only of the ropes which present problems to the trainee, they differ greatly from one of our training situations to another. As we have seen, it is not always made clear to the trainee who is in charge of him. If it is not, an important part of situational learning may be making a choice between two competing authorities, as in the program for nursing assistants. Similarly, sequences of study or work are not always laid down for him; the barber student has to decide for himself what to do and when. Moreover, the newcomer cannot be guided by the public goals of a program in deciding what courses of action are appropriate.

Success, as in the case of the intern, may entail the mastery of managerial skills apparently unrelated to graduate training in medicine.

In another and more abstract sense, the ropes are the same in all four training situations, but one program may be structured in a way that makes the learning of certain ropes difficult where another makes the same thing easy. In each situation, the newcomer takes the same steps. These include identifying persons and groups which affect his progress, learning what they do and what they know which may help him, and, if only by trial and error, how to interact with them properly.

Three of our studies include data which suggest that the trainee learns the ropes by making a social map of his new surroundings and relating the actions of others to his own. Although he is unlikely to formulate his ideas clearly unless action presents problems, he nevertheless defines his situation and acts on the definition. The business-machine student has a definition presented to him by the regular teacher; the barber student painfully achieves one by trial and error and observing his peers. The nursing-assistant trainee, despite his low status, sees that getting his work done has first priority, although he cannot anticipate the interruptions of staff from other parts of the hospital. Better placed in the hierarchy, the intern understands that his position permits him to search out the groups whose work affects his own in order to learn their habits and circumvent delays.

Our data indicate that teachers, books, customers, patients, bosses, subordinates, auxiliary personnel, and machines—in fact, any frequent contact—may become sources of situational learning. Moreover, we may infer that trainees are capable of considerable ingenuity in finding teachers. If their ordinary teacher is not available, they turn to peers; if peers are unavailable, they make use of client-subordinates; supplied with groups of superiors and subordinates, they tactfully exploit them all.

Perhaps we have said enough to suggest that the structure of a training program can facilitate or impede situational learning. The ingenuity of trainees further implies that they know that failure to learn the ropes may preclude learning anything else. If the intern does not learn whom to consult and how to secure his help, he will not learn what the consulting physician can teach him about medicine. If the barber student does not learn to get on with his fellows, they will not teach him to barber and, since they are a major source of substantive knowledge in the school, he may not learn much barbering.

We conclude that the ability to learn the ropes is closely related to successful negotiation of the training period. And, if there is a capacity for situational learning distinct from that for ordinary learning, as there may be, students who fail in training may fail because they have not learned the ropes—a kind of learning seldom included in the ordinary school curriculum.

Notes

1. For examples, see Donald Roy, "Quota Restriction and Goldbricking in the Machine Shop," *American Journal of Sociology*, LVII (1952), 427–442; Donald R. Cressey, ed., *The Prison: Studies in Institutional Organization and Change* (New York: Holt, Rinehart and Winston, Inc., 1961); and Erving Goffman, *Asylums: Essays on the Social Situation of Mental Patients and Other Inmates* (Garden City, N.Y.: Doubleday and Company, 1961).

2. We base our discussion on two studies presently under way: (1) a five-year study of the educational experiences of non-college youth and (2) a two-year study of medical interns. The study of non-college youth is supported by the National Institute of Mental Health (Grant No. MH09205–02) and carried on at Northwestern University under the direction of Howard S. Becker and at Syracuse University under the direction of Blanche Geer. The study of the educational experience of the medical intern is being supported by the U.S. Office of Education (Cooperative Research Contract No. OE–4–10–178) and conducted at the Florence Heller Graduate School of Brandeis University, under the direction of Stephen J. Miller. What we present here is necessarily preliminary, since full analysis of the data has not been completed.

3. See George H. Mead, *Mind, Self, and Society* (Chicago: University of Chicago Press, 1934). Edited by and with an introduction by Charles W. Morris.

4. See Everett C. Hughes, *Men and Their Work* (Glencoe, Ill.: The Free Press, 1958) and Howard S. Becker, Blanche Geer, Everett C. Hughes, and Anselm L. Strauss, *Boys in White: Student Culture in Medical School* (Chicago: University of Chicago Press, 1961). Work on a monograph dealing with undergraduates by Becker and Geer goes forward. Both studies were supported by the Carnegie Corporation and directed by Everett C. Hughes.

5. For discussion of the techniques of participant observation, see Becker *et al., op. cit.*, Chapters 2 and 3, and Blanche Geer, "First Days in the Field," in Phillip E. Hammond, ed., *Sociologists at Work* (New York: Basic Books, Inc., 1964), pp. 322–344.

6. Names of individuals, organizations, and machines have been changed throughout, except in one instance which will be apparent.

7. See Becker *et al., op. cit.*, pp. 158–184, for the problems of freshmen medical students in their efforts to determine "what the faculty wants us to know."

8. Peter L. Agnew and William R. Pasework, *Key Driven Calculator Course* (4th ed.; New Rochelle, N.Y.: South-Western Publishing Co.).

9. For discussion of this form of interaction, often called "binging," see F. L. Roethlisberger and W. J. Dickson, *Management and the Worker* (Boston: Graduate School of Business Administration, Harvard University, 1934), p. 8.

10. As the student continues his training, such a solution becomes less desirable as he must get through the legally required number of services to customers and be ready for his examination. The problem, however, is beyond the scope of this chapter.

11. See Julius A. Roth, "How Nurses' Aides Learn Their Jobs," *The American Journal of Nursing*, LXII (1962), 54–57, and his "Journal of a Tuberculosis Hospital Attendant" (University of Chicago: Committee on Human Development, 1959), mimeographed, unpublished. Although he followed experienced attendants around and learned the ropes from them, his analysis parallels ours in many respects.

12. The generally recognized system of divided authority in hospitals is the lay-professional structure. See Harvey L. Smith, "Two Lines of Authority: The Hospital's Dilemma," *The Modern Hospital*, I (1955), 59–64.

13. Freshmen medical students go through a similar, if more elaborate, process. See Becker *et al., op. cit.*, Chapters 8 and 10.

14. The presence of a staff person (teaching nurse) with authority over trainees conflicts with the authority of the floor nurses or line personnel. Each is oriented to a different set of values: the former emphasizes proper execution of procedures; the latter, the maintenance of the organization. The trainee has to resolve the problem of these conflicting expectations and demands, sometimes by covert means. See Melville Dalton, *Men Who Manage* (New York: John Wiley and Sons, 1961), Chapter 4, for elaboration of the conflict inherent in staff-line relationships.

15. For discussion of a similar relationship between janitors and their clients, see Raymond L. Gold, "In the Basement—the Apartment-Building Janitor," in Peter L. Berger, ed., *The Human Shape of Work* (New York: The Macmillan Company, 1964), pp. 11–14.

16. For discussion of the consequences of admission in cohorts, see Howard S. Becker, "Personal Change in Adult Life," *Sociometry*, XXVII (1964), 40–53; on irregular admission, see Stanton Wheeler, "The Structure of Socialization Settings," unpublished ms., 1965.

17. Stephen J. Miller is preparing a monograph on the intern's year which treats these and other topics in detail.

18. For discussion of the dominance inherent in the teaching role, see Blanche Geer, "Teaching," *International Encyclopedia of the Social Sciences*, (New York: The Macmillan Company & The Free Press, 1968).

19. This information is not needed, of course, by the several interns in the program who were at B.C.H. as students. For full discussion of the overlapping student-intern rotation, see Stephen J. Miller, "Training of a Physician," paper read at the annual meeting of the Midwest Sociological Society, 1965.

20. *Ibid.* The relationship between the intern and the assistant resident has been discussed as a bargain, the terms of which are based in an exchange of information.

21. For relevant analysis, see David Mechanic, "Sources of Power of Lower Participants," *Administrative Science Quarterly,* VII (1962), 349–364.

Part IV: Poor but Healthy?

Editors' Introduction   One of the few nearly universal values in our society is that it is better to be healthy than to be sick. Yet the opportunity to achieve and maintain health, like the opportunity to achieve and maintain wealth, is not the same at all levels of the society. Osofsky attributes the inability of the poor to participate fully in this segment of the American Dream to discrepancies in our values. Physicians share a common set of values with their middle-class patients, including the values placed on cleanliness, on a rational or scientific approach to health, on individual responsibility, on the postponement of immediate gratifications, and on conventional manners and morals. These same values, however, may not be so firmly entrenched among the poor. In his chapter, "The Walls Are Within," Osofsky suggests some of the ways in which such differing notions may affect the health and medical care of the poor. This chapter helps us better to understand the full impact of Rainwater's observation that when life is full of crises a health crisis is less likely to be seen as significant.

In his chapter, "The Lower Class: Health, Illness, and Medical Institutions," Rainwater's underlying theoretical thread is a lack of identity —a weak perception of one's "self"—among the poor. To the extent that his is a correct analysis, the appropriateness of the kinds of programs described by Haggstrom in Part II becomes manifest. Haggstrom's organizations are designed to create a feeling of self-worth—of power— among the poor. Implicit in Rainwater's chapter is the suggestion that such programs can alter the health of the poor as well as their social and economic conditions.

235

If Rainwater's description reveals the irrelevance of health and medical services from the perspective of the poor, Higgins shows us the other side of the coin. In his "Social Structure in Medicine," Higgins documents some of the ways in which the organized system for dealing with health problems may militate against the poor. It is not hard to read into Higgins' analysis the suspicion that these health services aren't for the poor. Rainwater, on the other hand, suggests that the poor aren't for those health services. With this combination of repelling forces—a rejection of poor people by the system and a rejection of the system by poor people—and with the limited alternative facilities of folk medicine, it should be no surprise that the poor are not so healthy as the rest of us. Local selective-service boards anywhere in the United States can probably verify this academic hypothesis.

Higgins provides us with some insight into a system. In that sense, his chapter might as well be in Part II as here. The personnel in his health agency "learn the ropes" as Geer and her colleagues have described that process and thus, in spite of the system, are sometimes able to adapt what Willie referred to as an "intercessor" role in behalf of those who need their services but are in danger of systematic exclusion. In "Social Structure and Medicine" we catch a glimmer of the quality of the encounters between the poor and the caretakers of health as, for example, in differences in the diagnosis of Negro and white children in the Southern county Higgins describes.

In Higgins' chapter we also have the story of an awakening—of the way in which sensitive investigators are able to break through the blinders of their "data" to a vision of the human beings and the human problems hidden behind. But it is Cassetta who confronts this issue directly. The final chapter in Part IV is an effort to assess the degree of confidence we can have in the reports of observers who participate in the observed phenomena: Cumming and his boys' gang, Deutscher and his public housing intake office, Geer *et al.* and their trade schools, Haggstrom and his organizations, Safa and her shantytown—in fact, the field method employed, with variations, by most of the contributors to this volume. If this book contained a section on methodology, then surely "Stranger in the Family" would have belonged in that section. But since the questions Cassetta deals with revolve around a study concerned with mental illness, the editors chose to include it in this section on "health."

Cassetta deals first with the knotty issue of the ethics involved in such field work relationships and then turns to the problems of the validity and reliability of participant observation data. The former section is based in large part on unpublished notes by Melvin Weiss, who was the participant observer in the schizophrenic families described and for whom the present volume is intended as a memorial. We find high-lighted here a description of a relatively uncommon form of encounter and a peculiar kind of relationship—that between the research field worker and his people. In sum, then, the middle-class agents encountered by the poor in Part IV include physicians, public health officials, other medical and paramedical personnel—and an anthropologist bent on his field work.

13 · The Walls Are Within

An exploration of barriers between middle-class physicians and poor patients

HOWARD J. OSOFSKY, M.D.

GOOD HEALTH for all members of society is a fundamental concern of American life. Since the turn of the century, medical advances in the United States have resulted in a life-expectancy increase of twenty-five years. Poliomyelitis has been virtually eradicated; tuberculosis has become less of a problem; infections have frequently been brought under control by antibiotics; hemorrhage has been treated by blood. The list could go on indefinitely.

In obstetrics, the figures concerning childbirth are most impressive. From 1930 to 1958, the number of maternal deaths per 10,000 live births decreased from 67 to 3.8.[1] Similarly, though not quite so striking, the number of infants born dead per 1,000 live births (fetal death rate) decreased from 38.1 in 1926 to 22.4 in 1952, and the number of infants dying during the first four weeks of life per 1,000 live births (neonatal death rate) decreased from 37.8 in 1925 to 19.8 in 1952.[2] The reasons for this progress are numerous; among them are blood for transfusion, antibiotics for infection, and improvement of prenatal care in general.

In the past twenty years especially, the desire both to increase life further and to decrease incapacity has led to the exploration of sociological as well as physiological aspects of patient care. Numerous studies have related death rates to socio-economic status. It has been rather conclusively shown that life expectancy at all levels can be correlated with social class. As Stockwell has demonstrated, even death from hypertension—which by stereotype has been popularly identified with executives—is in actuality more common among the lower classes.[3]

Obstetrics has been no exception to the rule. Although death rates for

239

mothers and infants have improved in all classes, the improvement in the more favored groups has been disproportionately higher than in the lower socio-economic classes. The disparity is striking when the national rates for white patients are compared with those for Negroes. The white maternal death rate per 10,000 live births decreased from 60 in 1930 to 2.6 in 1958; the Negro death rate decreased from 117 to 10.2.[4] Correspondingly, the white fetal death rate per 1,000 live births fell from 35.1 in 1926 to 19.5 in 1952 while during the same period the non-white rate fell from 73.0 to 39.8.[5] Within racial groups, too, striking differences can be shown on the basis of socio-economic class, such as in Pakter's 1958 study comparing Puerto Rican patients in Manhattan with those living in Westchester County; the Westchester County patients fared much better than those in Manhattan.[6]

With the availability of data demonstrating disparity of health on the basis of socio-economic class, studies have attempted to explore the etiology of class-related health differences. Koos has demonstrated the influence of social class upon attitudes toward medical symptoms.[7] The higher the patient's class, the more likely is he to consult a physician for a specific symptom. The lowest socio-economic class shows a marked indifference to symptoms. Simmons has further pointed out that public health precepts are based on middle-class norms and that lower-class norms may interfere with effective functioning of public health activities.[8] Middle-class norms place a high value on ability to defer gratifications in the interest of long-run goals. Simmons states that lower-class patients may not have the readiness to sacrifice the present for possible gain in the future. There may be a priority for immediate rewards. This has important implications in obstetrics, where so much of the care is of a preventive nature and where the patient is asked to defer gratification (for example, in quantitative and qualitative eating habits) for a prolonged time in order to achieve better care for both the mother and the offspring. Simmons further discusses the middle-class norm of a strong sense of individual responsibility. This contrasts with the lower socio-economic class in which the kin group is seen as being partially responsible for the patient's well-being. This, of course, could result in difficulties of patient acceptance of responsibility for medical care.

The individual's definition of health and illness has been explored by several researchers. Koos demonstrates the problem in relation to physician consultation by patients for specific symptoms.[9] Simmons,[10] Wellin,[11] and Paul [12] all refer to difficulties in eradicating disease because of folk medicine concepts which are different from those of modern scientific medicine. Kutner and Gordon point out the difficulties in getting the least-educated patients to seek medical care because of a lack of knowledge about the importance of the symptoms.[13] However, Mechanic and Volkart stress individual differences within the group.[14] They point out that individuals who have attitudes which allow them to accept medical care more easily tend to utilize medical services more often than do others with dissimilar attitudes.

The preceding paragraphs have pointed out possible effects of class and individual norms upon acceptance of medical care in general. In addition, the specifics of the doctor-patient relationship are of importance to the quality of medical care. Parsons discusses the traditional American concept of the warm and individual doctor-patient relationship.[15] The patient is expected to desire to get well and to cooperate fully with the physician. The physician is expected to be completely devoted to the welfare of his patients and to come to terms with them as individuals. He is expected to treat patients without regard to self-interest, emphasizing patient welfare at all times. The doctor-patient relationship has been further subdivided into three basic types by Szasz and Hollender.[16] The first is activity-passivity, usually characterized by the comatose patient. In this model, the patient is helpless and the physician does something to him such as a parent would to a helpless infant. The second model, which has its prototype in the parent-child relationship, is that of guidance-cooperation. Here the situation is less desperate; the physician tells the patient what to do and the patient follows instructions. The third model is that of mutual participation; its prototype is the relationship of adult to adult, with one having the specialized knowledge that the other needs. Under this scheme, which is the usual one for a medical state requiring prolonged treatment, the physician helps the patient to help himself. This model would seem most appropriate in the management of a pregnancy.

Parsons' description of the expected doctor-patient relationship,[17] while fulfilling the traditional American concept, has its pitfalls as regards the low socio-economic group of patients. In general, the marked increase in specialization and the rise of the medical-team approach to patient care have made the pattern of the individual doctor-patient relationship an increasingly difficult one to maintain. The economically poor patient has a further difficulty in building this relationship. Often care is received at a hospital or clinic. In addition to long

241

waiting times, the patient is frequently cared for by different doctors and nurses, often not even knowing their names. This fragmentation of care makes identification with the individual doctor difficult. But this in itself would not necessarily destroy the over-all image of the doctor as a dedicated individual with the sole interest of helping the patient. Of some interest, therefore, is Koos' observation that there is considerable feeling on the part of poor people that physicians do not want them as patients.[18] That the poor patient may be differentially perceived by the physician and may indeed be given less adequate care is borne out by the studies of Redlich, Hollingshead, and Bellis[19] and Myers and Schaeffer.[20] Though these studies deal with patients in a psychiatric clinic, the logical assumption is that patients receiving other types of medical care would undergo a similar experience. As Simmons states:

> It appears that the degree to which the qualities ideally defined as essential to the therapeutic relationship, namely mutual trust, respect, and cooperation, will be present in a given professional-patient relationship varies inversely with the amount of social distance. Conversely, the greater the social distance, the less likely that participants will perceive each other in terms of the ideal type roles of professional and patient, and the more likely that they will perceive each other in terms of their social class status in the larger society.[21]

Just as Parsons' description of the expected doctor-patient relationship in terms of an American ideal tends to have difficulty with patients of low status, Szasz and Hollender's description of the doctor-patient relationship in psychological terms also runs into some problems. The basic three models are unchanged, but the specific model anticipated for the situation may be altered. As mentioned, the usual middle-class doctor-patient relationship during a pregnancy would be expected to fall into the third model of mutual participation, with an adult-adult prototype. This is the relationship in which the physician and the patient usually feel most comfortable. As has been noted, however, patients of the lower social class may not have the middle-class norm of a high degree of individual responsibility. Therefore, the model which makes this patient most comfortable might be that of guidance-cooperation, with the prototype of the parent-child relationship. As Bloom points out, unless the physician can be flexible in his role, or unless the physician is willing—and able—to help the patient accept a new role, the difference in physician and patient expectations can lead to tension and difficulty in maintaining an adequate doctor-patient relationship.[22]

242

PATIENT ATTITUDES

The preceding section has reviewed some of the influence upon medical care and the doctor-patient relationship for members of low-status groups. Some factors tend to improve patient care and foster an effective doctor-patient association. At the same time, other factors may operate to hinder medical care and interfere with desired relationships. In this and the following section, these forces will be discussed in terms of specific situations. Material has been selected from interviews with patients and physicians, many of whom were participating in a project designed to learn more about pregnancy, maternal adjustments, and child care in low-income groups.

In our study is Mrs. E. M., a muscular twenty-eight-year-old white woman in her seventh pregnancy. She comes to the interview neatly but simply dressed, wearing no apparent make-up, and showing little concern for fashion. She answers questions in a direct and straightforward manner, explaining that she was referred to the clinic during her last pregnancy when her physician, a small-town general practitioner, discovered she was carrying twins and gaining an excessive amount of weight. The pregnancy had terminated successfully. Mrs. E. M. is most complimentary about the clinic, commenting that her physician had made the referral originally because he felt the doctors were specialists and could offer her better care. She shares this opinion, expressing extreme confidence in the physicians. In addition, she is pleased that a physician is always in the hospital; she believes that if an emergency should arise, a doctor familiar with her case would be available. Mrs. E. M. regards the amount of time spent waiting at the clinic as unavoidable; she reserves the entire morning for clinic when she has an appointment. What about the doctors' interest in her as an individual? Mrs. E. M. replies that she does not know the doctors well but feels that if she had questions (a situation which rarely arises) they would be glad to answer them.

Mrs. E. M. is married for the second time, her first husband having deserted her and their five children. She owns a farm, which she manages with the help of day laborers, whom she supervises. Her second husband is allergic to farm animals and cannot be of help on the farm. Because of this and because she desires an easier life, she is planning to sell the farm. She describes herself as self-reliant and thrifty. She is proud of being able to run the farm by herself and feels successful in that the farm is providing her with a living, even though the living is a

243

sparse one. She claims that she does not waste money upon herself and is not interested in "frilly things."

On the basis of income and savings, Mrs. E. M. fits the category of poor patient. Her personal goals and aspirations, however, seem to be middle class. She is oriented to the future and has the ability to work toward long-range goals, as seen in her thrift and her avoidance of "frills." Her pride in running a farm and keeping it a stable venture connotes a considerable amount of individual responsibility. Mrs. E. M.'s adjustment to the clinic appears to be good. She perceives the doctors as being helpful and interested and sees the disadvantages of the clinic as unavoidable and not as signs of lack of interest. Her relationship to the physicians lacks some of the middle-class private interpersonal depth. Yet at the same time there is considerable warmth, and a feeling is conveyed of a more adult-adult interaction than is seen with some of the other patients.

The second patient, Mrs. C. F., is a twenty-three-year-old white woman in her third pregnancy. She arrives for the interview appearing neatly groomed and fashionably, but inexpensively, dressed. She is the most poised of the five patients selected for this report, and her tone is friendly and warm throughout.

Mrs. C. F. has voluntarily referred herself to this clinic; her two previous deliveries were at another hospital clinic. She speaks glowingly of the other clinic and the care she received. However, she has been unable to pay her bill for the last delivery and is embarrassed to return with an outstanding debt. Though the clinic has not pressed for payment and she is certain she would be reaccepted for care, she feels awkward about returning at this time.

Mrs. C. F. regards waiting time at the clinic as unavoidable; private patients, she notes, also have long waits at their doctors' offices. Since this is her first visit to the clinic, she does not know her doctors well but is sure this will change after a few visits. At the other clinic she knew the doctors and felt close to them. Mrs. C. F. repeatedly mentions two doctors by name, the only patient in this study to do so. One was a resident and the other an intern, and she clearly identifies them as her doctors, discussing them much as a private patient does her physician. She adds that she had convinced her sister, a former private patient, to attend the clinic during her latest pregnancy because of the excellent care. Mrs. C. F.'s only complaint during the entire interview is related to the other patients. She feels she has little in common with them. She is particularly critical of Negro patients, saying that they dress and act inferiorly and that she feels uncomfortable spending long periods of time in the waiting room with them.

Mrs. C. F., like the first patient, has a relatively successful adjustment to the clinic. She also demonstrates, at least in part, middle-class orientations and values. Her sense of responsibility and pride, which prevents her from returning to her former clinic, allows her at the same time to relate to the physicians on a stronger footing and with more anticipation of obtaining their respect. By minimizing the class differences to herself, she is able to relate more fully to the doctors and to see them as warm, personal people. Her mobility and pride may in part explain her convincing a sister to see the clinic as an acceptable alternative to private care. Further, her unaccepting attitude toward other clinic patients may be related to a middle-class orientation. Mrs. C. F.'s concept of herself as a worthwhile patient, having much in common with clinic personnel, would make it difficult to identify with those patients whom she perceives as being less worthwhile.

Mrs. D. W., our third patient, is a twenty-nine-year-old white female receiving care for her fourth pregnancy. Her appearance is slightly untidy and her manner somewhat hostile throughout the interview. Mrs. D. W. comments freely upon the clinic, the physicians, and the other personnel, making disparaging remarks about everyone. She states that she is here only because she is on welfare and must have clinic rather than private care. She asserts that her care is bad, she has to wait long periods of time to be seen, and the physicians have no interest in her. When asked why she thinks this is so, she angrily replies, "Because I'm poor, and doctors and nurses don't like poor patients." She adds that her position is worse than that of some of the other patients because she is on welfare and physicians and nurses dislike welfare patients the most. Asked if the clinic physicians might be unaware of her welfare status, she says she is certain they are told by the nurses and that they look down upon her as a result.

Mrs. D. W. then volunteers further information about her experiences with medical care. Her six-year-old son had developed nephrosis the previous year. He had been treated at the pediatric clinic, where Mrs. D. W. was most dissatisfied with the care. The doctors, she said, looked down upon her because she had neglected the child's symptoms of lethargy, fever, and edema for a long time, believing them insignificant. She further disliked the doctors because they did not discuss the

245

case with her unless she asked questions. She felt that this was due to their disrespect toward her. Once, when an X-ray of the kidneys was ordered, she refused to allow it because she thought that no one had sufficiently explained it to her. Her husband, whom she described as never holding a job for more than a few weeks because of his bad temper, completely supported her on this and other occasions when she refused treatment because of feelings of being insulted.

Another time when Mrs. D. W.'s son had a "cold" with a cough, she brought him to the emergency room because by now she had refused further clinic care. She was kept waiting an hour for the doctor and was sure that this was related to her being on welfare. After this experience, she refused to give her child clinic or emergency-room care despite her welfare worker's urgings. Because of the renal problem, the worker finally arranged private care for the child with a physician of Mrs. D. W.'s choice. Her reaction to this was mixed. On one hand, she was pleased because she had attained her goal of private care. At the same time, she was again unhappy. The physician, by her statement, was pleasant to her. However, she felt that he looked down upon her, and as a result no longer liked him.

Economically, Mrs. D. W. easily fits into the poverty group, though her unhappiness with care could be considered a sign of mobility. Dissatisfaction with the present doctor-patient relationship and desire for more adult-adult pattern would be consistent with such mobility. However, her complete hostility to all doctors and medical personnel indicates difficulty in adjustment as playing a major role in her response. Her refusal to give her son medical care unless her terms are met, even though this might place him in jeopardy, would be opposed to middle-class mothering patterns and to middle-class values of rationality and gratification deferment. Her husband presents an additional factor in his support of her hostility and by his inability to hold a job. The patient herself presents a further problem. As has been pointed out, the American doctor-patient relationship norms include not only interest on the part of the doctor toward the patient, but also an active desire on the part of the patient to get well. The doctor working with Mrs. D. W., unless he was extremely flexible, would be apt to interpret her reactions as a lack of a desire to cooperate, and this could lead to diminished interest on his part. Even if he were to remain accepting of her, it would appear likely that her hostility might eventually result in her rejecting his offer of care.

246

Our fourth patient is Miss W. E., a neatly dressed, sixteen-year-old Negro being seen for her first pregnancy. Throughout the interview she is friendly and cooperative, obviously enjoying the talk but with a frequent tendency to giggle while answering questions. Now in her eighth month of pregnancy, Miss W. E. is generally pleased with her clinic care. She feels well and by her standards is having an uneventful and good pregnancy. She does not know the doctors but believes that they know her case well. She discusses little with them but is sure they would be glad to answer questions. Miss W. E.'s history is significant medically in that she has anemia of a familial nature. This concerns the doctors, and they have placed her on several pills. She is not worried, however, because she feels well and believes that feeling well means that she cannot be in bad health. In addition, Miss W. E. has gained forty-five pounds during the pregnancy and has been having ankle edema. The clinic physicians have prescribed a low-salt, low-calorie diet, which she has been unable to follow. They are now considering hospitalizing her, although this has been deferred for one week. Miss W. E. objects to the hospitalization, saying that the physicians are good doctors and interested in helping her but that they do not understand her and her needs. She is always hungry, she explains, and when a person is hungry she should eat because it means that her body needs food. She adds she enjoys eating a large amount and always has eaten more than other people. However, she plans to go on a diet in four weeks, when she will be two weeks from term. A girlfriend told her that such diets were effective, and she feels that she cannot diet for more than two weeks. If she dieted now, she would gain the weight back before the end of her pregnancy.

Miss W. E. is not worried about having or raising a baby. She is one of sixteen children and is very familiar with child care. As a matter of fact, her mother is again pregnant and will be attending this clinic. Miss W. E. is somewhat apprehensive over this, fearing that her friends may laugh at mother and daughter attending the clinic together. Her major concern, though, is with the Welfare Department. To continue receiving welfare, she must leave home and have an apartment of her own. This displeases her because she enjoys living with her family. However, in some ways it will be fun to have her own place, one in which things will be hers and in which she will be in charge. She hopes that the Welfare Department will find her an apartment near her mother's; one is available and her welfare worker is going to try to hold it until her delivery, even though this is unusual. Such an arrangement would make Miss W. E. happy because she enjoys being with her family and, in addition, if she has any questions about care of the child or the apartment, her mother could answer them.

Miss W. E., more than the other patients, presents some of the classical problems that arise in attempting to provide medical care for the low-status patient. Her concepts of illness are different from those of the higher-status person. She does not consider anemia, excessive weight gain, and ankle edema as significant problems since she has no symptoms which can be classified as disease by her standards. Such reactions certainly are consistent with Koos' findings concerning the meaning of symptoms to patients on the basis of social status.[23] Miss W. E.'s reaction to the weight gain is also opposed to middle-class values. Her inability to diet in order to gain less weight, have a safer pregnancy, and even to avoid hospitalization suggests difficulty in deferring gratification for long-range benefits. Her reliance upon the kin group for support and responsibility in the care of her child again suggests lower social-group norms. Her evaluation of the "good" doctor and her desires in a doctor-patient relationship strongly fit the guidance-cooperation pattern with the parent-child prototype. There is even a suggestion of an activity-passivity relationship, with the physicians thinking of placing her in the hospital and her resignation in awaiting their decision.

The fifth and final patient is Mrs. D. R., a thirty-seven-year-old Negro in her sixteenth pregnancy. She is a heavy woman, sloppy in appearance, with several teeth visibly absent.. When asked if she will answer a few questions, she replies that she will be glad to, but does not know of what use she can be. She does not believe in doctors. She believes in God. God heals; doctors cannot. She feels sorry for doctors. They mean well and spend much time with patients, but they cannot be of any help. Only God can cure illness.

Holding these feelings, Mrs. D. R. comes to the clinic because the law requires it. The doctors are good to her and she goes along with their requests, letting them draw blood and doing any desired tests. However, she takes none of the clinic medicines, believing only in herbs; she has gone through fifteen pregnancies safely this way so it must be all right. When asked about the doctors' attitudes toward this, she states that they do not like her because she is a Negro. She knows that I did not like her either. White people do not like Negroes. But she loves all people, including white people, because God says to love everyone. All people are God's children, regardless of color, and love is the most important thing in life.

Mrs. D. R. was born in the South, one of thirteen children. She had come north to this city for a brief period in 1945, and she and her husband have returned because he has a job here. She does not like the city because it has grown so. People seem less friendly. No one loves anyone, and she misses the South.

This patient easily fits into a low-status-group classification. Mrs. D. R.'s sloppy manner of dress and her apparent lack of concern with hygiene are inconsistent with middle-class norms which stress cleanliness to almost compulsive extremes. Her attitudes toward the value of medications, physicians, and medical care in general are opposed to the middle-class emphasis upon rationality, including awareness of and acceptance of scientific advances. Mrs. D. R.'s notion that the doctors see her as inferior because of her race appears unrelated to specific events in the clinic setting. Rather, it is more likely related to her concepts of white middle-class society in general, with her viewing the doctor as a member of this society rather than as a helpful, objective person. Of special importance, this patient demonstrates a problem often cited in discussions of medical difficulties in underdeveloped countries, but which would apply to certain low-status groups in this country as well. This problem is the reliance upon folk medicine and the rejection of scientific medicine as being of no value. In general, then, Mrs. D. R.'s beliefs and attitudes contribute to maintaining a gulf which considerably decreases the stability of the doctor-patient relationship and diminishes the effectiveness of medical care in general.

PHYSICIAN ATTITUDES

The preceding section described certain attitudes of low-status patients and their effects upon medical care and the doctor-patient relationship. This relationship, however, is not a one-way street. Just as patients, by their attitudes and expectations, affect physicians and the roles which they assume, so do doctors, by virtue of their feelings and desires, affect both the quality of care and the patient's perception of that care. An indication of the factors consciously or unconsciously put into play by physicians is given in the following discussions with two doctors, one a resident in Obstetrics and Gynecology and the other a general practitioner in the community. The two were chosen not because they necessarily personify all physicians but because their attitudes reflect some of the feelings which can influence the relationship between poor patients and their doctors. In addition, the difference in stage of professional development between the two physicians provides some basis for comparison.

Dr. C. A., a somewhat quiet individual, is a first-year resident in Obstetrics and Gynecology. His training consists of medical school and one year of internship in a general community hospital. His future training will include a three-year residency in Obstetrics and Gynecology before entering private practice.

At the time of the interview, Dr. C. A. is in the doctors' lounge waiting for a clinic patient to go into active labor. After discussing the mother-child relationship in clinic patients, the conversation turns to Dr. C. A.'s attitudes toward clinic and private patients, toward poor patients and wealthier patients. His first response is that he has never thought much about differences between clinic and private patients; he is not sure that he reacts differently to them. After thinking a bit, he notes that there are differences in his feelings toward patients but he is not certain that they are on the basis of poverty. For example, he reacts differently to the patients of some doctors because they reflect the doctor's temperament. He prefers calm, relaxed patients to those who are tense or anxious, and feels that certain physicians encourage their patients to be relaxed. However, he sees this as more a personality than an economic trait. In addition, Dr. C. A. prefers patients who are neatly dressed and who are clean; patients disheveled in appearance are not so pleasant to be around, and, he believes, generally have more difficult labors. He feels that untidiness is often related to lack of inner stability, and has the impression that these patients might be less cooperative, more demanding, and difficult to treat. Such patients, however, cannot be distinguished by social class alone. Though a higher proportion of clinic patients fit into this category, one also encounters a number of private patients who are unclean and uncooperative.

Are there any differences in Dr. C. A.'s reactions to patients when he makes rounds? Yes, he thinks he enjoys talking with private patients more than with ward patients. This is probably related to the higher educational and social level of the private patients; he has more in common with them. But this does not mean that he dislikes caring for ward patients. As a matter of fact, he enjoys caring for them more than for private cases. Although one day he will be in private practice, at this time the clinic patients are his practice. He feels more vitally involved with their care and considers himself to be their private physician. In Dr. C. A.'s hospital experience, would a welfare patient be kept waiting longer than a private patient in the emergency room—and would she be looked down upon for being on welfare? He thought this extremely unlikely. First of all, the residents would not know that a patient is on welfare when they are called to see her. In addition, if there were a choice, the resident would probably see the welfare patient first, since she is his patient and he will be responsible for her care. Thus, her case would be the more exciting and interesting one to him.

Dr. C. A.'s comments are of some pertinence, not because they reflect the attitude of all residents, but because they bring into focus some of the factors which influence the doctor-patient relationship. Obviously, Dr. C. A. holds value judgments concerning the types of patients who make him most comfortable and with whom he enjoys working. As he points out, these judgments are not on the basis of social class alone; he finds wealthy as well as poor patients with objectionable traits. Further, Dr. C. A. rates patients on the basis of the doctor they choose, believing that there is some relationship between the doctor's attitudes and those of his patients. However, the traits he finds most objectionable would be in part related to social status. While cleanliness and neat dressing are not alien to lower-class patients, extreme cleanliness is usually considered a middle-class trait, while a more casual attitude toward soap and water is associated with lower-status people. So, too, what Dr. C. A. refers to as inner stability might well be equated with rationality and individual responsibility, both middle-class norms.

These comments are not meant to imply that the care which Dr. C. A. offers low-status patients is of inferior quality. He states that he in some ways prefers the ward patient, who represents "his" patient. In part this may be related to his accepted professional status of clinic doctor and in part to his self-image of the doctor-in-training rather than the doctor-in-practice. To the extent that Dr. C. A. is able to see low-status patients as his patients, and to the extent that he can picture himself as their doctor with the inherent traditional concepts of professional responsibility, he would appear to offer adequate care. However, it is at least possible that his middle-class orientation to cleanliness and rationality and his greater comfort with the better-educated and more mobile patients might result in real barriers to a completely effective doctor-patient relationship with many low-status patients. Though such barriers might not be apparent to him, his attitudes could conceivably affect the role he presents to patients and the relationship which he develops with them.

The second physician in this study is a doctor in private practice. Dr. J. H. is a general practitioner in his mid-thirties, highly respected in his community and with a large and busy practice. His outgoing manner gives an impression of self-confidence and enthusiasm.

This physician lives in a medium-sized city. Because his community has no medical school, there are few clinics or residents to give ward care. Poor patients, including those on welfare, are usually seen by private physicians, and Dr. J. H. has cared for a considerable number throughout his years in practice. Despite this, he finds it difficult to assess his own attitudes toward poor patients, partly because it is hard to admit to oneself that a physician might react to patients differently because of their socio-economic status. We all have the concept, he states, that doctors should be humanitarians who want to cure the sick and help all patients. There should be no difference in one's attitude toward a patient because of poverty or education or even cleanliness. But this is being very idealistic. He knows that he does not react to all patients in the same way and, on the whole, he does not enjoy taking care of the poor patients as much as the others.

When Dr. J. H. first went out into practice, a considerable number of his patients were poor. Many of the established physicians in town discouraged welfare patients, and so the Welfare Department often sent patients to new physicians who needed the money. Dr. J. H. did not like these patients; he felt they understood that they were seeing him because he was newly in practice. In addition, they were often inconsiderate and more demanding than private patients, calling more frequently and not being concerned with the hour of the call. They often arrived in the office unkempt and unwashed. They tended to be noisy and rude, and he found it difficult to enjoy caring for them.

As time went on, Dr. J. H.'s practice grew considerably. His income rose sharply. He bought a lovely home in a desirable neighborhood, and his friends and acquaintances began to include more high-status individuals. The character of his practice also changed. His reputation in the community had grown, he was respected as a young, bright physician, and people of the class with whom he socialized now became his patients. At this point he began to notice further changes in his attitudes. He increasingly resented caring for the welfare patients. He at first explained this to himself by saying that they were noisy, abusive, and dirty, and that the nicer patients resented having to sit with them in the waiting room. But he now felt that this was not the only answer. It was evident that "nice" patients did not seem to be leaving him for other doctors. If anything, the prestige part of his practice kept growing. He knew, therefore, that his changing attitudes were related not only to patients' feelings, but to his own as well. What had happened, he thought, was that he had changed. He had become more affluent, had increased his standard of living, and had moved up considerably on the social scale. And just as he enjoyed socializing with high-status people after office hours because of more common interests, he enjoyed spending his professional hours with them. At first, this insight had upset him—it was not right, he should not feel this way. His professional feelings should be separate from social feelings. But then he wondered if his feelings might not be natural; as you move up the status scale you enjoy having your practice reflect your social life and prefer spending time with a teacher or an executive more than with an unwashed drunk.

Despite these attitudes, Dr. J. H. still sees many poor patients, though he feels that he spends less time with them than with other patients. In addition, he tries to schedule their appointments in blocks during less busy times, a practice that does not work out well since patients know that they may come at any time if they are acutely ill. He adds that his feelings are not on the basis of poverty alone, and gives an analogy of the medical student as a patient. The student might be poor and on welfare, but one would enjoy spending time with him because he is intelligent, of a higher class, and quite different from the drunk on welfare who is brought in with vomitus on his clothes. His own attitude, Dr. J. H. believes, is more accepting than that of many physicians. Some successful doctors no longer see welfare patients; others see them very superficially to make the fee. At least he tries to give them good care even if he does not feel so warm toward them as toward other patients.

As can be seen, Dr. J. H.'s attitudes parallel those of the resident in some areas but are considerably divergent in others. Part of the difference may be related to the variance in their professional and social status, while part may be due to individual differences. Yet, even though Dr. J. H. does not represent all physicians (just as Dr. C. A. does not represent all residents), he does illustrate some of the problems which threaten the relationship between the low-status patient and the doctor.

Interestingly enough, Dr. J. H. is concerned over the disparity between what he thinks he should feel and what he actually does feel. He recognizes emotionally the concept of the doctor who is devoted to the care of all patients and whose only interest is to make the patient well. Yet, while he feels that this is the ideal doctor role, he recognizes that he cannot fulfill it. Rather, Dr. J. H. exemplifies a concept discussed earlier: as the sociological distance between doctor and patient increases, the parties are less likely to perceive each other in terms of the ideal doctor-patient role and more likely to see each other in terms of social class. As Dr. J. H. notes, the further he progresses in social status, the more he dislikes working with low-status patients, partly because he sees them as threatening to his rising social status and partly because he views patients in a new light. These patients are not just sick people whom he would treat selflessly. In addition, they are individuals with whom he can maintain a pleasurable interpersonal relationship. With this change in concept, the low-status patient becomes a less desirable patient.

It is important to note that in spite of Dr. J. H.'s changing attitudes, he continues to see many poor patients and attempts to give them good care. At the same time, one may wonder if the low-status patient in his practice fully receives the care Dr. J. H. is trying to give. Some may realize that an attempt is being made to confine their visits to certain hours, an indication that they are less valued patients. Even if such a perception is not made, this doctor states that he feels differently toward low-status patients. Is it not possible that he treats them differently? He admittedly spends less time with these patients, and this could affect the care received. In addition to the quantity of time spent, the quality of the time might well be different, such as in talking *to,* rather than *with,* the patient. Thus he could be encouraging less of an adult-adult relationship and more of a guidance-cooperation relationship. Though this may be an easier role for the low-status patient to fulfill, it is not necessarily the most meaningful.

SUMMARY

Though this century has witnessed much progress in medicine, with both life expectancy and the state of health during life being considerably improved, a disparity has been noted in the benefits achieved by patients of different social classes. Quite simply, the state of health of the low-status patient is inferior to that of the higher-status patient.

This chapter focuses on the medical care received by low-status patients and the relationship of such patients to their physicians. Our goal is to explore some of the forces which either promote or hinder effective medical care within this group. Though the illustrative patient and doctor interviews are drawn from obstetrics, it is likely that similarities extend to other medical specialties.

In this small sample, the selected patients demonstrate a variety of adjustment patterns. Certainly the degree of successful adjustment is not related to poverty alone. However, if one considers low social status rather than poverty as the criterion, there appears to be a less successful patient adjustment. Though there are considerable individual differences, one does see less importance given to symptoms, less stress upon extreme cleanliness, less ability to defer gratification in the interest of long-range goals, and less individual responsibility. All of these are contrary to middle-class norms. Of more importance, all of these actions and attitudes tend to interfere with ideal patient care, especially if the doctor is not extremely flexible and accepting.

The two doctors selected for this study differ from each other and undoubtedly do not represent all doctors in their attitudes. However, we do find similarities which may apply to a larger group of physicians. One sees an unfavorable judgment of and a difficulty in relating to low-status patients. Once again, poverty alone is not the criterion. Rather, traits associated with low-status groups appear to result in discomfort for the physicians. This may well be related to the physicians' expectations both as doctors and as members of a higher-status group.

A troubling question raised by this study is: How do patient and physician attitudes actually affect the doctor-patient relationship and medical care? It appears that the low-status patient, because of certain attitudes, has a lesser chance of obtaining optimal care. This is related to such traits of giving less importance to symptoms, being less willing to sacrifice the present for future gain, and showing less individual responsibility. Even flexible physicians would have difficulty with these areas. To make matters worse, physicians may not be flexible and able to adjust to patient norms. In addition, the low-status patient sees the physician not only as a doctor but as a member of a higher-status group. This often suggests less physician interest and also makes the patient more apprehensive in relating to the physician. Similarly, the physician sees the patient not only as a patient but as a member of a low-status group. It appears that this can make the physician less understanding of and less interested in the patient. Though the picture is obviously complex, one fact emerges. The low-status patient is less likely to have as meaningful a doctor-patient relationship and as good over-all medical care as is his higher-status brother.

Notes

1. N. J. Eastman and L. M. Hellman, eds., *Williams Obstetrics* (12th ed.; New York: Appleton-Century-Crofts, Inc., 1961), p. 3.

2. R. E. L. Nesbitt, Jr., *Perinatal Loss in Modern Obstetrics* (Philadelphia: F. A. Davis Co., 1957), p. 14.

3. Edward G. Stockwell, "A Critical Examination of the Relationship between Socioeconomic Status and Mortality," *American Journal of Public Health,* LIII (1963), 956–964.

4. Eastman and Hellman, *op. cit.,* p. 3.

5. Nesbitt, *op. cit.,* p. 92.

6. Jean Pakter *et al.,* "Out-of-Wedlock Births in New York City. I. Sociologic Aspects," *American Journal of Public Health,* LI (1961), 683–696.

7. Earl L. Koos, *The Health of Regionville* (New York: Columbia University Press, 1954).

8. Ozzie G. Simmons, "Implications of Social Class for Public Health," *Human Organization,* XVI (1957), 7–10.

9. Koos, *op. cit.*

10. Simmons, *op. cit.*

11. Edward Wellin, "Implications of Local Culture for Public Health," *Human Organization,* XVI (1958), 16–18.

12. Benjamin D. Paul, "Anthropological Perspectives on Medicine and Public Health," *Annals of the American Academy of Political and Social Science,* CCCXLVI (1963), 34–43.

13. B. Kutner and G. Gordon, "Seeking Care for Cancer," *Journal of Health and Human Behavior,* II (1961), 171–178.

14. D. Mechanic and E. H. Volkart, "Illness Behavior and Medical Diagnoses," *Journal of Health and Human Behavior,* I (1960), 86–91.

15. Talcott Parsons, "Social Change and Medical Organization in the United States: A Sociological Perspective," *Annals of the American Academy of Political and Social Science,* CCCXLVI (1963), 21–33.

16. Thomas S. Szasz and Marc H. Hollender, "A Contribution to the Philosophy of Medicine: The Basic Models of the Doctor-Patient Relationship," *American Medical Association Archives of Internal Medicine,* XCVII (1956), 585–592.

17. Parsons, *op. cit.*

18. Koos, *op. cit.*

19. F. C. Redlich, A. B. Hollingshead, and E. Bellis, "Social Class Differences in Attitudes Toward Psychiatry," *American Journal of Orthopsychiatry,* XXV (1955), 60–70.

20. J. K. Myers and L. Schaeffer, "Social Stratification and Psychiatric Practice: A Study of an Out-Patient Clinic," *American Sociological Review,* XIX (1954), 307–310.

21. Simmons, *op. cit.,* p. 9.

22. Samuel W. Bloom, *The Doctor and His Patient: A Sociological Interpretation* (New York: Russell Sage Foundation, 1963).

23. Koos, *op. cit.*

14 · The Lower Class

Health, illness, and medical institutions

LEE RAINWATER

OUR CONCERN is with ways in which the characteristics of lower-class persons influence their behavior in connection with the issues of health, illness, and the utilization of medical services. The group characterized below constitutes some 25 to 30 per cent of the population of the country. It includes that segment of the society usually referred to by the term "lower lower-class" or "lower working-class" (some 15 per cent of the population) and a portion of the stable working class just superior to them in social status. A considerable body of research suggests that this group at the bottom of the social-status, occupational, income, and educational hierarchy has certain distinctive ways of looking at the world and of relating to it, as well as distinctive problems of adaptation to the world. Inevitably, these distinctive world views and modes of adaptation influence the ability of working-class people to take advantage of the standard services of the society, whether these be in the private or public sector.

The particular institutional activities considered in this chapter, those of medical care, represent but a very small part of the total adaptive activity of individuals. In the case of the lower class, we must at all times remain aware that lower-class ways of coping with different kinds of problems are much less subject to the elaborate systems of specialized role behavior and concomitant cultural techniques that are so characteristic of the middle class. Lower-class people find it much less easy or sensible to maintain different ways of coping and reacting to different situations and are more likely to bring to any one situation much the same approach that they bring to any other.

259

The lower-class person's experience of himself and his world is a highly distinctive one in our society. It is distinctive for its qualities of pain and suffering, hopelessness, and concentration on the deadly earnest present. It is distinctive for its problem and crisis-dominated character—as S. M. Miller has commented, "Lower class life is crisis-life constantly trying to make do with string where rope is needed." Having many problems at any one time and being constantly either going into a crisis, trying to manage during a crisis, or coming out of a crisis mean that for lower-class people any one misfortune does not stand out sharply and does not tend to call forth a focused effort at combating the misfortune. Thus, any one problem that lower-class people have (which as middle-class persons we believe should be solved immediately, if not sooner) appears to them as simply one among many fires that must be put out or controlled, or maybe just lived with.

This means that lower-class people (often with a considerable amount of realism on their side) will be inclined to slight health difficulties in the interest of attending to more pressing ones, such as seeing that there is food in the house, or seeking some kind of expressive experience which will reassure them that they are alive and in some way valid persons. The same kind of medical problem will stand out much more sharply to the middle-class person because he tends to conceive of his life as having a relatively even and gratifying tenor; his energies are quickly mobilized by anything which threatens to upset that tenor. (Studies of more stable working-class people who do not have the same chronic crisis situations suggest that the view of life as made up of a series of difficulties just barely coped with is not too far removed from their own impressions of the world they live in. While the overt character of daily life may seem quite stable, there is a constant theme of unease in stable working-class people, a constant sense that the world holds many potentialities for pushing them back into an unstable, highly punishing kind of existence.)

In the sections which follow we will take up particular aspects of the world view, belief system, and life style of the lower class. But it is important to keep in mind that behind any one particular orientation discussed is the problematic character of lower-class existence. This pervasive characteristic tends to make unreal the careful, meticulous, and solicitous attitude toward health which is held out by the health professions, and which is by and large subscribed to by the middle class and perhaps by an increasing proportion of the better-off parts of the working class. Such concerns will often seem empty and minor to lower-class people, who feel they have much more pressing troubles.

Another very general characteristic of the lower-class situation relevant to its crisis character is that these households are much more often "understaffed" than are stable working-class or middle-class households. That is, the complement of persons who normally maintain and run a household in our society, including at least a husband and wife, is much more often reduced. First off, households in which both husband and wife are present are less common in the lower class than in the middle and stable working class. For example, while in the St. Louis metropolitan area only 8 per cent of the white children under eighteen years of age do not live with both of their parents, 41 per cent of Negro children are in this position. If one looks at the census tracts inhabited mainly by poor Negroes, we find that well over half of the children under eighteen do not live with both of their parents. While marital dissolution among lower-class whites is perhaps not so common as it is among Negroes, it is certainly a great deal more common than in the white middle and stable working class. The understaffed households which result from this factor have many problems of coping with the normal pressures of daily living. Even when both the husband and wife are present, the typical patterns of lower-class marital relations have the result that husbands tend to be much less involved with what goes on in the home and to contribute less in the way of labor to maintain the family enterprise. Even when the household takes the form of a stem family in which there is some other relative present, our research suggests that the most frequent pattern is one in which one adult ends up having almost all of the internal family-maintenance responsibilities; the other adults see their role as either that of provider or of grown-up child who has a right to spend her time away from home engaged in activities for her own amusement.

This pattern of understaffed households in a situation of considerable family stress means that each individual's health receives relatively little preventive attention; when someone is sick, it is more difficult to care for him; and when the main adult is sick, she or he will be in a very poor position to care for herself properly or even to find the time to seek medical help. The attitude toward illness (even when it becomes chronic) in this kind of situation is apt to be a fairly tolerant one. People learn to live with illness, rather than use their small stock of interpersonal and psychic resources to do something about the problem.

THE LOWER CLASS AND THE BODY

In many ways lower-class people are heavily preoccupied with their bodies—a fact apparent in their heavy consumption of patent medicines, in the folk beliefs which researchers have documented as being common at this class level, and in the cultivation of various kinds of substances (alcohol, drugs) and activities (dancing, fighting) which have as one goal a heightened awareness of physical existence. Also frequently noted is that lower-class people tend to express their psychic difficulties somatically. It might be more correct to say that lower-class people do not differentiate psychic and somatic components of stress symptoms. For example, in our sample of some fifty intensively studied families, as many as one third indicated that at one time or another one member of the household had a "nervous" condition. It is usually apparent from the context that respondents are talking about some kind of undifferentiated state of unease which manifests itself both psychically, in terms of anxiety and confused feelings and cognition, and somatically, in terms of physical discomfort or other kinds of physical symptom. Considering all this, then, it would not be surprising to find lower-class people heavily preoccupied with issues of health and illness, and in a certain sense, they are. However, we know that rather seldom do lower-class people organize their lives around being ill, as in hypochondriasis; or, on a more constructive level, organize themselves instrumentally toward doing something about poor health.

Lower-class people perceive the world as a dangerous and chaotic place. This very primitive level of existential comprehension also carries with it a tendency to see the body as dangerous, or as potentially so. Thus, lower-class people seem fairly readily to think of their bodies as in some way injuring or incapacitating them. They view the body as mysterious, as not rationally understandable, and there is a tendency to relate to it in magical rather than in instrumental ways. When they talk about illness, lower-class people sometimes communicate a sense of alienation from their own bodies, a sense of distance from the illness processes going on in their bodies. They do not, like middle-class people, identify with their bodies and work toward a cure of physical difficulties in much the same way that they would work toward some lack in knowledge by discovering an appropriate solution to a problem.

This tendency to see the body as mysterious and potentially dangerous carries with it a rather poor differentiation of bodily parts and function. For example, in a study of how lower-class men and women think about the process of reproduction and about the bodily parts relevant to sexual relations, we found a rather low differentiation of the female sexual organs on the part of both men and women. A majority of lower-class respondents had very poor notions of the process of conception. This was found to be quite closely related to their inability to understand or trust chemical methods of contraception or feminine methods such as the diaphragm.

Another very general characteristic of lower-class persons is their tendency to have a low self-evaluation, to have as a chronic problem difficulties in maintaining a secure sense of self-esteem. Much lower-class behavior that appears flamboyant or deviant to middle-class people can be seen as an effort to compensate for lowered self-esteem. The reasons for this chronic lower evaluation of self are complex, involving a lifelong interaction between the symbolic communications others make and the more direct experiences of failure, punishment, and impotence that lower-class people have in striving to adapt to the harsh world in which they live. Lower-class people thus develop an attitude toward themselves characterized by a sense of being unworthy. They do not uphold the sacredness of their persons in the same way that middle-class people do. Their tendency to think of themselves as of little account is readily generalized to their bodies.

This is in sharp contrast to middle-class attitudes, which emphasize the intrinsic value and worth of the self and of the body. For the middle-class person, lowered body functioning is readily taken as an insult to both the body and the self, an insult which is intolerable and must be remedied as quickly as possible. For lower-class people, a body which does not function as it should, which has something wrong with it, simply resonates with the self that has these same characteristics. Just as lower-class people become resigned to a conception of themselves as persons who cannot function very well socially or psychologically, they become resigned if necessary to bodies that do not function very well physically. This is probably particularly likely to happen as lower-class people grow older and increasingly face a sense of failure because some of the adaptive techniques they have used to ward off a negative self-image begin to play out. Related to these interactions between self-concept and body image is a finding reported by Bernice Neugarten that lower-class people believe they become middle-aged at a much earlier chronological age than do working- and middle-class peo-

263

ple. Thus, lower-class persons are likely to accept impaired functioning in the thirties as a natural consequence of aging, whereas working- and middle-class people are less likely to see impaired functioning at this, or even later ages, as "natural." Rosenblatt and Suchman's characterization of blue-collar attitudes toward the body takes on a special significance when related to the differential notions of aging that the classes have:

> The body can be seen as simply another class of objects to be worn out but not repaired. Thus, teeth are left without dental care, and later there is often small interest in dentures, whether free or not. In any event, false teeth may be little used. Corrective eye examinations, even for those people who wear glasses, is often neglected, regardless of clinic facilities. It is as though the white-collar class thinks of the body as a machine to be preserved and kept in perfect functioning condition, whether through prosthetic devices, rehabilitation, cosmetic surgery, or perpetual treatment, whereas blue-collar groups think of the body as having a limited span of utility: to be enjoyed in youth and then to suffer with and to endure stoically with age and decrepitude. It may be that a more damaged self-image makes more acceptable a more damaged physical adjustment.[1]

The low "body esteem" which lower-class people have applies by extension to the persons under their care, including their children. Lower-class persons tend to develop rather negative images of their children as "bad" and/or "unsuccessful." This seems inevitable, given their conceptions both of themselves and of the nature of the world. The low esteem in which others are held as social beings easily extends to a minimal exercise of protectiveness and solicitude toward their physical needs and states. Thus we observe lower-class parents seemingly indifferent to all kinds of obvious physical illnesses their children have —particularly infections, sores, colds, and the like. Greater tolerance by their parents for children's physical disability or malfunctioning means that medical professionals cannot count on the parents to exercise careful observation or supervision of children's illnesses. And any program of treatment which does count on this is much more likely to fail than in the middle-class case.

The acceptance of something short of good health has implications both in terms of the care of people who are already ill and in terms of preventive medicine. Lower-class parents are much less likely to carry

264

out a consistent preventive regimen in the way the household is maintained and the children's activities controlled. The much higher accident rate among lower-class individuals, particularly children, is not only a result of the greater objective danger of their environment (more broken bottles around, more dangerous housing) but also results from the lack of consistent circumspection on the part of parents.

Low body esteem carries an important secondary gain. If one can regard one's body as in some sense not working right, then one has a legitimate extenuating circumstance for many failures to live up to one's own standards and those expressed by others. We have noted in our work with lower-class families that an enormous number of health complaints come up both in participant observations of daily living and in interviews. While these complaints are obviously related to many of the factors discussed in this chapter, one important function or consequence of the developing conception of oneself as not in tip-top physical condition is that of warding off allegations of irresponsibility or failure based on "not caring."

At the risk of unnecessarily proliferating role terms, it may be worth while to distinguish here between the "sick role," the "patient role," and the "disabled role." As used by Parsons and others, the sick role involves basically a notion of withdrawal from all normal responsibilities because of physical incapacity; the "patient role" is superimposed when the individual brings himself within the purview of healing agents. It may be true, as some researchers have suggested, that higher-status persons find it easier to accommodate themselves to these two roles, whereas lower-status persons champ at the bit to shed the sick and patient roles. However, it is also clear that lower-class people much more commonly regard themselves as in minor or major ways disabled from functioning "normally"—disabled in the sense of their physical condition not allowing them to function as fully active adults. We would suggest that the difficulties of coping with situations in such a way that self-esteem can be maintained tempts lower-class people to assume the role of the partially disabled. This assumption of the disabled role was described in its most dramatic form by Halliday in his discussions of the psychosomatic diseases of English workers during the depression. We also see it in a more moderated but chronic form in lower-class individuals, particularly women, where the connection with unemployment and the possibility of compensation is not at all in question. Once impaired functioning is defined as a "normal" state of the body and self, expectations of what one can and cannot do are greatly modified. It is possible for the individual to counter claims on the part of other individuals by pointing to his physical condition. To the extent that the disabling condition is thus defined as "normal," the individual's motivation to seek treatment is considerably lowered. Self-medication can then become a ritual which symbolizes the disabled state.

THE LOWER CLASS AND MEDICAL TREATMENT

The implications of most of what has been said so far for the kind of treatment regimen that will be maintained, and the likelihood of seeking medical treatment in the first place, are fairly obvious. Here we will simply focus the discussion on concepts of causality and initiative in connection with health and illness.

Lower-class notions of how things happen attribute a very great importance to good or bad luck—to "the way things are"—and tend to de-emphasize one's ability to affect importantly the course of future events by self-directed action. These beliefs, plus the deep commitment to self-maintenance in a difficult present, mean that lower-class people concern themselves relatively little with the long-term aspects of their problems. They do not plan for the future (how can they?), but rather live from day to day or, at most, from week to week. Such future-oriented plans as they do develop tend to be held much less tenaciously and are much more readily dropped under the impact of immediate crisis. Lower-class people tend to feel that the difficulties they encounter are the result of bad luck, rather than of failing to take proper care —indeed, the extent to which by taking proper care lower-class people can significantly affect their life chances is a very open question. The intense preoccupation with the immediate maintenance of the self in a given and difficult world makes it very difficult to take out of this system energy for planful action toward some future goal. The readiness with which lower-class people are distracted by immediate dangers or prospects for immediate gratification reduces the likelihood of their carrying out carefully tailored regimens of treatment and sharply limits preventive activities directed toward the future goal of avoiding an illness.

Health and illness, therefore, tend to be dealt with in terms of crises. That is, when the impairment of functioning becomes so great or so obvious in the immediate situation that the individual feels this problem stands out above the rest, some action is likely to be taken. Until that time, the illness problem recedes into the background as more pressing issues are dealt with. The immersion in the immediate situation also probably accounts for the difficulties lower-class people have in observing schedules of all kinds. It is difficult for them to keep appointments because something that seems more important is always going on. Clearly, any program that requires lower-class people to be as observant of highly time-bound schedules as middle-class people are capable of being is going to have only modest success.

The lower class is motivated to obtain medical care when there is a breakdown of bodily functioning such that a crisis is presented and essential activities cannot be carried out. Therefore I would generalize a bit from Rosenblatt and Suchman's statement:

> For the blue-collar workers, with their greater distance from the whole medical-care system, illness is related to dysfunction in work, primarily related to incapacitating symptoms. Symptoms which do not incapacitate are often ignored. For the white-collar groups, illness will also relate to conditions which do not incapacitate but simply by their existence call forth medical attention.[2]

In the middle class, any symptom that is obvious incapacitates because it takes away from the kind of more perfect person the middle-class individual likes to think of himself as being. The lower-class person cannot afford this conception of himself; he attends to physical symptoms, if at all, only when they pose a crisis in carrying out those activities he considers necessary.

THE LOWER CLASS AND MEDICAL INSTITUTIONS

Lower-class people tend to have mixed feelings about physicians. On the one hand, because of their involvement with their bodies as in some sense mysterious and unpredictable, they would like to be quite dependent on physicians and to have physicians behave in paternalistic, nurturant, and solicitous ways. On the other hand, the physician, representing middle-class views and a detached instrumental approach to problems, can be quite intimidating and difficult to understand.

Just as lower-class people tend to personalize all relationships, they tend to seek highly personalized relationships with physicians where this is possible. This is most likely when dealing with physicians in private practice. Women of the stable working class often develop close and trusting relationships with their private physicians, and are both heavily dependent on them and quite responsive to what the physicians tell them to do. This is less likely to be the case in the lower class. Persons here often must use public medical facilities, where it is difficult to form a relationship with one physician. In addition, the lower-class individual's distrust and uneasiness in dealing with middle-class persons often gets in the way of establishing the kind of dependent relationship he would like. Even so, despite the frequent difficulties lower- and working-class people have in paying high medical bills, we have found that seldom do women express hostility toward their own physicians as overcharging them or being unreasonable about payment.

It seems likely that the ability to form a trusting and dependent relationship with physicians increases as lower-class people grow older and feel a greater need for a nurturant figure because of increasing failure in managing themselves and their lives. In any case, even when dealing with private physicians, where the structure of the relationship allows greater personalization, it would seem that lower-class men and women have a good deal more difficulty in being really attentive to their physicians and in carrying out the regimens which the physicians prescribe.

The ability to form a close, trusting relationship with the physician is greatest in connection with the lower-class person's own medical needs. It would seem to be a great deal more difficult to develop this closeness when the patient is a child rather than the parent. The preoccupation with oneself and the touchiness that lower-class parents exhibit about somehow having failed their children make it difficult for them to sustain a relationship with a helping third party who is an authority and may make negative judgments about how one has behaved. In these situations, physicians need to be very careful that they do not alienate parents and make contact so uncomfortable that the parents cease to come back. For this reason, relationships with general physicians are much easier for lower-class people to sustain, since they count on the physician to treat both their problems and the problems of their children. Relating to pediatricians, uninterested as they are in the health needs of adults, will be much more difficult for the lower-class family.

When one shifts the focus of inquiry from the context of private practice to that of the large medical institution, the negative possibilities increase sharply. Many lower-class people are used to dealing with medical personnel only in the context of the large institution, and have had little opportunity to develop the kind of more personalized relationships that they would like to have with physicians. They are often inured to receiving poor service in low-cost or charity clinics and hospitals. They expect to have to wait long hours in order to receive medical service and to be shabbily treated by those with whom they deal. Because this is their experience and expectation, they tend to be rather docile and impassive in the face of such difficulties, but one should not be misled into thinking that these kinds of experiences have no effects. The lower-class person who must journey by public transportation for an hour to reach a public facility and then wait for several hours before receiving service is going to think two or three times before going for such service. The difficulty of receiving care serves to reinforce the tendency to seek it only when a crisis situation is reached. Clinic personnel who force patients to wait long hours in order to weed out the "poorly motivated" only deepen these tendencies.

One of the problems lower-class people have with bureaucratic organizations is that they are used to dealing with people in non-segmentalized ways. They expect a superior or someone with special knowledge to be able to cope with whatever problem is presented him, and they neither understand nor are tolerant of the great division of labor that obtains in such institutions. They want *someone,* rather than a *team,* to take care of them. It takes them quite a while to sort out the various functions represented by a team—whether this be a team of physician specialists or the nurse-physician-technician team.

While it is true that the middle class has a greater understanding of a division of labor, it should also be noted that because of their ability to purchase services they are better able to have someone inside the system represent them to the whole system. That is, middle-class people will turn to their own private physician to sort out any difficulties they have with the different specialties represented in the hospital. For the person who can afford his services, the private physician functions to moderate the impersonality of the medical division of labor. The lower-class person, in contrast, often feels he has no one person to whom he can rightfully turn with his gripes and have them listened to. In addition, middle-class people much more readily establish personalized relationships with many specialists, and can find pride and pleasure in having "my internist," "my pediatrician," "my obstetrician," and "my ophthalmologist." It takes a great deal of psycho-social energy for someone to form such relationships; lower-class people have enough trouble forming a trusting relationship with one middle-class professional, let alone several.

As many observers have noted, there are tremendous problems of

269

communication between middle-class professionals and lower-class clienteles. One of the most striking aspects of this communication is the amount of derogation and hostility that is covertly (and often overtly) expressed by the middle-class professionals. From the professionals' point of view, lower-class people are by definition "problem" people. It seems that over time professionals build up a considerable store of hostility and blaming attitudes toward such persons. The understanding that middle-class professionals develop of the peculiar characteristics of their lower-class clientele seems more often used as a way of avoiding blame for failure than of gaining insight into problems of dealing with this clientele and developing techniques that allow them to be more successful at their jobs. When lower-class people perceive the middle-class professional as blaming, derogating, or hostile toward them, they withdraw quickly into an adaptation of resentful docility, and are then much less available for any real communication or learning. While a few lower-class people develop an amazing ability to manipulate these situations toward their own ends, most simply retreat and get out of the situation as quickly as possible.

Lower-class people appear particularly prone to a sense of pervasive anxiety during hospitalization. They do not know what is going on nor on whom they can count for help. As patients, they also are likely to feel quite isolated. Their families' realistic difficulties in visiting them are often great, and the family ties may be weak enough so that, despite the best intentions, relatives just do not manage to make frequent visits. Thus hospitalization can be a painful experience for the lower-class person who spends most of his time alone in a situation in which he is frightened. There would seem to be a great need for facilities to be planned in such a way as to maximize the chance of establishing casual relationships with other patients. Also, visiting arrangements should be flexible so that when visitors do turn up, even at inopportune times from the point of view of the hospital, they can visit the patient.

The connections between class-related life-style characteristics and medical settings are illustrated by Rosengren's study of obstetric patients:

> Consider the blue-collar woman: the relative personal and social isolation in which she lives—isolated, at least, from the personal contacts and formal experiences by which one assimilates the meaning and significance of professional ministrations—the relatively minimal education she has achieved, and the life

270

milieu in which she lives, where illness, incapacitation, and the like abound; and also the very real, heightened chances that either she or her baby may encounter either insult or accident during pregnancy—all of these factors and others combine to make the pattern of high sick-role expectations among this group particularly understandable. Considering also that the blue-collar woman is likely to be cared for in a clinic setting rather than by a private doctor, it is easy to see why she might regard herself as "ill." The middle-class woman chooses her own physician—normally, on the basis of word-of-mouth advice from friends and relatives. She appears for her prenatal care in a treatment setting which has little of the symbolism of sickness—a quite "living-room-like" waiting room, perhaps occupied by a nurse without a uniform. This is in dramatic contrast to the clinic-attending woman who experiences her treatment within the confines of a hospital, with ambulances going to and fro, with uniformed nurses and interns scurrying about, sometimes in apparent anxiety, with stainless steel, tile walls, and medicinal odors intermixed with medical machinery and equipment. Not only, then, does the life milieu and its attendant contingencies conspire to move the blue-collar woman toward the enactment of the role of the sick, but so, too, does the peculiar character of her obstetric-treatment episode.[3]

The ecology of medical services can work to the disadvantage of the lower-class person. Such persons customarily organize their use of the resources of the environment in such a way that they do not have to go far to get the necessities of living. They tend to shop close at hand for food, clothing, furniture, and other items. While they do not mind going far on rare occasions for entertainment or visiting, traveling around the city is generally costly, uncomfortable, and inconvenient. This is particularly true of women who typically have several children to care for and who seem to develop a very special kind of anxiety about the outside world, particularly as they grow out of the late-adolescent and young-adult period.

In addition, there is the very real problem of the expense of traveling. Some lower-class people are so poor that even expenditures for carfare have to be carefully calculated. If emergencies seem to demand the use of taxis, there may just not be money available. For example, one woman in the housing project we are studying has a grandson with asthma. When he has attacks, she often has to spend precious time finding someone to drive her to the hospital or loan her money for cab fare. She cannot understand why the Well-Baby Clinic across the street from her building will not provide the necessary service at times like this. Again, middle-class people are often in a much better position to deal with the same problem. They have the money that allows them to travel (to own a car, call a cab, call an ambulance), and their demand for medical services is such that they are more likely to have the decentralized services of a suburban clinic or a medical office near them.

IMPLICATIONS FOR MEDICAL FACILITIES PLANNING

It seems clear that the steady growth of voluntary health insurance, as well as the increasing development of public programs such as Medicare, means that in the years to come more and more lower-class people will be asking for medical services, even though they ask for them with considerable trepidation and a certain touchiness. Voluntary health insurance seems to have permeated fairly well to the stable working-class level. For example, in 1962 a Social Research, Inc., survey in Chicago found that only 5 per cent of middle-class white and Negro families were without some form of health insurance. Figures for the stable working class were only slightly higher—11 per cent of the white and 22 per cent of the Negro upper-working-class respondents had no medical insurance. In contrast, however, a very large majority of the lower working class had no medical insurance—42 per cent of both whites and Negroes. (The peculiarities of the availability of medical facilities to Negroes in Chicago were such that even those who did have medical insurance, including Blue Cross, often could find medical service only at Cook County Hospital. The resentment thus built up because one is able to pay for but not obtain service because of color is especially strong.)

To the extent, then, that working- and lower-class families have a wage earner, it is likely that in the years to come a much higher proportion will have medical insurance and that this insurance will cover a wider range of services. We can expect that a continuation of the "war on poverty" will also extend medical services to those families where there is no wage earner or where he is not covered by health insurance. Medicare is apparently already placing heavy demands on medical facilities, and most of the new demand it is stimulating will come from working-class people. What, then, are some of the implications of lower-class attitudes in the areas of health, illness, and medical facilities for

272

designing programs and facilities that will most effectively accomplish medical goals?

At the very broadest level, one of the policy questions inevitably will be that of the relative balance of quality of service (in the abstract sense of the best possible service) and quantity of service (in the sense of the greatest number of patients treated at the least inconvenience to them). This is a constant issue in the extension of medical services of all kinds to less fortunate segments of a population. In family-planning policy, for example, there is a continuing debate over the extent to which one prescribes for lower-class populations the best possible contraceptive methods, even knowing that these methods (such as the diaphragm) are ones that lower-class people are most likely to have difficulty with, versus a strategy which argues for methods that have lower effectiveness in ideal circumstances but are much more likely to be used by lower-class populations.

In connection with medical services, the issue is likely to take the form of relative emphasis on centralization versus decentralization of medical facilities. One may argue that the greater the centralization, the better the medical services, because of (1) the greater availability of high-cost equipment and highly specialized personnel, and (2) the possibility of shifting rapidly from one treatment situation to another. All of the above discussion would suggest, however, that the more centralized medical facilities are, the less readily will lower-class people use them. Similarly, the more lower-class people have to deal with highly specialized personnel who take responsibility for only one aspect of treatment, the less likely they are to tolerate the treatment regimen or to learn what they must learn in it.

I believe that these considerations argue for the maximum possible decentralization of medical facilities and the expansion of subprofessional health personnel who can take over some of the more personalized functions that are lost in the highly specialized training which physicians and nurses now receive. One is likely to get furthest by letting physicians and nurses function as highly impersonal, specialized professionals while building around them a group of subprofessionals who can take care of the psycho-social needs that patients bring into the situation. (It does not seem very likely that we will ever succeed on a large scale in getting physicians or nurses to relate in highly personalized ways to lower-class people.) Subprofessionals could have another important function in preventive programs in that they could be

273

trained to pay attention to symptoms and conditions that are likely to have repercussions on the health of lower-class adults and children. These workers thus could serve an "intelligence" function which lower-class people are less likely to be able to perform for themselves.

In the location of medical facilities, it would seem useful to encourage decentralization and to sacrifice some of the "quality" that is presumed to come from the development of large complexes of medical institutions. This decentralization could take place in several ways. First, out-patient facilities should be spread throughout the city as widely as finances permit. Each facility should have the assigned function of doing preventive work and instituting treatment as early as possible when prevention fails. It would probably be useful to err on the side of attempting to handle on an out-patient level many conditions for which "best medical practice" normally requires hospitalization. In this way, the hospital itself would treat only those individuals who absolutely could not be sustained in their own homes. (Obviously, this strategy will require some reorganization of health insurance plans, since the current effect of many plans is to encourage hospitalization when it is not necessary in order that the illness be covered.) A comparison which comes to mind is that of the military organization of medical care. Because the military must take responsibility for the health of its personnel across the board, an elaborate hierarchy of medical facilities has grown up. Patients may move from the company aid station through successively better-equipped out-patient facilities to the field hospital and on to a few major medical institutions where the rare but more demanding kinds of treatment can be carried out. To be sure, city boards of health often operate many different kinds of clinics to provide services for underprivileged families. However, these clinics tend to be organized around a specialized function (maternal health, well-baby clinics, mental health clinics). A better plan would have them organized around the populations served, so that a clinic has the initial medical responsibility for a population in a given small area and can carry through that responsibility as patients are referred on to higher levels.

Planning for medical facilities for a lower- and working-class population will also need to take into account the rather different age pyramid of the lower class. The lower class is more heavily populated by children than is any of the other classes. This means that medical facilities serving the health problems of this group should be directed more toward children than is now the case. From all that has been said about

274

lower-class family life, it is clear that we cannot count on these parents to exercise the same close surveillance of their children's health needs that middle-class parents can be counted on to provide. And to a certain extent this is even true of the more stable working-class parents, who tend to be oriented to problems of incapacity rather than simply of ill health. This suggests that there is a greater need for more direct intervention in the health of children, both to deal with the health problems of any one time and also to work toward preventive goals. To a certain extent, medical professionals and subprofessionals will have to take over some of the responsibilities which parents are not able to carry out.

The school as a place where the great bulk of children are physically present several days a week becomes the most obvious focus for providing for the health needs of children. A much more active commitment needs to be made to the provisions of health services through the school. This has been, of course, one of the traditional avenues of preventive public health programs, but I have in mind a more active treatment orientation. There is no reason why the decentralized health services referred to above should not be located in or adjacent to schools, with the staff of schools given the responsibility for referring children to the facilities whenever there seems reason for this. It is simply ridiculous for parents to have to take children to a different place for health services when the children collect in the schools every day. If the Head Start programs, now recommended as a way of coping with the intellectual problems of lower-class children, are permanently established, it is very likely that schools will have most children from the ages of three to sixteen. In general, then, since schools are the one universal neighborhood institution in all parts of the country, they would seem an important focus for medical facility planning, just as they should become an important focus for all kinds of "war on poverty" planning that has to do with children. Some European countries, notably Denmark, have this kind of integration of educational and medical facilities for children, and an investigation of how these programs operate might be useful in our planning.

I have suggested that one solution to the hospital's problem of how to deal with increasing numbers of lower-class patients is that there should be facilities which minimize the number of such patients who ever appear at the hospital doors. However, there will undoubtedly be increasing numbers of such patients who do require hospitalization, and the way hospitals are organized must take this into account. For many reasons, it would seem worthwhile to minimize the traditional hospital atmosphere in facilities designed for increasing numbers of lower-class patients. (There are equally good reasons for doing this for middle-class patients as well.) A very hard look should be taken at the question of what proportion of hospital patients actually require the traditional hospital room. It seems likely that a rather high number of patients could be accommodated in a more hotel-like atmosphere in which their rooms would seem more like ordinary dwelling places, in which meals are taken in dining halls rather than in the room, in which it is possible to spend time in recreation rooms, socializing, watching television, and so on. A serious examination of this question would range all the way from determining the extent to which hospital design is presently dominated by an image of the typical patient as a surgical patient to a careful look at alternative designs of both hospital buildings and hospital furniture.

Finally, the subprofessional probably has a function in the hospital just as he does in out-patient clinics and in home visiting. I cannot say who these subprofessionals ought to be or exactly what they ought to do, but it seems to me that there would be a gain from having persons in the hospital to assist the lower-class patient in his multiple relations with specialized personnel much as the private physician functions for the middle-class patient. Such a person could take on responsibilities for interpreting hospital procedures and treatment regimens to the patient and to his family and also for coping with interpersonal problems that develop during the course of hospitalization. He would function as a liaison between the patient, his family and relatives, and hospital personnel. His role would be a central rather than a peripheral one, as seems presently to be the case with hospital social workers.

There are, of course, many things we do not know about how lower-class people take care of their health needs and, in particular, about how their coping behavior will change under arrangements which lift the heavy economic burden medical care now represents. This is but one example of a pervasive difficulty in understanding lower-class behavior. When one seeks to study lower-class peoples and their worlds, one is confronted with a complexly interwoven fabric of immediate situational responses, personal adaptations to life experiences, and an oral cultural tradition which represents the accumulation of generations of learning how to make out in a tough world.

276

Purposive social change operates on the situational factors of economic status, educational opportunities, possibilities for community participation, and the like. As these factors change, we expect individuals to change, to make new adaptations to new and more satisfying situations. But we know little about how lower-class individuals change as their world changes, about how to facilitate more rapid awareness of new possibilities, or about how to avoid untoward responses to such change. How could we, since our society has yet to make a major and permanent commitment to providing the needed opportunities and resources? If in the years ahead the nation does finally make such a commitment, the demands on health professionals (and social scientists) for rapid modification of their views, understandings, and procedures will be great, if the opportunity for increased understanding is not to be missed.

Notes

NOTE: This chapter is based in part on research supported by the National Institute of Mental Health Grant No. MH–09189, "Social and Community Problems in Public Housing Areas." The ideas presented have been influenced by discussions with the senior members of the research staff—Alvin W. Gouldner, David J. Pittman, and Jules Henry. The chapter was originally written as a background paper for a study of medical-facilities planning conducted by Anselm L. Strauss for the Institute of Policy Studies.

1. Daniel Rosenblatt and Edward A. Suchman, "The Underutilization of Medical-Care Services by Blue-Collarites," in Arthur B. Shostak and William Gomberg, eds., *Blue-Collar World: Studies of the American Worker* (Englewood Cliffs, N.J.: Prentice-Hall, Inc., 1964), p. 344. © 1964 by Prentice-Hall, Inc., Englewood Cliffs, N.J. This and subsequent quotations reprinted by permission.

2. *Ibid.*, pp. 344–345.

3. William R. Rosengren, "Social Class and Becoming 'Ill,'" in Shostak and Gomberg, *op. cit.*, pp. 338–339.

15 · Two Thirds of a Medical Equation

Pathology and patients

A. C. HIGGINS

ANALYTICALLY AT LEAST, sociologists acknowledge that the institutional arrangement which provides medical care to the poor is composed of three elements: physicians, patients, and the system interrelating physicians and patients.[1] Yet, judgmentally, it would seem that sociologists have used the patient's attitudes or some specific patient characteristics as the major independent variable predicting failure in the medical-patient system.

Implicit in the phrase "the culture of poverty" appears to be an ethnocentric evaluation that somehow the people of poverty are so different and so incomprehensible that the medical profession cannot deal with the poor effectively. If nothing else, the phrase "culture of poverty" seems to be a substitute for adequate description.

Rosenblatt and Suchman, for a recent example, suggest that the poor have their own concepts of disease and illness which differ from those of the middle class and, apparently, the middle-class physician. Similarly, these authors suggest that blue-collar workers are more skeptical of medical care, more dependent when ill, have greater difficulty in internalizing the sick role, and are less informed about illness.[2]

Coe and Wessen, reviewing the literature on the psychology of patients' use of facilities, suggest that response to illness varies with "age, sex, race, and ethnicity," and the "respondents who resisted or delayed seeing a physician tended to be more parochial, highly skeptical of the medical profession, and most often turned to their own ethnic group for advice and counsel."[3]

Quite simply, it seems to me that sociologists have spent a great deal of time and effort researching the poor and not enough time trying to understand the complex institution that is medical service. Sociologists, for reasons to which Straus[4] may well have alluded, have chosen to focus attention on the patient to the serious detriment of the systematic analysis which ought to concern sociology. Rather than study the system, sociologists have chosen one element within the system. Their choice has been a bad one, for the forces which determine patients' responses may be, and probably are, results of the system of providing care. That patient characteristics are found to be relevant in patients' care-seeking may relate to their correct perceptions of physicians and of medicine in general. In any case, studies of the institutional patterns are necessary before appraisal of patient-oriented studies can be made.

The facts that medicine does have a structure and that physicians do function in ways which are relevant for that structure seem to be underemphasized in the literature. The present chapter, therefore, focuses not on the poor patient but on the structure of providing care. The materials are illustrative of the ways in which one study came to reappraise patients in terms of medicine in one community. It is, in fact, a short history of what happened in one epidemiological study which began by focusing on patients and learned, rather slowly, that the way to understand patients was to understand the community, and particularly the subcommunity of professional care.

The sociological view that social structure has consequences on function is the point of departure for this analysis. In attributing consequences to structure, it should be understood that the issue of "blame" becomes unimportant. What is important is that everyone understand the influence of structure lest its influence be ascribed to the "uncooperative" poor. Misleading ascription of causality is not a useful way to approach a solution to a problem. Further, such a non-judgmental approach avoids the rancor which, Straus insists, derives from studies of the sociology of medicine.[5]

The materials which follow are used to illustrate the significance of medical structure. They are drawn from field work completed in Alamance County, North Carolina, and reported elsewhere.[6] These illustrations provide, hopefully, clear examples of the ways in which medical organization creates problems for its patients. By knowing what to look for, physicians as administrators may be able to make meaningful changes in the organization of medical care.

THE FIELD WORK IN ALAMANCE COUNTY

Alamance County is a community of about 90,000 in the central Piedmont of North Carolina. From 1961 through 1964, the county, and especially its major city, Burlington, was the locus of an intensive investigation of community needs and community services for handicapped children. The study of Alamance County began as straightforward, epidemiological study—survey of morbidity in persons under twenty-one years of age. At the end, the final report still contained those hallmarks of epidemiology, statistics, and more statistics, but the emphasis had changed considerably.

During the years of the study, the staff became aware of the context within which morbidity comes to be. The most exciting feature of the Alamance efforts was the gradual recognition by the study staff that the data on morbidity were not simple. For example, no medical records of orthodontic difficulties among Negro children were found. Either Negro children actually had no orthodontic problems or differential diagnoses and treatment were being offered to Negro children by the medical agencies of the community. Orthodontic problems being as frequently encountered as they are, the latter explanation seemed more reasonable: the agents working within the medical complexes of Alamance County were differentially defining problems of children. Interest therefore came to be centered not on the children but on the community itself. What kind of community was it that permitted differentials in service and diagnoses to exist? Further, to what factors within the community and within the medical agencies might these differentials be related?

What was exciting was that we were rediscovering the community by examining the records of health agencies and learning how these agencies operated. It became clear that making sense out of the data could be done only in the context of a subcommunity: each agency was understandable not only in terms of the social structure which was uniquely its own but also vis à vis the community. No longer was the staff focused on morbidity itself, but on morbidity as it came to be defined by agents acting within a community structure.

Interviews provided the first clues as to how structure affected function: complaints from parents had been heard in the upper echelons of medical administration concerning the treatment afforded multiply handicapped children. Tragic cases of disabled children, the deaf and

281

blind, were systematically being denied service. The medical-bureaucratic structure of the state had developed in a way which was apparently logical but which excluded the multiply handicapped.

The state system was established in terms of disease entities. Services were provided in terms of specific conditions. Children who were blind went to the school for the blind, and children who were deaf, to the school for the deaf. The child who was blind and deaf could not be admitted to the school for the blind because he was deaf. He could not be admitted to the school for the deaf because he was blind. Neither school could be "blamed" for its refusal to help, for each had to work within difficult enough limitations. Neither school could be expected to provide the extra kinds of services which the multiply handicapped child would require. The result was exclusion of that child from any kind of service. Some wit has characterized this disease of administrators as "hardening of the categories."

The provision of treatment in terms of diagnostic entities in the case of the multiply handicapped child illustrates one way in which service structures can be inimical to the provision of treatment. From a strictly logical point of view, the provision of care in terms of diagnoses does make sense. But the problems of handling the multiply handicapped child arise as a consequence of the very structure set up to solve problems. This kind of structure has debilitating consequences on the way the system works. Planners like to think that as all-encompassing a system as a one-to-one service for diagnosis ought to work. For every disease, there is a special service, and everyone gets help—and this seems fine and completely logical. Such a structure does not work because, try as bureaucrats might, the attempt to encapsulate a child and all his problems as a "condition" is impossible. Life is just too complex for that. Medical conditions are simplistic abstractions, while seriously disabled children are real, so very real. It is clear that a less parsimonious system of providing care, a more administratively acceptable procedure, is desirable for handling seriously disabled children.

This problem of hardening of the categories was known to the administrators of the medical programs in North Carolina. Efforts have been partially successful in correcting the situation. The illustration is given to suggest that the procedures, mechanisms, and structures established to solve a problem may really inhibit the solution to the problem. Having illustrated what the study's staff came to examine, knowing their frame of reference, it is possible to describe other medical structures which prevented care from being effectively given.

IDIOSYNCRATIC SPECIALIZATION

By idiosyncratic specialization is meant a more or less natural and unplanned concentration of services within agencies. By virtue of an agency's operation, the personnel within the agency develop procedures which come to be effective. By virtue of this effectiveness, the procedures come to be a form of specialization which, since it is uncoordinated and unexpected, is detrimental to the system.

Idiosyncratic specialization is different in its consequences from simple medical specialization. Legitimate specialization in terms of service can be planned for and can be allowed. The major problems of legitimate specialization are methods of providing coordination among specialists: communications, controls, and referrals are devices by means of which specialists cover the "whole patient." So long as specialization is allowed for in planning, medical specialization can be tremendously effective, though it does have its problems.

The major problem with idiosyncratic specialization is that it arises spontaneously. It comes as a consequence of success in providing care; it is caused by an agency being successful in establishing effective communications and referral policies. The successful channels tend to become the ones which are legitimated, and agents expect their continued use. As it turns out, such expected channels are often not the best ones from a medical point of view.

Legitimate medical specialization is supposed to induce in practitioners an awareness of a single area of competence. Thus, the specialist is supposed to make referrals. Specialization focuses attention and forces recognition of one's incompetence. Idiosyncratic specialization, on the other hand, does not promote referrals to other experts but to others who are "usually used as specialists." If one suggests that specialization produces a form of selective attention, then idiosyncratic specialization produces a form of selective perception, the consequences of which are not very difficult to understand.

Illustrations abounded in Alamance County of the effects of idiosyncratic specialization. In the large cerebral palsy facility in a nearby county, the medical director was a trained and excellent orthopedic surgeon. Though he was charged with handling cases of cerebral palsy, his treatment centered on orthopedic problems. A child with such problems could get superb care at his agency, but cerebral palsy has concomitants other than orthopedic difficulties.

In Alamance County, there were children who were being cared for as "mental retardates" but who were, in fact, suffering from a variety of other complaints. Such children who needed help could be given some kind of aid if their major diagnosis was that of mental retardation. The obvious solution in at least one major medical agency was to define the child as a mental retardate so that some help could be given. Once the child was appropriately labeled a retardate, there was a whole program within the state system from which he was eligible to draw.

Then, too, there were compensatory specializations of this type: the county lacked resources for the emotionally disturbed, but if something other than the emotional disturbance could be made as the primary diagnosis, some sort of help could be given. As a result, it was a practice to diagnose children in terms of categories for which services were available. This practice was legitimate from the viewpoints of those who sought to help children, since it made some service available; from the researchers' point of view, it complicated the task of defining morbidity. One must wonder, too, whether the child ever received the kinds of service he needed.

Thus, here are at least two kinds of consequences resulting from idiosyncratic specialization: first, children get fitted into plans and programs because those plans and programs work and not because the children can be helped by the service; second, conditions which should be recognized and served are left unattended because attention is given to something in which the idiosyncratic agent is interested.

A third illustration of idiosyncratic specialization was discovered by analyzing the referral patterns of the totality of medical services in Alamance County. The referrals from the Health and Welfare departments were different kinds of referrals: not only did the two departments not refer patients to each other, but within the community their usual referral links were quite different. The choice of a starting point was open to the patient. He could enter either system at the Health Department or the Welfare Department. But once that choice was made, where he would go for help and the kinds of help he would get were predictable.

Referrals were clearly being made on a basis of differential definitions by the referring agencies. It should be noted, however, that specialization in terms of referrals did not occur as a result of differential diagnosis. Whatever the diagnosis, the Health Department tended to send its patients into the private, fee-for-service system, and the Welfare Department tended to send its patients into the state system. These latter referrals were made regardless of the financial abilities of patients, and came to be the accepted, the usual, the normal ways of doing things within the department.

There was no attempt made in the Alamance County Survey to judge the effectiveness of the referral systems studied. There was no effort made to assay whether children in one service received better care than in another. That would require a much more sophisticated study than the preliminary one in Alamance County. However, the finding that even a general medical agency such as the Health Department used a referral system different from that of the Welfare Department leads to some question of how well the medical services of the county are integrated.

LEGALISM AND MEDICINE

Medical legalism is probably a form of complexity which is difficult for the majority of patients to understand. It is difficult for the physician to understand, and he is generally not reluctant to let his anger become known to the patient.

The plain fact is that the provision of medical services in a community is not only a medical problem but also a legal one. Public medicine must serve two masters: the physician who provides medical care and the lawyer-accountant who runs things from a political and financial angle. Thus, there is a joint responsibility for providing care and meeting operational criteria. Unfortunately, sound medical criteria and adequate business criteria are sometimes in conflict.

Medical legality includes such phenomena as the specification of responsibilities for disease control, the allocation of funds for specific disorders, and the administrative techniques of obtaining care. Consider this example of medical legality: a child could be covered by federal funds of the Crippled Children's Program only if he applied for those funds before admission to the hospital. In cases of accident or sudden trauma, the child was not eligible under the Crippled Children's Program because he did not apply in advance for the help. It makes sense to offer help in terms of a program for the seriously disabled where hospitalization can be planned; yet, by defining the admission policies rigidly, a great variety of problems are created for patients needing help now rather than at some time in the future.

Another example of a general nature is the rule that before medical services can be provided by publicly supported agencies a family must prove its poverty. Yet in one tragic case known to the author, a middle-class family first had to be financially ruined before its child could be helped. It just does not make medical sense, or social sense, that a family should be forced into bankruptcy before care can be given.

Laws are abstractions, while people's needs are very real. Admitting that some care must be given to control of funds, the expectation that children will meet legal or logical criteria makes medical solutions to medical problems very difficult. Medical ethics has it that medical care be provided in terms of need rather than in terms of what is best fitted to a program developed in generalities. People are too complex to fit legal categories of care. In Alamance, there were workers who were quite competent in "working the system" of medical-legal structure. These were agency people who, despite the complexities, managed to fit patients and programs—at least on paper. Until physicians learn to work with the legal system, they will remain poor workers. In short, administration must become a part of the medical art if physicians are to retain their self-control in a time of growing governmental control.

Legal and medical administrative viewpoints are different, and these differences serve to deter patients and services. Medicine has failed to control legalism by failing in sound medical administration, to the disservice of the patient. Several reasons for this failure may be evidenced: physicians do not like administration, and so relinquish their prerogatives; physicians are not trained in even the elementals of public administration; and physicians view medical problems as if they were independent of the communities in which they existed. Structurally, the administration of purely medical problems has passed to legal agencies, and the non-legal training of the physician and patient becomes a mounting problem.

MEDICAL ADMINISTRATION

The final organizational or structural consideration to be mentioned here is that of medical administration of the collectivity of services which exist within a community.

Alamance County's medical facilities were each unique in several ways. Specificity of service in terms of medical specialization was the least debilitating form this uniqueness took. Another characteristic illustrating individuality was the specificity of patients. In the Health Department, for example, 999 children were listed by the public health nurses as handicapped, or were cited in the files of the orthopedic clinic. At the same time, in the Welfare Department, 923 children were listed as handicapped by the social workers. The point here is that there was an overlap of only five children known to both community agencies. Children, for whatever reasons, were not serviced by the two agencies and were not even known to the agencies.

Two points should be made regarding the special problems of the Health and Welfare departments. First, the Welfare Department is legally the gateway for specialized services. For example, the family seeking a child's admission to a home for the mentally retarded must work through the Welfare Department. Hence, not all children known to or serviced by the department are medically indigent. Second, the Health and Welfare departments deal with similar patients in terms of disease and clientele, so there is no reason to assume that the observed referral failure can be explained as bureaucratic efficiency.

In the report on Alamance County, there is an entire chapter devoted to examining the linkages between agencies in terms of the referrals made by these agencies to one another. Here we may note that the community's facilities displayed a very clear structure: referrals to and from health resources showed a great deal of consistency. This referral giving was related to certain community factors, such as the existence of facilities and the diagnosis made. Referrals were also shown to be a function of the socio-personal characteristics of the child. In other words, behavior in referral giving and defining were functions of the structure and not of chance.

Interviews with the directors of the medical resources of Alamance County indicated that medical personnel were not aware, in most cases, of the structure that is medicine. The director of the Welfare Department, for example, thought his relations with the Health Department were excellent. So, too, did the Health Officer feel that his relationships with the welfare people were very good. If, however, the files of handicapped children are an adequate index, these relationships could be judged as only poor or fair.

It is not unusual to have a policy and a practice which are not related. Unless administrators are relatively sophisticated, they will not be aware of the consequences of structure. If on paper there are organizational charts indicating a linkage, then that linkage exists to the administrator. Observing in detail how the organization does work is much more difficult than drawing lines and believing the system works the way the lines indicate. In too many cases, health agents probably do not want to know whether the system is really working. It is much easier to describe the ways in which it is supposed to work; to speak and write of goals rather than operations.

Consider some of the reasons why a medical referral system might not work. The physician knows a handicapped child with certain needs, but if he refers the child to a specialized service agency over which he, the physician, has no control, the child may be lost to him as a patient. This would mean money out of the physician's pocket. Then, consider the physician who has medically managed a handicapped child for some time. He is aware, as are all physicians, that medical management can always be improved. The giving of a referral opens the physician to evaluation and criticism. This threatening situation is avoided by making no referrals. Referrals made by physicians to lay administrators of publicly supported health agencies are asking for criticism. It is simpler not to refer a patient and to retain control over medical management.

Whether or not these *post hoc* explanations are useful in explaining the reluctance of physicians to make referrals, the fact of the case in Alamance is that patients are not routinely sent to the various specializing service agencies of that community. Patients in the main are not referred to other agencies, despite the finding in Alamance that some, such as "handicapped children," tended to have more than one medically significant condition. If one considers that most medical services are specific and specialized, this system of non-referral can be seen as in need of explanation. One hypothesis which should be investigated is that service agencies do not make referrals because of structural pressures for retention of patients. Sending patients to other services means that they cannot be counted among the agency's clients, and, after all, budgets are provided in terms of numbers of people served.

Whatever explanations are found to be useful in organizing community resources, a fact is this: patients cannot be held responsible for making their own referrals. Patients do not create the structural consistencies which interrelate medical and paramedical resources; the creation of the structure is the responsibility of the administrators and physicians who run the agencies. If any gaps in service exist, the non-referred patient cannot be used to explain his not getting service. Yet, as a matter of fact, this is precisely what many medical personnel often try to do. In Alamance County, the staff heard that patients just do not follow up referrals. In studying this point, the staff did find that there were certain kinds of referrals which were not routinely followed by patients. For example, the severely handicapped child did not usually follow a referral. But as noted earlier, the multiply handicapped child would probably not be cared for because of the unique-service-per-agency concept. Here would appear to be information that the patient who does not follow a referral makes his decision for pretty realistic reasons. It would seem clear that the responsibilities of physicians and administrators do not end with the statement that the child should be seen by agency X. The physician has a responsibility to find out why a patient does not follow a suggested referral.

Another reason why referrals were not given and could not be followed is worthy of mention at this point. Alamance County lacked medical facilities of a variety of sorts: there was no legal agency responsible for treating emotionally disturbed patients and no program for the child with defective hearing. These gaps have been partly corrected with the construction of a community mental health facility. However, patients cannot be responsible for the recognition and provision of service for themselves. Some administrators must assume the responsibility for providing community health resources. It does no good to "blame" anyone here. What is needed are administrators who are willing to inform taxpayers of children's needs and undertake the research to document those needs. As a matter of fact, the taxpayers of Alamance responded very well to pleas for funds based on needs for handicapped children.

Unfortunately, physician-administrators have failed to provide the taxpaying public with leadership and the data on which to act. This failure may be attributed, in part, to the fact that physicians define their responsibilities in terms of service to the individual child. They have no responsibilities to provide the epidemiologic data which would be useful to planners. Further, the collection of such data would be, in some cases, a violation of the physician-patient relationship. Finally, physicians are trained to respond to demand rather than need: they do not know, in fact, what the needs of the community are, even if they are aware of the demands for service made by their own patients. As a result, the physician, a specialist in caring for those who demand care, does not know his community's needs or how to find out what those needs are. And then the state persists in appointing and demanding the appointment of physicians for responsible administrative positions when neither by training nor temperament are physicians equipped to deal with administrative problems. With the prodding and pushing of contemporary medical needs, as developed by government, the medical profession will have to assume greater responsibilities in preparing their trainees for administration.

A final illustration concerning administration should help clarify the significance of the medical system and its effects. In Alamance County, we conducted a medical clinic to which handicapped and normal children were invited. Following the medical examination, the physicians were to judge whether or not the child was receiving adequate medical care. Some of the children were receiving such care and others were not. An analysis of the data showed that several kinds of factors were related to the adequacy of care being received. Statistically, there were some medical conditions which were always adequately cared for. These conditions were orthopedics, heart difficulties, epilepsy, and cleft-palate cases. For these, all a physician had to know was the diagnosis, and he could predict that care was adequate. For another group of conditions, care was generally inadequate. These conditions were emotional disturbance, mental retardation, and hearing and orthodontic conditions. A third class of conditions were sometimes cared for and sometimes not cared for. These consisted of cerebral palsy, chronic respiratory conditions, vision defects, and speech defects.

It seemed simple enough to say that the structure which was medicine in Alamance County was responsible for the excellent care being given the first class of disorders—epilepsy, heart, orthopedic, and cleft palate. It seemed clear that medicine, and no one else, could be seen as the agent responsible for the inadequate care being given the emotionally disturbed, the mentally retarded, and so on. Another explanation was needed for the cases where care was sometimes adequate and sometimes not adequate.

Statistically, several factors operated in the provision of care for the third class of diseases—cerebral palsy, chronic respiratory conditions and vision and speech defects. Accounting for almost all of the variance were these four factors: age of the child, family finances, race, and the severity of the condition. In other words, social-psychological factors which had relevance for the child were important *given* the medical system which existed in Alamance County. The medical system itself could account for a large portion of the care being afforded the children of the county and, once these limits were set, aspects of the child as a part of the system then became important. Specifically, the older,

290

Negro, poor, severely disabled child consistently received less adequate care than the younger, white, wealthier, less disabled child. Poverty, race, age, and degree of disability were important, then, within the limits specified by the medical system itself. It would seem to make more sense, therefore, to examine that medical system than to study the poor, the Negro, the disabled, and the older children as "causes" of the difficulties within the medical system.

CONCLUSION

Medical specialization, idiosyncratic specialization, legalism, and medical administration cannot be explained in terms of the culture of patients. These structures are a part of the culture of physicians and are to be explained in those terms. Contemporary medicine has its own difficulties, to which physicians and others may, with profit, turn their attention.

Sociologists may be doing medical men a disservice by explaining medicine's problems in terms of patients. Physicians and sociologists should turn their attention to the complex organizations of medical service so as to eliminate the problems created for patients by medical bureaucracy. In this, sociologists should stop belaboring the poor patient simply because the patient is less threatening a study than is organized medicine.

The data from Alamance County provide clues as to the ways in which the organization of the subcommunity of medicine has consequences on patients, the ways in which function is affected by structure. The data from Alamance County were meant to be insightful and provocative; they are not definitive. Much work needs to be done regarding the medical problems of the United States. Yet, in focusing attention on the community and its social organization, Alamance County can become a most useful first step. There is no evidence to indicate that what happens in Alamance County is atypical of the organization of medicine anywhere else in North Carolina or in the rest of the United States. However, further research into the community is necessary. Efforts at understanding the social-psychological components of the medical-patient relationship will, perforce, miss the focus begun by Alamance County.

It seems fairly reasonable to say that no one but the physicians themselves can be held responsible for making the kinds of changes which will have to come to medicine soon. There will be great change in the next decade, and this change will come with the cooperation of physicians or in spite of physicians. Physicians stand in such high regard in the United States today that they could easily control the direction of orderly change shaping medical practice for years to come.

If medical care is, at this point in history, a shambles or a mess, the problems cannot all be placed on the patients' shoulders. There is a system operating here, one which involves patients and physicians in a complex and interdependent way. To grip this complex problem one must view the whole system: patients *vis à vis* physicians in terms of community. Realistic appraisal of the sources of difficulties is one way of approaching solutions.

Notes

1. Talcott Parsons, *The Social System* (Glencoe, Ill.: The Free Press, 1951), pp. 428–479.

2. Daniel Rosenblatt and Edward A. Suchman, "The Underutilization of Medical Care Services by Blue-Collarites," in Arthur B. Shostak and William Gomberg, ed., *Blue-Collar World: Studies of the American Worker* (Englewood Cliffs, N.J.: Prentice-Hall, Inc., 1964), pp. 341–349.

3. Rodney M. Coe and Albert F. Wessen, "Social-Psychological Factors Influencing the Use of Community Health Resources," *American Journal of Public Health*, LV (1965), 1024–1031.

4. Robert Straus, "The Nature and Status of Medical Sociology," *American Sociological Review*, XXII (1957), 200–204.

5. *Ibid.*

6. William P. Richardson, A. C. Higgins, and Richard G. Ames, *The Handicapped Children of Alamance County* (Chapel Hill: Department of Preventive Medicine, University of North Carolina, 1965).

16 · Stranger in the Family

RHONDDA K. CASSETTA

In 1959–1960, to collect data for a research project, Melvin Weiss became a participant-observer in eleven families, and as a stranger in the family was able to report on the family life and interactions he observed. While acting in this role, however, he suffered many qualms and consequently devoted considerable thought to the ethics of his situation.

The research project itself has not yet been completed, but from the data available we have selected two aspects on which to base this chapter: first, Weiss's qualms about the ethics of the participant-observer role; and, second, the attempts to assess the validity and reliability of the data he collected.

BACKGROUND

During the 1940's and 1950's, the concept of the schizophrenogenic family, having gained considerable attention among both scientists and laymen, was widely researched.[1] Studies reported in the literature were usually based on interviews with schizophrenic patients and their families, material gathered during treatment, and projective tests.[2] When controls were used, they were likely to be patients with neuroses, and data were gathered from them in such structured situations as the interview or the treatment session. Thus, while much was known about the members of families in which schizophrenia and other types of mental illness had occurred, little was known about the differences in the family process that might exist between these and normal families.[3]

In view of the limitations imposed by the methods of data collection and the undesirability of using other patients as controls, an exper-

294

iment was designed in the New York State Mental Health Research Unit in 1959 that would permit the collection of data in the family setting by a participant-observer[4] and would use "normal" people as controls. The purpose of the experiment was to test the validity of the schizophrenogenic-family concept.

At the time, Melvin Weiss, an anthropologist, was on the staff of the Mental Health Research Unit. He was selected as the participant-observer because of his previous experience in this role among migrant-worker families during the summer of 1956 and in an Indian society in 1959, his particular interest in continuing this type of activity, and his lack of information about theories of schizophrenia. Study planners felt that a more sophisticated knowledge of theories of schizophrenia in an observer would introduce bias in the selective reporting of patterns of interaction and family behavior.

As originally proposed, the detailed accounts of family interactions collected by Weiss in both control families and in families with a schizophrenic member would be presented to a research psychiatrist who would attempt to identify each kind of family on the basis of theories of schizophrenia. Plans were also made to describe the patterns of interaction in both kinds of families in terms of the allocation and stability of roles among the members, the communication patterns between the members, and the social-mobility and reference-group behavior of the members. Finally, the evaluations of the anthropologist, the research psychiatrist, and the clinical staff of the hospital treating the schizophrenic member were to be compared.

In a reconsideration of the study design two years later, plans were made to have episodes culled from Weiss's notes presented to a panel of judges for their grouping into families and subsequent identification as schizophrenogenic or normal. Because of the lack of funds to support this study, only the data-collection phase was completed.

The introduction of a participant-observer into the homes of the families was planned so that Weiss might report on the activities, the interactions, and the conversations that took place while he was there. In other words, he would be noting "who does what, with whom, when, and where, under what conditions, and how long does it take?"[5] The results were expected to be more descriptive of the usual behavior of the families than information obtained by other methods.

The participant-observer was expected to gain entry into the families, to become accepted by them so that his presence would not disturb routine family behavior, and to report accurately on the kinds of family activity. It was not necessary, and not even desirable, that he be able to analyze the situations, but he must be able to describe them.

THE SAMPLE

The two types of family under study were those that had produced a schizophrenic son and those that had not. Even though parents may interact differently with each child, it is assumed that there is a general pattern of family interactions, and that the interactions with a younger son are the closest approximations to the interactions that affected an older—in this instance, a schizophrenic—son. The first study group, then, consisted of white, working- and middle-class families in which a son seventeen to twenty-six years old had a first admission to a mental hospital for an acute onset of schizophrenia during 1959–1960. At that time the son was single and living at home with his biological parents and at least one younger brother. The control group was selected on the same characteristics, except that the son had recently been hospitalized for a moderately severe physical condition. Thus, each type of family had been subjected to recent stress in the hospitalization of a son.

The cooperation of five mental hospitals and six general hospitals in central New York was obtained in making their records available. After a particular patient was selected as a subject, his doctor was contacted by Weiss for permission to approach the family. Finally, the family had to agree to participate in the study.

Since our interest is in Weiss as a "stranger in the family," we shall not discuss the problems he encountered in locating his sample of families but proceed to a first visit with a family, and let Weiss speak for himself:

> One afternoon, I went to the house and knocked at the door and was let in by a small boy. "Is your mother home?" A woman in an apron walked into the living room, wiping her hands. She was followed by a young man. "I'm Mel Weiss, I'd like to talk to you about your son Albert. I'm from the New York State Mental Health Research Unit; I've spoken to Dr. ——" (the hospital physician who had authorized the contact with this family).
>
> "I'm Arline Applegate,[6] this is Arnold, my youngest son, and this is Albert," she said, introducing the boy and the young man. "Let me take your coat."

296

"I'd like to tell you about some work that is being started to try to study the illness that Albert had," I said, avoiding Albert and looking right at his mother. *I was quite flustered and really didn't know how to begin with Albert there in the room.* He must have felt this because at this point he half got up out of his chair and said in a hesitant voice, "Do you want me to go into the . . . ?"

"Of course not," I said, "there's nothing you shouldn't hear if you want to."

With that, he sat down, and I began to explain to Mrs. Applegate. The story I told was true and complete to the best of my ability. *There was enough anxiety for me in the situation as it was without having to consider in addition who was hearing what.* I gave the history of the project, what our interest was, why we had chosen it, and how we proposed to analyze the data. It took about three-quarters of an hour. I ended with, "You see, it is kind of like a detective story. We'd like to try to reconstruct Albert's life."

The entire procedure was as honest and as completely informative as I could make it, with two exceptions of emphasis: first, the overemphasis on reconstructing the patient's life (though there would be material collected in this area), and second, the underemphasis on parent-younger child interactions (though this too was mentioned as an interest).

This visit set a pattern that I found comfortable, and from some of the personal family concerns that were shared by the Applegates with me, led me to believe that they found comfortable, too. I made a practice of answering any question as honestly as I could and while I did nothing after the first visit to draw attention to my observer role, such as taking notes in their presence or asking other than ordinary questions, I did not avoid mentioning that I "worked downtown" or that I was ". . . on the job now."

During later introductions I felt it was necessary to add explicitly that their cooperation was voluntary, and that, even though they agreed to let me visit and I did so, if at a later time they wanted to stop they should feel free to tell me. In addition, it had to be made quite clear that what I was interested in was ordinary, everyday family life, and that I was not concerned with the unusual or the exceptional. I also assured them that, in addition to the regular procedures of anonymity and code letters for family names in office files, if something unpleasant should happen, the kind of thing they would not tell neighbors about, that material would not be recorded. This was offered as a condition of accepting access to a home and the family's hospitality. My guess is that when the purpose of field work is explained and a request for permission to visit is made, the parents, who generally grant the request, have really no clear idea of what is being asked of them, what they are expected to do or what the disposition of the data might be.

At a somewhat later date with another family, Weiss had become more at ease in the opening situation and more confident of himself. He described this first meeting as follows:

> In comes the mother; the mother is a woman of about fifty years of age, wears her hair long, loose, down to about the level of her jaw. It is pushed back from her head, kind of a wide black flap on each side of her head. She has strong bones, with heavy, saggy, white flesh over them; parts of her face move and jiggle as she speaks, but she has a kind of snap and bite the way she says things that might be a little intimidating.
>
> I gave her my name and my affiliation and had no sooner done this when in walked someone whom I took to be the husband. I walked over with my hand extended and said, "Are you Mr. ——?" and introduced myself. I said, "I'd like to talk to you about a study we are engaged in." I went on to explain the aims and attempts of the study and talked to them about why we were doing the research. The mother, during this time, sat back in her chair, nodded, and seemed to take, from the family point of view, rather complete charge of the situation.
>
> I described the purpose of the study as a comparison of life history materials, the two kinds of families that we are interested in, and said that most of the information that I would be getting would revolve around the reconstruction of the patient's life and about the kinds of things that had influenced him in the family situation, the people he played with, where he had gone to school, the sort of things that he had done when he grew up.
>
> In recounting various kinds of things that the parents felt would be material of this sort, the mother said at one point, "Guess we've had a lot of troubles in this family," and at that

point she broke down and started to weep rather freely and fully with her face distorted and a flood of tears running down her face.

Entry into a home was not always an easy process. In some instances, Weiss met resistance and only slightly veiled antagonism, as in the following:

I walked up to the house, knocked at the door, and was met by a boy of sixteen, Frank. I asked him if I might see his mother. "What do ya wanna see her about?" he asked. I looked at him, and then he said, "Is it about my brother?" I said, "Yes, I'd like to talk to her about it." He said, "Well, come in."

I came in and hesitated in the living room while he looked back over his shoulder, kind of stopping me, as he walked through a doorway, past the foot of a set of stairs, into a kitchen and said to his mother that there was someone here to see her.

The mother came out of the kitchen through the dining room and said to me, "Yes, what do you want?" I said, "I'd like to talk to you about some research that I'm doing," and began to explain the project to her.

She said, "Well, I can't tell ya anything; I don't know anything about that; we're just ordinary people; we have nothing to do with that; I don't know anything about that." She sat down on the couch, and I continued to stand there. She said, "Well, sit down."

I explained to her the general purpose and necessity for the project, and while I was doing this, she sat on the couch, half turned away from me, with her chin in her hands, looking at me over her shoulder, pulling her mouth awry and saying, "Yes, well that's all right, but, uh, we can't tell you anything here, uh, there's, there's nothing you wanna know here."

I indicated that what I was interested in was precisely that kind of situation; that they were a very hard family to find and that I had been looking for them for a long time, etc. She finally sat back and relaxed a little bit and began to ask me what I did and what my job was called, and whom I worked for.

Over a one-year period, Weiss made observations in six schizophrenic families and five control families. The time spent varied from a single two-and-a-half-hour visit in one family to eight visits with another family totaling twenty-six and a half hours. He recorded material from ninety and a half hours spent with the schizophrenic families and forty-two and a half hours spent with the controls.

Over time Weiss became aware of his changing role in the families and, as his image of himself shifted, he devoted some consideration to it. The families, he thought, visualized him as representing the mental hospital on his first visit; later he felt himself to be viewed as an authority on mental illness and many other subjects. As his acquaintance with a family deepened, he sensed that he became other things—sometimes a pawn in the power struggle between the parents and sometimes a sympathizer with the family in its relations with the hospital. Ultimately he hoped to be a family friend whose presence would be welcomed.

ETHICAL PROBLEMS

During the data-collection phase of the study, Weiss struggled with the ethical problems created by the presence of a participant-observer in a family. He was anxious over the possibility of his exploiting a family through entering the home, accepting refreshments and even meals, but all the while observing and recording the family interactions. He felt that only by some giving of gifts in return could he absolve himself of the exploitation.

On the first contact, Weiss gave in payment for being accepted into the home his rather lengthy layman's explanation of schizophrenia, of research, and of the necessity for obtaining information from the family. Having been a student for some years, he was also able to advise the family on such matters as continuing education for the sons, particular courses to be studied, and possibilities for employment. He also compared with the families his experiences in bringing up his children, and talked with the men about hunting and fishing and with the women about housekeeping problems. He loaned books and magazines to the families, and he took with him such gifts of food as doughnuts or frozen pastries.

At the same time that he was trying to resolve his ethical problems *vis-à-vis* the families, Weiss was also dealing with ethical problems that he recognized as stemming from the research itself. In a paper entitled, "Personal Ethics in Field Research: An Issue in the Study of Family Life," [7] he commented at some length on this problem:

> Since the design called for substantial amounts of time to be spent in the homes of the study families . . . personal factors would be quite important. First, there was the question of what

300

would be the best way to act in the field situation, and second, what effects extended contact might have on the investigator and the study families.

We considered, for instance, the alternatives of taking a stance either as a scientist or of trying to imitate a fly on the wall. In addition we thought about the changes that would occur in a family because of the presence of an observer or what might happen if the family got the investigator too deeply involved in its affairs. . . . Our decision was to play it by ear. . . . Over time a number of things occurred during the visits with the families and it is now obvious that, in effect, decisions were made and certain paths were followed that might as well have been the result of predetermined choices, although in fact they were not. . . .

What demands will the family make around the figure of the sick son? Will his progress or condition be associated with the investigator? How much information will they expect of him? What questions about the responsibility and possible help he may offer will the family put to the researcher? In view of his use made of the family's resources, space, attention, food, time, etc., what can he offer in exchange?

These questions in a sense define some major problems for the investigator. . . .

He has entered a situation that already contains anxiety-provoking elements, and his presence perhaps adds to them.

What he wishes to observe is not very predictable by time or place and a great deal of casual time needs to be spent in the situation to be on hand to see significant behavior as it occurs.

Then the problem arises, can what is observed be decently recorded and abstracted?

And last, as the work proceeds, the investigator will find himself the recipient of food as he joins the family for snacks and meals, of gifts for his wife, and of interest in his family as questions and advice are tendered about his children. One is conscious of something being used up by the investigator from his presence alone: space, convenience, ease, and attention. One seeks to find ways to return and replace some of these commodities.

301

From the family's point of view the situation is vague. The understanding that they have after three-quarters of an hour of clear, simple explanation is that they are going to be studied somehow in connection with and because of an illness. What is going to be done is not understood. They are aware that there is some sort of official sanction of this work, but beyond New York State or the Hospital, just what it is, is also unknown. About all they know for sure is that someone wants to spend time with them and come back occasionally.

There are, however, some feelings or attitudes that in our opinion they do have. Even though they are explicitly told that much time has been spent trying to find them or average families like them, they feel that there is something wrong with them or their relations to the son who was in the hospital. There is also some apprehension about what a stranger will see as he spends time with the family.

What will happen to them if neighbors find out? Then, too, they are not sure just what it is that they are supposed to do. Should they stay in when he comes? Should they "visit" with him? Is he supposed to spend time with the "sick" boy? And then maybe he can help them. There are things that puzzle them about the illness and problems that arise during home care. Can he get special treatment or will there be a private contact with the hospital that will help them to help their son?

My impression is, however, that the effect of a complete and forthright presentation is strongest on the investigator, that this kind of directness is what a parent responds to. I think that it is on the basis of the self-convinced honesty of the investigator that a father and mother grant access to their family for investigation.

Most of the time in the home after the first one or two visits was spent, as it were, hanging around playing cards with the children, eating a late supper with the father, drinking wine in a summer house with a grandpa, or just talking with the mother about children and family gossip of their family and mine. During these times it was possible to observe "natural" parent-child relations.

I've tried to draw a picture of informality, and directness of relation with the family, and it is one that I think has been fairly well maintained for all of the study families.

After visiting has begun, and the researcher is accepted as someone who is there in the home, by right as it were, one of the parents usually attempts to try him out. Sometimes it takes the form of discussing family matters which place the other spouse in a bad light.

An extended piece of invidious gossip is related about a defect in the spouse that shows what an excellent and long-suffering person the teller is. It has a number of effects. First it tends to elicit sympathy from the hearer. If simply accepted it would set the listener against the spouse. Or the teller would gain an ally if sides were being chosen. And to some extent it is, I would guess, an attempt to see if the listener is open to manipulation. These stories are told about various family members, the patient himself, the hospital or the physician. Many of them display, at some point, a logical error, a contradiction, or a missing part. They invite discussion and from the only semi-rhetorical questions that end them, they seem to demand that action (or at least a stance) be taken.

An example of a wife's trying to enlist Weiss on her side was recorded in an early visit to one family:

She sat up and leaned forward toward me and said, rather vehemently, "He's an alcoholic, you know; if you're gonna spend time with the family, you're gonna hafta know about that; he's a very bad alcoholic." The father hadn't been out of the room more than a few seconds when she said this.

In another instance, the parents tried to get Weiss to intervene in their son's treatment:

Then, the mother starts to describe the dosage of medicine that her son is getting, and she talks about it, and asks me questions about whether I have any information on it and who prescribes in this sort of thing. She turns to this dark-haired, quiet, rather handsome-looking boy and says, "You remember the time you went to get Bill at the hospital a few weeks ago, and he forgot his pills; you remember what happened when you went back to get them." What happened, apparently, was this: the younger brother went back to the hospital, was told that there were no more of the 100 milligram pills and that the patient would be given some 200 milligram pills. When he came back with this, and told his mother and Bill about this,

303

they were both quite disturbed and the mother related that the next time she and Bill went back to the hospital, she accompanied him into the office. A physician was called, but he could not get there so the social worker saw them. When the mother asked about the dosage, the social worker called up the ward and was told the following that she related to the mother. If the 100 milligram pills seemed to have unpleasant side effects, like too much sleeping, and were disturbing to the patient, then the dosage should be cut down to 50 milligram pills, and in the future he should take 50 milligram pills.

At this point the mother got very upset and wanted to know on what basis dosage was prescribed, and this was the reason for her big concern in trying to get information from me about it. The position she took was that a single dosage was appropriate; that the patient was on one dosage, apparently for the convenience, or because of accident; that it might be doubled; and on her complaint, or the patient's complaint, it might be halved; and she wanted to know in regard to this; she felt that the dosage should be controlled much more effectively than this.

She asked me if I knew what would help Bill; she said that they would be willing to do anything in order to get him better; that they didn't think he was getting better at the hospital; that he was unimproved for a long time. Then she started to talk about his lack of improvement, and with this she began to cry; her eyes filled up with tears and her voice quavered and I said something to the effect that this is a very difficult thing to bear, isn't it?

Weiss later wrote:

In general, a reasonable strategy might be to meet these demands for sympathy, commitment, or action with understanding and a statement of facts about the investigator's role; that he is not partisan in either direction; that he understands and sympathizes with the teller. If he does not offer to become involved in most cases, he will be permitted to play his role as he defines it. The same is true when an institution requests information about a family that they have helped to provide for study purposes. It can be explained to them that one of the bases on which access has been granted into the family is anonymity. A clear statement in response to a request of this kind

304

(which usually is presented on an informal level) to the effect that you cannot both get information and transmit it for use, if you are to remain in contact with the family, is acceptable to most people.

In social research it seems to me that, ethically, people are being used as means to ends that are not their own but the investigator's, and that there is something exploitative or potentially damaging in that use. An index of this is that social scientists are reluctant to have themselves studied in the same way that they study other groups. Now it is true that when a group is the subject of research they usually assent to cooperation where it is requested (or needed), but it is carefully elicited by suggestions and subtle pressures rather than freely offered. I feel that an investigator should try to use people as little as possible, to exchange goods and services where he can, and to accept the responsibility of at least maintaining the freedom of choice for people who are the objects of study. In short, his ethical goal ought to be the promotion of symmetrical relations between himself and society.

VALIDITY

As a member of a group, recording what he sees and hears, a participant-observer is always liable to question as to the validity of his reports. In this instance, the relevant questions were: Is the participant-observer able to report *what is going on?* Is he able to report *what it means?* This study was structured so that it was important that Weiss accurately report only "what was going on." The answers to "what it means" were to be supplied at a later time by the judges. In fact, Weiss's interpretations were not sought. Thus, only the first kind of validity was of concern at this stage in the study.

To test Weiss's ability to report what was going on in a group of which he was a part, arrangements were made for him to carry on a conversation with two other people in a room that was monitored by a one-way mirror and a microphone. Three staff members—a psychiatrist, a sociologist, and a statistician[8]—watched this interaction and then compared their observations with those made by Weiss. This test was repeated after a short interval. The consensus was that Weiss was able to observe and report accurately on the events in the interactions and on the content of the conversations. It was agreed, however, that his interpretations of what happened were doubtful. It must be borne

305

in mind that in the study his interpretations of his observations in the families were not sought and were, in fact, prohibited. Any editorializing that he did in his reports was deleted from the typescripts of his visits.

Following this test, the observer visited in the family of a schizophrenic boy for ten hours. After his observations had been tape-recorded and studied, an anthropologist and a psychiatrist[9] accompanied him to the home. Here it was agreed that his interpretations of the family situation were improbable, but the "gestalt" of the family that the descriptions had evoked was very close to their own perceptions of them. Furthermore, his descriptions of the interaction appeared to be remarkably accurate.

In planning for the main study, the research team felt that although the observer would be filtering the observations through his own personality, the descriptions of the families would be sufficiently literal and concrete to lessen the importance of this problem. Moreover, he would be a constant, although no doubt his relationship to different families would differ. Nevertheless, it would still be possible to discover the level of agreement about the kinds of cues that typify family interaction and culture.

Although the study was not completed, typescripts of the visits have been prepared and the majority of these subdivided into episodes, each pertaining to a single block of interaction. The design of the study called for a panel of judges to separate these episodes into family groupings and into schizophrenic and control families. Although this was never done, a psychiatrist and two sociologists[10] read 155 of the episodes and correctly classified 50 of the 83 schizophrenic, and 43 of the 72 controls.[11] The following are samples of correctly classified episodes on which there was agreement. Underneath each is indicated the reasons given by the judges for classification. These descriptions also illustrate the kind of picture of the "gestalt" of the family interactions that Weiss was able to evoke.

Schizophrenic Family

Helen is offered food at the table, but she refuses it, and says instead that she would like something to drink. The mother says, "Would you like some coffee?" and Helen says, "Well . . ." I said, "Maybe something cold to drink?" as if I were one of the hosts there. She says, "Yes," and the mother said, "Well, how about some tea? You always liked tea." Helen answered, "Well, all right." Then the mother goes in the house and comes out with a half of a quart bottle of orange pop, which she offers to Helen who takes some. Then the mother, Ralph,[12] Helen, George, Nancy and I are sitting at the table, nibbling, eating and talking. The mother offers me some cookies.

Ralph is still sitting there at the table and eating and smoking. George is leaned back in his chair. I offer him a cigarette which he smokes and makes comments about. . . . George says to Helen, "Oh, gee, it would be nice if you had your vacation the same time that I got mine." She says, "Well, I'm gonna take two weeks." He says, "Are you gonna get paid for it?" She says, "No." Then he says, "Yeah, boy, well you should be getting two weeks; how long have you been working there, two years?" She says, "No, three; they gotta bunch of girls there, y' know; you can do anything with girls," and shrugs her shoulders as if to say, "Well, what can I do about it?"

Comment: Even guest can't keep role straight.

Schizophrenic Family

While we were talking, a boy of thirteen came in, stood in the doorway off the living room, and said, "Ma, I'm gonna go out and play Pop Warner's." She said, "You are not gonna go out." He said, "Ah, it's all right; all the boys are my age." She said, "You're not gonna go out and break your leg again, like last time." He said, "I didn't break my leg playing football." She said, "Well, you're not gonna play football now, and that's all there is to it." He shrugged his shoulders; went back into the kitchen. A moment later, from the kitchen a voice said, "Jesus Christ," and a door slammed.

Comment: Irrationality: broken leg was blamed on football, which was apparently not the cause of it. Weakness and pseudo-decisiveness: the mother gives an order that is not obeyed. Somehow there is a suggestion that this is part of a pattern of lack of structure and clear messages.

Control Family

I arrived at the house a little before dark to find Ralph, the younger son of the family, getting ready for a prom. He was dressed in pants with a silk stripe down the sides, black shoes, which his mother said she had just bought him, and a beautifully fitting white dinner jacket. Just as I got there, he had evidently put the finishing touches on his dress, and was standing around in the kitchen, a little ill at ease. There were three girls and a boy, about sixteen years old, sitting in the kitchen, and altogether, in and out of the household, there are maybe ten or fifteen relatives. A half a dozen more high-school-age kids came around during the course of the evening, and there is a tremendous amount of going in and out, piling up in corners of people who stand and talk in little knots, who move in and out of the kitchen.

George says to Ralph, "Take it easy; you just relax, act natural. Pull your coat collar over a little bit." Ralph is a little confused and grabs his dinner jacket by the lapel button with the left hand, and shoves it up a little bit, pushing it away from his neck. His older brother says, "No, pull it down on your neck a little bit; pull it down on your neck," and again the boy pushes the coat up and away from his shoulders. His older brother finally walks over to him and says, "No, do it like this," and he puts his hands underneath the lapels of the jacket and smooths it down over his shoulder. Ralph is ill at ease and stands around, shifting from one leg to another. He has a foolish grin on his face. Everybody (everybody meaning the cousin, another woman relative of the family, his mother, his older brother, myself, three or four friends) is standing there admiring him, calling out advice to him, telling him how to stand, how to relax, what to do.

Comment: Sounds like home.

Control Family

We get up from the table and the five of us move into the kitchen, where the father puts a dish towel across his waist, and proceeds to wash the pots and pans in the sink, wipe off the dishes and put them in the dishwasher. The mother takes a rubber paddle and puts the gravy from the pan into a large jar. The boys help by bringing all the dishes from the table, getting a sponge mop out when some tea is spilled on the floor, and I try to help put some glasses into the dishwasher.

Again, here, there's kind of loud, animated conversation, part of which turns upon the fact that some months ago, an older brother, who had been recently married, visited the house and his wife had cooked for the two brothers; the father and mother evidently had been gone. The boys were complaining that their sister-in-law wasn't a very good cook, and that they had told her this. The mother defended the sister-in-law, saying, "Boy, if I'd been here, if I were in her place, you'd know whether I was a good cook or not; you would have eaten whatever I put on the table or not a thing at all." The father says, "Well, you have to give her time; after all, she's only been married a few months." Ralph says, "I guess when you've been married a few months, you don't really care what you eat." People kind of laugh and continue to do the dishes and clean up.

There is a dog in the house, a kind of a terrier-hound mixture, and a large cat. The mother feeds both of them in a little entryway and says that Fred had gone down to the dog pound and picked up the dog when he was a pup. He was getting kind of old now, but that they kind of liked having him around. The father is very busy, in a very work-like fashion, fixing up the kitchen and in about ten minutes the entire kitchen is spotlessly clean. As a kind of parting gesture, one of the boys, Ralph, takes the sponge mop and mops down the whole floor. Then he hangs the mop up after rinsing it out and goes to the telephone, where he makes a call.

Comment: Well organized.

RELIABILITY

Because of the method in which the data were collected, reliability as well as validity was of concern. Weiss did not take notes while visiting in the homes, since he felt it would distract from his ability to observe and would make the family members conscious that they were being studied. His usual procedure was to make notes shortly after each visit and to use these notes as the basis for a tape-recorded account of the visit. A staff member would then listen to the recording and question Weiss for further details or clarification, where indicated. She then edited the tapes to remove the use of any names or obviously identifying information, such as references to the mental hospitalization of the son. She also deleted Weiss's editorializing and images that were related to the stereotype of the withdrawn schizophrenic, such as, "He fades into the woodwork."

The time span between the note-taking and the taping varied from three days to, in one instance, as many as twenty-nine days. To what extent did this time span affect the reliability of the reports? To test this, Weiss undertook to retape from his notes the account of one visit. A family was picked at random and a representative visit selected. The original tape was recorded three days after the visit; the retaping occurred eight months after the visit and was done from the notes originally taken. So that the differences between the two tapings might be more apparent, the two accounts were separated into the same nineteen episodes, or natural blocks of interaction. The comparable sections were then typed beside each other on sheets of paper. The following differences were noted:

1. There was loss of detail in the retaping.
2. To compensate for loss of detail, Weiss interpolated descriptive material, generalizations, and commentaries on his impressions.
3. There was an over-all flatness in the retaped episodes. Dialogue that was reported originally in its colloquial form appeared in more correct English in the retaping. For example, "What kinda car you wanna ride in?," a quotation from the first taping, became, in the retaping, "Which car do you want to ride in?"

In addition, since the earlier taping can be assumed to have reported the incidents more accurately, there were errors in the retaping. For example, the father, who did not actually enter the living room until ten forty-five P.M., was reported in the retaping to have spent the whole evening in that room.

The episodes were then read by a college student[13] to whom the situation had been explained. She was instructed to decide in each case which episode had been taped first and to indicate the reasons for her choice. She identified sixteen of the episodes correctly, and her reasons were the same as those above: loss of detail, padding by generalizations, and flatness. Selected episodes were also presented to five other college students,[14] who were able to separate the two tapings.

Selected episodes from the two tapings follow. These illustrate the kinds of differences that were found throughout the tapes:

FIRST TAPE, *three days after visit:*	SECOND TAPE, *eight months after visit:*
On a weekday evening I arrived at the house of Family C about late dusk, approximately 8:30 in the evening. I drove into	I arrived at the house after supper on a weekday evening. Driving into the yard and parking, I met John, seventeen-year-old

the lawn, and there I passed the seventeen-year-old-son, John, walking with a friend, out toward the road. We greeted each other and as he and his friend walked to the road, I heard his friend say to him, "What kinda car you wanna ride in?" John said, "A red one." Red is the color of his car, which, I understand, has not been working in a year.

son of the house, and a friend of his. I got the impression they had been working on a car—a red, early 1950 Mercury that belonged to John. "Hey," they called out, "which car do you want to ride in?" The car is something of a joke in the family, since John has had it and been working on it, trying to get it in running condition, for over a year. "I'll take the red one," I said. I waved and went by toward the house.

From the boys' conversation, the murmuring of their voices that I could hear between them, and their relation to me, one got the impression that they were busy and businesslike. John certainly is somewhat older, more self-contained and mature than other boys of his age.

COMMENT:
Use of colloquial language. Factual reporting of incident.

COMMENT
English has been corrected. Error in people involved in interaction.

Addition of Weiss's commentary on boys [material set in italics].

FIRST TAPE, *three days after visit:*

While she is out, a boy of twelve or fourteen wanders into the house, stands in the doorway, goes back toward the kitchen, then comes into the doorway of the living room and comes in and sits down. The mother says,

SECOND TAPE, *eight months after visit:*

Then, as we continue to sit there, a heavy-set, fat neighbor boy with glasses comes in and sits down in a chair that Anne had occupied. He smokes a cigarette with exaggerated masculine gestures. The mother introduces

"This is Paul . . . a neighborhood friend." This boy has got a neck as thick as his head and has humps of fat and flesh all over him. He looks like a keg, and he is smoking a cigarette in a rather affected, young punk manner. He sits in the chair that Anne had been sitting in; Anne has gone into another part of the house, and he sprawls there, and he, too, comments, second guesses, and watches and approves the Emmy awards. He sits there until Anne has come back into the living room. After a few minutes the neighborhood boy gets up and wanders out.

him to me as Paul. His manner is quite different from that of the other children and people in the family. He seems quite aggressively self-possessed and he seems to have a swagger even as he sits watching television.

COMMENT:
Weiss gives emotional reaction to youth.

COMMENT:
Description is removed from actual observation.

FIRST TAPE, *three days after visit:*

Eleanor says to him, "Come on, it's late; we'd better be going; I've gotta get the baby home." He says, "Yeah, yeah, I know; just, just wanna see this; just wanna see . . ." and he continues to watch the Emmy awards.

Eleanor makes another attempt or two to get her husband to leave and says in a quiet, not very forceful, or not very authoritative voice, "Come on, we have to go; it is getting late, Sam." Sam shakes his shoulders and stands up and bobs up and down

SECOND TAPE, *eight months after visit:*

It is near 10:00 P.M. and about this time Sam, Eleanor, and the baby, who is bundled up, get ready and leave. There is no special leave-taking; the parents stay in the living room. Eleanor dresses the child and after coming back and sitting, waits until Sam has seen one or two more awards, then the two of them get up with their child and say a quiet good-by and leave.

312

with a gesture reminiscent of
boyish irritation and says, "Yeah,
yeah, we're going," and stands at
his chair and continues to watch
television. Then he kind of wanders out and says, "Well, so
long," and turns around and
watches television some more.
Eleanor gets up, gathers her
things, picks the baby up, takes
the baby out.

Sam is still standing in the doorway. Eleanor comes back to the
doorway. Sam has moved out of
the doorway, into the middle of
the living room now, still watching the television, finger in his
mouth, chewing his nails. Eleanor stands there with the baby,
dressed in outdoor clothes, on
her hip and waits patiently with
a very slight air of impatience.
Mostly she is just waiting patiently and after two or three
minutes Sam says, "Well, so
long; see ya," and waves to me
and to his mother and Eleanor
smiles and nods her head, and
they go out.

COMMENT:
Detail, dialogue, recorder seems
actually to have been present.

COMMENT:
Complete loss of detail. Description removed from observation.

The fact that the second taping was so far removed from the original
visit and from the first taping would maximize the differences, although
in one sense the similarities in the "gestalt" of the two accounts are as
striking as the differences in concrete detail. Nevertheless, one may
conclude in the case of Weiss that tapes made at a later date from his
original notes suffered loss of detail, introduction of extraneous material, and even gross errors that would have largely invalidated their

313

value as source information. It must be remembered, however, that none of the actual tapes was prepared as much as eight months from the visit; and the nearer the time of the visit, the more accurate the tapes are considered to be. The results suggest that in any future studies of this type, however, recording should occur within hours, and certainly within a day or two, of the visit.

SUMMARY

In 1960, in an effort to discover some factors that might differentiate patterns of interaction in families that had produced a schizophrenic son from those that had not, Weiss, as a participant-observer, was able to enter eleven study families that had been selected on specified criteria. Weiss's observations of what took place had to be accurate because these would later be the basis of study by a team of judges working within their theoretical framework of the schizophrenogenic family. Whether Weiss himself would be able to interpret what was going on was not necessary, since any interpretations he made were to be deleted before submission to the judges. Three tests of his accuracy were carried out, and the consensus was that Weiss was able to record the "gestalt" of the families. He was particularly skillful in recording details that evoked the picture of the family under study. On this basis his observations were adequate.

The reliability of Weiss's data was assessed by comparing the taping made immediately after a visit with a retaping made from field notes several months after the original observation. It was apparent that the later tape contained errors, loss of detail, and the addition of extraneous material. As Katz noted, "the worker cannot reconstruct from his notes his original observations after a lapse of time without some losses in completeness and accuracy." [15]

During the time Weiss spent with the families, he gave considerable thought to the ethics of a participant-observer under such circumstances. The fact that he had not resolved the problem to his satisfaction may have accounted for his early termination of contacts with many of the families. What he felt to be an uncomfortable, and eventually intolerable, involvement with at least two of the families caused a rather abrupt removal from them.

Thus, while typescripts of the completed visits have been prepared and subjected to some examination, the task, as a whole, remains unfinished. It has, however, raised several interesting questions and perhaps

314

suggests some answers that later research may confirm. First, can a participant-observer collect accurate data on interactions in a family that he enters as a stranger; second, what effect does the intervening variable of time have on the reliability of the data; and, finally, what effect does the participant observation have on the researcher and on the family? The answers suggested by this study are: it is possible for a participant-observer to collect accurate and detailed descriptions of interaction in families; the reliability of these descriptions decreases (probably geometrically) with the passage of time; and, finally, to be the stranger in the family is fraught with at least as much discomfort for the stranger as for the family.

Notes

NOTE: The research reported upon was supported by the New York State Department of Mental Hygiene, Mental Health Research Unit, Syracuse, N.Y.

1. See, for example, Gregory Bateson et al., "Toward a Theory of Schizophrenia," Behavioral Science, I (1956), 251–264; M. Bowen, "Family Relationships in Schizophrenia," in Alfred Auerback, ed., Schizophrenia, An Integrated Approach (New York: Ronald Press Company, 1959), pp. 147–178; D. L. Gerard and J. Siegel, "The Family Background in Schizophrenia," Psychiatric Quarterly, XXIV (1950), 45–73; Jay Haley, "The Family of the Schizophrenic; A Model System," Journal of Nervous and Mental Disease, CXXIX (1959), 357–374, and "An Interactional Description of Schizophrenia," Psychiatry, XXII (1959), 321–332; Jacob Kasanin et al., "The Parent-Child Relationship in Schizophrenia," Journal of Nervous and Mental Disease, LXXIX (1934), 249–263; Melvin L. Kohn and John A Clausen, "Parental Authority Behavior and Schizophrenia," American Journal of Orthopsychiatry, XXVI (1956), 297–313; Theodore Lidz, "Schizophrenia and the Family," Psychiatry, XXI (1958), 21–27; James McKeown, "The Behavior of Parents of Schizophrenic, Neurotic, and Normal Children," American Journal of Sociology, LVI (1950), 175–179; Suzanne Reichard and Carl Tillman, "Patterns of Parent-Child Relationships in Schizophrenia," Psychiatry, XIII (1950), 247–257; Trudy Tietze, "A Study of Mothers of Schizophrenic Patients," Psychiatry, XII (1949), 55–65; and L. Wynne et al., "Pseudo-Mutuality in the Family Relations of Schizophrenics," Psychiatry, XXI (1958), 205–220.

2. As examples, see Amerigo Farina, "Patterns of Role Dominance and Conflict in Parents of Schizophrenic Patients." Journal of Abnormal and Social Psychiatry, LXI (1960), 31–38; Norman Garmezy, Amerigo Farina, and Eliot H. Rodnick, "The Structured Situational Test: A Method for Studying Family Interaction in Schizophrenia," American Journal of Orthopsychiatry, XXX (1960), 445–452; and B. H. Roberts and J. K. Myers, "Schizophrenia in the Youngest Male Child of the Lower Middle Class," American Journal of Psychiatry, CXII (1955), 129–134.

3. John Cumming, "The Family and Mental Disorder: An Incomplete Essay," Causes of Mental Disorders: A Review of Epidemiological Knowledge, 1959 (New York: Milbank Memorial Fund, 1961), pp. 153–177.

4. The participant-observer has been the subject of a wide literature. See, for example, Howard S. Becker and Blanche Geer, "Participant Observation: The Analysis of Qualitative Field Data," in Richard N. Adams and Jack J. Preiss, eds., Human Organization Research, Field Relations and

Techniques (Homewood, Ill.: The Dorsey Press, 1960), pp. 267–289; Nicholas Babchuk, "The Role of the Researcher as Participant Observer and Participant-as-Observer in the Field Situation," *Human Organization,* XXI (1962), 225–228; Florence R. Kluckhohn, "The Participant Observer Technique in Small Communities," *American Journal of Sociology,* XLV (1940), 331–343; Morris S. Schwartz and Charlotte G. Schwartz, "Problems in Participant Observation," *American Journal of Sociology,* LX (1955), 343–353; Arthur Vidich, "Participant Observation and the Collection and Interpretation of Data," *American Journal of Sociology,* LX (1955), 354–360; and William Foote Whyte, "Observational Field-Work Methods," in Marie Jahoda, Morton Deutsch, and Stuart W. Cook, eds., *Research Methods in the Social Sciences* (New York: The Dryden Press, 1951), II, pp. 393–514.

5. Murray Melbin, "An Interaction Recording Device for Participant Observers," *Human Organization,* XIII (1954), 29.

6. All names are fictitious and were supplied by Weiss. All italics have been added.

7. Draft dated April 1961. Carbon copy on file at the New York State Mental Health Research Unit.

8. Respectively, John Cumming, Elaine Cumming, Rhondda Cassetta.

9. Respectively, William Mangin and John Cumming.

10. Respectively, John Cumming, Irwin Goffman, Elaine Cumming.

11. The episodes are not independent, since the thread of the account runs through single visits.

12. So that clues might not be given the judges in grouping episodes by families, the members of all the families were given the same names: each oldest son was renamed George, each second-oldest son, Ralph, and so forth.

13. Frani Cumming, Brandeis University.

14. James Cassetta, Ithaca College; Stephen Cassetta, University of Notre Dame; James Davenport, Plymouth State College; John Fay, Merrimack College; and Timothy Shevlin, Boston College.

15. Daniel Katz, "Field Studies," in Leon Festinger and Daniel Katz, eds., *Research Methods in the Behavioral Sciences* (New York: The Dryden Press, 1953), p. 73.

Part V: It's the Same Everywhere

Editors' Introduction   Most of the encounters described in this book occurred in the city of Syracuse, New York, although a few took place in other cities, and we were witness to the happenings in a rural classroom and a rural county. These few cases do not begin to reflect any systematic sampling of the range of poor people in the world, let alone in the United States. But there are poor people everywhere and, in some ways, wherever they are found, the poor are confronted with some of the same sorts of relationships with the vast impersonal "system" which seems to operate everywhere. In this closing section, we will raise our horizons first to another kind of American city, then to a Caribbean city, then to a comparison between a British city and Syracuse, and finally, to an overview of what seems to be the condition of peoples all over the world in the twentieth century.

In their study of four neighborhoods in a city which, although unique, is also typical, Freeman and Sunshine provide a reminder that there is a tight circle of consequences of prejudice and discrimination. That circle runs from inadequate employment opportunities, to low income, to poor housing in poor neighborhoods, to inferior schools and education, to inadequate employment opportunities, *ad infinitum* in a vicious downward spiral. To breach that tight circle, it must be attacked at all points simultaneously. For there is some justification, in fact, for the complaints of employers, city planners, realtors, educators, *et al.* that they cannot be held fully responsible for a totally reprehensible system, and they cannot separately be expected to cure the ills of a sick society. If treatment is to be effective, it must be applied in not

319

one, but in all areas at the same time. It is to the economics of residential ghettoization that Freeman and Sunshine draw our attention.

The venture into "Another Kind of City" differs from most of the chapters in this book in a number of respects. To describe its major difference at this point would be to reveal the last page of an O. Henry story. Let us leave it with the observation that there *is* a major methodological difference. There are other differences: for example, the perspective of this chapter is not a perspective from among the people, although it certainly deals with a crucial form of encounter between poor Negroes and whites who are better off economically—the residential encounter. Freeman and Sunshine consider some of the facts of neighborhood racial transitions from a market perspective, in a setting unlike those described in previous chapters, in "Another Kind of City."

In contrast to the impersonal operations of the marketplace described in "Another Kind of City," Safa draws us into the close personal networks existing within a San Juan shanty town. In Los Peloteros, a pattern of mutual aid, typical of an earlier era in rural America, persists among the poor. People share. They share labor, household appliances, tools, and, when necessary, even utilities and food. In Los Peleteros, where everyone is poor, people say, *"Nadie aquí pasa hambre"*—"Nobody here goes hungry." Safa illustrates the contrast between these close personal ties and the subservient impersonal encounters between the poor and outsiders. Perhaps the greatest contrast between the first two chapters in this final section is methodological. In part, Safa addresses herself to the problems of applying traditional anthropological field-work techniques to complex urban settings.

Rose's opening chapter in Part II delineated some types of poor people; Safa makes such distinctions, too, but without her more powerful magnification they are distinctions which are frequently less visible to the outsider. Noting the inclinations of the outsider to stereotype the shanty-town dweller, Safa illuminates status distinctions made within the community as well as the variations in life style which can and do exist within an apparently homogeneous slum community. One of the most important elements in Safa's chapter relates to the problems of power, identity, self-esteem, and organization among the poor, referred to earlier by Rainwater, Haggstrom, and others. We are provided in this chapter with a portrait of indigenous organization of sufficient power to attain indigenous goals. The poor in Los Peleteros have a political identity. They and their shanty towns are acknowledged as legal entities and political enclaves—a relationship with "The System" which bestows a degree of dignity and power almost unknown among the poor of the United States and the Old World. Thus we find public utilities, streets, and services provided for what is essentially a squatter community.

But if there are differences between the Puerto Rican shanty town and the American slum, there are also similarities. The San Juan shanty-town dweller, like the poor of the United States slums, must move out of his residential area into the broader community in quest of many services, goods, work, and recreation. But the relationships established with outsiders tend to be symbiotic, and the pattern of isolation in the shanty town persists. As Safa puts it, "despite their dependence on the outside world," the shanty-town dwellers, like the slum dwellers, "remain encased within a web of lower-class relationships."

There are commonalities among the poor—everywhere. And there are gross differences, too. The Sinfields, in their comparisons between unemployed men in a British and an American industrial town, choose not to deal extensively with the differences. Their focus is on similarities between the poor on two sides of the ocean—specifically, on how it feels to be out of work. It doesn't feel very good, either in Syracuse or in Shields. In this chapter, the "unemployables" come to life. Whether in Syracuse or Shields, children have their schools and playmates, housewives have their chores and daily rounds, and a man out of work and at home has nothing—nothing to do and no one to talk with. The loneliness, boredom, and idleness drive him restlessly from the home in search of something or someone. For a man to be out of work gives him the same feeling regardless of which side of the Atlantic he lives on.

Like the Americans, the British have their bureaucratic gatekeepers, making decisions on which of the poor are the more "deserving" and how much they "deserve." What differences exist seem to be less culturally derived and more related to differences in the programmatic efforts of the two nations to deal with the problems generated by what Meadows describes in the closing chapter as the "Mass Society." The Sinfields note, for example, that there does seem to be a difference in medical care. The general irrelevance of health facilities to the American poor, observed repeatedly in Part IV, does not appear to be so in Britain.

Whether in Britain, the United States, Puerto Rico, or "Another Kind of City," there seems to be a strange aura of sameness in the modern world. In the final chapter of this book, Meadows writes of the four

321

major technologies which have brought a degree of sameness to the contemporary scene in whatever corners they have reached. There are, indeed, few corners of the world that have not been touched by the industrial, political, social, and psychological technologies to which he refers. The nature of this "Mass Society" can be, and has been, viewed from a perspective of sheer numbers, from a psychological perspective, or from an organizational perspective. These three somewhat independent theoretical threads lead to essentially the same conclusion regarding man in the modern world: "A pervading sense of something wrong."

Meadows views modern man as the creator, through the organization of his efficient technologies, of his own vulnerability. However, although the problem is frequently perceived from all three of these perspectives, a great diversity of possible solutions is suggested both within each and among all three. There is little agreement among the many scholars cited by Meadows on effective solutions to the commonly perceived state of affairs. Meadows paints a pessimistic panorama of the inevitable future of modern man in mass society—everywhere on this planet. But is doomsday inevitable? Not necessarily, because *all men have the power to act*. "Here is the genius—the troubled genius, to be sure—and the eternal heritage of the society of free men."

Not to exercise this power to act, which each man holds, is, in effect, to betray that genius and eternal heritage of free men. *If* man in fact was consistent; *if* man was rational; *if* man was logical in his behavior, then pessimistic conclusions regarding his future would be justified. Fortunately, as a constantly changing and acting being, man is none of these things, and thus there is hope. Meadows concludes his chapter and this volume with an optimistic faith in man's ability to use his power to act, and his use of that power enunciates the philosophical underpinnings of many of the chapters in this book: "that human beings, all of them, regardless of color or class, must be trusted with the destinies of their own society, because they are human beings."

17 · Another Kind of City

A study of racial transition and property values

LINTON C. FREEMAN AND MORRIS H. SUNSHINE

THIS CHAPTER PRESENTS a study of the impact of racial transition on property values. Studies of this topic are not new. Since the early 1920's, sociologists and real estate analysts have examined the effects of Negro entry on the prices of houses in communities across the country. These writers have focused attention on two main questions: (1) What is the effect of race on housing values? (2) How is this effect achieved? So far, however, no clear-cut answers to these questions have been provided.

Until the 1930's, it was generally agreed that Negro entry into any neighborhood depressed property values. Abrams, for example, cites a book published in 1923 by McMichael and Bingham in which they say:

> With the increase in colored people coming to many Northern cities they have overrun their old districts and swept into adjoining ones or passed to other sections and formed new ones. This naturally has had a decidedly detrimental effect on land values for few white people, however inclined to be sympathetic with the problem of the colored race, care to live near them. Property values have been sadly depreciated by having a single colored family settle down on a street occupied exclusively by white residents.[1]

This is typical of earlier expressions; even the threat of Negro occupancy was thought uniformly to lead to lowered property values. This was seen as the automatic result of the unmodifiable refusal of whites to accept Negro neighbors.

323

During the 1930's and early 1940's, this pessimistic description was revised somewhat. Myrdal,[2] for example, argued that although Negro entry depressed property values, these values would rise again once racial transition was complete. His reasoning seemed to embody the notion of the self-fulfilling prophecy. Whites, he thought, would panic and sell when the Negro "invasion" took place. Thus, whole neighborhoods would change their racial character. After this transition, however, prices would return to a realistic level. In Myrdal's view, stereotyping and prejudice were still the critical explanatory factors.

In the late 1940's, a major change in thinking took place. Weaver[3] observed that Negro entry into a neighborhood did not invariably result in a decline in selling prices. Sometimes prices remained stable, and sometimes they increased. He concluded, therefore, that *"There is no one universal effect of Negro occupancy upon property values."* Weaver proposed four factors (in addition to prejudice) that might be relevant in an attempt to explain this observed variation: (1) non-white income distributions; (2) general business conditions; (3) long-run trend of values in the areas before entry; and (4) how non-white occupancy actually occurs.

Weaver's basic generalization has been confirmed by subsequent investigators. Abrams,[4] for example, concluded that "There are no fixed rules as to when minority neighbors raise or lower values; examples may be cited both ways and much study is still needed." More recently, after a large-scale empirical study, Laurenti[5] reported that ". . . no single or uniform pattern of non-white influence on property prices could be detected." Laurenti went on to specify a list of factors that he suspected were involved in determining housing prices under racial transition.

The major variables interacting in these local situations appear to be: (1) strength of whites' desire to move out; (2) strength of non-whites' desire to move in; (3) willingness of whites to purchase property in racially mixed neighborhoods; (4) housing choices open to whites; (5) housing choices open to non-whites; (6) absolute and relative purchasing power of non-whites; (7) absolute and relative levels of house prices; (8) state of general business conditions; (9) long-run trend of values in areas involved; (10) time.[6]

Thus, recent research has shown that a decline in price level is not a necessary consequence of racial transition. Other factors must be taken into account in any attempt to explain the observation that prices show no uniform response to Negro entry into what were previously all-white neighborhoods.

PROBLEM

Laurenti's work[7] provides a starting point. It suggests some hypotheses about the effects of factors other than racial transition on housing price levels. All of the items on his list can be classified either as manifestations of prejudice or as properties of the housing market. It seems entirely reasonable to assume that factors of both of these types are involved. As Laurenti has suggested, however, the problem is to determine how these factors interact to influence market prices. It is this problem that is the object of concern here.

Previous attempts to solve this problem have utilized either of two basic approaches: (1) they have described the history of racial transition in a single area, or (2) they have compared several areas over relatively short periods of time. An attempt to unravel the joint effects of several variables on the process of racial transition, however, requires that a study be both longitudinal and comparative. Comparable data on several communities must be collected over an extended period of time, but in order to collect such data tremendous resources are usually required. Still, we believe that this type of research should be undertaken, and in this report we will show the results of one such study. In some special kinds of cities, as we shall see, cost need not be a prohibitive consideration.

RESEARCH STRATEGY

The research design was—by current standards—rather simple. It called for the judicious selection and comparative study of urban neighborhoods. We were looking for neighborhoods that were almost identical in nearly every respect. Differences were permissible only in those factors that were assumed to have an impact on the prices at which houses would be sold during a racial transition period. In other words, we were seeking neighborhoods that could be expected to reveal certain clear-cut *types* of transition processes. Our method, therefore, is a simple extension of the "case study" approach.

Two types of variables were considered in selecting neighborhoods for study. Following Laurenti's analysis, we assumed that the price of houses in neighborhoods undergoing racial transition should result from the joint effects of variation in prejudice levels and variation in characteristics of the housing market. The market characteristics included were the purchasing power of applicants for housing and the number of prospective purchasers. These have an obvious intuitive appeal. It is evident that a white neighborhood will remain segregated either if Negroes cannot afford to buy houses in that neighborhood or there are no Negro applications for housing in the neighborhood. Moreover, these two variables—the number of buyers and sellers and their economic power to take part in the exchange process—seem to be the main features of *any* market. In summary, study neighborhoods were selected in terms of their differences in prejudice, the number of Negroes seeking housing, and their purchasing power.

Four neighborhoods were selected with great care. They were similar in nearly every important detail. All were relatively new subdivisions made up of single-family dwellings selling in the $12,000-to-$15,000 price range. They were similar in size (roughly 250 houses each), and all were strictly sales markets—rentals were not generally available. Moreover, at the start of our study period, all were occupied exclusively by white owners, but all were experiencing some pressure for Negro entry. In each case, observations were made over an extended period of time, and during the course of the observation period each of these neighborhoods experienced Negro entry. Observation was continued long enough in each case to establish the trend of its racial composition and price.

RESULTS

The first neighborhood studied was located in a metropolitan area with a small Negro population. There was, therefore, a small but steady stream of Negroes seeking housing. The purchasing power of these Negro applicants was markedly inferior to that of white housing applicants. In general, prejudice levels in the study neighborhood were high.

In this neighborhood, the entrance of Negroes was slow and difficult. In large measure the problem was an economic one: Negroes simply could not afford to pay the prevailing prices. This economic factor reflects prejudice in this region. In the first place, Negroes in this city were subject to discrimination in both jobs and salaries. Their income, therefore, tended to be lower than that of whites. Second, Negroes had difficulty in obtaining credit to purchase homes in a "white" neighborhood. Most Negro buyers, therefore, were simply priced out of the study neighborhood.

Those Negroes who could afford to buy houses in the study neighborhood were frequently shunted aside by realtors. In most cases, realtors simply refused to show available houses to Negro applicants. Negroes seeking housing were often led to believe that few, if any, houses were available in the study neighborhood. Comparable white applicants were, however, readily shown as many available houses as they were willing to look at.

White homeowners also constituted an additional obstacle for Negro purchasers. Our records show that Negro buyers were frequently unable to buy simply because the white owner refused to sell to Negroes. This experience was repeated many times. In this neighborhood, moreover, white hostility was so great that on two occasions Negroes who had purchased houses sold them almost immediately and moved out. However, the third Negro family was able to withstand this community pressure. For several months the family members served as lonely pioneers in an otherwise all-white neighborhood. Then a second Negro family moved in, and a third family followed shortly thereafter. At this point, the pattern of rigid resistance seemed to break. Five more Negro families entered the neighborhood during a brief period. Then realtors exhibited a change in policy. Instead of resisting Negro entry, they seemed perfectly willing to show available houses to Negro applicants.

The pattern exhibited in this neighborhood seems to be the classical one of an invasion-succession. Initially, white homeowners exhibited great (and successful) resistance to the entry of Negroes. Ultimately, however, this pattern was broken. By the time three Negro families had entered the neighborhood, resistance disappeared, and Negroes were freely admitted. In effect, the whites "gave up" the neighborhood to Negroes.

Before Negro entry, housing prices in this neighborhood rose gradually (along with a general regional increase in prices). The number of houses on the market at any time was small (about 2 per cent) and fairly steady. Once a few Negro families entered, however, a rise in vacancies to about 15 to 20 per cent was observed. White owners rushed to put their houses on the market, prospective white purchasers sought housing elsewhere, and the neighborhood was turned over to the Negro purchasers. But, for the most part, the potential Negro buyers were economically disadvantaged and relatively few in number. Prices began to fall, therefore, until they came into the range of the purchasing power of the Negro buyers. The net result was a marked decline in property values from about $15,000 to $10,000 in this neighborhood.

The second neighborhood studied was very much like the first. At the outset, it was inhabited exclusively by whites. The Negro applicants were poor. White prejudice levels were rather high. However, in this instance, the number of Negro applicants was much larger than in the preceding case. Negroes were in the majority in the community at large.

The pattern of white resistance previously described was repeated in this neighborhood. Realtors and owners refused to take part in sales to Negroes. Lending institutions were reluctant to extend credit to Negro purchasers who wanted to buy. Moreover, the first Negro pioneers were subjected to harassment and—as in the first case—several Negro families had to move out. But once a few Negroes became firmly established, the white-flight phenomenon was again observed, and again new white families were unwilling to take their place.

In almost every way the results of Negro entry into this second neighborhood paralleled the results in the first. The neighborhood progressively became a new Negro ghetto. In this case, however, after taking an initial decline, prices climbed back to their original level and stayed there. Thus, this seems to be the kind of situation described by Myrdal.[8]

The return of the price level to its original value in this instance seemed to be the result of the relatively large number of Negro buyers. Very simply, there were enough Negro applicants to restore demand to its previous level. The purchasing power of Negroes was, on the average, less than that of whites. But the population of Negro housing applicants was large enough to include a sufficient number of prosperous buyers to maintain price levels. In the long run, then, the new Negro market was able to generate about as much demand as had the previous all-white market. After the initial transition, therefore, prices returned to their original levels and stayed there.

Residential prejudice levels in the third test neighborhood were as high as in the first two cases. Here again the Negro population was large, but in this case ethnic employment barriers were weak and Negroes enjoyed about the same purchasing power as whites.

Even with economic equality, the previously described constellation of white resistance to Negro entry was observed. Here, however, resistance collapsed earlier. Their relatively advantageous economic status seemed to allow Negroes to compete more effectively in the housing market. Again, the first entry of Negroes caused a flurry of panic sales that led to a brief dip in prices. But as the neighborhood became increasingly populated by Negroes, prices rose until they greatly exceeded their original levels—the average price increased from $15,000 to about $20,000. The end result was another Negro ghetto, but this time it was characterized by unusually high house prices.

This over-all increase in house prices probably resulted from the fact that Negro buyers had a purchasing power equal to that of whites and at the same time were more numerous than whites. The increase, therefore, seems to reflect the effect of an increase in economic demand.

In all of the cases reported so far, high prejudice levels among whites resulted in initial resistance by whites and eventual replacement of white purchasers by Negro purchasers. A white market was, in effect, transformed into a Negro market. The ultimate price level seems simply to be a function of the strength of Negro demand. Where Negroes are few in number and poor, demand is weak and—as one might expect— prices fall. But when Negroes are more numerous or are better off financially, the consequent increased demand may result in house prices that equal or even exceed original levels.

In the fourth and last test neighborhood, white prejudice levels were extremely low. Although there were many Negroes in the area, most whites were insensitive to racial differences. Moreover, the economic status of Negroes in the area was similar to that of whites, and banks and realtors did not seem to discriminate in their business activities. Consequently, the entry of Negroes into this neighborhood was quick, simple, and uneventful.

Throughout the period of observation, this neighborhood displayed a balanced and integrated character. The neighborhood continued to be attractive to both Negro and white buyers. In this case, therefore, relatively low prejudice levels seem to have permitted the establishment of a stable interracial neighborhood. Occasional incidents did occur, but as a whole the transition from white to mixed occupancy was smooth.

In this fourth neighborhood, no dip in prices occurred at any time. Instead, prices climbed from the beginning of Negro entry until they finally seemed to stabilize at a level several thousand dollars above their original levels (nearly $25,000). In this last case, it seems, prices are again a function of demand. But here Negro demand did not *replace* earlier white demand. Instead, Negro and white demand schedules were coupled, and the result was a marked increase in total demand and consequent rise in price levels.

The picture revealed by a comparison of these four neighborhoods confirms Laurenti's observation on the variable effects of Negro entry on house prices. In our view, however, this variability is not surprising. The price at which housing stabilizes turns out, in every case, to be a simple function of supply and demand. With constant supply, neighborhoods where demand is high generate high prices; neighborhoods where demand is low generate low prices.

Ethnic factors are relevant only insofar as they affect supply and demand. Negro entry, *as such*, has *no* effect on price levels, but to the extent that prejudice influences market decisions, Negro entry conditions supply and demand and thus influence prices. It is evident that if Negroes cannot examine or buy houses with the same capability as white buyers, that this is—other things being equal—tantamount to a depression in demand. (Of course, from the perspective of the Negro applicant, this appears as an arbitrary constraint on supply.) Similarly, an equivalent depression in demand occurs whenever ethnic residential prejudice induces prospective white buyers to refuse to buy in a mixed neighborhood. Finally, prejudice may increase supply by encouraging white owners to sell their houses and move out of a neighborhood once it has become mixed.

In general, then, high prejudice levels lead to reduced house prices. This is true when prices under conditions of high prejudice are compared with prices in the situation where prejudice is low. In practice, the entry of Negroes into even a highly prejudiced neighborhood merely substitutes Negro demand schedules for white demand schedules. If Negro demand is greater, prices will rise; if it is smaller, they will fall.

A moderate prejudice distribution will tend to exclude some whites from competition for housing in a mixed neighborhood. The point of price stabilization in this case will depend upon the remaining demand —of Negroes and unprejudiced whites—after the prejudiced whites are excluded. In terms of the total economy, then, any residential prejudice is costly because it restrains trade and the potential expansion of the housing industry.

DISCUSSION OF RESULTS

A step has been made in this chapter to clarify the joint effects of economic and psychological factors in determining house prices in neighborhoods undergoing ethnic transition. Detailed observations were made in four neighborhoods over an extended time period. The results of these comparative observations suggested the way in which these general economic and psychological factors may interrelate to affect house prices.

It should be clear at this point, however, that the neighborhoods we studied were neighborhoods of a special sort. They were nearly identical in most respects; they differed only in terms of experimentally relevant factors. Thus, they dramatize the effects of several factors on the prices of houses in the ethnic transition process. It is often difficult to find neighborhoods exhibiting such stable regularities and such clear and consistent differences in any ordinary city.

The city we studied, however, was no ordinary city. It was, in fact, quite extraordinary in that it was a simulated city. A computer was programmed to "act" like a city undergoing racial transition and the behavior of the computer analogue was studied.

This same procedure is used by engineers to study the aerodynamic properties of a model of a proposed new aircraft in a wind tunnel. The properties of a whole range of basic wing designs can be studied without ever building an actual flying airplane. To the degree that the model faithfully reproduces the design characteristics of the proposed airplane, tests on the model are useful in predicting the aerodynamic properties of an actual airplane. In the present case, to the extent that we are successful in programming a computer to "act" like a city, we can learn about urban neighborhoods by observing and recording its activities.

The results reported here were obtained in the process of developing a larger computer model of housing segregation. A computer program was developed and a large number of runs were made. The details of the model and the over-all results of the simulation will be reported elsewhere.[9] Here we shall simply summarize the general characteristics of the simulation.

Almost any simulation defines a set of objects and a series of attributes or characteristics of each. Then a process is initiated that results in the modification of these attributes as events take place. In the present instance, our objects are houses and households. The attributes of houses are location and occupancy; those of households are ethnicity, purchasing power, economic acquisitiveness, and housing status. A string of events in this model begins when each occupied house in our hypothetical neighborhood is given an opportunity to be vacated. This

331

reflects the normal turnover of occupancy observed in all neighborhoods. Then each vacated house is priced by means of a mechanism that depends upon the "current market." Those families that are seeking housing are then exposed to the market of vacant houses. Their success in making a transaction depends—if they are white—upon their purchasing power and the price of the house, and upon the number and distance of Negro neighbors as conditioned by their own prejudice level.

If the family seeking housing is Negro, however, the family head may have difficulty in obtaining a loan, in seeing a vacant house, in closing a sale, and even in remaining in the house once it is occupied. All of these events depend upon the prejudice levels of whites in the neighborhood and upon economic factors. Then, depending upon these same factors, whites may leave the neighborhood because of the presence of Negroes, and those whites who are seeking housing may decide to look elsewhere. Finally, the prices of those houses that remain unsold are adjusted, and the whole chain of events is repeated.

A computer program was constructed that embodied these objects and events. Runs were made, and the effects of changes in prejudice levels, proportions of Negroes seeking housing, and relative economic conditions were observed. Data on vacancies, sales prices, proportion of Negro occupancy, and segregation within the neighborhood were recorded. In some cases, detailed observations of each transaction were made. In general, the results observed in this hypothetical world were not unreasonable in the light of the literature on racial transition in actual cities.

Clearly, this computer simulation does not "prove" anything. It is, however, a powerful technique for solving theoretical problems in complex social situations. In order to write a computer program, it is necessary to specify our variables and relations precisely. The computer tolerates absolutely no ambiguity. It often happens, therefore, that an expression that seems to be well defined—one that could pass in descriptive sociology—turns out to be fuzzy. In the process of writing computer programs all this hidden ambiguity is forcibly revealed.

A corollary of this result is the fact that the organization of axioms into simulation programs tends also to reveal areas where data are missing. The development of a simulation program involves the specification of numerical values for all relevant variables. In many cases, it turns out that existing data are insufficient for this task. Thus, in writing a program, the attention of the investigator is focused on areas of incomplete empirical information.

In short, computer simulation affords a powerful and convenient tool for organizing knowledge. Factual data suggest that under certain conditions important relations hold among a set of variables. A computer is programmed to reflect these constant conditions or parameters as well as the relevant variables and relations. This program governs the behavior of the computer and initiates a process in which the values taken by the variables may change. These changes are observed and, when possible, compared with changes observed in a natural setting. The set of governing variables and relations may be revised until any desired degree of correspondence is established. In this fashion, simulation may be used to build theory, and theory built in this manner has some hope of tolerating enough complexity to be useful in the solution of practical problems. In the present instance, computer simulation has helped to untangle a set of interrelated variables and thus to point the way toward solution of a significant problem of our society.

Notes

1. Stanley L. McMichael and Robert F. Bingham, *City Growth and Values* (Cleveland, Ohio: The Stanley McMichael Publishing Organization, 1923), p. 159, cited in Charles Abrams, *Forbidden Neighbors* (New York: Harper and Brothers, 1955).

2. Gunnar Myrdal, *An American Dilemma* (New York: Harper and Brothers, 1944).

3. Robert C. Weaver, *The Negro Ghetto* (New York: Harcourt, Brace, 1948).

4. Abrams, *op. cit.*

5. Luigi Laurenti, *Property Values and Race: Studies in Seven Cities* (Berkeley: University of California Press, 1959).

6. *Ibid.,* pp. 47–48.

7. *Ibid.*

8. Myrdal, *op. cit.*

9. Linton C. Freeman and Morris H. Sunshine, *Residential Segregation Patterns* (forthcoming).

18 • The Social Isolation of the Urban Poor

Life in a Puerto Rican shanty town

HELEN ICKEN SAFA

To THE OUTSIDER, the area along the northern border of the Martín Peña Channel appears to be an unbroken mass of tiny shacks packed one upon the other in hopeless confusion. There is no apparent order to this maze of narrow, twisting alleyways, few of which deserve to be called streets. Nothing appears to distinguish one section from the other, and so outsiders often lump the whole area together under the infamous name of El Fanguito (Little Mud Hole).

For people living in the area, however, El Fanguito is only one of the shanty towns, perhaps the best known. Each shanty town has a special name—Tras Talleres, Shanghai, Los Bravos de Boston—and with the name goes a distinct personality. No natural boundaries separate one shanty town from the next, though a street leading in from the main thoroughfare may come to serve as a dividing line. Nor do these boundaries always coincide with the political division into *barrios* set up for administrative purposes. The primary factor distinguishing one shanty town from another is a group sense of belonging together.

This chapter deals with one of these shanty towns, which we shall call here by the fictitious name of Los Peloteros. The author conducted field work in Los Peloteros for a period of fifteen months in 1959 and 1960 as part of a study aimed at measuring the effects of changes in family and community life resulting from the move from a shanty town to a public housing project. In this study, which was sponsored by the Urban Renewal and Housing Administration of the Commonwealth of Puerto Rico, Los Peloteros was used as a sample of a typical urban shanty town located in the midst of the San Juan Metropolitan Area.

335

In the following pages, we shall try to give the reader a look at Los Peloteros and the life its residents lead. We shall not attempt to summarize the results of the study, since this has been done elsewhere,[1] but instead shall view the shanty town, with its distinctive physical features, style of life, and patterns of association, within the context of the larger metropolitan community.

The field of urban research offers a new challenge to anthropologists because of the methodological difficulties involved in studying such a complex milieu. Traditional anthropological techniques of participant-observation with a limited number of informants would appear to be inadequate to ensure a representative sampling of all the heterogeneous elements of an urban population. Yet statistical data collected by standard survey techniques lose the color, the richness, and above all the meaning which direct observation of real people in real situations can provide.

The community study method developed by anthropologists such as Arensberg, Redfield, Steward, and others presents one solution to this dilemma. By limiting the scope of the study to a relatively small, well-defined community, it is possible to retain the standard anthropological technique of direct observation even in as complex a milieu as the modern metropolis. However, it is clear that an urban community is not a self-contained unit in the same sense as is a primitive tribe or even a relatively isolated peasant community. The methods employed in studying an urban community must therefore be designed to take into account the extra-local influences to which its residents are subject and their relationships with the outside world. Too many community studies, as Steward has pointed out, have failed to treat the community within its larger context.[2] We have attempted to correct this in the present study by constantly stressing the relationships between the shanty town and the wider metropolitan community of which it forms a part. We shall begin by tracing the growth of shanty towns as part of the over-all ecological pattern of the San Juan Metropolitan Area.

GROWTH OF SHANTY TOWNS

Metropolitan San Juan is the economic, political, and cultural center of Puerto Rico. This vast urban complex is the location of most of the island's manufacturing, financial, and trade activities; the seat of the Commonwealth Government and the headquarters of numerous local and federal agencies, as well as United States military and naval installations; and the home of the University of Puerto Rico, plus many primary and secondary schools, theaters, and movie houses. The past decade has seen the inauguration of a new international airport and expanded dock facilities for heavy transatlantic shipping; the construction of tall, ultra-modern office and apartment buildings; and the spread along the periphery of suburban Levittowns bordering on new superhighways with their large, bright shopping centers. The flourishing tourist industry has invaded the best beach front with a string of new luxury hotels, and brightly colored signs in English welcome the visitor and urge him to see the latest floor show at one of the fashionable nightclubs.

The present ecological pattern of metropolitan San Juan reflects neither the orderly class stratification of concentric zones characteristic of the North American factory city nor the nucleated Spanish pattern centering on a plaza, but rather a huge "mosaic of discontinuities" typical of the new metropolitan community.[3] Santurce, the busy commercial center of San Juan, is a hodgepodge of neighborhoods varying in type of housing, per capita income, population density, land use, and other socio-economic indicators.[4] But the old colonial two-class division between rich and poor is still noticeable in two relatively homogeneous areas remaining at the opposite ends of Santurce—the fashionable residential district along the beachfront and the sordid shanty towns along the Martín Peña Channel.

Shanty towns are a relatively recent phenomenon in metropolitan San Juan. The depression of the 1930's gave migration its real impetus. Many workers fled the rural area in search of employment in the city and, lacking resources, built their homes on public lands bordering the Martín Peña Channel. Despite the attraction of other cities, the largest number of rural migrants always headed toward the San Juan Metropolitan Area, which as early as 1935 to 1940 received over one half of all inter-regional migrants.[5] Though the great mass came from adjacent regions, particularly in this early period, migrants to San Juan have been drawn from all parts of the island. Thus, in Los Peloteros, the birthplace of rural migrants represents nearly every municipality on the island. There is no apparent tendency for families from the same region to settle in one neighborhood, as in some African and Asian cities. This may be true of a recently settled shanty town, but where a neighborhood has been established over one generation, as in this case, any initial concentration from one area has been dispersed and replaced by more recent migrants.

The formation of shanty towns appears to have started at a point close to the mouth of the Martín Peña Channel and to have spread in linear fashion along its banks inland, in the direction of Rio Piedras. Shanty towns have characteristically been confined to marginal public lands along the banks of the Channel or on the waterfront, property essentially unfit for either residential or commercial use. Residents never acquire legal title to the land, which remains public property, but shanties on it are bought and sold in perfectly legal transactions. Even the government compensates shanty-town dwellers for the loss of their homes in slum clearance programs.

This location along marginal, public lands distinguishes shanty towns from what may properly be called a slum. Slums are usually located in the center of the city, close to the central business district, and consist of once-adequate structures which have been converted from their original use to tenements housing many times their anticipated occupancy. Shanties, on the other hand, are from the outset inadequate structures; most are rather flimsily constructed with makeshift materials and unskilled labor provided by the owner and his friends. Thus, while slums are a form of blight or deterioration characteristic of highly industrialized cities, shanty towns are commonly found in the pre-industrial cities of the underdeveloped areas where marginal, public lands still exist on the urban fringe.

Approximately 86,000 people now reside in the five-mile belt of shanty towns extending along the Martín Peña Channel.[6] Though efforts have been made to reduce this figure through slum clearance and public housing programs, new shanty towns are constantly springing up as the stream of migrants continues to pour into the metropolis. A decade ago, it was estimated that from 800 to 1,200 families, mostly in the low-income group, migrated to San Juan every year.[7] Overcrowding can be measured by the fact that the average lot size in shanty towns is 16 by 24 feet, with an average density of nearly 100 persons per acre.[8]

Clearly, it is impossible to understand the growth of shanty towns without seeing them as part of the over-all pattern of urban development in the San Juan Metropolitan Area. Their emergence as distinct neighborhoods can be explained largely in terms of the need for an urban labor force to fill the demands of San Juan as the ever-expanding economic, political, and cultural center of Puerto Rico. Yet, the shanty town itself is characterized by a specific settlement pattern, life style, and other features which distinguish it from other neighborhoods in the metropolitan area.

338

THE SETTING OF THE SHANTY TOWN

Because of its location on marginal land, the shanty town is set off both physically and socially from the rest of the metropolitan area. The only residential area bordering on Los Peloteros is the string of equally squalid shanty towns leading off from its western boundary. To the south and east it is bounded by the waters of the Channel and to the north by a main thoroughfare, now a four-lane highway.

A total of 16,947 persons live in the political subdivision encompassing Los Peloteros, in an area covering approximately 82 acres, giving it a density of about 200 persons per acre.[9] Except for a narrow strip of land bordering the new expressway, every available inch of land has been utilized. Some houses even extend over the banks of the Channel, supported by wooden piles built into the water. These houses are considered the poorest in the shanty town and their inhabitants are referred to as *Los de abajo* (those below). Plank sidewalks just wide enough to allow two people to pass provide the only means of access. Further inland, conditions improve somewhat and houses are higher priced. Thus, residence within the shanty town itself is ranked differentially depending upon distance from the Channel.

Each shanty town has been built up gradually over many years through the joint efforts of the families settling there. Twenty-five years ago, for example, the first families arriving in Los Peloteros found only mangrove growing in the swampy land destined to become their home. They cleared and filled in a few plots to construct their houses and built plank sidewalks connecting different parts of the shanty town. Today street names such as O'Higgins, Colón, and Pablo Nuñez commemorate the struggle of these first families in the places where they established their homes.

For many years Los Peloteros was without water and electricity. The entire *barrio* depended upon a single public faucet. Now running water and electricity have been installed in almost every house, thanks to the work of *barrio* committees. As recently as 1959, a group of neighbors went to the Aqueduct Authority to complain about the shortage of water in one section of the shanty town. The Authority informed the group that no funds could be allocated for installing new pipes in Los Peloteros because the houses were soon to be demolished under an urban renewal program. The group then rallied support among their neighbors, who refused to pay their water bills. They collected signatures for a petition to Doña Felisa, the well-known Mayoress of San

Juan, and a few of the more articulate individuals went to see her personally. Eventually a new and larger pipe line was installed.

In the same way, committees were formed to protest the poor condition of the streets in the shanty town. They succeeded in having a few of the principal streets filled in with gravel, but still none are paved or lighted. When the weather is dry, the air is choked with dust churned up by passing vehicles. In heavy rains, the roads are closed to motor traffic and even become difficult for pedestrians. Because of the low level of the land, water drains into the shanty towns from higher ground, turning the streets to mud. Pools of stagnant water are left behind for days, creating additional health hazards.

No sewage system exists in Los Peloteros. Most families have latrines in the back of the house and a few have flush toilets that empty into the Channel. Refuse and waste are also disposed of in the Channel, since there is no garbage collection service. Until recently, the Channel served as a main sewage outlet for the city as a whole, and the polluted waters produce a foul, nauseating stench.

As we can see, shanty-town dwellers are still deprived of many essential public services—garbage collection, a sewage system, street lighting, and paved roads. They also must leave the neighborhood to do most of their shopping. At the main entrance to the shanty town is a cluster of old frame buildings housing a grocery store, a pharmacy, a barbershop, and a billiard hall. Scattered throughout the neighborhood are several small *tiendas* selling a limited variety of canned goods and other commodities, plus some still smaller *ventorrillos,* where the number of articles is reduced to a few non-perishable items such as lard, matches, or cans of tomato paste. For daily purchases, Pelotereños rely largely on these local stores, but usually the big, weekly purchase of food (*la compra*) is made at a larger *colmado* in Barrio Obrero, an old working-class district located across the avenue from the shanty town. Clothing and household goods are also bought in Barrio Obrero, where they are colorfully displayed on racks outside the store. This is where Pelotereños go to movies or dances on Saturday nights or where men meet at a favorite café. In a sense, Los Peloteros is considered merely a poorer offshoot of *el barrio,* as it is popularly called.

Of course, Pelotereños must leave the neighborhood to find work because there are almost no employment opportunities in the shanty town itself. As early as five or six in the morning, they board the buses on the main avenue and scatter to all parts of the city, from the docks in old San Juan to the new suburbs under construction in Rio Piedras. Here we

340

can see clearly the dependence of the shanty town on the wider metropolitan community.

Obviously, Los Peloteros is by no means a self-contained community. It is a one-class segregation, highly dependent on the resources and services of the wider metropolitan community. Shanty-town residents are in constant contact with people from other neighborhoods and other socio-economic levels in the city. The people they work for, the people they buy from, and their friends and relatives living in other parts of the city all represent part of the larger metropolitan community. Pelotereños depend on the city to provide them with water, electricity, and institutional facilities such as schools and hospitals. They participate in political parties, labor unions, and other organizations which link them to the larger urban area. Thus, we cannot study the shanty town as an isolated whole. Its heavy dependence on the resources, services, and institutions of the larger urban community make it an integral part of the modern metropolis.

VARIATIONS IN LIFE STYLE IN THE SHANTY TOWN

Despite the fact that the shanty town is a one-class segregation, it is not a homogeneous community. There is considerable variation in the standard of living of shanty-town families, and a limited amount of upward mobility is evident. We have already seen how lower status is accorded those families living on or near the Channel. Similarly, houses vary considerably in size and condition. Some have as many as three bedrooms, while the majority have only one. A few dwellings are just one-room shacks. Some are well kept and painted, others are in need of major repairs, and still others are completely beyond repair. To illustrate the variation in house values, three adjacent houses in Los Peloteros received assessments at the same time for $1,600, $600, and $100, respectively.

Shanties now are generally bought because of the lack of space in the shanty town for new construction. In some cases, old houses are bought cheaply and repaired and remodeled by the new owner, with the help of his neighbors and friends. The exchange of labor and skills in the repair and improvement of their homes constitutes one of the main avenues of cooperation among men in the shanty town. The only compensation in these cases may be in the form of food and drink and, of course, the expectation that these favors will be reciprocated. A man who fails to reciprocate will find himself without an assistant when he needs one.

Despite differences in size and state of repair, however, houses follow

341

a standard design which retains many rural features. Most houses are simple, single-story frame buildings with wooden floors and walls and with roofs of corrugated, galvanized iron. All of the houses are raised on wooden piles to prevent inundation in heavy rains as well as to forestall decay, since there is no basement. Because of the swampy soil, shanties must be periodically raised and the land underneath refilled with dirt and rocks. In this task, shanty-town families are customarily assisted by the local *compromisario* (ward boss) of the Popular party, who supplies men and materials for the operation. The *compromisario* is always a resident of the shanty town and his office in Los Peloteros, located prominently at the main entrance to the neighborhood, is often visited by residents requesting assistance of various kinds.

There are usually two entrances to each house, one in the back and the main one in front. Since the house is built high, it must be entered by a few wooden steps which, when expenses and space permit, are expanded into a small porch or veranda. Most casual conversation between neighbors is conducted on the porch or steps or from the window. Sitting on the steps, chatting and watching the passers-by, is a common pastime in the late afternoon.

The tempo of life in the shanty town accelerates considerably in the late afternoon when the men return home from work. In the morning, the women are busy washing clothes, cleaning the house, and preparing the main meal, which, as in the rural area, is still served at noon. The children are away at school, so the streets are almost deserted and the neighborhood is relatively quiet. But as the children and the men return and the women finish their work, everyone gathers outside, on the street, on the porches, and in the stores.

More formal visits are held in the living room. Some space in the houses is always reserved for receiving visitors, even if the only furniture consists of a few old wooden chairs. Where bedroom space is inadequate, as is often the case in large households, the living room will be converted into a bedroom at night by bringing out folding cots, which are stored away during the day. Better homes are furnished with a living-room set consisting of matching sofa and chairs and perhaps a coffee table. Brightly colored, cheap plastic covers have replaced the old rural wicker-and-wood combinations. The old-fashioned china closet has been shoved to one side, and the place of prominence is now occupied by a portable television set. Large painted photographs of family members hang on the wall, along with the school diplomas in

342

which the family takes such pride. The floor is lined with linoleum, which is always kept spotlessly clean.

No home has a separate dining room and few families ever own dining-room furniture since its value is mostly symbolic. Dining-room furniture is a sign of prosperity in the shanty-town household but has little practical use. The family rarely eats together and only the male head of the household or special guests are served at the table. Everyone else eats wherever he happens to be sitting or standing.

The kitchen may be an additional room or simply an extension of the living room, but, in keeping with rural custom, it is always in the rear of the house. A few families are fortunate enough to own a gas stove, with the gas supplied from a tank installed outside the house. Kerosene stoves are still found in most shanty-town households, increasing the danger of fire among the closely packed wooden shacks. A majority of families now own a refrigerator, sometimes second-hand, which is always prominently displayed in the living room. Others either have an old-fashioned icebox, for which they must buy ice daily from local delivery trucks, or are forced to store a few items such as milk in their neighbor's refrigerator. The amount of food stored is usually very small, since most perishable articles are purchased daily. Only staples such as rice, beans, lard, and tomato sauce are bought in quantity and in advance.

Bedrooms exhibit the same variation in living standards. Only the better houses in the shanty town have three bedrooms, permitting parents and children of the opposite sex to sleep separately. Even then, older children generally share beds with siblings of the same sex. A man and wife always occupy one bed alone, except when newborn infants sleep with them to aid the mother in breast-feeding. A baby may also be put in a small hammock strung across the parents' bed within easy reach of the mother. In one extreme case, a family of ten shared one bedroom, the parents occupying one bed and their eight children another.

Despite the overcrowding, there is great emphasis on personal cleanliness. Following rural custom, showers are taken daily, usually in the late afternoon when the men return from work. The shower is improvised in a closet-sized wooden shack at the back of the house near the latrine. The water drains off into the yard through a hole in the floor. Families without these facilities have to be content with a sponge bath.

Most persons do not own many clothes, so that washing seems to be an almost daily occurrence. Washing is usually done outside the house, where it is cooler; an aluminum tub and a wooden washboard are used for this task. Only a few families can afford the luxury of a washing machine, though most now own electric irons. Since closets are virtually unknown, clothes are hung from hangers on a pole nailed across one corner of the bedroom or, in more prosperous families, stored in a *ropero,* or wooden wardrobe.

The most common article in any household is a radio. All day long it is turned on full volume, blaring out mournful love songs and reporting the latest news, baseball scores, and winners at the race track. In recent years, television has gained increasing popularity and families without a set often gather together in a neighbor's house to see the latest *novela* (soap opera).

Differences in the quantity and quality of household furnishings, and in the size and state of repair of the house and its distance from the Channel, point up the socio-economic heterogeneity of the shanty-town population. Annual family incomes in Los Peloteros range from under $500 to over $5,000, and with increases in income goes a steadily improving standard of living. For example, in our sample, no family with an annual income over $3,000 is without a radio and a refrigerator, and most also own a television set. These more prosperous families commonly assist their less fortunate neighbors. Peletereños may donate the use of their refrigerator or invite a neighbor's children to watch television. Men cooperate in the repair and improvement of their homes. Small articles like tools or electric irons are constantly being borrowed, while very poor families may be forced to tap their neighbors' electricity or to draw on their water supply. Even food is shared. Some old men living alone in the shanty town depend almost completely on neighboring families for their meals, for which they contribute little or nothing. As one of my informants remarked when a neighbor passed by with a plate of rice and beans: *"Nadie aquí pasa hambre."* (No one goes hungry here.)

The pattern of sharing and mutual aid acts as a leveling device in the shanty-town community, much as the sponsoring of religious fiestas redistributes wealth in the peasant community.[10] The person who shares his possessions with others is rewarded with greater prestige than the one who withholds them for his own use. By his ability to help others, he demonstrates his own relative prosperity. Thus, sharing supports status distinctions based on differences in living standards; at the same

344

time it prevents these distinctions from becoming too great. By distributing benefits which might otherwise be confined to a few families, sharing tends to equalize some of the differences in socio-economic standing in the shanty town. Too high a degree of internal differentiation would weaken neighborhood solidarity by destroying its basic homogeneity. The pattern of sharing, on the other hand, ties Pelotereños together in a system of mutual aid; community cohesion is reinforced through the interdependence of its members.

PATTERNS OF ASSOCIATION WITHIN THE SHANTY TOWN

Relationships between residents of the shanty town are reciprocal, highly personal, and largely non-utilitarian. We have seen how Pelotereños cooperate with one another and share the little they have with less fortunate neighbors. Their closest contacts tend to be with people living in their own immediate neighborhood, and these relationships often persist over long periods.

The first place of settlement for most newly arrived lower-class rural migrants is the shanty town, from which they are gradually absorbed into other areas of the city. In this movement also can be seen the interconnections between the shanty town and the wider metropolitan community. Despite this constant turnover of personnel, however, there is a core of "old-timers," made up of some of the original settlers of the shanty town, that contributes greatly to neighborhood stability. These residents form a stable nucleus to whom new migrants can attach themselves and they also provide an important source of leadership and continuity to the community. Don Andres, who is president of the Housing Cooperative in Los Peloteros, has lived in the neighborhood for twenty years, and his wife for thirty. He is steadily employed as an electrician at the docks, where he is secretary of his labor union. All of his children have been born in Los Peloteros, all are receiving at least a high school education, and one son plans to become a lawyer. Thus, long-time residents are not necessarily the least progressive, for, as we have pointed out, there is considerable room for upward mobility within the shanty town.

Newcomers to the shanty town often settle near a relative who helps them adjust to urban life. Frequently the relative will have found a home for the migrants and sent for them to come. He assists them in finding employment, shows them where to shop, and takes them to the hospital. The house of one old couple in Los Peloteros was surrounded

345

by the houses of their children and grandchildren, copying the same settlement pattern to which they had been accustomed in the rural area.

Kinship provides an important link between residents in the shanty town. More than half of the Pelotereños in our sample had relatives living in the neighborhood and they generally see each other daily. Though they may not occupy the same dwelling unit, such a kin group is often a tightly knit functional unit, cooperating extensively in the care of children and other household tasks. Thus, Doña Ana's niece was a frequent visitor to her aunt's house and her children were often left there for days at a time. Shortly before the birth of her third child, the niece moved into a house across the street so that she would be close to her aunt. Doña Ana assisted during the delivery, which took place in her home, and took care of her niece and children until the young mother was able to resume her household duties.

Relatives are particularly important to women, for bonds of kinship are emphasized in the maternal line. Though they associate extensively with their neighbors, women often remark that their only real friends are relatives—usually other females such as a mother, sister, or daughter. Children come to know their mother's relatives far better than those of their father, simply because they see more of the former. The bond to the maternal grandmother may be particularly strong, reflecting her dominant position in the kin group.

Effective social contact is generally restricted to relatives living in the same or nearby neighborhoods. Visiting with nearby relatives is a favorite Sunday pastime, particularly among women, who usually take their younger children with them. Even when men are present, there is little mixed conversation. A group of women gather in the kitchen or the bedroom to talk over family gossip or admire a new household appliance, while the men remain in the living room, discussing incidents at work or the latest political news. Most social life is centered in the home, as the following quotation from my field notes illustrates:

> The barrio was very much alive when we returned about six, with visits in every house. Carmen's mother was there, and a friend with a teen-age girl. The nurse's husband lay on the porch playing with his child, until his mother came to take her in. Don Francisco talked to a male friend in his living room. Lorenzo was drinking with two or three friends in his house. Children of all ages played together in the street.

346

Blood ties between neighbors in the shanty town are amplified by ties of marriage. There is no stated preference for endogamy, but marriage between members of the local neighborhood seems to be fairly frequent as a natural consequence of limited contact with the outside world. The social life of girls in particular is largely confined to the shanty town. Two teen-age sisters in Los Peloteros were severely criticized by their neighbors because their mother allowed them to go unchaperoned to dance in Barrio Obrero until late at night. Their mother lived alone with the children of two consensual unions, and it was generally assumed the girls would end up the same way.

Many *compadres* are also chosen from among immediate neighbors. *Compadrazgo* is a ritual kin tie important in Latin America because it establishes a bond between the baptismal godparents of the child and his real parents; thus *compadrazgo* serves very often to incorporate neighbors and close friends into the kinship system. The choice of neighbors as *compadres* in Los Peloteros hence reinforces already existing neighborhood ties.

Ties of kinship, marriage, and *compadrazgo* also integrate a neighborhood indirectly, since they provide an additional point of contact among unrelated people. For example, Pedro does not only know Uncle Juan in the next block, but also Luís, who is Juan's next-door neighbor. Thus, Pelotereños live in what Bott has termed a "highly connected network" of relatives, neighbors, and friends.[11] This leads to a closely integrated neighborhood with a strong sense of group identity and cohesion.

Los Peloteros is a very friendly neighborhood. Almost everyone in the shanty town knows everyone else, and the outsider is spotted immediately. Even men tend to find most of their friends in the immediate neighborhood and spend much of their leisure time in a local *cafetín,* or bar. The same crowd of men commonly congregates in a favorite locale nightly to drink, gab, listen to the jukebox, or play a game of dominoes. The proprietor often becomes one of the "gang" and it pays to be his friend, since he may be called upon to extend credit when cash is low.

Stores are a favorite meeting place for people of all ages in the shanty town. Like the *cafetínes,* the small *tiendas* and *ventorrillos* in Los Peloteros usually serve a rather steady clientele drawn from the immediate vicinity. Customers who stop to talk as they shop are customarily neighbors for whom this functions as an additional point of contact.

There is no central authority in the shanty-town community, or even a central point at which people may gather, such as the plaza in the Puerto Rican rural town. The integration of the community, instead of being based on a hierarchy of established authority, is built up through a series of overlapping segmentary groups, each of which is composed of perhaps half a dozen neighbors. Contact between the groups is maintained by persons who are members of more than one group because of close friends, *compadres,* or relatives living in other parts of the neighborhood. These persons serve as connecting links through which the more extensive associations of kinship and friendship operate to build up an over-all neighborhood unity.

Cooperation is most evident in times of crisis. We have already referred to the help given by female relatives or neighbors at the birth of a child. Crises such as fire enlist the aid of all able-bodied men in the neighborhood. Neighbors know that a fire can spread rapidly in the wooden, tightly packed houses of the shanty town and are quick to form bucket brigades to help extinguish it. Fires are often brought under control long before the fire trucks arrive, particularly in areas difficult to reach near the Channel.

Social control in the shanty town rests not so much on outside authority as with the neighbors themselves. The highly connected network of relatives, neighbors, and friends permits no deed to go unnoticed, and deviant behavior reflects not only on the person himself but on his family and friends as well. Responsibility for the regulation of neighborhood affairs rests largely with the men. For example, men may attempt to end a fight between neighbors or tell a drunkard to do his drinking elsewhere, while women are hesitant to intervene in non-family affairs. The previously mentioned *barrio* committees to improve conditions in the shanty town are also made up largely of men.

The close integration of the shanty-town community serves an important function for both the newly arrived migrant and the older low-income residents of the modern metropolis. The shanty town provides a stable setting within which migrants may gradually adapt to the new way of life in the city. While shanty-town residents live in San Juan and work at urban jobs, their life in Los Peloteros retains important folk-like characteristics, with a strong emphasis on primary group ties. Prestige accrues to a man as he serves on *barrio* committees, or becomes an officer of the local housing cooperative, or helps a neighbor repair his house, or beats him at a game of dominoes. This prestige may not add to his status in the larger society, but it does give him a position of importance within the primary reference point of the shanty-town community. Thus, the cohesion of the shanty town permits the urban poor to retain an integral, meaningful style of life despite their position at the bottom of the social ladder.

THE SHANTY TOWN AND THE OUTSIDE WORLD

The cohesion of the shanty-town community clearly distinguishes it from the anomie normally thought to characterize urban neighborhoods. In his classic article on "urbanism as a way of life," Wirth has described the weakening of kinship and neighborhood bonds and the replacement of primary group ties with the secondary associations which usually accompany the urbanization process. In the urban community, according to Wirth, relationships are generally utilitarian and specialized, leading to widespread depersonalization and the growth of competition and formal control mechanisms.[12]

Our description of the highly personal nature of life in the shanty town stands in sharp contrast to Wirth's analysis. In this chapter we have attempted to identify some of the sources of this cohesion. Thus, one fact of obvious importance is that the shanty town was built up through the joint effort of newly arrived migrant families, struggling to establish a home in the city and facing similar difficulties in their adjustment to the urban milieu. Many of these families have lived in the area for a long time, so that despite the constant turnover of personnel in the shanty town, there is a core of "old-timers" to whom new migrants can attach themselves and through whom they become incorporated into the network of neighborhood relationships. Many of the formal and informal leaders of the shanty town are drawn from this core of old-timers, such as the ward boss or the president of the local housing cooperative. Bonds of kinship, friendship, and *compadrazgo* unite the shanty town, which is the center of social life for men and women alike. In Los Peloteros, there are many small, intimate meeting places such as stores or bars scattered throughout the neighborhood, where neighbors and friends may get together and exchange the latest gossip or news. The pattern of sharing and cooperation draws neighbors together in common endeavors and concerns and reduces the impact of socioeconomic differences among families in the shanty town. The visibility of neighbors in the shanty town, promoted by the single-family dwellings with their open windows and porches, also leads to greater sociability than is typically found in the more enclosed setting of apartment houses.

The highly personal nature of relationships in the shanty town contrasts markedly with the impersonal nature of relationships with other classes in the metropolis. Pelotereños may meet people from other classes in church, for example, but only in the impersonal setting of public worship. Persons from other socio-economic levels seldom participate in the more important life-crisis ceremonies such as weddings and baptisms, which are confined largely to the immediate network of relatives, neighbors, and friends. Most transactions with persons of higher status leave the lower-class person in a subservient position, as a customer in a store, a worker in a factory, or a patient in a clinic, dependent upon others ". . . who own the instruments of production, provide the work opportunities and sell the commodities to be bought." [13]

Participation by Pelotereños in this outside world is highly selective. The stores at which they shop, the bars and theaters they frequent, the places at which they work, and even the church services they attend, all cater to the lower class. Their use of public schools and public medical services is further proof of their proletarian status. Because of the large number of parochial and other private schools on the island, students in public elementary and secondary schools are drawn largely from the lower class. Similarly, few shanty-town families can afford the luxury of private doctors or clinics when there are public health services available to them free of charge. This pattern of interaction does not break down the physical and social isolation of the shanty town. On the contrary, it draws Pelotereños into closer association with members of their own proletarian class within the wider metropolitan community, while in effect minimizing contact with other classes in the city. Thus, despite their dependence on the outside world, Pelotereños remain encased in a web of lower-class relationships.

Hence, a class subculture may be defined not only in terms of shared norms and values but also in terms of distinct patterns of interaction. The pattern of utilitarian, specialized, and impersonal relationships described by Wirth properly applies only to relationships *between* the classes in a metropolis. *Within* the shanty town and within the class subculture, relationships tend to be highly personal, reciprocal, and nonutilitarian. Despite the diversities of socio-economic status among them, shanty-town families know that they face essentially similar life chances and follow essentially similar life styles. They are drawn together by

350

their common position at the bottom rung of the social ladder and by their physical and social isolation from other classes in the metropolis.

Not all urban neighborhoods are characterized by the highly connected network of relatives, neighbors, and friends found in Los Peloteros. According to Bott, highly connected networks are usually associated with neighborhoods strengthened by bonds of kinship, continuity of residence, and a fairly homogeneous social structure.[14] These requirements are more easily met in long-established lower-class neighborhoods such as Los Peloteros than in the new middle-class suburbs or even in the transient Negro ghettos. Yet if we break down the modern metropolis into its constituent subcommunities and class subcultures, we see that within each of these there is a style of life different from the impersonal nature of relationships that characterizes the city as a whole.

Notes

1. Helen Icken Safa, "From Shanty Town to Public Housing: A Comparison of Family Structure in Two Urban Neighborhoods in Puerto Rico," *Caribbean Studies*, IV (1964), 3–12.

2. Julian Steward, *Area Research: Theory and Practice* (New York: Social Science Research Council, 1950), p. 50.

3. Conrad Arensberg, "American Communities," *American Anthropologist*, LVII (1955), 1156. Reprinted in Conrad Arensberg and Solon Kimball, eds., *Culture and Community* (New York: Harcourt, Brace and World, Inc., 1965).

4. Theodore Caplow, Sheldon Stryker, and Samuel E. Wallace, *The Urban Ambiance: A Study of San Juan, Puerto Rico* (Totowa, N.J.: The Bedminster Press, 1964), pp. 38–39.

5. Robert Parke, "Internal Migration in Puerto Rico" (Master's essay, Columbia University, 1952), p. 13.

6. Theodore Caplow *et al.*, *op. cit.*, p. 41.

7. Eduardo Barañano, *Master Plan for the San Juan Metropolitan Area* (rev. ed.; San Juan: Puerto Rico Planning Board, 1955), p. 56.

8. Theodore Caplow *et al.*, *op. cit.*, p. 56.

9. *Ibid.*, p. 55.

10. Eric Wolf, "Closed Corporate Peasant Communities in Mesoamerica and Central Java," *Southwestern Journal of Anthropology*, XIII (1957), 4–5.

11. Elizabeth Bott, *Family and Social Network* (London: Tavistock Publications, 1957), especially pp. 52–61 and 92–96.

12. Louis Wirth, "Urbanism as a Way of Life," *American Journal of Sociology*, XLIV (1938), 11–17.

13. Sidney Mintz, "The Folk-Urban Continuum and the Rural Proletarian Community," *American Journal of Sociology*, LIX (1953), 141.

14. Bott, *op. cit.*, p. 64.

19 · Out of Work in Syracuse and Shields

DOROTHY AND ADRIAN SINFIELD

IN THE 1930's, unemployment struck widely and more or less indiscriminately. The general disaster aroused general sympathy: there was the feeling on seeing the queue before the employment exchange of, "There, but for the grace of God, go I." Today unemployment is confined more and more to certain groups in certain jobs in certain areas, and the rest of the work force has greater security. Some groups are particularly vulnerable—the unskilled or the disabled, the Negro high school dropout, the older worker in a declining industry in a depressed area.

At the same time, programs and services for the unemployed have both improved and increased. The drop in the number of unemployed and the existence of these services are often taken as proof of the diminished problem of unemployment. While this may be true for the community at large, it tells us little about what happens to those who do experience unemployment today. It is not unusual to hear, "Of course, these people think they're hard up. I tell you, they don't know what it's like to be out of work. I can remember when my father and my brother were out in the Thirties—all the families in the street were on relief. That's when times were bad."

Instead of recognizing the industrial facts of life, some are likely to put their greater security down to their own efforts. The creed of the old Poor Law of Britain and the United States—"any man can find work who really wants it"—still has many subscribers, and as unemployment has dropped after the recent depression in both countries it has gained new circulation. In 1964, when there were ten vacancies for

353

unskilled laborers known to the local employment exchange and over 450 laborers registered as unemployed, a town clerk said, "They're only the dregs left on the dole: there's nothing you can do for people like that." This remark recalls the many reports of the 1930's which identified the number of "unemployables" in millions. What was surplus labor at a time of peace became essential manpower in war.

This is a report on two surveys of unemployed men and their families which sought to describe the experience of unemployment in terms of what it meant to these people. In the winter of 1963–1964, we interviewed a random sample of ninety-two unemployed men living in North Shields in northeast England. The following winter we interviewed a second group of sixty men in Syracuse, in upstate New York. Syracuse is a modern manufacturing town of 200,000, located about 280 miles from New York City. North Shields forms half of a county borough of 70,000 on the eastern end of the old industrial area of Tyneside. The traditional industries are shipbuilding, heavy engineering, fishing, and mining. During the period of the first interviews in each town, the rate for male unemployment was between 4 and 5 per cent, and this dropped to below 4 per cent at the time of second interviews in the late winter and early spring. This meant that Syracuse had less unemployment than the rest of the country, while North Shields was about twice as badly hit as the average town in Britain, although it was better off than the rest of the northeast.

Differences between towns some three thousand miles apart in different countries are not hard to find. To an Englishman, Syracuse often appeared wastefully and widely sprawled out. Vivid patches of color caught the eye from vast billboards by day or neon signs at night. The perpetual flutter of service station flags added a false note of gaiety. An American in Shields might notice first the old narrow streets and terraced houses of stone or deep-red brick. Where the house did not front on to the street with a highly polished doorstep, wooden fences or brick walls separated even the smallest and most ill-kept garden from the road and its neighbors.

But the similarities were also there. The worst housing seemed to be near the factories and the railway yards. The all-purpose corner store, the pub or bar, and the thrift or bargain shops often provided the only color in these streets. Although there was some good public housing in both towns—where we found few unemployed—there was much that might be described as "purpose-built slums," in which the local housing

354

department seemed to have lost all interest apart from collecting the rent. The lines of washing, the children playing, the general air of shabbiness were common to both areas.

For the rest of the people living in North Shields, the public housing estate of "The Ridges" was a tough, dirty, and disreputable world. Everyone knew what was meant by "Of course, they live in the Ridges." The worst of fates was to be in "lower Ridges," where, we were frequently told, lived the problem families, the work-shy, and "the dregs" of North Shields. "You can see their sort a mile off," said one shopkeeper, "and I know them because I've been doing youth work with them for years." "I bet the cruelty man [the National Society for the Prevention of Cruelty to Children officer] has his time cut out there," one local government official hinted ominously. The social distinctions were made easier by the geographic isolation of the estates: two school playing fields and a garden allotment separated the old town from the public housing. The "lower Ridges" nearer the river Tyne had been built before the war as the first part of the borough's redevelopment scheme. In this estate were now many residents of the old slums. The houses were often in poor condition, with cracked and twisted metal windows that would not close properly and which let in the vigorous northeast winds that blew across the estate from the North Sea. The responsibility for the bad state of the houses was disputed, the housing council blaming the tenants and the tenants the council. Most of the families seemed anxious to move out and many had relatives who had already done so. There was often little contact with, and much disapproval of, the neighbors in this area—contrary to the picture often presented of great neighborliness in poor working-class areas. "The gasman said ours was the only meter in the street which had not been broken into," said one man. "The sooner we're out of here the better."

In Syracuse, the living conditions of those without jobs were pictured as follows:

> Most of the unemployed were found either in the older public housing projects and the surrounding areas, or in old neighborhoods—some still lined with trees in memory of richer days. At first glance these older areas seemed fairly attractive. They looked better in winter; the white of snow was prettier than dirt where grass should be. The houses were sometimes still quite handsome, but upkeep and repairs were minimal. In some, handwritten signs announced that decent people live

355

here; that women are not permitted in men's rooms; that doors must be closed; and please do not litter the hallways.

The living quarters themselves had walls covered with layers of cheap paint that could never be washed. Cracks and holes in the walls were not repaired; the remains of gas line connections and no-longer-functioning electrical outlets were left in place —everything was just painted over. Rough floors with wide boards were covered with crumbling linoleum, rugs worn past color, or nothing. In some old buildings people seemed to be tucked into every available corner. In cutting up these places there appeared to have been but one concern—that no place that might yield a rent check be wasted. There were apartments in attics and sheds and cellars, and down the long, dark hallways. It was not safe to assume that two or four or six mailboxes meant two or four or six living spaces. The landlord did not live there—it was his business, a lucrative business with low overhead.[1]

Even while the sample was still being collected, differing attitudes to unemployment became evident. In tidy little crescents of semidetached, mock-Tudor private homes in North Shields, the caller who inquired if there were any unemployed living there might be told with marked coolness, "My husband has a very steady job. I should try the other side of the main road, you'll find plenty of *them* over there," or, as if it were a joke, "Oh, goodness no. No one out of work here." In both towns the receptions in such areas (in Syracuse, the equivalent would be tree-lined streets with pleasant, well-decorated houses and tidy lawns) could be short and businesslike, even abrupt. You have to explain clearly who you are and what you want. People may show annoyance at being bothered and occasionally refuse to speak to you.

In the poorer areas, the frequent reply to the inquiry about unemployment was, "No, thank God." On the whole, people seemed more cooperative, or at least more passive. One sometimes felt that, although a man had not refused or complained, he had agreed to the interview because he knew no other response to someone who spoke with the right accent and carried papers to fill in. We realized that to a Negro in a Syracuse housing project our routine "Hello, I'm —— from the Syracuse Research Unit" registered as "Hello, I'm a well-dressed white and so I must be from the Housing Authority or the employment office or the welfare and therefore have the right to ask questions and use your time."

356

There seemed to be both less suspicion and less passive acceptance in North Shields. Maybe unemployment there was accompanied by less feeling of alienation because it was more accepted by the community. At the time that we first called, everyone in the town knew that the local shipyards had no work to do. In Syracuse, unemployment was more an admission of defeat. There seemed to be a greater tendency to dodge rather than refuse a question or an interview there than in North Shields, where we were more likely to meet with a curt refusal. The tactic of agreeable and courteous evasion seemed to be practiced particularly by Negroes, and it is tempting to ascribe it to their greater consciousness of being in an inferior position. On the other hand, much of the difference may have been quite simply due to their greater experience, and therefore greater docility, in being interviewed in this sort of way. In answer to an apology for taking up his time for nearly two hours, a man said, "Oh, that's nothing; the last fella took seven."

The effect of unemployment on the life of a man and his family was hard to measure in one or two brief interviews. It was clear that men played down the impact while they were actually unemployed. Interviews with men back at work could often be very different. "Do you remember that black eye I gave you?" a man teased his wife, and they both roared with laughter and told the story. Once the crisis was over it seemed that some of the more central issues could be discussed openly: the need to present a united front was over. Perhaps this in itself indicates how deeply unemployment could strike at a family's security.

Another factor was the laconic way men referred to their misfortunes. Hard-luck stories were very rare, and few men seemed to be trying to impress us. Beside the element of self-respect, there was the fact that for many unemployment was now part of their way of life, a way they had come to regard quite fatalistically as "just one of those things." "What effect does it have on you being out of work?" was regularly greeted in North Shields, for example, by "It's serious, man, it's serious"—a term that was used about the weather, the performance of the local football club, the rising cost of living, and so on. Further probing might be greeted with "It makes you grumpy" or "Aye, it gets you sometimes." But from all the brief remarks, a general pattern emerged: "When you're at work, you're keeping the family and you know this; then when you're out, it's as they say, idle hands make idle thoughts." "It's like this: if you've got a definite aim you can put your backbone into it. When you've no objective, you're living on hope. Your standard of living deteriorates, your morale drops, it's an unpleasant way of living."

A few men said, "It's just like a holiday." This may have been bravado to cover up their loss of face, but it seemed that such remarks usually came from men who had relatively large wages, small family responsibilities, and little experience of unemployment. They were often engaged in work that was especially demanding of their time. Mr. Franklin,[2] an electrician in his twenties with a wife and one young baby, had been working six and one-half days a week at the end of his last job, receiving both overtime and incentive payments so that the job would be completed on schedule. "At first it seemed just like a holiday. I was glad to stay at home and rest and get up when I wanted to. Then after a couple of weeks I got worried and started looking very hard. I got bad-tempered and grumpy."

As the time out of work grew longer, the general attitude of the men was reflected by Mr. Robertson, a fifty-six-year-old fitter, who said, "I don't want sympathy, I want a job." Meanwhile, men had to find some substitute for their accustomed routine of work. The children still went to school and the wives still had their housekeeping and, amid this continuing meaningful activity, the men felt lost. In small houses where only the living room and the kitchen were warm in winter, young children were noisy and constantly under foot, and their father's power to keep them quiet seemed to diminish if he were always in the house. Conflict often arose between man and wife because he wanted the children to be quieter and more orderly than they usually were while he was out at work. He felt in the way when his mother-in-law, a sister, or a woman friend of his wife dropped in for a chat. In Syracuse and Shields, men said "You have to go out. You can't sit in there staring at those four walls any longer. But when you get out, there's nowhere to go. So you stand around, get cold, and then come in again." One woman whose husband and son were both out of work laughed and said, "That poor dog doesn't know what's happening to him. He gets taken for a walk by one after the other."

The search for somewhere out of the house and out of the wind and rain took some men to the reading room of the local public library in North Shields. Men sat silent at the tables, gazing blankly or slumped with their heads on their arms. Others stood in front of the racks of papers, swaying with their eyes closed in front of *The Daily Mirror* or *The Financial Times*. One or two muttered or sang to themselves. Here presumably were some of the old and lonely who could not stay any longer in their single rooms and came here for warmth and maybe the mute companionship. Although some officials remembered this happening in the 1930's, few were aware that it still happened today.

Most of the men said that they missed the company of workmates. "I like company when I'm out of work. We all like company, animals like company. I met one man the other day. 'How are you feeling, George?' I said. 'Rotten, I've been out since ten in the morning, it's now three, and never a soul has spoken to me!' I couldn't help laughing at that. 'What do you want then, George? Do you want someone to come and put their arm round you?' But it's hard, you know."

Those who declared least frustration and seemed to have adapted themselves most to being out of work were not always the ones who had been longest out of work. They were often men in their twenties or thirties who had few doubts about their chances of being re-employed shortly. They were most likely to refer to the opportunities unemployment provided to see more of the children, to baby-sit while their wives went out with friends, to get on with some decorating in the house or repairs on an old car, or just to be one's own boss. In contrast, the rest appeared reluctant to make even minor adjustments, perhaps because they regarded these as acknowledging that they might be unemployed for some time.

For wives, the greatest problem was the cut in their housekeeping money. A man would say, "I miss the money for my baccy [tobacco] or my beer," but the problem of keeping house on less money was something usually left to the wife: "We seem to eat as well" or "We manage" or "You'd better ask the wife. I leave all that to her." The women spoke of the struggle to keep the children's clothes in good shape longer and the ways in which they managed to ensure that they could still put a good meal on the table at weekends for Sunday dinner. The narrowed economic aspirations were often brought home vividly. "What have you cut down on, now that your husband's out of work?"—"Well, we've never had many luxuries lately." "What are luxuries?"—"Oh, fresh or tinned fruit, cream, biscuits, and cheese." Or, "Is there anything you bought while your husband was out of work that you felt you really shouldn't have because you couldn't afford it?"—"Well, yes. On a Friday night when Jack collected his money at the dole [Employment Exchange], he would stop at the shop on the corner and buy us a pasty and bacon and eggs. I know it was extravagant, but we had to have something to cheer us up." Again, collecting data after the man had returned to work often proved more revealing. A man in Syracuse said, "We can be a little more extravagant with the groceries now—we can have cookies, desserts, and sodas." One family with five children kept shopping lists for us both in and out of work: cakes, biscuits, and fresh and tinned fruit were bought only when the family wage earner was back at work.

Many families received nearly as much money out of work as working, but this was more an indication of the lowness of the wages than of the generosity of their social security payments. Very few earned as much as two thirds of the average weekly industrial wage for the area —£15–£16 in North Shields and $100–$110 in Syracuse. For these families, the question of cutting down could mean little. Family resources were so low that it was hard to pull in an already tightened belt. Economic crises were so common an event that families rarely bothered to mention them, and we only discovered their great difficulties sometime later.

In both towns, a general distinction could be drawn between the unemployment experience of the skilled and unskilled. The semiskilled shared the characteristics of one or the other of the two groups, but this did not obscure the major differences. First of all, unemployment came less often to the skilled than to the unskilled, and when it came it usually ended sooner. Although the skilled workers were therefore less accustomed to unemployment and might react more anxiously (as Mr. Franklin above), they seemed on the whole better equipped to meet it. They were usually better paid, and their less interrupted working career meant that in Britain they were likely to qualify for a longer unemployment insurance coverage. Since they usually found work sooner than the average unskilled, they had less need for this protection.

A skilled man, particularly one who had been able to establish some sort of seniority, seemed less likely to be affected by the general ebb and flow of the labor force in either town. At the same time, there were two skilled groups—the construction workers in Syracuse and the shipyard tradesmen in North Shields—who were likely to experience regular seasonal unemployment. The construction workers were usually recalled through their union and the shipworkers through the Employment Exchange. There was little pressure on either to join the dispiriting search from worksite to worksite and from shipyard to shipyard which characterized the experiences of the less skilled and less well established.

360

The worries of the craftsmen were mainly twofold. There might be no further demand for their trade because of new advances in technology or because of a declining demand for the product, as in the Thirties, when many shipyards closed for good. Or they might lose their jobs to younger men. Mr. Jenner, who at sixty-one was fighting bronchitis, had this fear, and was one of the few skilled men who tramped the yards along the Tyne in search of work. Mr. Armstrong, a Syracuse carpenter in his late fifties, said, "I've been sick and I've lost weight. You have to struggle harder to keep up with the younger fellows." If they did not expect a call back from their old works, or their family responsibilities or their own inclinations did not permit them to wait so long in idleness, the skilled men looked for work through newspapers, the unions, and the "bush telegraph"—the informal contacts between men who knew each other and their abilities.

Men with skills in short supply had greater control over their work. A New York welder said, "I've got lazy—I've made no effort to find work. As long as I don't have to put up with any nonsense, I find things comfortable enough. Just sitting and reading, I find life enjoyable that way." This man, who was unmarried, was supporting himself on his savings alone. Another skilled single man related how he managed to dodge seniority and so was laid off every winter: "I don't like working in the cold, and I've got enough to get by on."

An illustration of the greater power of the skilled was provided by a British foreman. "If you get a skilled man come up to you and say, 'This is a bloody place to work. I can get another £2 down the road,' you don't say, 'Well, why don't you go and get it?' because you're not going to be able to replace him. But there are plenty of unskilled signed on up at the dole. If any laborer said that to you, he'd have his cards and be out of the door in five minutes." An employment official pointed out that there was always more license allowed the senior tradesmen: "They're the ones who can come in late on a Monday morning and get away with it. But a laborer might be paid off for that, and then he wouldn't be eligible to pick up his benefit because he had been sacked."

The plight of the unskilled was more severe, and so it is not surprising that they expressed more despondency: "Everything seems hopeless when you're out of work. You get grumpy and there are times when you feel really depressed." "It's no life at all—but what can you do about it?" There was less chance that an unskilled worker would be called back to his old job, and the competition for jobs was much greater. What was perhaps even more influential in molding attitudes

361

was the belief that there was no right way to look for work—the search was dominated by luck. This did much to account for the fatalism often expressed by the unskilled: "I'm a great fatalist; whatever comes along, that's your fate." But this was not, as some have said, apathy. The same man continued, "But you've got to go out and look for work; you've got to push yourself. Perhaps you will be going to one place and there won't be work; at another there will be. That's your fate."

The part of luck or fate was brought out time and again in the descriptions by the unskilled of how they found their last jobs. This was in marked contrast to the men, mostly skilled, who said in Syracuse, "I always go to the union," and in North Shields, "I wait to hear from the Exchange." This regular and predictable experience stands out from the many "I just happened to go" and "sheer luck." For example, one unskilled worker recounted, "I got my last job myself—not that I can say I got it by looking for it. I'd been down to the yards looking and no luck. On the way back I stopped to talk to some men working on the corner just outside the house—and I got taken on because they were a man short." This was the picture one built up in both towns. "You get up early and go down to the yard and along to the factories—nothing—and you go home cold and tired and irritable. The next day you lie in bed and crawl out shamefacedly mid-morning when your wife's out shopping. You're depressed and frustrated, and you go out to the bar for a quick drink, hoping that none of your neighbors see you. You meet a man you know who says, 'Are you looking for a job?' and you say, 'What do you think?' And he tells you about his brother who needs extra men. So that's it, you're on again and no credit to you."

The value of these informal contacts to the unskilled cannot be exaggerated. Frequently laborers said, "It's not what you know, but who you know." The lack of these contacts made it especially difficult for the Negro, especially the school-leaver, to enter into the steady-job world. It was in the unintended way of breaking through this barrier that the various training centers in Syracuse seemed to be of most value. A boy learning to repair electric toasters or to become a clerk would be told of someone who needed a window cleaner or a janitor. It might be of little relevance to the skill he was acquiring, but up at the Employment Service they had offered him only short dishwashing jobs.

Jobs seemed to be getting scarcer for particular groups: for example, school dropouts in both towns. At the same time, the growth of private work-related benefits of all types—the title "fringe benefits" is increasingly misleading—anchored the established even more firmly to their company, and the labor-turnover rates were slowly falling in many industries. As job openings became more difficult to find, the importance of informal contacts slowly increased, and there seemed to be a danger that the gulf between those in work and those out of work would widen.

Attitudes toward the unemployed were apparently becoming less sympathetic as the total volume of unemployment dropped. Certain types of unemployment were more acceptable than others: there was more sympathy for the man laid off than the man who quit, whatever his reason. These distinctions were often applied in class terms. The skilled craftsmen were respectable. It was taken for granted that such men would return to work as soon as they could, and they were spared the harassment many suffered to go out and find work. In Syracuse, the Employment Service unemployment insurance offices left it to the unions to find their members work, so a union member—nearly always skilled—drawing unemployment benefits was not subjected to an interrogation as to what active searches he was making for work. No alternative work was suggested by the Employment Service, partly because of union rules and partly because unskilled or non-union jobs would probably have lower wages. Such men were not suspected of malingering, although, as described above, there were some instances of job dodging. If a skilled workman did have to apply for welfare—maybe for medical costs—he was likely to receive more courteous and considerate treatment than the average applicant. He was described as a man who had had bad luck "through no fault of his own," and was thought more deserving than "those who are always in and out of here. If you give them one thing, they'll be back for another."

The ordinary laborer, in contrast, seemed to be regarded as a potential malingerer by many Employment Service and welfare officials. Welfare or assistance regulations were interpreted as tightly as possible, while the man himself was often grateful for getting less than his entitlement because he did not know how to obtain his full rights. Yet the effect that the level of income while out of work has upon men's willingness to work is very hard to assess. All of the interviewers formed their own ideas as to how much particular men wanted to get back to work: it seemed impossible not to make one's own interpretation while recording responses about efforts to find work. What is noteworthy is the number of times our impressions were proved false. The apparently "eager searcher" might remain out of work, while the patently "work-shy"—"I'm all right. No, I'm not looking. It's O.K. being out of work"—might be back at work a few days later.

Financial incentives and deterrents appeared to bear little relevance to the issue of persistent unemployment, but financial support was essential for participation in society. Where statistics are available, they show that the rates of unemployment are higher for the single and the separated than for the married. Unemployment also lasts longer for the single and the separated. Yet these are the groups who, if the argument about financial incentives has any weight, would be the most attracted to work.

The major resources open to the men in the two towns to supplement their own meager savings and occasional earnings were unemployment insurance benefits and national assistance or public welfare. About 35 per cent of the Syracuse sample and 65 per cent of the North Shields sample were drawing unemployment benefits. Nearly 40 per cent in Syracuse and just over 40 per cent in Shields were receiving assistance or relief payments, some of these payments in North Shields being a supplement to the insurance benefits. Just under a third of the Syracuse men were managing without either of these resources, although some would undoubtedly have qualified if they had applied for welfare. In North Shields, it was calculated that maybe another fifth would have qualified for an assistance grant in addition to their insurance benefits if they had applied. Although unemployment insurance played an important part in income maintenance, the welfare or assistance program is of more interest here, since this was intended to supplement other payments where necessary and to provide the income level beneath which, it was believed, no one need fall.

In Britain, the fear that a man might not work if he could obtain as much on relief is reflected in a National Assistance Regulation—known as the "wage-stop"—stating that a man's grant should not exceed the amount of his net weekly earnings if he were employed full time in his normal occupation. Because the size of the grant depends on the rent he has to pay and the number of people he has to support, this regulation affects mainly men with large families and low-paying jobs. In New York State, this procedure did not apply; in fact, welfare could be paid to a man in full-time work to supplement his earnings if these were inadequate to meet his needs. Some of the welfare workers resented this subsidy and appeared to behave more harshly toward those large families with grants at or above the level of what they might earn.

A number of factors in the New York program seemed actively to depress the family's resources before aid could be given. These included the requirement that families should hand over their rights to certain possessions—a house, a mortgage, insurance policies—as a condition for receiving relief. A single man was required to move to cheaper accommodations, while another was compelled to give up an apartment and move into the county home. When he was financially able to support himself again, he would have to build up his position from nothing once more. The family-responsibility regulations provided a further deterrent to applying for welfare. Until recently in New York State—and still in many of the others—it was impossible for an able-bodied unemployed man to obtain welfare for himself and his family: he had to leave the home, and his wife had to take out a petition of non-support against him in order to receive any welfare. This breakup of the family still seemed to be demanded on a number of occasions. Finally, an unemployed man was likely to find himself on work relief. In theory, at least, a rehabilitative measure to help preserve a man's skill, it seemed likely to become a punitive deterrent for the unskilled.

With so many restrictive regulations in existence, the would-be welfare applicant often had a quite unrealistic impression of what application would mean. On the other hand, the experiences of many on welfare indicated that visits to the welfare office could be not only time-wasting but humiliating and distressing: "You take what they give you and get out before they change their minds." There was little sense of any entitlement.

Apart from the regulation reducing grants to earning potential—the wage-stop—the British system of National Assistance appeared in principle much simpler, less punitive, and more generous. Both schemes had a common heritage in the Elizabethan Poor Laws, but National Assistance had advanced further from social control to income maintenance. Yet in practice in North Shields, it seemed that the attitude of many of the officials was still close to that of their New York counterparts. Although assistance officers had wide discretionary powers to increase or restrict grants—for example, an officer might make a special grant of up to £20 without having to see higher authorization—they tended to exercise their extra powers only to reduce grants beneath the basic scale of "needs" laid down by Parliament, frugal as this already was. Their estimates of what a man might earn, for instance, were often £2 or £3 less than his previous wage and what he did earn when he later returned to work.

365

While the Act itself and higher officials encouraged greater assistance and less deterrence, local officers often seemed to take their standards from those who had been longest in the office—men who had perhaps been recruited in 1948 from the Poor Law authorities and who retained the harsher attitudes of the past. Some young officers described how they had to accept the prevailing standards of the office on certain points or just act in silence. One had suggested giving a grant for some new linoleum to a young married couple and remembered the consternation of the older men in the office: "I shouldn't start doing things like that, son. You'll have the whole street in."

Under these conditions, financial hardship was common among the unemployed. There was often little recognition of this and, in particular, scanty awareness of where the burden fell hardest. We heard frequent, though unproven, criticisms of the man with a large family to support. "It's all right for them; they can get as much out of work as in—if not more." Such accusations came from many sources: officials, social workers, neighbors, and other unemployed—"I'm not like the fellow next door. He's got eight children and he doesn't need to work."

The few people expressing any degree of satisfaction with the level of their income while out of work and who might, therefore, be prepared to malinger were usually single men or married men with only their wives to support. Some of these were in a better position because of savings or support from their family: the boy living at home who received full board and pocket money from his parents; the man whose wife went out to work and supplemented his unemployment benefit or whose children were working and paid in more to the housekeeping. In Britain, the single or small family man was often helped through unemployment by involuntary savings. While employed, he paid income tax at a higher rate than the man with many dependents; unemployed, he was able to claim this back within the month as a tax rebate. Some men were receiving as much again from this income-tax rebate as they did from National Insurance Unemployment Benefit, at least for a few weeks.

There were also the men who appeared satisfied with their income because they seemed to expect so little. Mr. Simpson, a bachelor in his forties living with a stepbrother, had been out of work for eighteen months. Since a nervous breakdown in 1947, he had never had regular employment and was registered as a disabled person at the Employment Exchange in an area where there was a surplus of able-bodied unskilled labor. He received £3.7s.,0d. a week[3] from the National

Assistance Board. "I'm that used to living on short money, I wouldn't know what to do with a full wage of fifteen pounds. I would if I got married, but I'm never out and I don't meet people, so how could that happen? I'd like a job, a part-time job. I'd take anything like that, but most of these jobs are kept for pensioners." All the officials who knew him said, "Of course, he's ill—he couldn't really work." But twice a week he was required to make the three-mile trip to the Employment Exchange and join the queue to register as unemployed and draw his assistance. It is difficult to decide whether this ritual depresses a man more, constantly bringing home to him his failures to return to work, or whether it buoys him up with the hope that when things get better, his chance will come.

But not all men with few family commitments were satisfied. The greatest problem for the single man, especially if he was living by himself, was loneliness, although this in turn was aggravated by lack of income. Sixty-four-year-old Mr. Connor was a short, stocky man with rheumy eyes and a pale face which suggested that he did not go out much. Before the war he had taken part in the Jarrow march of the unemployed, nearly three hundred miles from the Tyne to London. Now registered as disabled, he had been out of work for two years and received £3.18s.6d.[4] from the National Assistance Board. When asked if he had any friends, he said, "I've got my radio, that's far better than bringing in people you don't want, and it keeps you company. If you eat out, half your week's money has gone. But being out of work sends you dopey. When I was a nightwatchman, the men on nightwork would come and have a natter [talks]. When you're closed in like this, you don't know where to go when it's pouring with rain. You need someone to help you with the cooking and cleaning; you get fed up doing it by yourself. You shut yourself off from other people. When you've got nothing, you're afeard of going amongst them in case they think you're sponging on them."

This suggests the existence of a vicious circle. Loss of work means loss of company; lack of income restricts the search for company; with more unemployed men than vacant jobs, contacts are essential for finding work. In this way one sees the longer unemployment of the single or separated man, particularly as he gets older, connected with his loneliness and meager resources. While these impediments remain, the incentive of a wage some three or four times above his present income can play little part.

Although a working wife or working children lessened the financial problems of unemployment, this in itself often exacerbated the man's own discontent and sense of powerlessness. When her husband was out of the room, Mrs. Fletcher said, "He gets so edgy now; he's the only one out of work in the house now and he can't stand it." An old fisherman said, "I've worked since I was nine. I've always supported my family and now I'm even dependent on them for a fag." But although families without young children often had to make considerable adjustments in their income as unemployment continued—drawing on savings intended for retirement or the deposit on a house, or canceling a long-planned vacation—their standard of living on the whole suffered less than that of most large families. This may be because some were older and had already furnished their homes and completed the payments, or, brought up during the Twenties or Thirties, were more accustomed to restraint on their expenditures. A more important reason is that some needs can be deferred until the return to work, while others—particularly children's needs for shoes and clothing for the winter—cannot be. As a result, these needs must be met more expensively, by buying on credit or by buying cheaply and having to repair or replace sooner.

In both communities, the largest families seemed to be the hardest pressed by poverty, and there would seem to be urgent need for research into the costs of supporting families of different sizes and ages. In neither area did the extra grants made for children—and in Britain this included the Family Allowance[5] paid to men in and out of work—appear to be in proportion to the extra costs borne by the families. When, in North Shields, the wage-stop regulation operated to reduce grants, the problem of supporting a family on relief was even greater. One man had to support his wife and eight children on an income reduced to the standard allowance appropriate for a man, wife, and one child.

Our surveys gave no evidence that larger families were more wasteful of their money than smaller families. There were many indications that men with large families accepted that an ever-smaller proportion of their wage should be left them for their own "pleasures," and wives resigned themselves to the fact that their clothes would have to last longer. Some of the women who had given birth to five or six children were wearing dresses around the home that they had bought after their second pregnancy: the clothes were, not surprisingly, badly fitting and out of date. Oddly enough, this in itself seemed likely to work against their gaining sympathy or understanding from some of the officials that visited them. Caseworkers complained how badly or poorly dressed these women were, as if this were confirmation of an inferior and less deserving status and not the inevitable result of having to make a little money go a long way.

Inadequate resources also meant that the homes of such families were usually in need of decoration, and the furnishings old, battered, and insufficient. There were rarely enough chairs for all the family to sit up to the table to eat. This often overlooked fact helps to explain why teachers may complain that children from large families "have such appalling table manners: they just won't sit still at mealtimes." This point was made by some teachers as both illustration and proof of the parents' inadequacy and inability to bring up their children properly, rather than their poverty.

In Syracuse and North Shields, some of the officials and case workers visiting the homes had little awareness of the normal behavior of a large family. Many came from middle- or upper-working-class homes where families were smaller; many were unmarried. The mother of four or five children seemed to them casual, slaphappy, and even callous. At least part of this, it seems, should be put down to the change in behavior and attitudes on the part of parents as they gain in experience and confidence; and this is equally true whatever the income or social class. A colleague with four children remarked that he and his wife recently looked at a diary they kept of their first baby and were both amused and horrified by what seemed to them now to be an overanxious and overprotective concern.

Discussion of the economic hardships of large families is often countered with references to the need for self-control and family planning: "the rich get richer, and the poor get children." Unfortunately, we did not collect any detailed data on this subject, but some of the comments made spontaneously by the men or their wives indicate the difficulties some encountered in their attempts to find an adequate method of birth control. A few wives had been refused sterilization by their doctors after a fourth or fifth child and after they had tried different types of contraception. One woman wryly pointed out that she and the woman across the road were both taking the same pill—she because she did not want any more children, having suffered a prolapse, and the other because she did want children and the doctor had given her the pill to make her more fertile.

The area of medical care for the unemployed showed marked contrast between Syracuse and North Shields. Those of us coming from

Britain were very sensitive to the differences in the costs and quality of care in the two towns and were perhaps particularly quick to notice that many in our Syracuse sample put off obtaining medical care until they could do so no longer. By this time, the costs were not only much higher but the treatment more urgent and the period for recovery much longer. For this reason, the impact of ill-health on the lives of these people seemed to us to be unnecessarily heavy. Men often returned to work not yet fully recovered, and bound down by weighty medical bills. We could not help wondering how much connection there might be between the strain caused by long-untreated physical ill-health and the fact that at least ten of the sixty unemployed in Syracuse had been in a mental hospital at least once in the last ten years.

Throughout this chapter we have drawn attention to the similar position of similar groups in different communities. The contrasts between skilled and unskilled persist beyond the experience of unemployment, although it is in their ability to meet such crises that the differences become clearest. They have different degrees of power in the labor market, different opportunities to exercise choice, and different access to resources. Although unemployment brings certain hardships for all, the problems of the single and lonely man are distinct from those with families, and large families make different demands from those of small ones. The part played by the official agencies of income maintenance is an important one, although the official and unofficial policies of incentive and deterrence may hamper the overriding responsibility to provide for the welfare of those in need. Evidence suggests that we should be more concerned that some people receive as little in wages as they do when unemployed than that big welfare grants destroy the will to work.

When there is increasing prosperity among the majority, it is perhaps not surprising that the problems of the rest should be seen as psychological or environmental; that there should be talk of personal failure or social decay, and the need for adjustment or control, for re-motivation or retraining to escape the restricting, frustrating life of poverty. All these may have their place and their value, especially in dealing with "hard-core" groups. But the experiences of the unemployed we interviewed in Syracuse and North Shields draw attention to the effect that the simple lack of resources, and of access to resources, has on men and their families. In bringing new skills and new techniques to bear on the poor, we should not neglect this basic fact.

370

Dorothy and *Adrian Sinfield*

Notes

NOTE: The surveys on which this chapter is based were financed by the London School of Economics (1963–1964) and the New York State Mental Health Research Unit in Syracuse (1964–1965). We are grateful for the help we received from our colleagues in London and Syracuse and would particularly like to thank Professor Peter Townsend and Mr. Robert Fish.

1. Mary Lou Wilkins, "Observational Aspects of a Study of Unemployment" in *Unit Report* (Syracuse, N.Y.: New York State Department of Mental Hygiene, Mental Health Research Unit, 1965).

2. All names used in the text are, of course, fictitious.

3. About $9.50, although this gives little idea of purchasing power. This figure is just over one fifth of the average industrial wage for the area. (All dollar-pound equivalents are as of 1965.)

4. About $11.00, a quarter of the average industrial wage.

5. At present, these are eight shillings per week for the second child dependent and ten shillings for the third and later dependents. The official exchange rate of $1.15 and $1.50 understates the buying power. The payments have been increased only once since their introduction in 1948 and have not been adjusted to meet the rising cost of living.

20 • Human Concerns in a Mass Society

PAUL MEADOWS

"There are possibilities for me, certainly; but under what stone do they lie?"

—FRANZ KAFKA

A HISTORIC SEQUENCE of maps of the globe displays enlarging size and perspective. The globe as man has known it has literally expanded as human contacts and inquiry have been extended. If we possessed maps of the social world of man, they too would show an expanding universe. And in a historic sequence of such maps, the most pronounced, even revolutionary, shift would appear in those for the last hundred years. For in that span of time human beings, and particularly Euro-Americans, have moved from localized and isolated communities to large-scale and interactive mass societies.

The mass society of modern man is a product of four major technologies. The *industrial* technology of massed mechanization evolved a new human productive organization: industrialism. The *political* technology of centralized government brought a new state organization: the nation-state system. The *social* technology of urbanization and commercialization, building on the decline of the folk culture, erected a new form of social organization: urban, contractualistic, secondary society. The *psychological* technology of mass-mediated communication has molded a new organization of human interests and involvements: an age of mass communication and mass movements. What has been created is unquestionably a historic novelty—modern mass society. The modern man, particularly of the industrial West and increasingly in the rest of the world, lives in a mass age.

How have these new patterns of human relationship been described? What are the human risks, the human vulnerabilities of the new mass culture? What kinds of compensatory patterns of adjustment and response have been developed? In brief, what has happened to the pattern and dynamics of human concern in the society of mass culture?

MASS SOCIETY IN THEORY

Three major styles of describing and interpreting the culture of modern mass society may be noted: the numerical, the psychological, and the organizational. Each approach selects an aspect of mass society which is considered to be of strategic importance in the understanding of the mass culture: numbers, psycho-social traits, and institutional characteristics. Each theme serves as a special kind of portraiture of modern man.

The numerical portrait of modern man in a mass society provides a view of mass culture in terms of the predominance of huge masses of human beings, aggregated, conglomerated, and more or less organized in sprawling human settlements. Such massed human contacts create conditions widely different from those of the relatively circumscribed interactions of earlier societies. Thus, sociologist Kimball Young has described contemporary society as "a vast mass of segregated, isolated individuals, interdependent in all sorts of specialized ways, yet lacking in any central unifying value or purpose." [1] He adds: "The interconnections and the totality rest chiefly on external, more or less mechanical relationships of persons and groups." Elsewhere, he refers to the manner in which "the loss of traditional ties, the greater interdependence which is nevertheless fragile, in large part, tends to foster mass society." [2] French social theorist Lucien Romier has stressed the manner in which the massing of human beings produces mass patterns. "With the spread of specialization in labor, in knowledge and even in thought, each individual is aligned with a group possessing similar interests. These groups form economic units or masses, whose size varies. . . . It is within the organization of these masses and in their relations with each other that the new balance of society finds its basis." The masses become in themselves a source of power. "The mass . . . never feels any doubt about the justice of claims which it possesses." [3]

Mass theorists are often not so restrained in their appraisals. "Masses" is a term which is often, as Hardman has suggested, an "elastic epithet." [4] The kinfolk of the term masses is a polyglot crew: *hoi polloi,* the rabble, *canaille,* "the great unwashed," Jacobins, proletariat, *narodniki,* the common people, the common man. The mass theorist, working this vein, may be an ironist, as in the case of Ortega y Gasset. Starting with a "visual experience"—the "fact of agglomeration, of plenitude"—he notes that "the multitude has suddenly become visible, installing itself in the preferential positions in society." [5] The mass man is the average man in a position of power. "The masses, without ceasing to be the mass, is supplanting minorities": "hyper-democracy." The historic irony lies in the fact that the commonplace, continuing to be commonplace, imposes a power which it does not understand—what Weimar Foreign Minister Walter Rathenau called "the vertical invasion of the barbarians" and what English sociologist Herbert Spencer termed at the end of the nineteenth century "barbarization." [6]

The numerical theorists of mass society strike out in different directions from their mutual initial observation, the fact of unprecedented agglomeration of human numbers. Mass society, whatever else it may be or become, is a society of masses of human beings. There is, however, a basic theme: mass is a force, almost in the physical sense, determining social variations and shaping social organization. It is a theme seldom better developed than by Georg Simmel.[7] To his careful analysis has been added the variegated and burgeoning literature of the social alienationists, ringing the changes on such characterizations as anonymity, the fragmentation of interests, impersonality, and loss of individuality, among others. All of these qualities of modern behavior are thought to derive their nature and their influence from the sheer massing of human numbers, which industrialism and urbanism have demanded.[8] Quantitative change has produced a series of revolutionary qualitative changes.

A second group of theorists of mass society has been interested in the socio-psychological traits of this historically novel kind of society. An earlier school, denominated by sociologist Luther Bernard as "the planes and currents" school,[9] concerned itself with the psychological consequences and implications of intensified and extended human contacts. Their thinking was colored by the impression of human agglomeration, and they were, for the most part, epithetic and ironical in their portrayals of the "mentality" of the mass society. Typical of this school, most of whose publications appeared before World War I and whose psychology most certainly belongs to that period, were the French social psychologists Le Bon and Tarde, the Americans Ross and Martin, the Englishmen Wallas and Trotter, and the Austrian Freud.[10] Two of them will be selected for consideration here.

Trotter built on the contradictions between "reason" and "herd suggestion." He posited a herd instinct, which he thought of as manifested in three different types of "herds": the aggressive, the protective, and the socialized—paralleling the paradigms of the wolf, the sheep, and the bee. Man's "social instinct"—this earlier group was almost always instinctivist—"must follow one of these three activities and reactions." [11] He himself was most interested in the conditions which encourage the socialized herd type. His optimism, shared by Tarde and Ross, is in contrast to the pessimism of Martin, Freud, and Le Bon. Thus, Le Bon argued that a mass society spawns a "dictatorship of discontent." [12] "The Great Civilizations," he wrote, "grow complex as they develop, leaving behind them in their rapid progress a host of human beings who have not had the capacity to keep pace with them. They form the vast army of the unadapted, the incapable. These people are naturally discontented and, therefore, the enemies of society, in which they do not hold the position of which they consider themselves to be worthy." [13] Le Bon found the idea of a dictatorship of discontent "a natural enough consequence of the illusion which attributes intellectual superiority to numbers." [14]

A later group of psychologically oriented mass theorists, writing in terms of the totalitarian movements of the 1920's and 1930's and against the background of newer developments in the social sciences, reversed the approach of the earlier writers. They did this by assuming that the collective behavior of the masses is a function of their mass cultural patterns. These latter are regarded as giant frames of manipulation and control, at the disposal of unscrupulous and designing minorities posturing as friends of the masses. The masses as such are not the source of behavior so much as the targets of concentrated and perfected social controls made possible and matured by mass technologies. Thus, Sergei Chakhotin writes of "the psychological rape" of the masses through persuasion and suggestion and by means of such devices as doctrine, myth, rites and slogans.[15] "In our opinion," he writes, "collective action, especially of the masses, is the result of political acts within the governmental machines of the present day."

A similar vein of analysis runs through the writings of Franz Neumann and Emil Lederer.[16] The mass state of the totalitarians has utilized a novel type of leadership, the "charismatic" leader, who, it is devoutly asserted, "is endowed with qualities lacking in ordinary mortals." [17] Evolving along the lines of the historic model of the ancient "thaumaturgic kings," the totalitarian state becomes an "adulterated form" of the messianic idea. Like Le Bon and Martin, Neumann feels that "the least rational strata of society" turn for refuge and salvation to the state as the modern *Mysterium Tremendum*.[18] The conditions which transform "man" into "mass man" are those associated with "modern industrial capitalism" and "mass democracy."[19] Monopoly capitalism and mass democracy, Neumann writes, "have imprisoned man in a network of semi-authoritarian organizations controlling his life from birth to death, and they have begun to transfer culture into propaganda and salable commodities."[20]

Lederer is closer to the Le Bon-Tarde approach in that he, too, starts with the fact of "great numbers of people." His initial concept is "the multitude," composed of persons who are "in no respect psychologically homogeneous."[21] Unlike the multitude, the mass or crowd includes "a great number of people who are inwardly united so that they feel and may possibly act as a unity."[22] "Masses are therefore amorphous; social stratification is effaced or at least blurred. The point of unity for the individuals comprising a mass is always emotional. A crowd can be united only by emotions. . . ."[23] The mass is the acting crowd, integrated by a leader who is skilled in evoking "hidden qualities" in the crowd upon the occasion of some crowd-sensed crisis. The relationship between the crowd or mass and the leader is a magical one.[24] The function of the leader of the mass state is to keep this relationship alive by shrewd and dramatic strategy and through the agitation of amorphous and generalized or perhaps paranoid attitudes, capable of being specifically defined and explosively directed upon the felt need of the leadership. Totalitarian parties are ironclad but frenzied crowds. The charisma of the leader varies with his skill in pulverizing the forms of the society into fluid and undefined crowds, in "melting together" all "the various layers of society into crowds . . ."[25] However, a vicious circle is set up: "crowds can be kept together and in order only if they can be moved and satisfied emotionally. . . ." The mass state "must constantly race to action."[26]

A third school of theorists of mass society centers attention on the social forms evolved by the mass technologies, and derives the traits of mass culture from the analysis of the operations and interrelationships of these forms. These protagonists do not agree in their approaches to the mass culture; some make a cultural analysis, others an associational, still others a political, and a fourth group an administrative interpretation. But all four share what may be called a technological point of view: they regard the various technologies of modern society as responsible for the development of certain mass attributes, which are, however, differently listed and treated by them.

The cultural or anthropological approach to mass society theory enlarges on the contrast between folk and urban-national cultures. Thus, positing a logical sequence from tribal to city culture, Redfield finds that when peasant is compared with tribal village, town with peasant village, and city with town, certain differential traits show up. The first named in each pair of contrasts is less isolated, more heterogeneous, more specialized, and secular in its specialties, more dependent, more impersonal in the functioning of its institutions of control, freer in the choice and action of the individual. These traits, of course, are most extreme in the industrial or commercial city. The polarity between the folkic and the urbane is the background of the discussion of mass society by Bennett and Tumin.[27] Employing as their nuclear concept the idea of pattern—"a very flexible concept which refers to any regularity in social behavior at different degrees of observability and at different levels of abstractness"—they distinguish between mass culture as congeries and as uniformity or standardization. Thus, in American culture "what we see is an incredible mass of detail, variation, vast elaboration and change of ideas, forms, structures, fads and fancies. . . ."[28] They speak of American society as "a large number of intersecting and overlapping subcultures—ethnic, religious, class, organizational, communal, and regional." Searching for uniformities "overlying" these diversities, they find them in a composite phenomenon, "mass culture": "a kind of least common denominator . . . a kind of film hiding the diversity beneath."[29] The ineptness of the figures of speech perhaps suggests the nominalistic character of their conception. Nonetheless, there does emerge from their characterizations the idea of a "bipolar quality" in mass culture: the presence of common denominators and of ideals which may have only a loose verbal relationship to reality. The behavioral functions of mass culture as they identify them overlap considerably: unification, communication, association, and catharsis.

A second approach to the portrayal of mass society in terms of organization makes use in a rather neutral sense of the concept "collective," and draws implications from the fact that modern mass technologies have brought together a vast network of collective habits, interests, and organizations. Perhaps the most notable integrative interpretation of mass society in terms of these concepts is the prize-winning study by

Robert M. MacIver, *The Web of Government.*[30] Seeking a central culture theme, MacIver finds it in the concept "myth," first developed profitably by Georges Sorel and later (and in a much different manner) by Suzanne Langer.[31] "All social relations are myth-sustained." Moreover, "all changes of the social structure are mothered and matured by appropriate new myths. Social myth at every level enjoins some kind of order among men, and involves that order in a context of value-impregnated lore and legend, in tradition and in philosophy." [32] Moving from simple to complexly institutionalized societies, MacIver finds an increasing institutionalization of the "central" myth. This process is rendered urgent by the fact that "a multigroup society is a multi-myth society." *Pari passu,* the pyramiding of social power—"the capacity to control the behavior of others"—develops. A struggle among the power units for the direction of the central mythology and for the defeat of all competing myths takes place. A sharp and decisive alternative ultimately appears: "the conception of the all-inclusive, all-regulating State"—"a pre-Copernican conception of the social system"—versus the conception of the accommodative and pluralistic state.[33] Both conceptions have in common the heightened institutionalization of human relationships as the necessary counterpart of the mechanization of the productive processes, and both remove "the levers of social control" from the "reach of the common man." Both master patterns of mass society face two sets of possible human reactions. A negative set of tendencies includes managerialism, anomie, bureaucracy, cultural decadence, and formalism. A positive set embraces the strategic role of government in social change, the increasing importance of science-technology, the expansion of the world of interaction, and reformulations of the democratic idea.

Unlike the psychological theorists of mass society, who link the leadership of mass society with the emotional dynamics of crowd behavior, the organizational theorists are inclined to see the problem in terms of administrative skill. There is, however, a sharp difference of opinion among writers who have focused on this aspect of mass society. One group,[34] writing from the vantage point of liberal-democratic ideology, regards the leadership of mass society as a social process in which all persons involved in problem-solving—at different levels of involvement and at different levels of skill—can and must participate. Leadership is a cooperative effort, and as such it must rely on communication; participants must be able to get together. Lines of interaction must extend to all; they must be kept open, freely used, and sincerely respected—the basic formula for democratic administrative management. Central to this concept is the administrative man, neither the economic man of classical economics nor the mass man of totalitarian economics. The administrative man is that member of a public, or of a state agency, or of a community, who in the plan-actions of policy determination (administration) and policy execution (management) moves in a reciprocal and mutually helpful system of communication with all concerned. The power of such leadership is a "power with," not "power over," others.[35]

Another group of writers elevates to primary place the administrative elite, skilled in all of the technologies of a mass culture. The elite theorists form a distinguished and apparently growing company.[36] Perhaps the most influential was Karl Mannheim, who was bold in tracking down "the crisis" of mass culture to the failure of the customary modes of elite-formation and elite-elevation. "The crisis of culture in liberal-democratic society is due . . . to the fact that the social processes, which have previously favored the development of the creative elites, now have the opposite effect, i.e., have become obstacles to the forming of elites, because wider sections of the population still under unfavorable social conditions take an active part in cultural activities." [37] But Mannheim was careful to qualify this thesis. Administrative elites should be selected on the basis of achievement, a rule which contemporary mass societies have abrogated: Mannheim called it "the breakdown of the exclusiveness of the elite." Elites should be cosmopolitan and outward-bound, a rule being rejected, he felt, by mass societies in favor of localistic and class-bound choices. "Inarticulated publicity" disturbs the "ultimate pre-requisites of social creativeness and its transformation into concrete action." [38]

Less restrained in his elite theory of mass culture is Burnham.[39] Starting with the commonplace observation that we are now in the midst of a major social transition or revolution, which he defines as a shift from capitalist society to managerial society, Burnham characterizes the latter as a social order with publicly owned production, indirect exploitation of masses, and control of economic decisions and operations by a new ruling class, the managers. Working hand in glove with the politicians—a symbiotic but not necessarily harmonious relationship—the managerial elite mobilize ever greater areas of control through the skilled exploitation of mass-accepted managerial ideologies (MacIver's

379

"myth"). New economic mechanisms and social relationships are thereby coordinated in the realization of elite-selected goals having a decreasing significance for the individual. It is a mass culture *of* and *for* but not *by* the masses—the goal being a *minimum* "feasible participation" by the masses.

MASS SOCIETY IN TROUBLE

It requires little skill to observe that in all of the portrayals of modern man in mass society which have thus far been reviewed there is a pervading sense of something wrong. Indeed, the very formulation of the concept of mass society seems to have been provoked by the observation that all was not well. Thus, the writer who really dramatized the idea for Euro-American thinkers, Karl Mannheim, dwelt on the "novel element" in modern society, the presence of two interactive factors— "the fundamental democratization" of modern society and the "process of growing interdependence"—both of which, he felt, had made inescapable "the ultimate incompatibility" of rationality and morality in the contemporary social order.[40]

Democratization promotes this conflict by its permissive concentration of the material culture and by its enlarging demands for more and more areas of social living to come under the control of rationality, as imaged in technology. "As a large scale industrial society, it creates a whole series of actions which are rationally calculable to the highest degree and which depend on a whole series of repressions and renunciations of impulsive satisfactions. As a mass society, on the other hand, it produces all the irrationalities and emotional outbreaks which are characteristic of amorphous human agglomerations. As an industrial society, it so refines the social mechanism that the slightest irrational disturbance can have the most far-reaching effects, and as a mass society it favors a great number of irrational impulses and suggestions and produces an accumulation of unsublimated psychic energies which, at every moment, threatens to smash the whole subtle machinery of social life." A specific danger appears in the fact that "In a society in which the masses tend to dominate, irrationalities which have not been integrated into the social structure may force their way into political life." [41] A twin danger lurks in the possibility of irrationality in morality. "The more modern mass society is functionally rationalized, the more it tends to neutralize substantive morality or to sidetrack it into the 'private' sphere. In public matters it seeks to confine itself to universal standards which have a purely functional significance." [42]

380

Consider for a few moments some aspects of the hazard to human values and to human organization inherent in some sources and forms of vulnerability to modern man in mass society.[43]

Shortly after the close of World War II, a New York editor set people across the United States talking about a powerful editorial, later expanded into a brief book. I refer to Norman Cousins and his *Modern Man Is Obsolete*. This arresting title adumbrated the threat to man's existence contained in the atomic bomb. Since then, modern men by the millions have shown little evidence that they were concerned about their becoming obsolete. On the contrary, if the mounting stockpiles of nuclear weapons mean anything, they suggest that we have perhaps connived at our own demise.

Beyond the physical annihilation inherent in the A-bomb, there is the menace, fully as lethal, in the vulnerability of modern man as a dweller in modern mass society. The conquest of atomic energy was the fruit of a disciplined, highly organized, and far-flung collective effort. The engineering genius of modern man in all of its many specialized departments—physical, mental, governmental, financial, technological —was levied upon in order that the first ominous bomb-burst might take place. It was not enough that in making the bomb modern man made himself infinitely more vulnerable than ever before in history. In so doing he actually professionalized his vulnerability! In this, his newest threat to his own existence, he sought out, pooled, and refined all the professional skills known to modern society in order to extend not only his mastery but also his vulnerability. That is to say, he *organized* his vulnerability.

The mushrooming cloud at Los Alamos, Hiroshima, Bikini, and at all other future experimental or military testing grounds is an image, dark and forbidding, of the existence of modern man. For it is in fact an outgrowth of modern organized ways of living. It is itself the harvest, by no means random but calculated with fabulous professional ingenuity, of all the arts of organized living today. Designed as a weapon of invulnerability, the nuclear weapon has rendered modern man incredibly vulnerable. It is not easy to find a more immediately poignant symbol of the life of modern man in mass society.

This is not the first time that the search for sanctuary has created nightmares where there were only bad dreams. The collective arts of discovery and invention perfected the machine, and now modern man must fight against the vulnerability of mass unemployment and machine displacement. The collective arts of specialization and division of labor engineered a new economy, industrialism; but in the midst of fragmented and scattered interests modern man must seek for a new unity of common interests that can maintain a human community. The small, parochial village surrendered dominion to the megalopolitan city, and the human measure lost its usefulness in a megalonthropic age. Small and self-sufficient states coalesced into vast, interdependent nation-states, and the autonomy and peace of the parts are swallowed up in the uninterrupted crises and tensions of the whole.

All the advances in the arts of human society are defended and hailed as new bulwarks of human security. And yet in daily fact they cast dark, long shadows across the future edges of personal experience. The more intricate the organization, the more easily it is disrupted; the more massive the scale, the more sweeping the telltale consequences. Mass has assumed the significance which once dwelt in the individual, and shrunken egos must find solace in swollen coffers and momentous issues. It is easy to attack the integrity of nations, to decry the inconsistencies of corporations, to castigate the contradictions of groups; but the quiet integrity of a man's own life seldom can withstand the shocks of the tiniest and most timid assertion of personal conscience. The glorious cause and the monumental decisions dwarf the austerities of a single human defiance. The inspired protest is lost in the labyrinths of administrative protocol and hierarchical disavowals. Form must substitute for feeling, and the priestly rituals of collective self-interests quench the fires of prophetic judgment. The expert, the technician, the artists in obscurities replace the armed vision. Where men were once persons, they are now members; and they must, according to the pathetic irony of human involvements, live within group walls that always shut out far more than they shut in.

In organizations, modern man in mass society has sought to explore the outermost ranges of his collective capacities; but in so doing he finds it difficult, perhaps impossible, to restore or to maintain his powers as an individual human being. Consider in this respect the problem of human loyalty. Among tribal peoples loyalty is simply and easily defined—to the tribal gods, rituals, mores, routines, lineage group. But how can the loyalty of modern man in mass society ever be so simply and easily defined?

For the social universe of modern man in mass society is a pluriverse. His living is identified with a meshwork of groups and interests and causes. In associations he names his loyalties. In groups he forges the links that bind. In causes he is knit to issues and ideas that transcend his day-by-day involvements of living. In interests he pursues goals that may have no roots in principles. Herein lies the difficulty of modern man's loyalties in a mass society. There are so many of them, and they exist in so many different varieties. They often compete with one another; and if not by day then by night in the unconscious strivings, like Jacob with his angel, they clash for possession of his soul. His group memberships time and again force him into acquiescence in decisions in which he was not really—though perhaps ceremonially—consulted, perhaps in which he has been defied or even ignored. In anger he may denounce the neglect, while doing violence to even more fundamental loyalties.

In what ways can modern man lay claim freely and honorably on his loyalties? For he knows he should be able freely and honorably to stake them out and to declare them. Indeed, he experiences the greatest security of his living in the loyalty that stands unimpeachably clear and firm. But where and how can he discover such free and honorable loyalties? If he joins this group, he cannot share in that; if he holds this faith, then he must reject that; if he prizes this way, then he must spurn that. Nor is this all. By affirming his loyalty to this or that principle or program or cause, he often, if not usually, finds that semantic subterfuges, legal technicalities, judicial sonorities, legislative "whereases," and administrative procrastination have repudiated, where they have not humiliated, his loyalties.

The delicacies and sensitivities and anxieties of national security are a case in point. Bureaucratic predilection and inclusive but ambiguous law make a farce of membership. Admitted membership, concealed membership, past membership in a party or in a group now under fire are no less censured and actionable than assumed membership, or likely membership, or reputed membership, or membership in a group with known or suspected sympathies paralleling at some past or present or possible future points the sympathies of a hated group.

But the anomaly of modern loyalties goes far beyond contemporary secularized witchcraft. In an organized society modern man protects and promotes his particular interests through organized groups. But any group membership, imputed or established, can be rendered suspect. Any loyalty can be defined as disloyalty, any conscience as the lack of it. The only conformity that apparently can survive the merciless crossfire of privileged criticism can be only the most universal, the most

383

flattened out, the least assertive, the most innocuous and mediocre conformity. Heresy is the idea hated by men who have no ideas, it has been said. Bigotry becomes the *deus ex machina* of a machine-processed acquiescence. And in an age of mass conformity, bigotry—"the appalling frenzy of the indifferent," as Chesterton called it—slashes out at the "heretical" novelty, at the "traitorous" sensitivity, the "treasonable" criticism. In numbers, it seems, there is safety for very little—save numbers!

Modern man in mass society has indeed industrialized his vulnerability: he has mass-produced it, standardized it, serialized it, streamlined it, credentialed it, mass-merchandised it. In such a society every bounding line becomes a boundary, every affection an alienation, every inclusion an exclusion, every approach a withdrawal, every sympathy a suspicion, every faith a heresy.

Consider again the sources and forms of human vulnerability in a society of mass culture in terms of the mass society's impact on human conflict.

Two generations ago Hebert Spencer set about to prove that an industrial civilization has nothing in common with a militaristic one: aggression is not good business. The hopes of his day were for a peaceful world in which the vexing problems of human relations would be efficiently attended to and dispatched. But the generations since the *fin de siècle* days of Spencerian optimism have seen how modern industrialism has in fact increased and has continued to increase the probabilities of conflict in human relations. Indeed, it has so revolutionized the conflict process as to create a not unimportant revulsion toward the whole culture structure of a scientific, industrial technology.

This change in the scale and tempo of conflict has occurred at each and every stage in the conflict process. The impact of industrial mass culture on human conflict may, in the first place, be seen in the way in which it has broken down the walls of human isolation. Immobility—induced by the barriers of space, time, fear of the unknown, dread of the stranger, love of the past or of the next world—has yielded to the technic-ways of mechanical invention in communication and transportation. "Men on the move" are the dramatic symbols of an age which has given wings to feet and speech. This breaking up of vicinal isolation, together with the mental mobility which it created, has sent men on great voyages of discovery of their globe and space. The sixteenth century discovered "the environment." The nineteenth century harnessed it. The twentieth century has engaged in spectacular probes and thrusts of exploitation of it. The new mental mobility has created an impressive expressiveness of the human spirit which has unfolded in all directions. The friction of time in human contacts has been overcome. Incredible swiftness—across land space, through air space, into outer space—has signaled some of the greatest achievements of the mass age. Mechanization has become the classless servant of the masses, diffusing the intentions and contentions of human minds to all men. The frequency and the variety of human contacts have responded to the technological tempos of the mass culture. Who can say that this process will cease— or even slow down?

The impact of the industrial mass culture on the conflict process may, in the second place, be seen in the phenomenal increase in human differences. It is true, of course, that the basic types of human interests and functions have remained fairly stable: men have always and everywhere been religious, economic, familial, political, and so on. But within these frames of human expression they have manifested astonishing variability. Industrial mass culture is an impressive monument to this singularity of man's interactions with his world. The machine technology of modern mass culture has incredibly multiplied the specializations of human functions, the division of human labor, the variability of human interests—the extent, therefore, of human differences. Modern industrial mass culture has put the human species on a thousand revolving stages where man enacts his dramatic rendezvous with meaningfulness. The mass society is a factory; but it is also a playground, a hospital, a laboratory, a church, a library, a school, a home. For specialization within *mechanical* technology has also made possible specialization in all the other cultural technologies. Moreover, the technological differentiation of the mass culture has pulled man out in manifold directions. It has succeeded in shifting him from localism to cosmopolitanism; from the sacred to the secular; from the provincial to the national and international; from locality and blood groups to special interest groups; from primary society to secondary or derivative society. Man has become highly multivalent.

The impact of industrial mass culture on the conflict process may, in the third place, be seen in the emergence of exclusive and irreconcilable human differences. In all of the shuffling and reshuffling of the cards of human destinies, the stakes have become higher and higher. For men made differently, act differently. They become aware of their differences, justify them, sentimentalize them, strive to make them irreconcilable and immortal. They come to see their differences through the glasses of exclusion; they set their sights on the far hills of exclusive realization. This shift in human thinking and feeling is commonly ascribed to the work of ideology and the ideologists. Just as the provincial conflicts of the medieval and early modern period had their mercenaries, so the world conflicts of our own day have their hirelings. Janizaries have been replaced by ideologists, and primary fealties by secondary apologetics. Fragmented world views become supported by segmental rationalizations, and the towering spires of passionate imperialisms (known by many different names!) are strengthened and adorned by the flying buttresses of idea-systems, slogans, and stereotypes. This reorientation is apparent in most of the competing ideologies of war. In one century it is the "White Man's Burden"; in another, it is the *Herren Volk,* the world proletariat, the "Greater East Asia Co-Prosperity Sphere," or indeed the "Great Society's" alliances for the protection of freedom. The logic becomes more subtle, more intricate, perhaps more persuasive. In a world of differences, we refine our philosophies of differences, and we call them ideologies. Henceforth, ideological irreconcilability is wedded to the strategy and tactics of group thwart or group annihilation.

The impact of industrial mass culture on the conflict process may, finally, be seen in the costs and damages to human existence which have accompanied all these changes. The conflicts of the external social universe become the mirror of the self. The personal imbalances of insecurity and fear are the tribute money modern man pays for the privilege of the technological exploitations of his new mass culture. Of course, one hardly needs to be reminded that man has always been victimized by his fears. "In the beginning was fear," writes Lewis Browne in *This Believing World,* "and fear was in the heart of man, and fear controlled man." A thousand vestiges in religion and art and family life bear testimony to this truth. And yet, can we say that modern mass culture has been guiltless in provoking this fear? Prehistoric man lived in a world of the unseen, the supernatural. That world had to be coerced. Magic is our name today for early man's wish-fulfilling "controls" over that world. But this primitive system of technology only fed fuels to the flames of man's fears, as the ritual prayers and ceremonies of his "rites of passage," among many others, show. In like manner, man's newest "controls," industrial mass culture, continue to play on his fears. Despite the spread of tools and knowledge and skills, few people can deny the great increase in human anxiety. "Be not anxious about tomorrow" was an injunction to an agricultural people who knew little about business cycles, cutthroat competition, technological displacements, the perils of distant markets, or planetary rivalries.

There are many who feel that the parade has gone up a dead-end street. First came the liberation of the mind: we call it the Renaissance. Then came the liberation of the conscience: we call it the Reformation; and it was followed by the liberation of the body—the Industrial Revolution. Then emerged the liberation of the human will: we know it as the Liberal Revolution. But now, whither bound? Shall modern man seek safety, as Erich Fromm has wondered, in escape from freedom? Shall he find security in the protective fortresses of his besieged national economies? Shall he find surcease from the turbulent waters of a changing, competitive society in the still waters of a status culture, by whatever name it may be known?

Or perhaps something else has been going on in modern mass culture which is moving in a new direction, creating new forms, arousing new fealties, seeking in the creative experiences of social invention some counters, some compensations for these deficits in human values and in the human spirit?

TOWARD A COMPENSATORY MASS SOCIETY

Clearly, the answer is sure to be more impressionistic than quantitative, more intuitive than formal, for the question seldom attracts the more systematic scientists. Yet it is a perfectly natural question, and the answer, even if impressionistic and intuitive, is the kind of answer with which many generations of human beings have learned somehow to live.

The clue to an answer lies, as it does in so many areas of human questioning, in the nature of human expectations and actions—their directions, their continuities, their strengths, their fulfillments. Suppose we start there.[44]

It has been suggested, in several different ways in these pages, that there is not a single area of modern mass society which does not have its clinical aspects. And in each clinical examination of danger spots to contemporary civilization, attention points to some kind of drift in human values. Such a focus of attention is primary, for the enduring power of any society is, after all, in its human values—whatever hap-

387

pens to them is the key to the future of every other aspect of the society. The ubiquitous clinics of our society point to a problem of action, a problem which has to do with nothing less than the permanence of the industrial mass culture itself.

Such a statement differs, of course, in many important ways from that of a number of writers on the contemporary social landscape. It contrasts sharply with the fanatics of a mass industrialism who think only in terms of continuing technological expansion, or of more efficient markets, or of scientific ingenuity. On the other hand, such a statement does not diverge widely from that of the socialist movement which, for several generations now, has been speaking ominously of the collapse of "the system" and of its replacement by a "new order." But their "new order"—whether communist, nationalist, or whatever—involves little change in the basic structure of industrial mass society. In fact, that structure is assumed; the changes, if any, are political and imposed upon it. Thus, Marxian socialism states its case very largely in terms of individual income distribution, and national socialism in terms of national income distribution; in neither instance is the new centralization of production or the concentration of power, to mention only two matters, considered. In other respects, the whole pattern of industrial mass society is left intact.

However, the socialists have put us in their debt on one important score: their insight that the future of industrial mass society is bound up with the processes and fortunes of politics. Classic liberalism boycotted government and sought its neutralization; even the early socialists, not uninfluenced by the anarchist tradition, were unimpressed by the political order. But there is an inevitability about politics which even the most determined classical economist and Marxist is unable to deny or resist. For politics is the process of public decision and action. It emerges when the changing tempos and tensions of a society upset or redirect the balance of interest and power and a new equilibrium of social forces must be found. Industrial mass society is, as we have been saying, a set of vastly disequilibrating forces, and the political process becomes the technic of social compromise and social decision. In consequence, the sharp demarcation between the economic and the political is a fiction of the myth-minded.

But the political process is not a patent of the state. Every human situation in which the settlement of any social situation and the provision and control of any social function becomes necessary is a political

388

situation. All human associations are thus units of political action, in much the same sense and certainly for some of the same reasons that the state is. The difference between these associations on the one hand, and the state on the other, seems to be this. Whenever social ends and means transcend the sphere of action of any single group and thus become "affected with public interest," as the phrase has it, the processes of political action which are the special province of the state are initiated. Increasingly, the problems and means and meanings in modern living become "public," so that the growth of the state has paralleled the development of industrial mass society. Business collectivism, for example, has its counterpart in "public" collectivism. It is no historical accident that both liberal and totalitarian countries in the last generation have experienced a rapid assumption of social and economic functions by the state: the evolution of industrialism itself is the most natural explanation.

However, these same evolutionary processes also explain the mounting tension and feeling which surround the expanding power of the state in our day. Recourse to the state as the arbiter of conflict and the channel of collective action spells, so it is thought, the surrender of personal and group autonomy, or at least of a good share of it. In the name of public interest, demands can be made and sacrifices exacted which less dynamic societies might not experience. Yet the loss of autonomy is hardly the whole story behind the resentments, misgivings, and conflicts over the enlargement of state power. Perhaps even more important is the fact that as the state itself becomes an enterpriser in area after area of the society and economy, the struggle to control its policies and activities becomes intense and acrimonious. There spring up ideologies which rationalize motives, attract support, state issues, and press for well-selected though not always publicly avowed objectives. The lines of struggle are fluid, the forces sometimes latent, the partners changing (as manifest issues change), the slogans and sentiments artfully chosen and carefully phrased. The strategy is warlike, the tactics brutal, for the stakes are high—the life or death of systems of property, codes of behavior, patterns of expectations, particular group controls.

A maturing industrial mass society and the processes of its decision-making and decision-enforcement are ineradicably colored by ideological precommitments and entrenched group interests. This clash of forces is a normal phase of politics in an expanding industrialism, as

389

any textbook on the industrial history of the United States shows, and it is likely to be constructive and wholesome, as a long record of social legislation indicates. But it loses its character as mere politics in a contracting or in a maturing industrial mass society: it becomes revolutionary, violent. There is no reason to believe that the kind of tensions and unsettlement which industrial mass society seems now to induce can ever again be handled by the neutralization of government. Nor can they be handled by the spirit of political planlessness and postponement which characterized the problem-solving of nineteenth-century industrial societies. The society of industrial mass culture in these days of its maturity has reached a new age, a plan age, and its leadership has problems which the leadership of earlier industrialism neither recognized nor was prepared to solve.

Gone are the days when the "time for decision" is solely an occasion for individual human action. The forces of industrial mass society are collective, institutional forces working within giant frames of thought and action: "business," "industry," "labor," "agriculture," "markets," protest groups of all kinds, and so on. If this point of view be true, then the future of industrial mass society, partly because it is tied to these mass patterns of life, is likely to be more emotional, less rational, less a matter of cold, calculating determination than nostalgic partisans of the past are prepared to believe. To be sure, there is in this prospect little aid and comfort to the apologists of a planned or planning future, for it seems to run completely counter to some of the traditional definitions and rights of a free society. The rhetoric of those definitions swung around "liberty" and "freedom"; the absence of restriction and the capacity to act; the rights and the powers of free men. And yet surely it must be plain that there is no primitive pattern, no pristine liberalism. The free man, or the free society, is concerned with the power to act; the power to act in such a way that the deepest demands and the highest insights of his being can be known and can be fulfilled. And this human concern can never be fixed, made final or inviolate, embodied in unchanging forms.

However, whatever the forms they may take, the human concerns of a free society in an age of mass industrialism must continue to hold fast to one conviction: in the free society, all men have the power to act. Here is the genius—the troubled genius, to be sure—and the eternal heritage of the society of free men. It is this genius which sparks the deeply felt necessity of such collective actions as would enforce the

390

principles of the free market and the free mind: the provision of real opportunity for all men to produce and buy, to live and let live, to say and to listen, to teach and to learn, to act and to respond without prejudice or injury to any man. This social freedom in an age of industrial mass culture, which has been sought in so many different ways by anarchists and communists, by socialists and capitalists, has yet to evolve a common speech, though all are dedicated to that measure of the free society—the common good. It is a freedom in process, yet its direction is clear: the discovery of ways and means of enabling modern man to act in a mass industrialism through the technics and techniques of social organization. Sometimes called humanism, optimism, humanitarianism, social politics, social planning, it is the really novel revolution of our times. Its turning point is the human power to act, its essence is the mobilization of social resources to be put at the disposal of such power, and its obstacles are all those vested claimants who have laid through law and custom a death-hold on those selfsame resources.

A free society in an age of mass industrialism is by no means a finished one; its historic task is incomplete. Moreover, the completion of its task lies far more in the realm of politics than protagonists of freedom have ever dreamed. The unique historic opportunity of the free society of this age of mass industrialism lies in the perfection of a state essentially and supremely "*by* the people." The totalitarian ideologies of Europe and Asia have notoriously failed in this enterprise: there is no mistaking their incapacity to bring to maturity a state which reposes complete faith in the skill and the devotion of the common man to administer it, a state with which the common man can identify himself without misgivings and without human loss.

The state problem of the free society today, then, is the invention of political methods which will be expressive of the spirit and power of liberal bases and purposes and which will lie well within the scope and province of democratic government. Such a political conquest must begin with a recognition and acceptance of a *new* liberal state system as the imperative need of modern industrial mass society. Free men have never been wholeheartedly persuaded of this necessity. Their social legislations have been too often cautious improvisations—hopes against the hope, as it were, that something bold must be undertaken. But that day is dead. The policy of patchwork reform, successful during the epoch of expansion of mass industrialism, can never save a liberal mass society.

391

The social politics of the past served to surrender the outworks of liberalism without solving the crucial issue of the inner citadel's stability. "The ideal of masterly inactivity," to use Lippmann's phrase, is not only an antique in a mature mass industrialism; it is suicide. The initial step in a renascent liberalism, suited to the problems and possibilities of an industrial mass society, is the acceptance and commitment to the fact that the free man can live, so long as he lives in an industrial world, in an organized society. The precise political formula of that organization —if that is at all a possibility—must surely be a matter of experimentation; but its basic variables are "freedom" and "authority." Such a formula imposes upon the modern liberal state responsibility for the total national economy and society, but neither total nor unquestioned nor final responsibility. The insistence upon freedom—the *ability,* quite literally, *to respond*—must temper the urge for authority, and the liberal genius for compromise must evolve a political pattern in which both state and people collaborate in the construction of a free collectivism.

Nobody has any right to expect this task to be painless, or without conflict. The free society is a coat of many colors. Nor should anyone expect the opposed interests of an industrial mass society to settle their own differences unaided and to work out their own arrangements. This work has been the historic role of the state. But in this task the liberal state of a mass society can no longer be regarded simply as a broker of these interests. It must exercise the power which in point of fact it has always had in the nation-state system, the power which it has, as the "Great Association," as the supreme system of legal imperatives, to organize industrial mass society in the interests of free men. That power, according to the traditions of freedom, rests not upon coercion but upon consent: successfully to plan, it must be able successfully to arrive at agreement. The business of the liberal state is the satisfaction of effective demand. But demand is not unitary; it is dispersive and competitive, occasionally collusive, often latent. To organize such a society is not easy, but it is not impossible. For freemen it is inescapable.

It is difficult for any person to describe, even in slight detail, the form of this new liberal state. It is emerging from the experiences of depression and war, from the planning of river valleys and cities, from the administrative law of social politics, from the social vision and the professional skill of technicians and administrators, from the myriad forms of agencies and groups, public and private, brought into life and activity around some human need or interest. Most notably of all, it is coming from the experiences of crisis government in war and in peace. Many terms and phrases suggest the texture of its thought and the quality of its effort: executive leadership, planning, due process of administration, public participation, decentralization, industrial jurisprudence, industrial democracy, conservation of human resources, administrative authority, the managed market, public administration, public corps, and public programs. The pattern is plain: public initiative in order to provide private power. The release of human and physical resources through representative and participative administrative as well as legislative action is the clue to this new constitutionalism to which the new liberal creed is giving birth. The goal is clear: the forging of instruments of public power ("the free society") through which the individual in an age of industrial mass culture can still be a free man, having the power to act. To use that power is to prove again and again what free men have always believed: that human beings, all of them, regardless of color or class, must be trusted with the destinies of their own society, because they are human beings. The free society of an industrial mass culture must create and revise its structures of action around such simple convictions—that the people count, that they must be counted in the processes and products, the forums and agencies, the potentialities and the limits of the politics of their own social existence. This is the free society's answer to a mass culture in being but in trouble.

Notes

1. Kimball Young, *Sociology* (New York: American Book Company, 1942), p. 25.

2. *Ibid.*, p. 182.

3. Lucien Romier, *Who Will Be Master? Europe or America?*, translated by Matthew Josephson (New York: Macaulay, 1928), p. 20.

4. J. B. S. Hardman, "Masses," *Encyclopedia of the Social Sciences*, (New York: The Macmillan Company, 1933), X, 195–201.

5. José Ortega y Gasset, *The Revolt of the Masses* (London: Allen and Unwin, 1932), p. 13.

6. For a recent exposition of this theme, anticipated in the nineteenth century by Matthew Arnold in his *Culture and Anarchy*, see T. S. Eliot, *Notes Toward a Definition of Culture* (New York: Harcourt, Brace, and Company, 1949).

7. Georg Simmel, *The Sociology of Georg Simmel*, translated by Kurt H. Wolff (Glencoe, Ill.: The Free Press, 1950).

8. Typical of this perception are the writings of Lewis Mumford: *The Culture of Cities* (New York: Harcourt, Brace, and Company, 1938); *The Condition of Man* (New York: Harcourt, Brace, and Company, 1944).

9. L. L. Bernard, *An Introduction to Social Psychology* (New York: H. Holt and Company, 1926).

10. Gustave Le Bon, *The Crowd* (Paris: F. Alcan, 1895) and *The World in Revolt* (New York: The Macmillan Company, 1921); Gabriel Tarde, *The Laws of Imitation* (Paris: F. Alcan, 1890); Edward A. Ross, *Social Psychology* (New York: The Macmillan Company, 1905); Everett D. Martin, *The Behavior of Crowds* (New York: Harper & Brothers, 1920); Graham Wallas, *The Great Society* (New York: The Macmillan Company, 1916); William Trotter, *Instincts of the Herd in Peace and War* (New York: The Macmillan Company, 1926); and Sigmund Freud, *Civilization and Its Discontents* (London: Cape and Smith, 1930).

11. Trotter, *op. cit.*, p. 197.

12. Le Bon, *The World in Revolt*, p. 13.

13. *Ibid.*, p. 154. Freud, it might be noted, attributed the discontent to something quite different—to a relapse into conditions which make individuals very much alike. This atavism consists in the fact that "each individual is bound by libidinal ties on the one hand to the leader . . . and on the other hand to the other members of the group." See his *Group Psychology and the Analysis of Ego*, translated by James Strachey (London: International Psychoanalytical Press, 1922), pp. 44–45. The role of cultural repressions is, of course, accepted, as in his *Civilization and Its Discontents*.

14. Le Bon, *The World in Revolt,* p. 164.

15. Sergei Chakhotin, *The Rape of the Masses: The Psychology of Totalitarian Political Propaganda,* translated by E. W. Dickes (New York: Alliance Book Corporation, 1940), pp. 284 ff.

16. Franz Neumann, *Behemoth* (New York: Oxford University Press, 1942); Emil Lederer, *The State of the Masses: The Threat of the Classless Society* (New York: W. W. Norton & Company, 1940).

17. Neumann, *op. cit.,* p. 85.

18. The writer who popularized this theme was Max Weber; see his *The Theory of Social and Economic Organization,* Talcott Parsons, ed. (New York: Oxford University Press, 1947), pp. 358 ff.

19. Neumann, *op. cit.,* p. 367. There is a strikingly romantic quality in this view, recalling the romantic writers of the post-revolutionary and Napoleonic epoch: Bonald, de Maistre, Chateaubriand, Taine. See the present writer's "Viewpoints on Revolution," *Social Education,* X (1946), 14 ff.

20. Neumann, *op. cit.* For a further development of this general theme, see Sigmund Neumann, *Permanent Revolution* (New York: Harper & Brothers, 1942).

21. Lederer, *op. cit.,* p. 29.

22. *Ibid.,* p. 30.

23. *Ibid.,* p. 31.

24. Much earlier, Freud developed this point; see Appendix I, "On Group Psychology and Magical Thinking," in *Group Psychology and the Analysis of Ego.*

25. Lederer, *op. cit.,* p. 77.

26. *Ibid.,* p. 78.

27. John Bennett and Melvin Tumin, *Social Life: Structure and Function* (New York: Alfred A. Knopf, 1949), Chapters 30 and 31, "The Mass Culture."

28. *Ibid.,* p. 604.

29. *Ibid.,* p. 609.

30. Robert M. MacIver, *The Web of Government* (New York: The Macmillan Company, 1947).

31. Georges Sorel, *Reflections on Violence* (Paris: 1912) and Suzanne Langer, *Philosophy in a New Key* (Cambridge: Harvard University Press, 1942).

32. MacIver, *op. cit.,* p. 51.

33. *Ibid.,* pp. 621 ff.

34. See Chester I. Barnard, *The Functions of the Executive* (Cambridge: Harvard University Press, 1938); Mary P. Follett, *Creative Experience* (New York: Longmans, Green and Co., 1924); Alfred M. Bingham,

The Techniques of Democracy (New York: Duell, Sloan and Pearce, 1942); Edward P. Herring, *Public Administration and the Public Interest* (New York: McGraw-Hill Book Company, 1936); T. V. Smith, *The Legislative Way of Life* (Chicago: University of Chicago Press, 1941).

35. See the present writer's "Planning in Mass and in Differentiated Society," *Journal of Legal and Political Sociology*, II (1944), 17 ff., and the chapter "The Administrative Revolution of the Liberal State," in his *The Culture of Industrial Man* (Lincoln: University of Nebraska Press, 1950).

36. See Gaetano Mosca, *The Ruling Class*, translated by Hannah D. Kahn (New York: McGraw-Hill Book Company, 1939); Vilfredo Pareto, *The Mind and Society*, translated by Bongiorno and Livingston (New York: Harcourt, Brace and Company, 1935); Marian W. Beth, "The Elite and the Elites," *American Journal of Sociology*, XLVII (1942), 746–755; James Burnham, *The Managerial Revolution* (New York: The John Day Company, 1941); Roberto Michels, *Political Parties* (New York: International Library, 1915); Suzanne Keller, *Beyond the Ruling Class: Strategic Elites in Modern Society* (New York: Random House, 1963); Gabriel A. Almond and James S. Coleman, eds., *The Politics of the Developing Areas* (Princeton, N.J.: Princeton University Press, 1960); Harold D. Lasswell, Daniel Lerner, and C. Easton Rothwell, *The Comparative Study of Elites* (Stanford, Calif.: Stanford University Press, 1952).

37. Karl Mannheim, *Man and Society in an Age of Reconstruction* (New York: Harcourt, Brace and Company, 1937), p. 85.

38. *Ibid.*, p. 111.

39. Burnham, *op. cit.*

40. Mannheim, *op. cit.*, pp. 43–44. By rationality, Mannheim had in mind the fact that "a series of actions receives a functional position and role." Hence, everything which breaks through and disrupts this fundamental ordering is functionally irrational. In this sense, the industrial mass society is supremely and necessarily rational.

41. *Ibid.*, p. 67.

42. *Ibid.*

43. Adapted from the writer's "Technological Change and Human Conflict," *The Personalist*, XXIX (1948), 396–402; used by permission.

44. Some of the following materials have been adapted from two articles by the present writer: "The Leadership of an Industrial Society," *American Journal of Economics and Sociology*, VII (1948), 257–263, and "The New Tasks of the Liberal State," *ibid.*, 205–214.

ACKNOWLEDGMENTS

To the *American Journal of Economics and Sociology* for permission to print a revised version of Arnold M. Rose's "The New Problem of Large-Scale Unemployability," XXIII (October 1964), pp. 337–350.

To Holt, Rinehart and Winston, Inc. for permission to reprint a condensation from *My People Is the Enemy* by William Stringfellow. Copyright © 1964 by William Stringfellow.

To Prentice-Hall, Inc. for permission to quote from two chapters in Arthur B. Shostak and William Gomberg, eds., *Blue-Collar World,* 1964: (1) William R. Rosengren, "Social Class and Becoming 'Ill,'" pp. 338–339; and (2) Daniel Rosenblatt and Edward A. Suchman, "The Underutilization of Medical-Care Services by Blue-Collarites," p. 344.

Index

INVENTORY 74   SUMMER 77

INVENTORY 1983